Born in Macedonia, **Aristotle** (384–322 B.C.) left his provincial home at age seventeen for Athens, where he remained for twenty years as a pupil and colleague of Plato. After Plato's death, Aristotle returned to Macedonia to become tutor to the prince who would become Alexander the Great. In 336 B.C., he established a school in Athens called the Lyceum, which put him in perpetual conflict with supporters of the rival Platonic Academy. Eventually he retired to the island of Euboea.

Renford Bambrough (1926–99) held various appointments from St. John's College, Cambridge, including Supervisor in Classics and Moral Sciences, and Director of Studies in Moral Sciences. In addition to two books—*Reason, Truth and God* and *Moral Skepticism and Moral Knowledge*—he published numerous reviews and articles in leading magazines and journals, including *Cambridge Review*, *Philosophical Quarterly*, and the *London Times Literary Supplement*. He also served as editor of the journal *Philosophy* from 1973–94.

Susanne Bobzien is Senior Research Scholar in Philosophy at Yale University. Previously she was Professor of Philosophy at Yale and tenured CUF Lecturer in Philosophy at Oxford. She is the author of several books, including *Determinism and Freedom in Stoic Philosophy*, and of numerous articles in top philosophy journals. Among her awards are a Fellowship of the National Endowment for the Humanities and a British Academy Research Readership.

THE PHILOSOPHY OF
ARISTOTLE

A SELECTION WITH AN INTRODUCTION
AND COMMENTARY BY
RENFORD BAMBROUGH

WITH A NEW AFTERWORD BY
SUSANNE BOBZIEN

TRANSLATIONS BY
J. L. CREED AND A. E. WARDMAN

SIGNET CLASSICS

SIGNET CLASSICS
Published by New American Library, a division of
Penguin Group (USA) Inc., 375 Hudson Street,
New York, New York 10014, USA
Penguin Group (Canada), 90 Eglinton Avenue East, Suite 700, Toronto,
Ontario M4P 2Y3, Canada (a division of Pearson Penguin Canada Inc.)
Penguin Books Ltd., 80 Strand, London WC2R 0RL, England
Penguin Ireland, 25 St. Stephen's Green, Dublin 2,
Ireland (a division of Penguin Books Ltd.)
Penguin Group (Australia), 250 Camberwell Road, Camberwell, Victoria 3124,
Australia (a division of Pearson Australia Group Pty. Ltd.)
Penguin Books India Pvt. Ltd., 11 Community Centre, Panchsheel Park,
New Delhi - 110 017, India
Penguin Group (NZ), 67 Apollo Drive, Rosedale, North Shore 0632,
New Zealand (a division of Pearson New Zealand Ltd.)
Penguin Books (South Africa) (Pty.) Ltd., 24 Sturdee Avenue,
Rosebank, Johannesburg 2196, South Africa

Penguin Books Ltd., Registered Offices:
80 Strand, London WC2R 0RL, England

Published by Signet Classics, an imprint of New American Library, a division of
Penguin Group (USA) Inc. Previously published in a Mentor edition.

First Signet Classics Printing, June 2003
First Signet Classics Printing (Bobzien Afterword), January 2011
20 19 18 17 16 15 14 13 12 11

Introduction copyright © Renford Bambrough, 1963
Afterword copyright © Susanne Bobzien, 2011
All rights reserved

 REGISTERED TRADEMARK — MARCA REGISTRADA

Printed in the United States of America

CONTENTS

EDITOR'S PREFACE

Every writer on Aristotle owes a great debt to his predecessors. The list of Books for Further Reading includes some of the works that have helped me most. My specific obligations are too numerous to set out in detail, but I should like to acknowledge above all the help that I have received from the writings of Sir David Ross.

At every stage in the preparation of this book I have received generous help from Mr. Creed and Mr. Wardman; and I should like to record here my warm gratitude for their hard work, sound judgment, and kindly collaboration.

—Renford Bambrough

TRANSLATORS' PREFACE

The passages from the *Ethics* and *Politics*; the "Posterior Analytics"; and chapters 1, 4–9, and 21 of the *Poetics* were translated by A. E. Wardman. J. L. Creed was responsible for translating the passages from the *Physics,* the *Metaphysics,* and the *Psychology;* the "Categories" and "On Interpretation"; and chapters 13–15 and 23–26 of the *Poetics.*

We should like to acknowledge particular indebtedness to the following commentaries and translations, which we consulted:

Ethics

Joachim, H. H. *Aristotle: The Nicomachean Ethics. A Commentary.* D. A. Rees (ed.). New York and London: Oxford University Press, 1951.

Logic

Ross, Sir W. D. *Prior and Posterior Analytics.* New York and London: Oxford University Press, 1949.

Metaphysics

Ross, Sir W. D. *The Metaphysics.* 2 vols. New York and London: Oxford University Press, 1924.

Physics

Ross, Sir W. D. *The Physics.* New York and London: Oxford University Press, 1936.

Poetics

Else, Gerald F. *Aristotle's Poetics: The Argument.* Cambridge, Mass.: Harvard University Press, 1957.

Potts, L. J. *Aristotle on the Art of Fiction.* New York and London: Cambridge University Press, 1953.

Politics

Barker, Ernest. *The Politics.* New York and London: Oxford University Press, 1946.

Psychology

Hicks, R. D. *De Anima.* London: Cambridge University Press, 1907.

The Oxford translation and the translations in the Loeb Classical Library were useful throughout.

We have usually followed the text of Aristotle given in the Oxford Classical Texts.

—J. L. C.
A. E. W.

GENERAL INTRODUCTION

The importance of Aristotle in the intellectual history of Europe is too well known to need explanation or defense. The range and power of his achievements place him without question in the shortest of short lists of the giants of Western thought. To many generations of thinkers he was known simply as "The Philosopher." Dante, with reverence but without exaggeration, honored him with the proud title of "master of those who know." Darwin testified to his huge achievement as a biologist: "Linnaeus and Cuvier have been my two gods, but they were mere schoolboys to old Aristotle." All studies in formal logic until very recent times were footnotes to his work. In the study of ethics, politics, and literary criticism he set standards of sanity, urbanity, and penetration by which his successors two thousand years later may still be severely judged. His theological speculations are still the basis for the natural theology of the Roman Catholic Church. There is no problem in any of the branches of what is still called philosophy—ontology, epistemology, metaphysics, ethics—on which his remarks do not continue to deserve the most careful attention from the modern inquirer.

And yet, it can be claimed that his historical importance and influence do not constitute the most important reasons for continuing to study his writings at the present time. Indeed, there are two points of view from which his great historical influence can be charged to the

debit side of the account. In the first place, the sheer
weight of his authority has often inhibited his successors
from making their own independent contributions to
thought. In logic and the natural sciences especially, his
disciples have been slow to see when the time had come
to go further than their master, or in a different direction. Secondly (and this is more important for the purpose of this book), the *historical* interest of all his
writings is inclined to obscure the interest that some of
them have, not merely as documents for antiquarian
study, but as living contributions to fields of inquiry in
which the most important writings, however ancient,
never go out of date.

There are several possible views about the relation
between historical studies of a philosopher's work and
the independent study of the primary questions of philosophy themselves; there are, consequently, several possible views about how to select from the works of
Aristotle and present them in translation. Most of the
standard selections from Aristotle have a heavily historical bias. They have been made by and for those whose
primary concern is with Aristotle's place in the history
of Greek thought or with his effects on the literature
and thought of later ages. The aim of this book is to
stress the importance of Aristotle's discussion of problems that still perplex and preoccupy philosophers of the
present day. The book has been prepared in the belief—
which is finding increasing favor among students of ancient thought—that there has in the past been too sharp
a division between philosophy as a living and continuing
activity, and historical studies of the work of earlier, and
especially of ancient, philosophers. There is a proper and
important place for historical studies that relate a philosopher's work to that of his predecessors and successors,
and to the general nonphilosophical background from
which his problems emerged and against which his solutions must be understood; for the kind of study, in fact,
that is characteristic of the history of science. But the

work of an important ancient philosopher has an interest quite independent of any concern for these purely historical matters. The present-day astronomer need take no account of the work of Ptolemy or Aristarchus; all that is valuable in the work of his predecessors has been absorbed into the tradition into which he is initiated in his early training. Biologists do not read Darwin except from antiquarian interest. But philosophy is different. In philosophy there is nothing recognizable as a single line of advance. Its questions remain open, its debates continue, in such a sense that a classic work of philosophy must continue to concern all who deal with the main philosophical questions.

For this book I have chosen a selection from the texts of Aristotle that relate most directly to philosophical questions still being debated today. It was part of Aristotle's own achievement to help forward the process of division of labor among the arts and sciences, to distinguish the types and branches of knowledge, with the result that much of what he included in his encyclopedic scope is now in the hands of specialized experts—physicists, chemists, botanists, zoologists, logicians—whose fields are sharply distinguishable from philosophy. Much of his work therefore joins that of Aristarchus and Darwin on the history-of-science shelves. Those of his questions that have been definitively answered, whether by himself or by his successors, will be those that least concern us here. But his answers to many questions remain of primary interest and importance. What is the nature of knowledge, and what are its ultimate grounds? What are the ultimate categories of thought and the basic constituents of the universe? What is the relation between language, thought, and their objects? How is the mind related to the body? To what end or ends is human life to be directed? What is the place of the individual in human society? How is pleasure related to goodness? What is the function and purpose of literature? All these questions are still alive, and Aristotle's answers to them are still among the most prominent candidates in the field. His treatment of these topics, therefore, has an interest quite different from the historical interest we may still take in his treatment of those problems of logic or science to which his answers are either known to be true or known to be false.

This contrast between the steady advances of logicians and scientists and the apparent unsettleability of philosophical questions leads to a more particular reason why the present time is opportune for the kind of book that this is meant to be. Philosophy has been going through one of its recurrent periods of self-consciousness and self-examination. Philosophers are sensitive to the achievements and pretensions of mathematics and the natural sciences. Some have held that philosophy must now yield to science all the privileges and responsibilities she has had for two thousand years. Those who feel that there is still a place for philosophical inquiry face a challenge to declare how their activity fits into a new intellectual landscape. At such a time a study of the work of Aristotle is especially rewarding. Although he made important contributions to many fields that are now cultivated by specialized experts, he never lost sight of the aim of unifying knowledge, of understanding the world as an organized whole. In him we find what is not always found even in philosophers of his stature, a meeting of the two main philosophical motives: a desire to understand the world and a desire to understand man and his place in the world. The first of these motives is what philosophy has in common with science, and the second is what philosophy has in common with religion.

Now, the effect of the heart searchings of twentieth-century philosophers has been to concentrate attention on the connections between philosophy and science, at the expense of those between philosophy and religion. What is more, even those philosophers of the past whose main motive was a disinterested curiosity about the nature of the universe have been attacked for trying to understand the world by large-scale a priori theorizing rather than by piecemeal empirical research. Consequently, recent analytical philosophy, in spite of taking pride in its noble descent from Locke, Berkeley, and Hume, has tended to be indifferent or hostile to studies in the history of philosophy because it has been hostile to so much that was characteristic of the work of the philosophers of earlier ages. The issues are raised in their sharpest form by the writings of the school known as Logical Positivism. This movement originated in Vienna, but later became influential in many British and American universities. According to these thinkers, philosophy was to be seen, not as "the queen of the sciences," but rather as their humble handmaid. Speculative and constructive philosophy of the traditional type was to be abandoned. The task of philosophy was seen as purely critical, in the first place exposing the pretensions of the metaphysical philosophers of the past and in the second place elucidating the discoveries of the various branches of positive knowledge, and studying the relations between them. This approach naturally led to the neglect of many of the important philosophers of the past, whose work was held to be in principle misguided. There has been a reaction against this uncompromising school, and although most British philosophers and many in other countries have been greatly influenced by these philosophers and their successors, a more tolerant approach is now preferred. There are still some unrepentant logical positivists, but most philosophers of the so-called linguistic school would now wish to reassess and to present in different terms the achievement of the early positivists.

The principal thesis of positivism is that there is a precise criterion by which all significant discourse may be accurately distinguished from meaningless discourse, and that according to this criterion most of what has passed for philosophy in the past is strictly senseless. Many philosophers would now maintain that what is really shown by the positivistic arguments is not that traditional metaphysics is meaningless, but that all or most metaphysicians have misconceived the nature of the inquiries upon which they were engaged. Metaphysics is the study of the logical character of statements and questions, and in particular the search for answers to questions of the form, "What are the ultimate grounds on which such and such a type of statement may be justified?" Some metaphysical remarks are explicitly concerned with these tasks; others are disguised as descriptions of what purport to be the most general features of the actual world, or as laments on the impossibility of the very types of knowledge that they are implicitly portraying. The positivistic thesis is itself a typical piece of metaphysics in this sense. What it disguises as a distinction between the meaningful and the meaningless is an implicit comparison of some types of meaning with other types, coupled with an unfavorable evaluation of one of the classes of inquiries between which it distinguishes. The study of the logical characters of types of statements and questions and of the relations between the various types may be carried on without any hostility to any particular type and without any presupposition that there is one use, or one set of uses, of language and logic that is the paradigm from which the others decline. Those who bring to this study an openminded recognition that language and reason function differently when they are used for different purposes and on different subject matters will naturally be more interested in the history of philosophy than those who do not. Hume, the patron of positivism, was prepared to "commit to the flames" any book of philosophy that did not contain either "abstract reasonings concerning quantity or number" or "experimental reasonings concerning matter of fact or existence," since he claimed to know in advance that it could contain "nothing but sophistry and illusion." The positivists echoed these words and these principles, but their more moderate successors have returned to a study of the classic philosophers of the past, and they have also shown a renewed interest in departments of philosophical inquiry—ethics, politics, aesthetics, philosophy of history, philosophy of religion—that early extremists neglected on principle.

It therefore seems appropriate, in this new translation of selections from the works of Aristotle, to bear in mind especially the needs and interests of students and teachers of philosophy, and the requirements of those general readers whose interest in ancient thought is more than purely historical. In this Introduction and in the introductions to the separate sections will be found references to the current problems and the contemporary books and articles that are most akin to the problems Aristotle raised and discussed.

Aristotle himself made it a mark of the man of education that he would expect of each inquiry only the types of reasons appropriate to it, and only such exactness as it can afford: he did not expect mathematical rigor from an orator, nor allow a mathematician to offer rhetoric in place of proof. The energy, insight, imagination, and, above all, the sense of proportion that he brought to the study of the character of the various types of knowledge, and of the ultimate reasons for them, make him an excellent companion in that endless and inexhaustibly absorbing investigation.

ARISTOTLE'S LIFE

Aristotle was born in 384 B.C. in the Macedonian town of Stagira. His father was physician to King Amyntas II of Macedonia, and to this royal connection Aristotle owed his appointment as tutor to the boy prince who later became Alexander the Great. At the age of seventeen he left his provincial birthplace for Athens, the cultural capital of Greece, and he remained there for twenty years as a pupil and colleague of Plato. After Plato's death in 347 he left Athens to take up residence in Asia Minor, first at Assos, with whose ruler, Hermeias, he was on friendly terms, and later at Mytilene, on the island of Lesbos. While at Assos, Aristotle married Pythias, the niece of Hermeias. In 342 he returned to Macedonia to take up his tutorship of Alexander, and remained there until 336. It was in that year that Alexander succeeded to the throne of Macedonia. Aristotle went once more to Athens, and he now set up his own school, the Lyceum, side by side with the Platonic Academy, which was in the hands of Platonists whose interests were unsympathetic to Aristotle. After the death of Alexander in 323, Aristotle was in danger from the anti-Macedonian party at Athens, who trumped up a charge of impiety against him. To save himself from the fate of Socrates, and the Athenians from a second crime against philosophy, he retired to Chalcis on the island of Euboea, where he died in 322. He left behind him a daughter, who was called Pythias after her mother, and a son, Nicomachus, who was born to Herpyllis, a woman with whom Aristotle had formed a permanent liaison after the death of Pythias.

Aristotle's master and his pupil were the two greatest men of his time, with the possible exception of Aristotle himself. The association between Aristotle and Alexander has naturally excited the imagination of later ages: the future master of the known world at the feet of the "master of those who know" makes a romantic picture. The probable truth is that neither had any marked effect on the other. Aristotle's careful study of existing political institutions, and his theoretical speculations on the nature and purposes of human society, betray no greater consciousness than Plato showed in the *Republic* that the days of the Greek city-state were numbered and that henceforward the distinction between Greek and barbarian would be no more important than that between Athenian and Spartan. Alexander's achievement was to transform the world on lines of which his tutor had no inkling, and there is little evidence that he shared Aristotle's academic aspirations. He is reported to have given financial support to Aristotle's researches in biology and to have instructed his subjects to help Aristotle with his search for objects of scientific interest. But there is no historical evidence to support the legends that have flourished from the time of Plutarch onwards.

With Plato we are on firmer ground. Aristotle's twenty years in the Academy left a deep impression on his intellect and outlook. Although the commonsense cast of his mind and his early connection with the science of medicine made him primarily a biologist rather than a mathematician, it remains true that what his philosophy has in common with Platonism is as striking as the differences. Aristotle's temperament was not such as to make him show his debt in just the way that Plato had chosen to pay his debt to Socrates, but it was a profound debt, and he shows in many passages of his works that he recognized and acknowledged it. In a celebrated passage of the *Ethics* he indicates that his affection for Plato takes second place only to his love of the truth: "both are dear to us, but truth must be preferred." In some of the passages in which he is most critical of Platonism, he speaks in such terms as to associate himself closely with the school he is criticizing. The three greatest Greek philosophers form a compact intellectual dynasty, with Aristotle as the philosophical grandchild of Socrates.

ARISTOTLE'S WRITINGS

If the whole body of Aristotle's writings had been preserved for us, there is no doubt that the strength and the directness of Plato's influence on his thought would be even more clearly visible. His earliest works, of which we can form an impression only from isolated fragments and from the testimony of those who read them in antiquity, were dialogues in the Platonic manner, expounding the familiar themes of Plato's philosophy. The surviving fragments confirm the judgment of Cicero and other ancient authorities that Aristotle had a flexible and graceful literary style, but there is little in our evidence to suggest that the lost works contained any important original philosophy. They were more or less faithful expositions of the philosophy he imbibed in Plato's Academy. Like the early Socratic dialogues of Plato, they were the apprentice works of one who was only later to reveal himself as an outstanding original thinker.

The writings on which Aristotle's immense reputation is based, and by which he must now be judged, are quite different both in form and in content from the lost dialogues. Their exact purpose and their mode of production are among the most vigorously debated topics of Aristotelian scholarship, and it may be that fully agreed solutions to these problems will never be reached. What does seem clear is that the surviving treatises were not intended for wide public dissemination, but were primarily meant for use within the narrower circle of Aristotle's friends and pupils. They bear a close relation to his oral teachings in the Lyceum, and have been variously thought to be Aristotle's own notes for his lectures, or the notes taken down by pupils under his instruction. Their style is crisp and workmanlike rather than smooth or elegant, and although there are some passages that have a high polish, there are strong indications that the treatises were not prepared by their author as finished works for general publication. The quality of their content is unquestionable. They reveal a mind grappling, confidently but carefully, with an unparalleled range of academic problems; the mind of a man who is always prepared to recognize and discuss an objection or an alternative solution, but who is convinced that questioning need not be endless, that knowledge is not only attainable but has been attained. And yet Aristotle is not dogmatic. He pays explicit attention both to commonly received opinions and to the pronouncements of his predecessors; in fact, the history of philosophy is one of the many specialized studies of which he was a pioneer. When he rejects a popular or plausible view, it is never for paradoxical effect, but because "truth must be preferred"; and he is careful to give a full argument for every position he adopts.

The distinction in subject matter between the lost dialogues and the surviving treatises probably corresponds roughly with the distinction between the popular, or "exoteric," and the private, or "acroamatic," teaching of the Lyceum. Besides providing advanced and specialized instruction for specially qualified pupils, Aristotle also carried on the Platonic tradition of offering more popular fare for the general educated public. But a more important difference between the dialogues and the treatises is connected with their probable dates of composition. The dialogues were mainly written during Aristotle's membership in the Platonic Academy, whereas the treatises embody his own teaching to his pupils in the Lyceum. The dialogues are orthodox expositions of Platonism; the treatises give us the independent and original philosophy of Aristotle.

The relation between the dialogues and the treatises and, indeed, the whole question of the dates and purposes of Aristotle's various writings have been the subject of much valuable study in this century. Professor Werner Jaeger's notable book *Aristotle: Fundamentals of the History of His Development* has helped modern scholars to a new understanding of points about which, it is now clear, the easy assumptions of earlier scholars are untenable. Until Jaeger's book appeared, there were two remarks that almost any lecturer or writer on Aristotle felt bound to make at the beginning of his account, and two corresponding assumptions that would govern the whole manner in which he presented Aristotle's philosophy. The first was that the philosophy of Aristotle, unlike that of Plato, formed a single, coherent, unchanging *system*. It was recognized that there were overlappings and even contradictions between one work and another or between one passage and another; but these difficulties were always overcome by supposing that the manuscripts of the treatises had been badly edited in antiquity or that there had been unauthorized interpolations, or, indeed, by any ad hoc hypothesis that would preserve the dogma that Aristotle's doctrine was systematic and static. The assumption was a natural one, and not purely arbitrary. Aristotle does attack a philosophical problem in a much more formal and systematic manner than Plato does, and he makes much greater use of technical and semitechnical expressions. He does give the impression that he is expounding the one known and settled truth about the matters with which he deals. Both his division of knowledge into clearly separated branches and his habit of making reference from one book or topic to another help to foster the impression that he is presenting a single, fixed body of doctrine. When we further remember the extent to which Aristotle was revered in the Middle Ages as "the philosopher," the authority with a ready answer to every important problem, we can see what a weight of tradition and what strong prima facie evidence Jaeger had to resist. But there is no doubt of his success. Although work is still in progress on the detailed development of Aristotle's philosophy, Jaeger has established to the satisfaction of all serious scholars that there was such a development and that in outline it consisted of a gradual movement away from the Platonism of the dialogues toward a scientific world-picture, centered in biology and the concrete individual substance rather than in mathematics and the abstract universal substance.

Professor Jaeger's detailed discoveries will concern us when we come to look more closely at Aristotle's philosophical doctrines. But we can see at once that his work disposes of the second traditional assumption—namely, that Plato and Aristotle are natural opponents in philosophy, that their approaches to philosophy represent two irreconcilable polar opposites. The truth is that Aristotle's departure from Platonism was very gradual, and that even in his latest works we can still see the clear influence of his master. What once was thought of as a sudden reaction can now be understood as an organic growth. The hesitations that can already be seen in the dialogue *On Philosophy* grow into the severe criticisms of the "Theory of Forms" that are to be found in the *Metaphysics*. But we shall see that in Aristotle's most mature philosophy, and perhaps especially in his ethical and theological doctrines, there remains the deep impress of the philosophy of Plato.

ARISTOTLE'S PHILOSOPHY

The rejection of these two assumptions does not radically alter the character of a general exposition of Aristotle's philosophy. It remains true that his mature philosophy, as we find it in the extant treatises, is a coherent and systematic account of the branches of knowledge in which he was interested in the later periods of his teaching life. The main difference made by Jaeger's work is in our understanding of the *spirit* of Aristotle's philosophy. We may no longer think of him as grimly expounding a lifeless system of doctrine. We can now see and understand the indications in the works themselves that he adopts, in his approach to each new problem, a dialectical, tentative, exploratory technique. Many of the difficulties that commentators have made for themselves in the past have arisen from a failure to notice that Aristotle habitually expounds and elaborates lines of thought that he will in the end reject. He takes care to review the received opinions on any given topic before deriving and announcing his own conclusion, and he is constantly pausing to deal with difficulties and objections that might be raised against his provisional formulations. The difference in form and technique between the Platonic dialogue and the Aristotelian lecture or treatise is easily exaggerated. For the mature Aristotle, almost as much as for Plato and for the young Aristotle of the lost dialogues, philosophy is a debate rather than a monologue. Jaeger writes in his Introduction that "it is one of those almost incomprehensible paradoxes in which the history of human knowledge abounds, that the principle of organic development has never yet been applied to its originator." By applying the principle, Jaeger has shown that features that were for many centuries believed to belong to the philosophy of Aristotle were, in fact, in the eyes of misguided beholders.

Accounts of the separate departments and doctrines of Aristotle's philosophy will be found in the introductions to the separate sections of this book. In this General Introduction, I propose to concentrate my attention on the unifying elements in Aristotle's work. In spite of the manifold variety of his intellectual and scientific interests, he never lost sight of the unity and coherence of knowledge. There are several distinct binding agents, each of which makes an important contribution to the unifying of his work, and which combine to form the essence of Aristotle's philosophy. Chief among these are his logic, his doctrine of the four causes, his conception of substance, and his all-pervasive notions of development and end or purpose.

The importance of the *Logic* for an understanding of the unity of Aristotle's philosophy is twofold. Its primary function as a link consists in the fact that it is not a specialized branch of knowledge, side by side with physics, psychology, and "first philosophy," but rather the basic method of reasoning that is indispensable to these and to all other special intellectual disciplines. The function of logic as the tool of the sciences is well marked by the title *Organon*, or "Instrument," which was attached to the logical works at an early date (although not in the time of Aristotle himself). Aristotle was the first to grasp the importance of the *formality* of logic, its neutrality as between the subject matter of one study and another or one proposition and another; this enabled him to make great contributions to the study of the patterns of reasoning that are the concern of formal logicians. Although Aristotle recognizes that the detailed methods of particular sciences do and must differ according to their particular subject matters, he rightly insists that there is a need for and a possibility of a study of reasoning in general, which will exhibit the patterns of inference which are valid regardless of what subject matter they are applied to. For example, the rule "If all A is B and C is A, then C is B" justifies our inferring from two premises in a given *form* a conclusion in a given *form*, regardless of the *content* of the propositions that appear as premises and as conclusion in any particular application of the rule.

Formal rules of this kind enable us to proceed from knowledge to knowledge, to argue from premises whose truth is known to conclusions whose truth was hitherto unknown; but they do not give us the original and ultimate premises of our knowledge. They tell us what *must* be so *if* such and such is the case, but they do not answer the prior question—whether our *premises* are themselves true or false. Formal reasoning will increase our knowledge only if we already have some knowledge. Aristotle therefore distinguishes sharply between the demonstrative and dialectical argument. In the "Prior Analytics" he treats of the principles of reasoning from a purely formal point of view. In the "Posterior Analytics," which is concerned with the acquisition of scientific knowledge, he deals with the prior and more difficult question, "What are the principles upon which new knowledge, i.e., knowledge of *new premises*, is to be acquired?" This book does not contain any selections from the "Prior

Analytics," the contents of which are standard portions of all introductory textbooks on traditional logic. There will be found in this book, however, a translation of Book I of the "Posterior Analytics," since the topics with which it deals continue to be of live interest to logicians and philosophers. Before setting out to construct his system of knowledge, Aristotle rightly feels it necessary to show that knowledge is possible, and to deal with a number of skeptical arguments that might be raised against the initial assumptions of his program of inquiry.

It is characteristic of Aristotle that a great deal of his treatment of topics that might nowadays be included under the heading of "logic" should be found in his treatise on *Metaphysics*. Much of what he has to say in the *Metaphysics* about the law of contradiction and the law of excluded middle is closely related to what he says in the "Posterior Analytics" about the possibility of demonstrative knowledge.

It will be clear from these remarks, and still more from the content of the logical writings included in this book, that although Aristotle maintained a sturdy commonsense approach toward the questions of philosophy, he did not disdain to answer at the outset of his investigation the skeptical difficulties that had been raised by some of his predecessors, and notably by the Sophists of the preceding century.

There is a second and more fundamental sense in which the logical writings help to unify the diverse philosophical writings and doctrines of Aristotle. For this second link, the most important documents are "Categories" and "On Interpretation," two short treatises in which Aristotle deals with the logic of terms and the logic of propositions, respectively. The two have long been recognized as valuable introductory works on the topics with which they deal. What concerns us here is not their *contents*, which can be seen in the selected translations to be found later in this book and will be discussed in their proper place, but rather the assumption from which they start, and which not even their logical radicalism prompts Aristotle to doubt—namely, that all significant assertion consists in the attribution of properties to things. This assumption remains unchallenged throughout the whole of Aristotle's logical and philosophical work. The formal doctrine of syllogistic inference as expounded in the "Prior Analytics" wholly depends upon it, and we shall see later that the metaphysical doctrines of Aristotle are heavily influenced by it. Moreover, the same assumption, sometimes in the original Aristotelian form, sometimes modified by later reflection, but never wholly abandoned, dominated logical and metaphysical thinking for many centuries after Aristotle's death, and has only recently been explicitly challenged and rejected by any considerable body of philosophers. The importance of this assumption in philosophy and in the history of philosophy, and especially its centrality in any understanding of the philosophy of Aristotle, requires that it should be constantly borne in mind as we go on to consider the metaphysical doctrines to which it naturally led.

The character and importance of this assumption are at once clear from a brief glance at the doctrine of the "Categories." This work is intended to answer the question: "What kinds of questions can be asked about the things that are in the world, and what kinds of answers are appropriate to such questions?" Both the form in which the problem is propounded and the manner in which the topic is treated presuppose without argument that anything that can be spoken of is either a thing or an attribute or property of a thing. In the "On Interpretation," it is expressly stated that although there are uses of language to which no considerations of truth or falsehood are relevant, every *proposition*, every remark of which it may appropriately be said that it is true or false, consists in assigning a predicate to a subject. We shall see later why this presupposition is so attractive and so tenacious, and also why in the last analysis it must be given up. For the present, it is sufficient to stress its fundamental role in Aristotle's philosophy as the basis on which he builds and the mortar by which he binds together his logical, physical, metaphysical, biological, psychological, moral, and political doctrines. It serves not only as one of the links that unify his philosophy but also as a link between the links themselves.

Its effect on the doctrine of the four causes is clear and decisive. Because of modern developments in the physical sciences, we have come to think of causation primarily as a relation between *events*; but for Aristotle, the four causes were primarily causes of *things* or *substances*. The doctrine is intended as an account of how particular substances originate or "come to be" and why they have those properties that we recognize in them. When we think in these terms, and escape from our customary preoccupation with *events*, we can see at once how natural and how closely interconnected are the four questions to which Aristotle's four causes indicate the relevant types of answer: *What is it? What is it made of? How was it made? Why was it made?* These are the questions that Aristotle asks of everything that comes within his purview; but it is clear that there are two subjects to which the questions are especially relevant, and with which Aristotle is especially concerned.

For Aristotle, the principal sources of all motion and change, and therefore of all "coming to be and passing away," are nature and mind. Hence, it is no accident, but an essential feature of his causal theory, that the four causes should be illustrated so often and so effectively in terms of examples drawn from biology and from human skills of manufacture. It is primarily and most typically the man, the horse, or the tree and the house, the ax, or the statue whose character, composition, origin, and purpose are to be understood and explained in terms of form, matter, efficient cause and end: and by "man" or "house" is meant primarily *this* man or *this* house; the particular, individual substance and not the universal. It is true that in one sense all things have the same causes, "by analogy;" but every individual substance has its own individual causes: "Peleus is the father of Achilles, and your father of you." The sense in which all things have the same causes might be paraphrased by saying that there is a single framework of causal conceptions into which the causes of all individual substances can be fitted. Every substance has *a* form, but not every substance has *the same* form: every man has *a* father, but not every man has *the same* father.

The primacy of the individual thing, which is presupposed in the *Logic* and is implicit in the account of the four causes in the *Physics* and the *Metaphysics*, becomes explicit in those parts of the *Metaphysics* that deal with the notion of substance. It is here, too, that the insistence on the subject-predicate form as the essential form of all significant assertion exerts its most profound influence, both for good and for ill, on Aristotle's philosophy. The search for substance is the search for that which most truly and essentially *is*, that which can only properly be made the subject of predication, and not predicated of something else. Aristotle here shows his awareness of the distinctions between logical form and grammatical form and between logical form and what used to be called "the form of the fact." The grammatical subject of a particular sentence may not denote the logical subject of the proposition expressed in the sentence; the logical subject of a particular proposition may not be something whose only proper place in a proposition is that of logical subject. There are many things that *may* be the logical subjects of propositions; the search for true substance is the search for what *must* be the logical subject of a proposition if it is to be accorded the status in thought and speech that belongs to it in the order of being. By an investigation whose stages are traced in Book VII of the *Metaphysics*, and which will be expounded later in this book, Aristotle arrives at the conclusion that the concrete individual thing is substance in this primary sense.

We are now in a position to see the closeness of the connection between Aristotle's metaphysical doctrine and his concern with biological investigation. For Plato, pure mathematics had been the paradigm of clarity and certainty by whose standards all other branches of knowledge were to be judged. Consequently, the emphasis in Plato's metaphysical doctrine is on the universal and the abstract. Aristotle does not abandon the Platonic conviction that knowledge is of what is universal, but his distinction between what is most knowable *in itself* and what is most knowable *to us* enables his formal theory to give to the concrete individual substance the important place that it must necessarily have in the researches of the biologist. We have already seen that the individual plant or animal is one of the two types of substance whose character and genesis can be most easily studied in terms of the theory of the four causes. If we now pay particular attention to what is for Aristotle the chief among the causes—the *end* toward which every substance, whether it exists by nature or by human agency, is striving, and in terms of which it must be understood—it becomes more than ever clear that the logic, the theory of substance, and the theory of causation are not isolated doctrines. They are united into a coherent picture of the world and of our knowledge, and prominent in the foreground are the science of biology and the plants and animals that are its subject matter.

The same notion of end or purpose, with the related conception of growth and development, gives its characteristic stamp to Aristotle's treatment of ethics, politics, and literature. Just as "God and Nature do nothing in vain," so that the questions "What is it for?" and "What is the condition in which it reaches its fullest maturity?" are the right questions to ask about a plant or animal or any one of its separate parts or organs, so are the lives and activities of men to be studied and understood in terms of aims and ends. An individual man, a community, or a tragedy has a function and a purpose, in relation to which it is to be judged a good or bad specimen of its species, and hence it is more than a manner of speaking to say of Aristotle's *Ethics, Politics*, and *Poetics* that they, no less than the *Historia Animalium* or the *De Partibus Animalium*, are biological works. It is no accident that it was a pupil of Aristotle's who wrote the first detailed account of types and traits of human personality—the *Characters* of Theophrastus. Aristotle himself, in the *Ethics*, gives much of his space to a description of human characters and motives, to the discomfiture of those for whom the ethics of Plato constitute the pattern by which all moral inquiries must be judged. Similarly, his suggestions for the constitution of an ideal community are based on an empirical study of actual cities and their constitutions, and his remarks on the writing of tragedy are informed and directed by a careful attention to actual tragedies. In a passage in the *Politics*, he explicitly draws the analogy between biology and the human sciences on which he implicitly operates in the *Ethics* and the *Poetics*. Just as we form our conception of a good oak tree or a good lion by inspection of actual individual oak trees or lions, so we may come to see what a man or a city or a tragedy *ought* to be like by seeing what the actual specimens of the species *are* like.

Here again, Aristotle is concerned with the concrete and particular, whereas Plato deals in the general and the abstract. Plato, the mathematician, tries to arrive at external and universal norms by which the conduct of men may be governed and judged. Aristotle adopts a more piecemeal approach because it is natural for him to judge men by internal, that is to say, by *human*, standards. Those who prefer the Platonic approach are inclined to dismiss Aristotle's ethics as "merely descriptive" or even as "subjective"; but this is to miss the point of Aristotle's treatment. He is as keenly concerned as Plato that we should acquire moral understanding in order to become better men and to lead better lives, and he shares Plato's conviction that there is an objectively determinable answer to every well-formulated moral question. The difference is that Aristotle is not a moral innovator or reformer: he wishes to keep us up to the mark, not to set us a new mark to aim at. Here, as elsewhere, we find him identifying nature and purpose in such a sense that to study one is to come to understand the other: if we rightly understand the nature of man, we shall rightly conceive the end for man.

This intimate connection between nature and end or purpose is itself one of the links connecting the various departments of Aristotle's philosophy. In Aristotle's own terms it is seen as a close connection between form and end. The character of a substance—what it is for it to be a substance of the kind to which it belongs—is comprehensible only in terms of the condition in which the substance reaches its proper fulfillment. We therefore distort the picture if we say without qualification that the end is for Aristotle the primary cause. It is, rather, that end and form are aspects of a single principle of explanation. To know what something is is to know what it is *for*; to know what something is for, we must learn what is its nature, its character, its *form*. But even this is not the whole story. The primacy of end or purpose, which involves, as we now see, the primacy of form, is a natural consequence of Aristotle's view that motion and change are to be attributed to the operation of human purpose, or of a nature that is itself a purposive agency. (The only exceptions—namely, spontaneous and chance events—are, significantly, explained as *privations* of the powers of nature or the human mind; they are the cases in which what *might have been* the outcome of purposive action transpires without such action.) It follows that the final cause, or end, is to be identified not only with form but also with the efficient cause, or cause of motion. The end is understood not as something purely passive, but rather as an active influence on that which is in process of growth or development toward its complete condition. This element in Aristotle's doctrine is best understood by taking account of his distinction between potentiality and actuality. The efficient cause is always something that *actually* possesses a given form and that is therefore capable of transmitting it to something else that *potentially*, but not so far actually, possesses that same form.

More must be said of all these separate doctrines in their proper places, and at each stage it will be necessary and possible to underline the patterns of relationship between one doctrine and the rest. But it will already be clear what flexibility and adaptability Aristotle's conceptions display, and yet how well fitted they are to mark the connections between one aspect and another of our knowledge and of the world that is its object. Plato was obsessed with *likenesses*; and hence his metaphysical doctrine is likely to give the impression, in the words of Professor H. H. Price, "that the world is a tidier place than it is." Some philosophers, like Hume for example, have given the impression that the world is more discrete and disconnected than it is. Aristotle permits himself to mark similarities without forgetting differences and to draw distinctions without overlooking connections. His respect for the concrete individual saved him from the oversimplifications of Platonism. His Platonistic insistence that knowledge is of the universal, that knowledge is knowledge of causes, and that the causes of all things are causes of the same specifiable *kinds* enabled him to do justice to the variety and complexity of the world without making it too disordered for human comprehension.

This is not to say that Aristotle makes things easy for us. His doctrine is by no means always clear, and some of the greatest difficulties arise from precisely those features of his thought that I have just been stressing. For example, Book VII of the *Metaphysics*, in which he gives his principal account of the concept of *ousia*, or substance, is notoriously difficult, and the difficulty consists in this: that Aristotle appears to be giving several different and incompatible answers to the question "What is substance?" when he is in fact stressing the analogies between form, matter, the compound of form and matter, substratum, universal, and genus, which make it plausible to think of any one of them as a possible candidate for the title of substance in the primary sense of the word. All these candidates are prima facie suitable because each one of them is well fitted to be the subject of predication. Although *being* is ambiguous, as Aristotle declares at the very beginning of the book, it is not *merely* ambiguous. It is not for nothing that the same word is used, even if it is used in many different ways. Similarly, it is not for nothing that all the causes are called causes: although we must carefully differentiate them one from another, we must also see that they all contribute in their different ways to the search for a single unified understanding.

Every comprehensive philosophy constitutes a scaffolding on which the whole world can be constructed. Few philosophers would now claim that there is one framework of concepts that uniquely corresponds with the structure of the actual world; some have explicitly maintained that in order to understand the world rightly, we need to follow out to its conclusion each of the great metaphysical theories in turn. For all who do not despair of constructive philosophy in all its forms, the system of Aristotle must remain of absorbing interest. It shows its vitality by its very independence of the particular circumstances of its composition and of the inevitable limitations, long ago transcended by his successors, of Aristotle's knowledge in this or that branch of specialized inquiry.

This Introduction did not set out to review every one of Aristotle's doctrines in turn so much as to portray the character of his philosophy as a whole; more detailed comments on the most important particular doctrines will be found in the introductions to the separate sections. But it may be briefly indicated here how all-embracing the fundamental framework of his philosophy is by mentioning one or two doctrines of which little or nothing has so far been said and showing how each derives its nature and its power from the same central principles—the theory of substance and the theory of causation—which in turn are derived from the fundamental role assigned to the subject-predicate form of proposition.

His theory of universals depends heavily on his distinction between form and matter. What is universal is the form, which characterizes a number of individual instances, but is separable from the particular individuals only in thought and not in fact. The concepts of form and matter are again prominent in his account of the relation between soul and body. Each organism is a compound of formal and material principles; and the body of an animal is its matter, whereas the soul is its form, moving cause and end. Finally, Aristotle's theology is to be seen as a study of pure form and actuality. The God, or Unmoved Mover, of Book XII of the *Metaphysics* stands at the summit of the hierarchy of substances as the ultimate moving cause whose activity is the source of all motion and change: God is pure form, pure moving cause, and pure end, the supreme instance of the identity of all the three nonmaterial causes.

No attempt to summarize Aristotle can be successful. Like any other philosopher, he stands or falls by the detail of his work, by the *texture* of his arguments and discussions. It is time to turn away from signposts to the road, from charts to the voyage.

THE PHILOSOPHY OF
ARISTOTLE

METAPHYSICS

Introduction

For an understanding of Aristotle's metaphysical doctrine, it is necessary to consider further the nature and influence of his presupposition in favor of the subject-predicate form of proposition, and to say more about the relations between logic, language and the world. Whether we see metaphysics in its traditional light, as an attempt to portray the most general features of the world and its structure, or in more recent terms, as a search for the nature of the ultimate justifications of our statements about the world, it is clear that, in either case, some conception of the relation between language and the world will be necessary for the metaphysician. Philosophers from Plato to Wittgenstein have always inveighed against the treacherous fascination of language and have pleaded with us to look at *things as they are* and not at mere words. But as the work of even the greatest philosophers amply illustrates, this advice is easier to give than to take. Language is the necessary medium of philosophical as of all other communication. Great perplexity inevitably lies in store for us when we try to make the clear distinctions between language, thought, and the world that we must make if we are to see any of them as it is in itself, unaffected by its contact with the others. For each is inseparably intertwined with the others, and the philosophical desire to separate them cuts us loose from our usual moorings and puts us to sea with no chart and no landmarks.

This reference to navigation suggests an analogy that may help us here. It is clearly necessary (and, at first sight, quite easy) to distinguish between those features of a map that correspond with features of the land that is mapped by it and those that are features conferred on the map by the mode of its projection and do not correspond simply and straightforwardly with any features of the land that is being mapped. For example, in a map on Mercator's projection, the general shapes and relative positions of the continents are fairly directly represented. If we could see the whole of South America from an earth satellite, it would look roughly carrot-shaped, as it looks roughly carrot-shaped on Mercator's map; and on Mercator's map, just as on the surface of the earth, if we move from Sweden to Italy and then continue in the same direction, we shall arrive in Africa. Thus, we may come to think that the correspondence between the map and the earth's surface is closer than it is, or more direct than it is, and this will lead us into error. If we suppose that one inch on the map of Ecuador represents the same distance on the earth's surface as one inch on the map of the Sudan, all will be well. But if we suppose, again, that one inch on the map of Greenland or of Tasmania represents the same distance, we shall be mistaken. There is a systematic distortion of relative size and distance in a map on Mercator's projection. Landmasses near the poles are made relatively larger and those near the equator relatively smaller than they actually are; Greenland occupies a much greater proportion of the map than it does of the surface of the earth. The point is most strikingly illustrated by noting that on the map the North Pole and the equator are represented by lines of equal length, whereas on the surface of the earth the pole is a point and the equator is a line of approximately 24,000 miles in length.

If we know and understand the projection, we do not have any serious trouble with a map; and since the projection was deliberately devised, it is quite easy to come to understand and to use it. But the modes of projection by which our language portrays the world are not set out for us in any elementary textbook; and although they are human products, they were not *deliberately* devised by any human beings. It is therefore a matter of the most stubborn difficulty to know and to explain at what points and in what respects our language does and does not directly represent the world that it is used to describe. The struggle with this difficulty is a very large part of the task of metaphysics. The group of treatises that we know as Aristotle's *Metaphysics* is primarily concerned with this central problem.

Aristotle's own name for metaphysics was "first philosophy," and his conception of its nature and function is expressed in rather different terms from those I have used so far. If we now go on to look in more detail at some of his metaphysical doctrines, I think it will become clear that the differences of idiom are merely a superficial disguise for an underlying identity of aim and scope. We can most conveniently begin by examining the influence on Aristotle's thought of the subject-predicate form of his language. We see in the "Categories" how natural it was for Aristotle to take as his starting point the fact that in his native language, as in ours, the grammatical form most frequently and prominently used for making assertions about the world is that in which an attribute or property, designated by a grammatical predicate, is ascribed to a thing or substance, designated by a grammatical subject. Although he is well aware that this grammatical form is not an infallible indication that the sentence in which it occurs is making an assertion of this type, he sees it as fundamental because he holds that every other form of proposition presupposes propositions of this type. He accordingly concludes that the world that we describe in language must have a structure whose basic elements are the concrete particular substances of which the subjects of these fundamental propositions are the names, and that everything in the world that is not such a substance must be an affection or attribute of such a substance. We shall need to consider later whether Aristotle is justified in his assumptions and conclusions, but it is already clear that, rightly or wrongly, he is presupposing a fairly straightforward correspondence between the structure of his language and the structure of the world—or, in the terms of our analogy, between the features of the map and the features of the landscape.

The outline of this picture of the world is simple enough, but Aristotle finds it necessary to complicate the scheme if he is to reconcile it with other prominent features of language and of the world. The word *ousia*, which is usually translated as "substance," and which is Aristotle's word for his concrete particular substances, is in fact the abstract noun formed from the Greek verb "to be," so that "being" or "essence" would be a more literal translation of it. Now, Aristotle conceives of his metaphysical inquiry as a study of *ousia*, or "being" in general, and he recognizes, and indeed insists, that the verb "to be" is used in many and various ways, not only existentially and predicatively. In Book VII of the *Metaphysics* Aristotle studies the relations and distinctions between these various senses. The book is in effect a dialectical inquiry, in which the reasons for and against a number of possible candidates for the position of primary substance are considered. For example, matter, or the underlying substance, is in a sense substance because it is of the matter that we predicate the qualities that constitute the form. Again, form or essence is substance in a sense, for we know what something is if, and only if, we know its essence. The universal and the genus also have some of the qualifications that we require in what we shall be prepared to regard as the basic *being* that is the object of our search.

This is one of the most difficult books in the whole corpus of Aristotle's works, but it is also one of the most rewarding to the student whose interest in philosophy is more than purely historical; and the difficulties are in any case not so great as some commentators have made them out to be. Some have failed to recognize the tentative, dialectical, aporetic character of this book and have therefore tried to elicit from it an answer to the question "What is substance?" that will consist in choosing one of the possible candidates and wholly rejecting all the others. This attempt implies a serious misunderstanding of Aristotle's aim and achievement. The effect of his discussion, and probably also its intention, is to exhibit some of the formal analogies between the multifarious uses of the verb "to be." Being is an ambiguous concept, but its ambiguities are systematic rather than casual. It is not merely accidental, but essential, to the structure of the Greek language that the verb *einai* and the subject-predicate sentence-form in which its parts are so often put to work should be so readily adaptable to a variety of purposes between which there are striking differences as well as striking similarities. We have seen that Aristotle's causal theory can be understood as a logical framework or structure that is itself firm and fixed but that may be applied in an indefinite variety of contexts. Similarly, the substance-attribute conception is to be seen as a logical framework, always exhibiting the same internal structure but capable of being variously applied.

This account is in danger of being as obscure as the doctrine it is meant to elucidate. A simpler illustration from another context will help to clarify it. We make a sharp distinction between means and end, but it is certainly not the case that every action we perform must be classified without qualification as *either* a means *or* an end. A train may be the means by which I travel to London, and arriving in London is therefore the end to which the train journey is the means, but my going to London may itself be a means to some further end, say, that of looking at the Elgin marbles in the British Museum. The means-end distinction has the same *sense* in all the instances of its correct use, and whenever we speak of an end, it makes sense to ask for the means, and vice versa; but the activities or objects that may serve as means or ends are infinitely various, and what is now a means may at another time be an end, and vice versa.

The same point can be made about the distinction between cause and effect. To say that something is a cause or an effect is to say that it has an effect or a cause, but there are no events which are always and necessarily causes and never effects, or always and nec-essarily effects and never causes.

Aristotle himself does give a special status to one par-ticular use of the subject-predicate form, namely, that in which the subject is a particular concrete substance such as a horse or a statue; and he has been criticized by later philosophers for failing to see that there is no *necessity* for giving primacy to this use. He has been accused, with some plausibility, of reading into the world itself a structure that is suggested by the structure of his lan-guage but that need not be supposed to be the actual metaphysical structure of the world. But many critics have made too much of this objection, and some have even gone so far as to say that Aristotle was placing a heavy weight of doctrine on what is "merely an accident of language." This extreme accusation overlooks the important fact that Greek and other Indo-European lan-guages have the structure that they have, not as the re-sult of a mere accident, but because that structure equips them very well to deal with the world as it is in terms of the interests and purposes of the speakers of those languages. It is true that Aristotle did not know that among the actual languages of men there are some whose structure is very different from that of Greek; and it did not occur to him that, quite apart from the *actual* cases, there is an infinite variety of *possible* language structures. But his critics forget that if the structure of a language bore no relation to the nature of the world in and of which it is used, then it would not be a viable and effective instrument for the purposes of its speakers. Aristotle's metaphysical doctrine is an account of the-world-as-we-know-it, and he was right in supposing that this is closely connected with the-world-as-we-describe-it. His mistake consisted in supposing that the relation between language and the world is simpler and more direct than it is, not in supposing that there is such a relation.

Aristotle's metaphysics is of the kind which P. F. Strawson calls "descriptive," as opposed to "revisionary." He set himself to reveal and describe the systematic relations that can variously be understood as relations between terms in a language, between the concepts expressed by the terms, or between the things or phenomena described in the language. Recent philosophers have been much concerned with questions about the relations between grammar and logic, and philosophy and metaphysics or ontology; and these questions are important for us if we wish to understand and describe the nature of philosophical thinking. But in reading a descriptive metaphysician like Aristotle we shall gain little and lose little by understanding his work in any one of these three ways rather than in any other. The structure is the same whether we think of it as linguistic, logical, or ontological, just as the course of a game of chess may be exactly the same whether the game is played with ivory chessmen, with a makeshift set consisting of coins and buttons, with live human beings, or with no physical pieces at all.

If Aristotle were to enter into the modern dispute to which I am now referring, there is little doubt that he would describe his metaphysical work as ontological rather than as linguistic or logical. In Book VII, Chapter 4, he remarks that our concern is with how things are, and not with what we should say. But he frequently speaks in the other idioms, often using "what we say" as an indication of how to answer a philosophical question. His treatment of the "coupled terms" like "snub" shows how closely connected in his mind, and in fact, are the idioms of a language and the things that are described in language.

The conception of metaphysics that I have illustrated by special reference to the important and central concept of being or substance applies also to the other important concepts that Aristotle discusses in these books, and all his metaphysical writing is to be understood in the same spirit. The conceptions of potentiality and actuality, and of substratum and contraries, as well as those of form, matter, efficient cause, and end that we have met in other contexts, are all derived from a study of the ways in which language-as-we-use-it is applied to the-world-as-we-know-it.

But there are two further topics that call for separate treatment: his theory of universals and his theology. Aristotle's discussion of the so-called "problem of universals" is one of the most perennially interesting parts of his metaphysical work, both because of the importance and the constant recurrence of the problem itself and because it is here above all that we can see how he absorbed and yet transcended what Plato had taught him.

Language and thought would be impossible if the world consisted wholly of particular things of which each was unique in all its features. We cannot speak or think at all without attending to or marking connections or similarities between things or events, without dividing things into *kinds* or attending to *properties* that are found in numerically different individuals. The problem of universals may be expressed in the following questions: "What does it mean to be of a certain *kind*?" "What is the nature of the connection between a number of *different* things when they are all of the *same* kind?" "What is the justification, if any, for applying the *same* word to *different* things; for example, the word 'man' both to Socrates and to Callias?"

Plato's answer to this "problem of the one and the many" had consisted in saying that the many particular instances that fall under the same general term were all related in the same way to a *form*. The form was conceived as a substance existing in its own right and independently of the particular instances, and on which the instances depended for their existence and nature. The forms constitute a real but invisible, intangible, suprasensible world; they are the substance of which the world that we see and touch is a mere shadow. In Shelley's words, "The One remains, the Many change and pass." We can make a particular table that did not exist before; we can destroy this or that particular table, and even *all* particular tables; but the universal form of table is beyond change and decay.

Plato himself, toward the end of his life, had become conscious of some of the serious logical difficulties that face such a theory. In the first part of his *Parmenides*, he sees that these difficulties come to a head in the problem of describing the relation between the form and the instances. If we say that the particulars participate or share in the form, we seem to be destroying the form's essential and indispensable unity. If we say that the particulars resemble the form or are copies of it, we seem to need an extra form to explain the connection between the members of the class consisting of the-particulars-and-the-form, and so on to a viciously infinite regress. (This is the difficulty that Aristotle refers to as "the third man.")

Aristotle believed that these insoluble problems arose from the initial false step of treating the form as a separate substance, existing in its own right and apart from the particulars. Only concrete particular things can exist by themselves. To say that Socrates and Callias are both men is not to say that over and above Socrates and Callias there is a third thing, *man*, to which they are both related in the same way. It is indeed to say that they both have the same character or form; but as Aristotle makes clear in his general account of the four causes, the form of something is not a separate *element* either inside or outside the particular thing itself, but its *nature*. It follows, as G. E. M. Anscombe has pointed out (in *Three Philosophers*, by G. E. M. Anscombe and P. T. Geach), that Aristotle does not, as is often said, believe in *universalia in rebus* any more than he believes in Plato's *universalia ante res*. He complains that Plato's reduplication of the world is a reduplication of the problem, not a solution of it. It must also be emphasized how far Aristotle is from the *nominalist* position that things that are called by the same name have nothing in common except that they are called by the same name. In thus mediating between nominalism and both kinds of realism Aristotle anticipates some of the important work of Wittgenstein on this topic in *The Blue and Brown Books* and the *Philosophical Investigations*. There is a particularly modern ring about Aristotle's remark, in Chapter 24 of Book I of the "Posterior Analytics," that a word may have *one meaning* without necessarily referring to *one thing*. The assumption that he is there rejecting is among the prime sources of Plato's theory.

It is in Book XII of the *Metaphysics* that we find Aristotle's main account of his theology. Aristotle uses the word "theology" for his study of the highest and purest substance, and we shall misunderstand his intentions unless we disregard some of the most important and familiar associations of the word. His God is the ancestor of that "God of the philosophers and scholars" whom Pascal rejected, and as far as any God could well be from the God of Abraham and of Isaac and of Jacob. It is true that Aristotle urges us to aspire after that life of contemplation that is God's life intensely and eternally but that man can achieve only intermittently and in low degree. On this point, *Metaphysics* XII must be read in close association with Book X of the *Ethics*. But in no other respect is the God of Aristotle a God who will satisfy the religious needs of men. He is an answer to philosophical and cosmological problems, rather than an object of worship or a source of spiritual redemption.

The two main functions of God in Aristotle's philosophy are to account for the continuous occurrence of motion and change and to provide a principle of unity for the world. He argued that change and motion must be eternal since change is inseparable from time, and it is absurd to speak of anything that is "before time" or "after time." The observable revolution of the fixed stars seemed to him to confirm that change was continuous and eternal. Now, the ultimate source of motion cannot be something that is itself moved, since its own motion would need to be attributed to some source outside itself. The ultimate source of motion is therefore an *unmoved* mover; and this is God. He is pure form and pure actuality, for any admixture of matter or potentiality would destroy his primacy and independence. In a comparison that reminds us of the Platonic origins of his metaphysical thinking, Aristotle likens the action of the unmoved mover to the effect of love or desire. The object of love is the cause of a change in the lover, without itself being changed. Similarly, God is the object of the aspirations of other substances but is not himself susceptible to change or motion. God unifies the world by being the ultimate end toward which other things aspire; he is the pinnacle of Aristotle's teleological hierarchy. There is only one world and only one God; for if there were two or more worlds, and consequently two or more Gods, the Gods would have to be differentiated by matter and therefore could not be pure form and actuality.

The activity of God is thought, which is the highest activity; and thought about God himself, for he is the highest object of thought.

There is clearly no place in Aristotle's scheme for the creation of the world by God, although the world depends on him as the ultimate cause of all that happens within it. Some commentators have tried to accommodate divine providence into the scheme, but the task is impossible. In Chapter 10 of Book XII, Aristotle says that the *good* in the world is both its immanent order and the perfection of the transcendent God; but there is no suggestion that God himself is immanent in the world, or even that he is aware of anything outside himself.

Book I

1. All men by nature desire to have knowledge. An indication of this is the delight that we take in the senses; quite apart from the use that we make of them, we take delight in them for their own sake, and more than of any other this is true of the sense of sight. For not only when we want to do something, but even when we have no intention of doing anything at all, we prefer sight to practically every other sense. The reason for this is that, more than any other sense, it enables us to get to know things, and it reveals a number of differences between things.

Animals have senses by nature when they are born; from this, memory develops in some of them, but not in others. Consequently, those animals in whom memory does develop are more intelligent and learn more readily than those in whom it does not. (Those that, while they have memory, cannot hear sounds—bees, for instance, and any other animals that are of this kind—are intelligent but cannot learn; those that have this sense as well as memory do learn.) Other animals, then, live by impressions and memories and have only a small share of experience; but the human race lives, too, by art and by calculations. Experience is produced in men from memory, since many memories of the same thing produce the effect of a single experience. Experience seems to be almost the same sort of thing as science and art; but, in fact, it is through experience that science and art occur among men, since, as Polus says, "experience produces art, but inexperience chance." Art comes into being when, from many notions derived from experience, one universal judgment is formed about things that are alike. If one judges that when Callias was suffering from a particular illness, a particular thing did him good, and that the same was the case with Socrates and with many other individuals, this is all part of experience; but if one judges that it does good to all people of a particular kind, who are thus defined as belonging to a single class and who are suffering from a particular illness— phlegmatic or bilious people, for instance, suffering from a burning fever—this is part of art.

As far as getting things done is concerned, experience does not seem to differ at all from art; in fact, we observe that those who have experience meet with more success than those who have grasped the principles of the subject without having any experience. The reason for this is that experience is knowledge of individuals, whereas art is knowledge of universals, and all activities and processes have to do with individuals. The doctor does not treat "man" except accidentally; he treats Callias or Socrates, or someone else described in this way, who is accidentally "man." So, if someone has grasped the principles of the subject without having any experience, and thus knows the universal without knowing the individuals contained in it, he will often fail in his treatment; for it is the individual that has to be treated. Nonetheless, we do regard knowledge and understanding as belonging more to art than to experience; and we regard those who possess an art as wiser than those who just have experience, on the grounds that in every case wisdom follows on knowledge. We have this attitude because those who possess art know causes, whereas the others do not. Men who have experience know that a thing is so, but not why it is so; those who know why a thing is so also know its cause. This is why we regard the master craftsmen in any field as more deserving of respect, more knowledgeable, and wiser than manual workers: because they know the causes of the things being done; the manual workers are like certain inanimate objects in that they do things without knowing what they are doing—fire, for instance, burns in this way; however, whereas inanimate objects do all of these things somehow by nature, manual workers do them by habit. Thus it is not on the grounds of their greater success in doing things that we judge some people to be wiser than others, but because of their grasp of principles and knowledge of causes. In general, too, what distinguishes the man who has knowledge from the man who does not is the ability to teach, and this is why we regard art as being more truly knowledge than experience: those who possess art can teach, those who do not cannot.

Further, we do not regard perception by any of the senses as wisdom; yet it is these perceptions that form our most authoritative knowledge of individual things. But they do not answer the question "Why?" about anything; they do not, for instance, tell us *why* fire is hot, only *that* it is hot.

It is therefore probable that the man who first discovered any kind of art that went beyond man's ordinary perceptions was admired by mankind not just because of anything useful that there might be in his discoveries, but also on the grounds that he was wise and superior to everyone else. It is also probable that, as more arts were discovered—some dealing with the necessities of life, others with its recreations—those who discovered the recreational arts were thought of as wiser than the others because their sciences were not developed to be useful. Hence, it was when all such sciences had been fully developed that those other ones were discovered, those that aimed neither at providing pleasure nor at coping with the necessities of life; and this happened first in those places where people had leisure. Thus it was in Egypt that mathematics was first organized, since the priestly class there was left with leisure.

I have explained in the *Ethics* what the difference is between "science," "art," and the other terms of this kind. My purpose in embarking on this discussion is to show that everyone regards what he calls wisdom as being concerned with first causes and principles. Thus, as we have said earlier, the man with experience is regarded as wiser than those who have just sensations, of whatever kind; the man who possesses an art as wiser than those who just have experience; the master craftsman as wiser than the manual worker; and the theoretical sciences as more important than the productive ones. It is, then, clear that wisdom is a science that is concerned with certain principles and causes.

2. Since this is the science about which we are trying to find out, we must inquire the kind of causes and principles of which wisdom is the science. This will perhaps become clearer if we look at our own notions about the wise man.

In the first place, we suppose the wise man to know everything, as far as that is possible, although without having knowledge of every individual. Secondly, we regard as wise the man who grasps things that are difficult and not easy for man to grasp. (Perception is common to everyone, so it is easy and in no way a mark of wisdom.) Further, with regard to every science, we think a man wiser the more accurate he is and the more he can tell us about causes. Then, among the sciences, we hold one that is desirable for its own sake and for the sake of knowledge to be more truly wisdom than one that is desirable only for what follows from it, and one that involves the giving of directions as more so than any that is subordinate to it; for the wise man ought not to be given instructions, he ought to give them, and he ought not to obey anyone else, someone less wise than he should obey him.

Such, then, are the notions that we have about wisdom and wise men. To take them in turn, knowledge of everything necessarily belongs to the man who more than any other has knowledge of universals, since such a man knows in a way all the individuals that are included in them. Further, the things that are the most universal are pretty well the most difficult things for men to get to know, since they are the furthest removed from the senses. Then, the most accurate sciences are those that are most concerned with first principles, since those that are derived from fewer principles are more accurate than those that have additional ones; arithmetic, for instance, is more accurate than geometry. Again, the science that studies causes is more informative than any other, since the people who really give us information about anything are those who tell us its causes. Then, knowledge and understanding for their own sake belong most of all to the knowledge of what is most knowable; for the man who chooses knowledge for its own sake will above all choose what is most truly knowledge, and this is knowledge of what is most knowable; and the things that are most knowable are first principles and causes, since it is through and from these that we get to know everything else: it is not from the particulars that we get to know first principles. Further, the science that most involves the giving of directions, and that does so more than any subordinate to it, is the one that knows the purpose for which each thing has to be done; and this purpose is the good of each thing, and in general what is best in the whole of nature. From all these points it follows that the name into which we are inquiring applies to one and the same science: this must be the one that studies first principles and causes, for the good and the purpose of things are among these causes.

That this science is not a productive one is clear from the first people who practiced philosophy. It is from a feeling of wonder that men start now, and did start in the earliest times, to practice philosophy. Originally they wondered about strange things that were at hand; then, as they went forward bit by bit on this line of inquiry they got bewildered about larger issues, like the changes of the moon, the sun, and the stars and the origin of the universe. Now the man who is in a state of bewilderment and wonder thinks that he is ignorant (hence, even a man who is fond of myths is in a way a philosopher, since a myth is made up of wonders); so, if it were to escape ignorance that men engaged in philosophy, plainly they were pursuing science for the sake of knowledge, and not for any practical purpose. This is borne out by what actually happened. It was when all the necessities of life and everything conducive to ease and enjoyment were already there that this kind of wisdom began to be studied. Plainly, then, we do not study it for any use beyond itself; rather, just as a free man is one who exists for his own sake and not for anyone else's, so we study this science as the only one that is free, since it is the only one that is studied for its own sake. For this reason, one would be justified in regarding the possession of it as more than human, since human nature is in many respects enslaved; in this case, as Simonides says, "this privilege would belong to God alone," and man should not seek any knowledge that is not at his own level. Indeed, if there is anything in what the poets say, and the divine nature is such that it can feel envy, it is in this case that it is most likely to happen, and that all the outstanding people will meet with misfortune. But in fact neither is it possible for what is divine to feel envy—rather, as the saying goes, "poets tell many lies"—nor ought we to regard any science as more precious than this. For what is most divine is also most precious, and only this science can be called most divine, on two counts. In the first place, a divine science is one that God himself would most of all possess; and secondly, it is any science that is concerned with divine matters. This science alone has both these characteristics: God is agreed by everybody to be one of the causes of things and to be a first principle; and a science like this would be possessed only by God, or at least by him more than by anyone else. Thus, although all other sciences are more necessary than this one, none is better.

Our state when we possess such a science ought in a way to be the reverse of our state when we embark upon our inquiry. For, as I have remarked, all men start from wondering that things are as they are—puppets, for instance, or the solstices, or the incommensurability of the diagonal; for it is a source of wonder to all who have not yet studied the cause that anything cannot be measured by its smallest unit. But we ought to end up in an opposite and, as the saying goes, better state, as people do in these cases, when they understand them. For nothing would cause a geometrician to wonder more than if the diagonal were to become commensurable.

We have thus explained the nature of the science into which we are inquiring and the aim that our inquiry and our whole investigation should attain.

3. It is plain, then, that it is of ultimate causes that we must obtain knowledge, since it is when we think that we have grasped its first cause that we say that we know a thing. Now causes are talked of in four different ways: one cause is the being and essence of a thing, what it is for a thing to be what it is (for the reason why a thing is as it is is ultimately reducible to its definition, and the ultimate reason why a thing is as it is is a cause and first principle); a second is a thing's matter and substratum; a third is the source of its movement; and the fourth, the counterpart to the third, is the purpose of a thing and its good—for this is the goal of all generation and movement. We have studied these causes adequately in the *Physics*; nonetheless, let us review those who have proceeded before us to the investigation of reality and who have practiced philosophy in the hope of discovering the truth. For quite clearly they too talk of certain principles and causes, so that it will be of use in our present inquiry that they be brought before our notice. Either we shall find some other kind of cause or we shall have more confidence in the ones that I have just mentioned.

Most of those who first practiced philosophy thought of the principles of everything only in the form of matter. What they declare to be the element and principle of all that exists is that from which all that exists comes, that from which it originally comes into being and into which it is finally resolved when it perishes—a thing whose substance persists although it is changed in its affections. For this reason, they do not think that anything at all either comes into being or perishes, since a natural substance of this kind is always preserved. Just as we do not talk of Socrates coming into being outright when he comes to be handsome or musical, or of his perishing when he loses these qualities, since Socrates himself persists as a substratum, so it is with everything else: there must always be some natural substance, either a single one or several, from which everything else comes into being while it persists itself. But they do not all agree about the number and form of such principles. Thales, who began this kind of philosophy, says that the principle is water, and this is why he declared that the earth rested on water. He perhaps got this idea from seeing that everything is nourished by what is wet, and that even heat comes into being from it and lives by it— for what things come into being from is the principle of everything. This was one thing that led him to this idea; another was the fact that the seeds of everything have a moist nature, and that water is the principle of the nature of all moist things. Some people think that even those who lived far back in antiquity, long before the present age, and who were the first to discourse about the gods, held this kind of view about nature. For they made Oceanus and Tethys the parents of all that has come into being, and said that what the gods swore by was water, which they called Styx; for what is most precious is what is most ancient, and it is by what is most precious that people swear. Whether this opinion about nature really is an ancient one and does go back so far is perhaps not clear, but certainly Thales is said to have made this kind of statement about the first cause. (Hippon scarcely deserves to be classed with these thinkers because of the smallness of his intellect.) Anaximenes and Diogenes declare air to be prior to water and make it above all the principle of simple bodies. Hippasus of Metapontum and Heraclitus of Ephesus say that it is fire, and Empedocles says that it is four of them, adding earth to the three that we have already mentioned; these elements, he holds, always persist, and do not come to be except in respect to their being many or few through being brought together into a unity or separated out from it. Anaxagoras of Clazomenae, who was older than Empedocles although his works were written later, says that the principles are infinite in number: all those things, he declares, whose parts are of the same kind as the whole, like water or fire, come into being only in so far as they are brought together and separated; otherwise they do not come into being or perish, they persist forever.

From all this, one might think that the only cause was that which is said to be in the form of matter. But as these thinkers went forward in this way the subject itself gave them guidance and joined in compelling them to seek further. For if all coming-to-be and all perishing does in fact proceed from one thing or even from several, why does this happen, and what is the cause of it? Certainly the substratum does not cause itself to change. Neither wood nor bronze, for instance, is the cause of its own change: the wood does not make a bed, nor the bronze a statue; something else is the cause of the change. And in looking for this we are looking for another principle, which we would call the source of movement. Those who originally embarked on this kind of inquiry, and said that the substratum was one, felt no dissatisfaction with their views; but some of those who say that it is one, as though they were defeated by this second inquiry, say that the one and the whole of nature are immovable; and in saying this they are not referring merely to coming-to-be and perishing (for with regard to these, the view is an ancient one on which everyone agrees), but to every kind of change as well; this is the peculiarity of their view. None of those who regarded the substance as one ever formed any idea of such a moving cause, except possibly Parmenides; and he did so only in so far as he laid down that there was not just one cause but in a way two causes. But it is more feasible for those who say that there are several substances to talk of a moving cause—for those, for instance, who make the hot and the cold the substances, or fire and earth—for they make use of fire as being something whose nature is to move things, and of water, earth, and such things as having an opposite nature.

After these thinkers and the search for principles of this kind, since these principles did not seem adequate to generate the nature of everything that exists, people were again driven on, as I have said, by the truth itself, to seek the next principle. For it is not reasonable that the cause of some things that exist being in a good and fine state, and of others getting into such a state, should be fire or earth or any other such thing; nor is it reasonable that they should have thought so. And it was not satisfactory for so important a matter to be entrusted to spontaneity and chance. So when someone said that there was a mind in the world, as there is in animals, and that it was the cause of all the order and good arrangement of things in nature, he seemed a sober man as compared with his predecessors, who had been throwing out random statements. We know for certain that Anaxagoras adopted these views, but Hermotimus of Clazomenae is credited with having made the statement before him. Those who have held such views, then, have regarded the principle in things that exist to be whatever is the cause of things being in a good state, and the cause of motion being imparted to things.

. . .

6. After the philosophies that I have mentioned came Plato's system. In most respects this followed the Pythagoreans, but it had certain peculiarities that were not shared by the philosophy of the Italians.

Plato had, first of all, ever since his youth been familiar with Cratylus and with the opinions of Heraclitus, according to which all sensible things are always in a state of flux and there can be no knowledge concerning them. This view of sensible objects Plato continued to hold later on. Then there was Socrates, who was concerning himself with ethics and not at all with nature as a whole, but who was nonetheless seeking universals in the field of ethics and was the first person to apply his mind to definitions. Plato accepted Socrates' views, but held that definition must be concerned with other things than the objects of sense, since it is impossible for there to be any common definition of sensible objects because they are always changing. To these other things he gave the name of "ideas;" and he held that all sensible objects were named after them by virtue of their relation to them, since those things that share the names of the forms exist by virtue of their participation in them. In talking of "participation," he was merely changing the name: the Pythagoreans say that things exist through their "imitation" of numbers, Plato that they do so through their "participation" in them; just changing the name, as I say. But what exactly this participation in or imitation of the forms was, they both alike neglected to inquire. Further, in addition to the objects of sense and the forms, Plato says that in between these there are the "mathematical objects." These differ from the objects of sense in being eternal and immovable, and from the forms in that there are many of them which are alike, whereas each form is unique.

Since the forms were the causes of everything else, Plato regarded their elements as the elements of everything that exists. Thus, he thought of "the great and the small" as the material principle, and "the one" as the essence. For the numbers, he held, come from "the great and the small" through participation in "the one." In treating "the one" as a substance, and not as something else that is said to be one, he was saying practically the same as the Pythagoreans, as he was, too, when he talked of the numbers as the causes of other things being what they are. But in making the infinite a pair instead of a single unit, and in deriving the infinite from "the great and the small," he was doing something original. Further, Plato says that the numbers are apart from the objects of sense; whereas the Pythagoreans say that things themselves are numbers, and they do not place the "mathematicals" in between them.

The separation of "the one" and the numbers from ordinary things—as opposed to what the Pythagoreans did—and the introduction of the forms were due to Plato's inquiries into logic, for his predecessors had known nothing of dialectic; but his reason for making the other element a pair was that the other numbers, apart from the first ones, could readily be generated from it, as from some waxlike material. And yet what actually happens is the reverse, and the Platonic view is not reasonable. The Platonists make many things from their matter, although their form generates once only; but clearly only one table comes from one piece of matter, whereas a single man who imposes the form onto it makes many tables. The relation of male to female is similar: the female is made pregnant by one act of fertilization, but the male makes many females pregnant. And these phenomena are imitations of the ultimate principles.

These, then, were the points that Plato made about the subject into which we are inquiring. It is clear from what has been said that he made use of only two causes, the essential and the material; for the forms are the essential cause of everything else, and "the one" is the essential cause of the forms. It is clear, too, that the underlying matter, on which the forms are said to be imposed in the case of sensible things, and "the one" in the case of the forms themselves are a pair—"the great and the small"; also that the cause of things being in a good or a bad state is assigned in one case to one of these elements, in the other to the other; this is like what we said of the inquiries of some of the earlier philosophers, such as Empedocles and Anaxagoras.

■　■　■

9. The first point about those who maintain the theory of forms is this. In seeking to find the causes of the things that are around us, they have introduced another lot of objects equal in number to them. It is as if someone who wanted to count thought that he would not be able to do so while the objects in question were relatively few, and then proceeded to do so when he had made them more numerous. For the forms are equal in number to, or at any rate no fewer than, the things whose causes the Platonists were seeking when they turned from them to the forms. For in the case of every substance there is something that shares its name, and this is true, too, in all other cases where one term can be applied to many things: it applies both to things in the world around us and to things eternal.

Further, the existence of the forms is not made evident by any of the arguments by which we try to prove it; from some of them, nothing necessarily follows; according to others, there will be forms even of things which we do not believe have them. For according to the arguments based on the sciences, there will be forms of all the objects of scientific knowledge; according to the argument based on one term applying to many things, there will be forms, too, of negations; and according to the argument which points out that we can think of something even when it has perished, there will be forms of perishable things, for of these, too, we retain an impression. Then, of the more rigorous arguments, some involve there being forms of relational terms, of which we say that there is no class on its own, whereas others mention the "third man." In general, the arguments about the forms demolish views whose truth we are more anxious to maintain than the existence of the forms. One consequence is that it will not be the pair that is primary, but number; another, that relational terms will be prior to independent ones; and there are all the other views which people have held through accepting opinions about the ideas, only to find themselves in contradiction with the first principles of the theory.

Further, according to the view which leads us to say that there are ideas, not only will there be forms of substances, but of many other things, too. For it is not only about substances that a single conception can be formed, but about other things as well; and the sciences, too, have other things besides substances as their objects; and there are countless other consequences of this kind. But according both to logical necessity and to the views held about them, if the forms are such that they can be participated in, there must be forms only of substances. For things do not participate in the forms accidentally; rather, things must participate in each form in a way different from that in which something is asserted of a subject. What I mean is this, for example: anything that participates in doubleness participates, too, in everlastingness, but only accidentally, since it is only accidentally that the double is eternal. Thus the forms will be substance. And the same words must indicate substance both here and there; otherwise, what will it mean to say that there is something apart from the things that are here or to talk of the single unit set over the many particulars? If the ideas and the things that participate in them have the same form, there will be something shared in common by them. For why should there be a single identical pair common to all the perishable pairs, and to all those which though eternal are multiple, any more than one that is common both to this pair itself and to any other individual pair? But if the ideas and the things that participate in them do not have the same form, they will be sharing no more than a name; and their similarity to each other would be like that between Callias and a bit of wood, if one were to call them both "man" without looking for anything really in common between them.

But one is most of all bewildered to know what contribution the forms make either to the sensible things that are eternal or to those that come into being and perish; for they are not the cause of their movement or of any change in them. They are no help either towards the knowledge of other things, since they are not the substance of these other things—they would be in them if they were; nor do they contribute to their existence, at least not so long as they are not inherent in the things that participate in them. If they were inherent, they might seem to be causes, in the way that whiteness is the cause of a white thing's being white by being mixed in it. But this argument, which was used first by Anaxagoras and later by Eudoxus and others, is only too easy to dispose of: one can readily produce many objections to such a view that make it quite untenable. Nor do other things derive from the forms in any of the other ways that they have usually been said to. To say that the forms are patterns and that other things participate in them is to talk in empty phrases and to utter poetic metaphors. What is it that works by looking towards the ideas? It is possible for anything at all that is like something else to exist or to come into being without its being modeled on that other thing: whether Socrates did or did not exist, someone could still be born who was like him, and clearly this would be equally true even if Socrates were immortal. Then there will be several patterns, and thus several forms, for the same thing: in the case of man, there will be the form of animal and the form of biped as well as the form of man himself. Further, the forms will not be patterns only for sensible objects but also for themselves; the genus, for instance, which contains species, or forms, will be a pattern for them, and thus the same thing will be both pattern and copy.

Again, it would seem impossible for the substance and that of which it is the substance to be separate. Then how can the ideas be substances of things even though they are separate from them? Yet this is how they are described in the *Phaedo*: the forms are said to be the causes of things existing and coming into being. But even if there are forms, the things that participate in them do not come into being unless there is something to impart movement to them; whereas many other things, like houses and rings, come into being as well, of which we say that there are no forms. Clearly, then, it is possible for anything else both to exist and to come into being for the same kind of causes as those that apply to the things that we have just mentioned.

Further, if the forms are numbers, how can they be the causes of things? Is it because different things are different numbers? Is one number, for instance, "man," another "Socrates," and another "Callias"? Even if this is so, how does it make the numbers the causes of these people? Nor will it make any difference for the numbers to be eternal and the people not. But perhaps numbers are causes because things here are ratios between numbers, like a musical concord. But in that case there is clearly some single class of things of which they are ratios. And if there is this something, which is in fact the matter, clearly even the numbers themselves will be ratios between one thing and another. I mean, for instance, that if Callias is a ratio between the numbers of fire, earth, water, and air, the idea too will be a numerical ratio with certain other things forming its substratum; and the form of man, whether or not it is in a sense a number, will nonetheless really be a ratio between numbers and not a number itself, nor are these grounds for regarding any idea as a number.

Further, from many numbers one number comes into being; but how can one form come from many forms? But if numbers do not come from numbers, but from the constituents of numbers—the constituents, for instance, of ten thousand—what about these units? If they are all of the same kind, many strange consequences will follow, but so too if they are not all of the same kind, either each individual unit like every other, or each group of units like every group. How can they differ from each other, if they have no qualities? Such a view is neither reasonable nor consistent with the way in which we conceive of units.

Further, it is necessary to set up a separate class of numbers with which arithmetic deals, quite apart from the intermediates of which some talk. But how can these intermediates exist? From what principles can they come? And why should there be intermediates between what is in the world around us and the ideal numbers?

Then, each of the two units in "the pair" must derive from another pair, which is prior to them. Yet this is impossible. Also, why should a number taken together be one?

In addition to the points that I have made, if the units are different from each other, they ought to be described in the way in which those thinkers describe the elements who say that they are two or four in number. For none of these philosophers describes the thing that is in common to them—body, for instance—as the element; but whether or not there is such a thing in common, like body, they describe the elements as, say, fire or earth. But the Platonists talk as if the one were of the same kind as its parts, like fire or water; if that is so, then the numbers will not be substances. But if "the one" is something on its own and is a principle, clearly the term "one" is being used in a number of different ways; otherwise the view is impossible.

In our desire to refer substances back to first principles, we derive lengths from "the short and the long"—

that is from a particular instance of "the great and the small"; plane surfaces from "the broad and the narrow"; and solid bodies from "the deep and the shallow." But how can a plane surface contain a line, or a solid body contain a line and a plane surface? "Broad and narrow" are of a different genus from "deep and shallow." So, clearly, just as number cannot be contained in any of these—since "the many and the few" are a different genus from them—none of the genera can be contained in any of its successors. On the other hand, neither can "the flat" be the genus in which "the deep" is contained; if it could, a solid body would be a plane surface. Then how will points come to be contained in things? Plato indeed even used to contest the existence of this genus of things; he regarded it as just a geometrician's hypothesis. The ultimate principle of a line—and this was a point that he would often make—he would call "the indivisible lines." Yet there must be some limit to these; and thus the same argument which leads us to say there is a line must also lead us to say that there is a point.

In general, too, although philosophy seeks the cause of visible things, we have ignored this, and say nothing of the cause which is the source of change in things; and when we think that we are giving some account of the substances of things, we are in fact merely saying that there are other substances, and our account of how they are at the same time the substances of things here is meaningless because, as we said earlier, "participation" means nothing at all. And as for what we saw earlier to be the cause of the sciences, which makes all mind and all nature active, on this the forms do not touch at all although we maintain that it is one of the first principles of things; instead, with the thinkers of the present day, philosophy has become just mathematics, although people maintain that mathematics should be studied only for the sake of other things.

Again, one might think that this underlying substance was of a rather mathematical kind; one might suppose

that things like "the great and the small" were such as
to be asserted of substance and matter, and to be distinguishing characteristics of them, rather than being matter
themselves. For that is what the natural philosophers say
of "the rare and the dense," that they are the primary
differentiating characteristics of the substratum, since
they involve excess and deficiency. Then, with regard to
movement, if "the great and the small" are movement,
clearly the forms will be moved; but if they are not,
where has movement come from? In this way the whole
inquiry into nature is done away with. Further, what
seems easy to prove, that everything is one, in fact turns
out not to be so; even if one grants all their assumptions,
and makes forms of every class of things, one does not
establish that everything is one, but only that there is a
"one itself"; and not even this will follow unless you
grant that every universal is a class, which is impossible
in some cases. Nor is there any account of the things
that come after numbers—lengths, planes, and solids—
of how they exist, or how they can exist, or what force
they have. They cannot be forms, since they are not
numbers; they cannot be intermediates, since they are
not "mathematicals"; and they cannot be perishable
things; rather they turn out to be another, fourth, class
of things.

In general, we cannot find the elements of the things
that exist without previously analyzing the ways in which
they are said to exist, especially when we are inquiring
in this way into what kind of elements things are made
of. It is impossible to decide what "action," "suffering,"
or "straightness" are made of; if this is possible at all,
it is only so with regard to substances. Thus, it is false
to look for elements of all the things that there are, or
to suppose that one has found them.

How could one learn the elements of everything?
Plainly one could not have any preliminary knowledge
before one started. It is possible for a man who learns
geometry to know other things before he starts, but he

knows nothing in advance of the objects of this particular science, or of what he is going to learn; and it is the same with all the other sciences. So, if there is some science of everything, of the kind that some people say, the man who learns it must start off knowing nothing at all beforehand. But all learning proceeds entirely or partially by means of things that are previously known. This is true of learning through demonstration and of learning through definition (since one must know beforehand the terms of which the definition is composed, and they must be familiar to one); and it is the same with learning by induction. But if in fact this science should turn out to be innate, it is astonishing that we should possess the best of all sciences without realizing it.

Then how is one to know what things are made of? How will it become clear? This, too, involves difficulties. One might have doubts about it as one does about some syllables. Some people say that *za* is made up of *s* and *d* and *a*, others that it is a quite separate sound, composed of nothing that is already known.

Again, how can one know the objects of the senses without having senses? Yet one ought to be able to, if everything is made up of the same elements, in the way in which complex sounds are made up of their own elements.

Book II

1. The study of the truth is in one way easy, in another difficult. An indication of this is that no single person can adequately understand it, although it cannot be the case that everybody fails to hit upon it. Everyone has something to say about nature; and even though one person's individual contribution is of little or no account, from all our joint contributions something substantial emerges. Thus, if this study seems to correspond with our proverb "Who can miss the gate?" in that sense it is easy. But the difficulty of the subject is shown by our being able to gain some grasp of it as a whole, but not of any particular part of it. Perhaps, since difficulty can be of two kinds, the cause of it here lies not in the content of the subject but in ourselves; for the intellectual faculty of our souls reacts to what are by nature the brightest of all things, as bats' eyes react to daylight.

But it is not only to those whose opinions we may share that we should be grateful, but also to those who have dealt with the subject more superficially. They, too, made a contribution by forming in us a disposition for the subject. If there had been no Timotheus, we should have missed a great deal of music; but if there had been no Phrynis, there would have been no Timotheus. It is the same with those who have talked about truth. From some we have received certain opinions; others have

35

been the causes of their being in a position to hold these opinions.

It is quite right for philosophy to be described as the knowledge of the truth. Truth is the aim of a contemplative study, action that of a practical study; for even if practical men do study the state of a thing, they do not study its cause for its own sake, but for some immediate and relative purpose. We do not know the truth about anything without knowing its cause; and in every case that thing more than any other possesses a quality that causes other things to share its name and character; fire, for instance, is of all things the hottest and is the cause of heat in everything else. Hence, too, that thing is the truer that causes things subordinate to it to be true. Therefore, the first principles of things that exist forever must be of all things the truest. They are not just sometimes true, nor is anything else the cause of their being; rather, they are the cause of the being of everything else. Thus, everything has as much truth as it has being.

■   ■   ■

3. Our attitude toward what we listen to is determined by our habits. We expect things to be said in the way in which we are accustomed to talk ourselves; things that are said in some other way do not seem the same at all but seem, rather, incomprehensible and strange because of their unfamiliarity; for it is what is familiar that we find comprehensible. The power that familiarity possesses is shown by the laws; there, because of habit, the mythical and childish elements in them carry more weight than does our recognition of them for what they are. Some people will not listen to anyone who does not talk in the manner of a mathematician, others will not listen to anyone who does not use illustrations, others again expect a poet to be adduced as an authority. Some people want rigorous treatment in everything, whereas others are annoyed by it, either because they cannot follow it or because of its pettiness; for rigorousness does carry with it something that makes some people feel that in arguments, just as in business transactions, it is rather illiberal.

Thus, one needs already to have been educated in the way to approach each subject: it would be strange to be inquiring at one and the same time into a science and into the way in which it should be acquired, for it is not easy to grasp either of these things even on its own. We must not look for mathematical rigor in every subject, but only in those fields where there is no matter involved. So it is not the right way to approach nature, since all nature presumably contains matter. We must, then, first of all inquire what nature is, since in this way it will become clear what natural science is about.

■   ■   ■

Book IV

1. There is a science that studies being qua being, and the attributes that belong to it by virtue of its being itself. This science is different from all those that are said to deal merely with a part of being. None of the other sciences makes a universal inquiry into being qua being; they cut off a bit of being, and then study its attributes—the mathematical sciences, for instance, do this. But since we are seeking for the first principles and the ultimate causes, plainly it is of some nature considered just as itself that they must be causes. So if those who looked for the elements of everything that there is were in fact looking for these first principles, the elements of being must be elements of it qua being, not accidentally. Hence, we too must understand the elements of being qua being.

■   ■   ■

4. There are some people who, as we have said, both maintain that the same thing can be and not be and say that it is possible to hold this view. This is the view of many who study nature. We have assumed here that it is impossible for the same thing to be and not to be at the same time, and on the basis of this we have shown that of all principles this is the least open to question.

Some people, through their lack of education, expect this principle, too, to be proved; for it does show a lack of education not to know of what things we ought to seek proof and of what we ought not. For it is altogether impossible for there to be proofs of everything; if there were, one would go on to infinity, so that even so one would end up without a proof; and if there are some things of which one should not seek proof, these people cannot name any first principle which has that characteristic more than this.

However, the impossibility of a thing both being and not being can be proved by refutation, if only one's opponent says something. If he says nothing, it is absurd to seek to give an account of the matter to a man who cannot himself give an account of anything; for insofar as he is already like this, such a man is no better than a vegetable. Now, the difference that I maintain between proof by refutation and straightforward proof is this: a man who proves a thing seems to ask for the initial premise to be granted; but when someone else produces the premise, then we have refutation, not proof. In all such matters, the right way to start is not to ask one's opponent to say that something is or is not so (since this might be thought to be begging the question), but rather to ask him to say something that has meaning both for himself and for someone else. For this he must do if he is to say anything at all. Otherwise, he could not engage in discussion either with himself or with anyone else. But if he grants this request, proof will be possible, as there will already be something defined. The responsibility, however, then rests not with the man who is conducting the proof but with the man who is accepting it. For while he is trying to do away with reason, he is also accepting it. Furthermore, the man who makes this concession has conceded that something is true quite independently of the process of proof.

Firstly, then, this much is clearly true: that the phrase "to be" or "not to be" means something definite, so that not everything can be both in a given state and not in a given state. Then, we would allow that "man" means one thing only—let it be "two-footed animal." What I mean when I say that something "means one thing" is this: if man is such and such, then for anything that is a man that is what being a man will be. Nor does it make any difference if someone says that a word means more than one thing, provided the meanings are limited in number; for each different account could be given a different name. I refer to cases where, for instance, one might say that "man" meant not one but many things, and that "two-footed animal" was the account of one of them, but that there were many others, though they were limited in number; then one could apply a particular name to each different account. If, however, this were not the case, and one were to say that a word had an infinite number of meanings, then plainly there could be no account of anything; for to mean no single thing is to mean nothing; and if words mean nothing, there is an end to discussion between people and, indeed, really to reflection with oneself. For it is not possible to think without thinking of some single thing; and if it is possible to think of this single thing, it must be given a single name.

Let us assume then, as we said at the outset, that a name means something, and means just one thing. It is then not possible for "being a man" to mean the same as "not being a man," if "man" means not only something that can be attributed to only one thing, but means also just one thing itself. (For we do not expect everything that can be attributed to one thing also to mean just one thing; if that were so, "musical," "white," and "man" would all mean one thing, so that all things would be one, since they would share the same definition.) It will not be possible, either, for a thing to be and not to be the same thing, unless one is talking ambiguously—as, for instance, if what we call "man" were to be called by others "not-man." But our problem is not whether it is possible for the same thing to be and not to be man in name, but whether it is possible in fact. If "man" and "not-man" do not mean different things, plainly "not being a man" will also be the same as "being a man," so that "to be man" will be "to be not-man," since they will be one. (That is what "being one" means, being like "cloak" and "garment," with one and the same account being given of both.) So that if these two are one, "being man" and "being not-man" will mean one and the same thing. But in fact it has been shown that they mean different things.

It is, then, necessary, if it is true to say of anything that it is man, for that thing to be a two-footed animal (for that was what "man" meant). And if this is necessarily true, it is not then possible for this same thing not to be a two-footed animal (for that is what "it is necessary for something to be" means: "it is impossible for it not to be"). So it is not possible for it to be true to say at the same time that the same thing both is and is not man.

The same argument applies to "not being man." "Being man" and "not being man" must have different meanings if "being white" and "being man" have different ones. For "not being man" is much more an opposite of "being man" than "being white" is, so that it must have a meaning different from it. But if someone says that "white" means one and the same thing as "man," then we shall be saying exactly what was said earlier; and everything, not just opposites, will be one. If, however, this is not possible, what we have maintained does follow, provided only that our opponent answers the question.

But if our opponent replies to our simple question by adding the denial to the assertion, he is not answering the question. For there is nothing to stop the same thing being "man" and "white" and an immense number of other things; but, nonetheless, when someone asks whether it is true or not to say that this or that is a man, one's answer should have one meaning, and one should not add that he is also white and large. It is impossible to go through all a thing's accidental attributes, since they are infinite in number; and a man should go either through all of them or through none. Even, therefore, if the same thing were on innumerable occasions man and not man, one should follow the same rule; and if someone asks whether this or that is man, one should not answer that he is at the same time not man unless one is going to go through all the other accidental things that he is or is not. And if one does that, one is not engaging in discussion.

Those who maintain this view utterly do away with substance and essence. For they must necessarily say that everything is an accidental attribute, and that there is no such thing as being a man or an animal essentially. For if there is such a thing as being a man essentially, this will not be the same as being not a man or as not being a man (although it is these which are its negations); for there was only one thing that being essentially a man indicated, and that was the substance of something. And by indicating the substance of something we mean that its essence is that and nothing else; and if for that substance being essentially a man is the same either as essentially being not a man or as essentially not being a man, the essence will be something else; thus they will have to admit that there cannot be any account of the substance of anything, but that all attributes are accidental. For this is the distinction between substance and accident: "white" is an accidental attribute of "man" because man is white but not essentially so. But if all things are said to be accidental, there will be no primary subject for them—if, that is, what is accidental always indicates something being asserted of a subject. The process would necessarily go on to infinity. This, however, is impossible; no more than two accidents can be combined. One accident is not the accident of another except insofar as both are accidents of the same thing. I mean, for instance, that "white" is "musical" and "musical" is "white" insofar as both are accidents of man. But it is not in this way, that is, through their both being accidents of something else, that Socrates is musical. Some things are said to be accidental in that way, others in the way that "white" is said to be an accident of Socrates; but in the case of things said to be accidental in the latter way, one cannot produce an infinite series of accidental attributes by saying, for instance, that there will be something accidental to "white Socrates." For no unit comes into being from all these terms. Nor will anything—such as "musical"—be accidental to "white." For "musical" is no more an accident of "white" than "white" is of "musical," and we have already distinguished between what is accidental in this way and what is accidental in the way that "musical" is accidental to "Socrates." In the case of accidents of this latter kind, no one accident can be accidental to any other; it is only with things that are accidental in the other way that this can happen. Hence, we cannot say that everything is accidental. So, on the basis of arguments of this kind, too, there will be something that indicates substance. And we have shown that, if this is so, it is impossible for contradictory assertions to be made of it at the same time.

Further, if all contradictory assertions made about the same thing are true, all things will clearly be one. A trireme, a wall, and a man will all be the same thing, if it is possible to assert or to deny anything of everything—as indeed must happen with those who maintain the view of Protagoras. For if anyone thinks that man is not a trireme, according to their theory he clearly is not one; but in this case he also will be a trireme, if the contradictory statement is also true. Thus the situation described by Anaxagoras arises—"All things are together"—so that no single thing truly exists. These people, then, seem to be talking of the indeterminate; and although they think that they are talking of what is, they are in fact talking of what is not. For the indeterminate is what is potentially but not actually. But they must maintain that everything can be either asserted or denied of everything. For it would be strange if its own denial were true of each thing, but not the denial of something else that was not true of it; I mean, for instance, that if it is true to say of man that he is not man, it is clearly also true to say either that he is a trireme or that he is not one. If, then, the assertion that he is a trireme is true, the denial that he is one will necessarily also be so; and if the assertion that he is one is not true of him, the denial that he is one will at least be truer of him than the denial that he is a man. If, then, the denial that he is a man is true of him, so will the denial that he is a trireme be; and if that is true, the assertion that he is one will be true, too.

These consequences, then, follow from maintaining this view. In addition, it is no longer necessary either to assert or to deny a thing. For if it is true to say that he is both man and not man, it is clearly also true to say that he is neither man nor not man. For the two assertions each have their denial; or, if there is one assertion formed out of the two, there will also be one denial, opposed to it.

Further, either their view is true of everything—and a thing is both white and not white, both existent and not existent, and similarly with all other assertions and denials—or it is not true of everything, but only of some things and not of others. If it is not true of everything, then the exceptions will be admitted as such. But if it is true of everything, then either in all cases where assertion is possible denial will be possible, and in all cases where denial is possible assertion will be possible; or in all cases where assertion is possible denial will be possible, but assertion will not be possible in all the cases where denial is possible. In the latter case, there will be something that definitely is not, and this will be a firm belief; and if the fact that it is not is definitely known, the opposite assertion will be even more clearly known. But if one can equally assert all that one can deny, either one must be speaking truly when one divides the terms and says, for instance, that this is white and that this is not white, or one must not. If one is not speaking truly when one divides the terms, one is not in fact making these assertions, and nothing exists—but then how can what does not exist speak or walk? Then everything will be one, as we have said before, and "man" and "god" and "trireme" and their contradictories will all be the same thing; for if one can make these assertions alike of everything, no one thing will differ from any other; for if it does differ, it will be true and unique. Similarly, even if it is possible to speak truly when one divides the terms, the consequence that we have just mentioned follows; in addition, everyone would be speaking truly and everyone would be speaking falsely, and our opponent himself would be admitting that he himself was speaking falsely. At the same time it is clear that one cannot engage in any inquiry about anything with such a man, since he is saying nothing. For he is saying neither that things are in a particular state nor that they are not in a particular state, but that they both are and are not in it. And then again he denies both these statements, saying that things are neither in a particular state nor not in it. If he did not do this, he would already have made some definite statement.

Further, if, whenever an assertion is true, its denial is false and, whenever a denial is true, the assertion of what it denies is false, it is not possible truthfully to assert and to deny the same thing. But people might say that this is to beg the very question that is at issue.

Again, is the man who supposes that things either are or are not in a particular state mistaken, and the man who supposes that they both are and are not correct? If the latter is correct, what is the point of saying that the nature of the things that exist is such and such? But if this man is not right, but more right than the man who

holds either of the other views, things are already in
some particular state; and this last statement is true without being at the same time not true as well. But if all
men alike say both what is false and what is true, the
man who holds this view will not be able to speak or
make any utterance; for he is at one and the same time
saying that this is so and that it is not. And if he holds
no opinion, but at the same time thinks and does not
think things to be so, what difference is there between
him and a vegetable? This above all makes it clear that
no one really has this attitude either among those who
maintain this view or among the rest of mankind. Why
does a man walk to Megara instead of staying quietly
where he is when he thinks that he ought to walk there?
Why does he not walk one morning straight into a well
or a ravine? Why is he instead so manifestly cautious,
thus showing that he does not think falling in is both
good and not good? Clearly he regards the one course
as the better and the other as not. And if he does this,
he must regard one thing as man, another as not man,
one thing as sweet, another as not sweet. For he is not
seeking everything equally or regarding everything as
equal when, thinking it better to drink water or to see
a man, he proceeds to look for them. Yet he ought so
to have regarded them if the same thing were alike a
man and not a man. But, as we have said, there is nobody who is not manifestly careful to avoid some things
and not others. So everyone, it seems, does suppose that
things are in a definite state, at least with regard to what
is better and what is worse, if not in every respect. If
they do so on the basis of opinion rather than knowledge, they should pay that much more attention to the
truth, just as a sick man has to pay more attention to
his health than a healthy one. For the man who has mere
opinions is not in a healthy state, with regard to the
truth, as compared with the man who has knowledge.

But, however much things may be both in a given
state and not in it, differences of degree are inherent in

the nature of things. We would not say that two and three were equally even numbers or that the man who thought four was five and the man who thought four was a thousand were equally mistaken. If they are not equally mistaken, clearly one of them is less so, and so is saying what is right more than the other. If, then, "more true" means "nearer the truth," there must be some truth to which what is truer is nearer. And even if there is no such truth, we already have something that is firmer and more genuine, and we are free of the extreme view that prevents our defining anything with our intellects.

5. The doctrine of Protagoras, too, springs from this same opinion, and the two alike must be either both true or both false. For if all opinions and appearances are true, everything must be at once true and false; many people hold views which are opposed to one another's, and they regard those who hold different opinions from their own as mistaken; and thus the same thing must both be and not be. On the other hand, if this last proposition is true, all opinions must be true. For those who are mistaken and those who are right hold opposite views; if, then, the facts correspond to these opposite views, everyone will be right.

It is plain, then, that both these views spring from the same attitude of mind. But one should not always adopt the same method to meet these arguments. Some people need to be met with persuasion, others with compulsion. The ignorance of those who have adopted this view out of bewilderment is easily cured; it is not with their arguments but with their mental attitude that one has to make contact. But those who merely talk for the sake of argument must be cured by refutation of their actual words and utterances.

Those who are in a state of complete bewilderment have been led to this opinion by observation of the sensible world. They believe that contradictories and opposites can be true at the same time because they see opposites coming into being from the same thing. If, then, they argue, it is not possible for what is not to come into being, the thing must have been there beforehand, being both opposites alike, as Anaxagoras says when he talks of everything having been mixed in everything, and Democritus too; for he says that the empty and the full are present alike in every part of things, and yet that the one of them is "what is" and the other is "what is not." To those who base their opinions on these considerations we shall say that in one way they are quite right in what they say, but in another they do not understand. For there are two ways in which one talks of what is: in one way it is possible for something to come into being out of what is not; in another way it is not possible; and it is possible for the same thing to be "being" and "not being" at the same time, but not in the same respect. For it is possible for the same thing to be potentially two opposites, but not actually. We shall, further, ask them to believe that there is another kind of substance among the things that exist, in which neither movement nor decay nor birth is present at all.

It is, similarly, from an observation of the sensible world that some people have been led to the view that truth is concerned with appearances. They do not think it right for the truth of an opinion to be judged by the number—large or small—of people who hold it; but nonetheless they observe that the same thing seems to some people sweet, to others bitter, so that if everyone were ill or mad and only two or three were healthy or sane, it would be these two or three who would seem to be ill and mad, not the others.

Further, they say, many of the other animals receive from the same objects impressions that are the opposite of ours; and even in the case of a single individual things do not always appear the same to his senses. It is not at all clear among these impressions what kind are true and what kind are false; for these are no more true than those; they are all in the same position. Hence Democritus says that either nothing is true, or at least the truth is hidden from us.

And in general it is because they hold that knowledge is sense perception, and that sense perception is a process of change, that they say that what appears to the senses is necessarily true. It is on this account that both Empedocles and Democritus and practically all the other thinkers have got involved in views of this kind. For Empedocles says that it is through changing their condition that men change the state of their knowledge: "It is as things come before them that counsel increases in men"; and elsewhere he says that "When they change their natures and become different, it happens to them that they think things that are just as different." Parmenides, too, talks in the same way: "For as the mixture is that each man has in his much-bent limbs, so is the mind that is in men; for it is the very thing that thinks that is the substance of the limbs of every man; for that of which there is most is thought." Anaxagoras, too, is reported to have made the remark to some of his companions that things would be for them such as they supposed them to be. They say, too, that Homer clearly held this opinion when he made Hector, after he had been stunned by a blow, lie "conscious of other things," as though even those who are out of their minds are conscious of things, but not of the same things. Clearly, then, if these are both of them kinds of consciousness, things that exist are in fact both in and not in a given state at the same time.

The consequences of this view are indeed very serious. If those who have seen the most of such truth as it is possible to see—and they are those who most of all seek and love it—if they have opinions of this kind and talk in this way about the truth, those who are only just beginning to practice philosophy might well despair. For seeking the truth would seem to be like pursuing a will-o'-the-wisp.

The reason these people held this opinion is that, although they were investigating the truth about things that exist, they thought that "things that exist" comprised only sensible objects, and among these objects there is a great deal of what is indeterminate by nature, and the nature of what there is is as we have described it; so what they say is plausible but not true—it is more fitting to put it like this, than as Epicharmus did to Xenophanes. Then, seeing that all this world of sensible nature was in motion, and knowing that no truthful statement could be made about what was changing, they concluded that it was certainly not possible to make any truthful statement about what was everywhere and in every way changing. It was from this view that there grew up and flourished the view, more extreme than any that we have mentioned, that was held by those who professed to be following Heraclitus; it was a view such as Cratylus held, who in the end thought that one ought not to say anything, and used to merely move his finger; he rebuked Heraclitus for saying that it is not possible to step into the same river twice; he thought that one could not do it even once.

Our reply to this argument will be that, while there is a certain reasonableness in thinking that what changes "is not" when it does change, yet the view is open to question; for what is losing anything still retains something of what is being lost, and when a thing is coming into being something of it must already be there; and, in general, if something perishes, there will still be something left which "is," and if something is coming into being there must be something from which it comes and by which it is generated; nor can this process go on to infinity.

But leaving these points aside, let us note that change in respect to quantity is not the same thing as change in respect to quality. We will admit that in respect to quantity there is nothing stable; but it is by its form that we recognize each thing.

We may also find fault with those who hold this view on the grounds that they have based their view of the whole sensible world upon what they have observed in a mere minority of the objects of the senses. For it is only that part of the sensible world that surrounds us that is continuously involved in coming into being and perishing, and this part is practically nothing as compared with the whole; they would have been more justified in denying to this portion of the world these characteristics because of the rest than in asserting them of the rest because of this portion.

Further, we clearly must say to these people what we said some time ago; we must point out to them and persuade them to believe that there is a class of things that are by nature unmoved. (Yet the consequence of saying that things are and are not at the same time is that everything is at rest rather than in motion. For then there will be nothing into which things can change; every quality will belong to everything.)

As far as truth is concerned, we must show them that not every appearance is true. For, firstly, even if our sensation of a particular object is never false, appearance is not the same thing as sensation.

Then, we may feel some surprise if these people are really uncertain whether sizes and colors are such as they appear to those who are far off or to those who are near at hand, whether things are as they feel to the healthy or to the sick, whether weights are as they seem to the weak or to the strong, whether the truth is what appears to the sleeping or to the waking. Clearly they do not really think these questions difficult; certainly nobody who imagines at night that he is in Athens when he is in fact in Africa then goes off to the Odeum. Further, with regard to the future, as Plato too remarks, the opinion of the doctor is presumably not of equal weight with that of the layman about such questions as whether a man is going to get better or not.

Then, in the case of the senses themselves, the perception of an object extraneous to a given sense has not the same weight as that of the sense's proper object, nor has the perception of what is merely akin to a sense the same weight as that of what is the sense's own. In the case of color it is sight, not taste, that is valid; in the case of flavor, it is taste, not sight. But none of these will ever assert about the same thing that it both is and is not in a given state. Nor, indeed, would any of them disagree about the actual sensation even at different times, though they would disagree about the object of which it was a sensation. For instance, the same wine may seem, through some change either in itself or in one's own body, to be at one moment sweet, at another not. But sweetness itself never changes from being such as it is whenever it is present; one is always right about it, and what is going to be sweet is necessarily so. Yet all their arguments make this impossible; just as there cannot, according to them, be any substance of anything, so there cannot either be anything which happens of necessity. For it is not possible for what is necessarily so to be both in one state and in another; so if there is anything that is as it is of necessity, it will not be both in and not in a particular state.

In general, if it is only what is perceptible by the senses that exists, nothing would exist if there were no living beings; for then there would be no sensation. It is perhaps true that there would be no sensible qualities and no sensations in such circumstances, for they are the experiences of the person who has the sensation. But that the substrata that produce the sensation should not be there even apart from sensation itself is impossible. For sensation does not exist on its own; there is something else apart from it which is necessarily prior to it, for what moves things is necessarily prior to what is moved, and this is no less true if the terms are correlative.

6. Both among those who are really convinced of these views and among those who merely express them for the sake of argument, there are some who raise this further difficulty. They ask who is to judge what man is healthy, and in general who will make correct judgments in any given field. Such problems are like the problem of whether we are now asleep or awake, and they all amount to the same thing. These people are asking for a reason to be given for everything; they are looking for a first principle that they hope to grasp by demonstration; it is clear from their actions, however, that they are not convinced of the reality of the problem. This, however, as I have said, is what has happened to them: they are looking for a reason for things for which no reason can be given, for the starting point of demonstration is not a demonstration. These people will readily be persuaded of the truth, since the point is not difficult to grasp. But those who are looking only for a compelling argument are looking for the impossible. For they are claiming the right to contradict themselves, and in so doing are in fact at once contradicting themselves.

If all things are not relative, and some things do exist on their own, it will not be the case that all that appears is true. For what appears appears to someone; and so the man who says that all things that appear are true is making everything that there is relative. Therefore, those who are seeking a compelling result in their argument, and at the same time expect to engage in discussion, must take care not to say that what appears exists, but that it exists for the person to whom it appears, at the time when it appears, to the sense to which it appears, and in the way in which it appears. If they maintain an argument but do not maintain it in this way, they will soon turn out to be contradicting themselves. For it is possible for one and the same thing to appear as honey to the sight but not to the taste, and for the same things to appear different to the sight of the two eyes, if they are different from each other. For we can reply to those who, for reasons which we went into some time ago, say that what appears is true. They say that because what appears is true, all things are alike true and false; for things do not appear the same to everybody, or even always the same to the same person, but often we have contrary impressions at the same time: touch says that there are two things when the fingers are crossed, whereas sight says that there is only one. Our reply will be that this will never happen to one and the same sense, or to the same part of it in the same way and at the same time; appearances will be true with this qualification. Perhaps it is for this reason that those who maintain this view, not because they are puzzled but for the sake of argument, are compelled to say that this is not true in itself but only to the person who perceives it. And indeed, as we have remarked earlier, they are compelled to make everything relative to opinion and to sensation, and thus nothing has ever come into being or ever will do so unless someone has thought of it beforehand. For if anything has so come into being or should do so in the future, it will clearly not be the case that everything is relative to opinion.

Further, if a thing is one, it is relative to one thing or to some determinate number of things; and if the same thing is both half and equal, yet the equal is not relative to the double. If, then, in relation to what is thinking, man and what is being thought of are the same thing, man will no longer be what is thinking but what is being thought of. And if everything is relative to what is thinking, what is thinking will be relative to an infinite variety of things.

We have, then, said enough to show that the most indisputable of all beliefs is that it is not possible for contradictories to be true at the same time, to indicate what are the consequences of saying that they can be true, and to explain why people maintain this view. Since it is impossible for contradictory assertions to be made truthfully of the same thing, clearly it is not possible, either, for contraries to belong to the same thing. For one of the contraries is as much a privation as it is a

contrary and it is the privation of some essential nature;
it is the denial of something's belonging to a defined
class. If, then, it is impossible truthfully to assert and to
deny anything at the same time, it is also impossible for
contraries to belong to anything at the same time; either
both must belong to it only in a way, or one must belong
to it in a way, and the other absolutely.

7. But it is not possible, either, for there to be any
intermediate between contradictory assertions; any one
thing must be either asserted or denied of any other.

This will become clear if we first of all define truth
and falsehood. To say that what is is not, or that what
is not is, is false and to say that what is is, or that what
is not is not, is true; so the man who says that anything
either is or is not will be speaking either truly or falsely;
but where there is an intermediate assertion, neither
what is nor what is not is being said either to be or not
to be.

Further, any intermediate between contradictories either will be as gray is in relation to black and white, or
will be like what is neither man nor horse in relation to
man and horse. In the latter case, it would not change;
for change is from what is not *x* to what is *x*, or from
what is *x* to what is not *x*. But in fact it is clearly always
changing, since there is no change that is not into contraries or intermediates. If, on the other hand, it is a real
intermediate, such as gray, then we will have a process
of change into white that is not from what is not white;
but such a process is never seen.

Then, everything that is thought or conceived is either
asserted or denied by the intellect whenever it is thinking either what is true or what is false, as is plain from
our definition of the terms: when the intellect combines
terms in one way in an assertion or a denial, it is saying
what is true; when in another, what is false.

Again, if the view that there are intermediates is not
just being maintained for the sake of argument, it must

hold true of all pairs of contradictories. In that case there will be people who are neither saying what is true nor not saying it, and there will be something else besides what is and what is not, so that there will be another kind of change besides coming-to-be and perishing.

Further, in all the classes in which the denial of a term implies its contrary, this rule will apply too; among numbers, for instance, there will be a number that is neither odd nor not odd. But this is impossible, as is evident from the definition of the terms.

Again, the process will continue ad infinitum, and the number of things that there are will not be just half as great again, but a great deal larger. For it will be possible to deny in their turn both the assertion and the denial of the intermediate; and this further intermediate will be something, for it will have a separate substance.

Then, if someone is asked if a thing is white and says that it is not, he has denied nothing other than that it is white; and the statement that it is not so is a denial.

Some people have reached these opinions in the same way that other paradoxical opinions have been reached. Unable to refute captious arguments, they have surrendered to them, and have agreed that what has been concluded is true. This is the reason why some people hold the view; others do so because they seek a reason for everything. In reply to all these people, the right way to start is with a definition. And a definition is formed because it is necessary for these people to mean something, for the account of what a name means will be its definition. The doctrine of Heraclitus that everything is and is not seems to make everything true, and that of Anaxagoras that there is something intermediate between contradictories seems to make everything false; for when everything is mixed up, the mixture is neither good nor not good, so that it is not true to say anything.

8. Now that all these distinctions have been drawn, it is clear that it is impossible for the one-sided statements and generalizations that some people make to be true; some of them say that nothing is true, since there is nothing to stop every statement being like the one that the diagonal is commensurate; others say that everything is true. These views are practically the same as that of Heraclitus; for the man who says that everything is true and everything is false is also making each of these statements separately, and if they are impossible when taken separately, they are also impossible taken together.

Further, there clearly are contradictory statements that cannot be true at the same time; nor indeed can they all be false, though from what has been said this would seem to be more possible. But in dealing with all views of this kind, we must ask to be granted, as we said further back, not that something is or is not, but that something has meaning, so that we can argue on the basis of a definition, after having grasped what truth or falsehood means. And if what it is true to assert is nothing other than what it is false to deny, it is impossible for everything to be false; for one of any pair of contradictories must be true. And if one must either assert or deny everything, it is impossible for both statements to be false; only one of the two contradictories is that. Indeed, all views of this kind have the consequence, which has often been noted, that they refute themselves. The man who says that everything is true makes the view opposed to his own true, and thus he makes his own view not true, since his opponent does not think that his view is true; and the man who says that everything is false is making his own view false as well. And even if they make exceptions and say, the one, that only his opponent's view is not true, the other, that only his own view is not false, they will still have to ask for an infinite number of true and false statements to be granted as exceptions; for the statement that the true statement is true will also be true, and this will go on ad infinitum.

Plainly, those who say that everything is at rest are not right either, nor are those who say that everything is in motion. If everything is at rest, the same things will always be true and false; but in fact it is evident that there is change in this respect; at one time the speaker himself did not exist, and at some future date he will no longer do so. But if everything is in motion, nothing will be true; and so everything will be false, which we have shown to be impossible. But yet it is not the case that everything is sometimes at rest and sometimes in motion and that nothing is always one or the other. For there is something that is always moving the things that are moved, and the first mover is itself unmoved.

■   ■   ■

Book VI

1. What we are seeking are the principles and causes of the things that are, and clearly of things that are qua being. There is a cause for health and physical fitness; there are principles, elements, and causes in mathematics; and in general every completely or even partially intellectual science is concerned with principles and causes, which it treats with a greater or smaller degree of accuracy. But all these sciences have marked out for themselves some particular thing that is, some particular class of objects, and concern themselves with that; they are not concerned with being considered on its own, or qua being, nor do they give any account of the essence of what they are dealing with; rather they work from the essence, some of them making it plain to the senses, others forming an assumption as to what it is; and then they show, more or less rigorously, what are the essential attributes of the class with which they are concerned. Hence, it is clear that there is no demonstration of the substance or essence through this kind of procedure; there is some other way of making it clear. Similarly, they say nothing about whether the class of things with which they are concerned exists or not, since it is part of the same intellectual process to show what a thing is and whether it exists.

Natural science is concerned with a particular class of

being; it is concerned with the kind of substance the source of whose motion or rest is in itself. Plainly, then, it is not a practical or a productive science; for in the case of things that are produced, the source of the movement is in the producer, being his mind, or his art, or some capacity of his; in the case of what is practical, the source is in the doer, being in fact his decision; for what can be done and what can be decided upon are in fact the same. Thus, if every science is either practical or productive or speculative, natural science must be speculative; but it will speculate about the kind of being that can be moved, and generally it will study only substance in the sense of form when it is not separable.

But we must not fail to grasp the way in which the essence and the account of it exist; for if we do not grasp this, our inquiry will come to nothing. Among things that are defined and that are essences, some are like "snub," others like "curved." These differ in that "snub" is combined with matter, since "snub" means having a curved nose, whereas "curvedness" is devoid of any matter that is perceptible to the senses. All natural objects are talked about in the way that "snub" is—nose, eye, face, flesh, and bone, for instance, and animal in general; or leaf, root, and bark, and plant in general; for no account can be given of any of them without reference to movement, and they all always contain matter. If all this is so, it is clear how we ought to look for and define the essence in natural science, and why it is the business of the natural scientist to study the soul too to some extent, insofar as it is not devoid of matter.

From these considerations, then, it is plain that the science of nature is a speculative science. But mathematics, too, is a speculative science; it is not, however, clear whether its objects are immovable and separable, although it is clear that some of them are treated as immovable and separable.

But if there is anything that is eternal, immovable, and separable, plainly it is the business of a speculative science to know about it; it is not, however, the business either of natural science (since it is with movable objects that natural science is concerned) or of mathematics, but rather of a science that is prior to both of them. Natural science is concerned with things that are separable but not immovable; whereas some of the objects of mathematics are immovable but perhaps not separable, since they are contained in matter. But the primary science deals with things that are both separable and immovable. All causes must be eternal, but especially these, since they are the causes of such divine objects as are visible.

Thus, there are three kinds of speculative philosophy: mathematics, natural philosophy, and theology. For it is quite clear that if what is divine belongs anywhere, it belongs to something that is of this nature, and that the most valued science must be concerned with the most valued class of objects. The speculative sciences, then, are to be preferred to the other sciences, and among them this is to be preferred.

People may be at a loss to know whether first philosophy is universal or whether it is concerned with a particular class of things, with a kind of being. There is not even uniformity in mathematics in this respect; geometry and astronomy are concerned with one particular kind of being, whereas universal mathematics applies alike to everything. If there is no other substance apart from those that have come together by nature, natural science will be the first science. But if there is a substance that is immovable, the science that studies it is prior to natural science and is the first philosophy; and it is thus universal insofar as it is first. It is the business of this science to study being qua being, and to find out what it is and what are its attributes qua being.

2. There are many ways in which the simple term "being" can be used: one is of "accidental being," another of being as truth (and not-being as falsehood); and in addition to these there are the various categories, such

as what a thing is, quality, quantity, place, time, and any
other term that has this kind of meaning; and besides all
these, there are potential and actual being. Since being is
talked about in these many ways, let us first of all discuss
accidental being and show that there can be no study of
it. An indication of this is that no science, whether practical, productive, or speculative, is concerned with it. The
man who produces a house does not also produce all its
accidental attributes. For these accidents are infinite in
number, and there is nothing to stop the house when it
has been made from being pleasant for some people,
harmful for others, and advantageous for yet others, nor
to stop its being different from practically everything
else that there is. But none of these qualities is produced
by the building art. Similarly, the geometrician does not
study what are in this way the accidents of shapes, or
whether "triangle" is different from "a triangle whose
angles equal two right angles." It is reasonable enough
that this should happen, for what is accidental is little
more than a name. In a sense, therefore, Plato was not
far wrong when he made sophistry deal with not-being,
for the sophists do discuss what is accidental more than
practically anyone else. They discuss, for instance,
whether "musical" and "literate" are the same, whether
"musical Coriscus" is the same as "Coriscus"; they inquire whether everything that is but has not always been
has therefore come into being; in that case, they say, if
anyone has become literate while he is musical, he will
also have become musical while he is literate; and they
discuss any other questions that are of this kind. For the
accidental does seem to be very close to not-being. This
is made clear, too, by the following argument: in the
case of things that are in any other fashion, there is
coming-to-be and perishing; but in the case of things that
are accidentally, there is not. Nevertheless, we must as
far as possible say what the nature of the accidental is,
and what the cause of its existence is. For perhaps it will
become clear at the same time why there is no science
of it.

Among the things that exist, some are always and of necessity in the same state—I do not mean the necessity brought about by violence, but the kind we talk of when it is not possible for a thing to be other than it is; others are as they are neither of necessity nor always, but only for the most part. This is the origin and cause of the existence of the accidental, for we talk of accidental being in the case of what is as it is, neither always nor for the most part. If there is a storm and it is cold during the dog days, we say that this is accidental, but not if it is sultry and hot then, for that is what it generally or always is then; the other is not. Then of man we say that he is accidentally white, since he is neither always nor generally so; but not that he is accidentally an animal. It is accidentally, too, that a builder makes someone healthy, since this is not what it is a builder's, but a doctor's, nature to do; it was an accident that the builder was also a doctor. A cook who aimed at giving pleasure might make someone healthy, but it would not be by virtue of his cookery that he did it, so we say that this was an accident; and although he did it in a sense, strictly he did not. Whereas with other things there are productive capacities, in the case of these there is no definite art or capacity involved. Of things that are or come into being accidentally, the cause is accidental too. Thus, since not everything that is or comes into being is as it is of necessity or always—most things are only so for the most part—there must be accidental being. For instance, the man who is white is neither always nor generally musical; but since he sometimes becomes so, he will be so accidentally. If this were not so, everything would be as it is of necessity. Thus, it is matter, which admits of things being other than they generally are, that is the cause of what is accidental.

We should take as our starting point the question of whether there is nothing that is neither always nor generally in whatever state it is, or whether this is impossible. The fact is that, in addition to what is always or generally as it is, there is what happens as it may chance to, and what is accidental. But is it the case that things are as they are generally but that nothing is so always? Or are there some things that are eternal? We must look into this question later; but it is clear that there is no science of what is accidental, since all science is of what is always or generally so. Otherwise how could one learn or teach anyone else? What one learns must be defined by being either always or generally so; one can say, for instance, that honey-water is generally beneficial to a man with a fever. A science will not be able to say what is contrary to this, for if one tries to say when honey-water is not beneficial—at the new moon, for instance—one will already be saying that this is either always or generally so. But what is accidental is what runs counter to this.

We have then shown what the accidental is, what the cause of its existence is, and that there is no science of it.

■　■　■

Book VII

1. There are many ways in which the term "being" is used, corresponding to the distinctions we drew earlier, when we showed in how many ways terms are used. On the one hand, it indicates what a thing is and that it is this particular thing; on the other, it indicates a thing's quality or size, or whatever else is asserted of it in this way. Although "being" is used in all these ways, clearly the primary kind of being is what a thing is; for it is this that indicates substance. When we say *what kind* of thing something is, we say that it is good or bad, but not that it is three feet long or that it is a man; but when we say *what* a thing is, we do not say that it is white, hot, or three feet long, but that it is a man or a god. All other things are said to be only insofar as they are quantities, qualities, affections, or something else of this kind belonging to what is in this primary sense. For this reason, people might wonder as to "walking," "being in good health," or "sitting down" whether any of them exist; and they might do the same with any other terms of this kind. For none of them exists on its own, or can be separated from substance; if anything, it is what is walking, or what is sitting down, or what is in good health that exists on its own. These clearly do more truly exist, since they have a definite substratum, which is the substance and the individual, as is clear in the way that we use the terms. Neither what is good nor what is sitting down can be referred to independently of a substratum. Clearly, then, it is because of the substance that each of these terms "is"; so what is primarily—not in the sense of *being something*, but of just quite simply *being*—is substance.

There are many ways in which the word "primary" is used; but in whatever way it is used, substance is primary; it is primary in definition, primary in knowledge, and primary in time. No term in any other category is separable; only substance is. Then, it is primary in definition, since the definition of the substance must be present in the definition of anything. Finally, we think we know anything most fully when we know what it is—what man or fire is, for instance—rather than when we know what kind of thing it is or what size it is or where it is, since even with these questions we know the answers only when we know what quality and size *are*. And, indeed, the question that was raised long ago, is raised now, and always will be raised and puzzled about—namely, "What is being?"—is really the same as the question, "What is substance?"; it is of substance that some people say that it is one, others that there are more than one; some that there is a finite number of them, others an infinite number. So the main, the first, and almost the only question that we have to study is what is being in this sense.

2. Substance is thought most clearly to belong to bodies. That is why we say that animals, plants, and their parts are substances, as are also natural bodies, such as fire, water, earth, and anything that is of that kind; all their parts; and everything that is made up either of some or of all of them—the heaven, for instance, and its parts, the stars, the moon, and the sun. But we must see whether these are the only substances, or whether there are others as well; or whether only some of these are substances, and some other things are too; or whether none of them is, but only certain other things are. Some people regard the limits of body—the surface, the line, the point, and the unit—as substances, and as being more so than body and what is solid.

Then, some people think that there is nothing substantial apart from sensible objects; others that there are eternal substances, more numerous and more substantial than the sensible ones. Plato, for instance, regarded the forms and the "mathematicals" as two kinds of substance, with sensible bodies as a third kind. Speusippus thought that there were even more kinds of substance; he started from the one and assumed a first principle for each kind of substance, one for numbers, one for magnitudes, and then one for the soul; and in this way he extended the number of substances. Some people, too, say that the forms and numbers have the same nature and that everything else, such as lines and plane surfaces, is dependent on them, going right up to the substance of the heavens and of the sensible bodies. We shall have, then, to see which of these statements are right, which wrong; what things are substances; whether or not there are substances apart from sensible bodies; how these sensible substances exist; whether or not there is any separable substance apart from sensible ones, and, if so, why and how. But before we do this we must first give an outline of what substance is.

3. There are four chief ways, if not more, in which we speak of substance. In the case of any particular thing, the essence, the universal, and the genus are all thought of as being its substance; and, fourthly, so is the substratum. The substratum is that of which everything else is asserted; it is not itself asserted of anything. So we must first of all determine its nature, for it is the primary substratum that is most of all thought of as being substance. In one sense, matter is talked of as the substratum; in another sense, the shape; in yet a third, the product of the two. (By matter I mean, for instance, bronze; by shape, the pattern of the form; and by the product of the two, the statue, the combined whole.) If, therefore, the form is prior to and more truly existent than the matter, it will by the same argument be prior to the product of the two.

We have now given an outline of what substance is. We have said that it is what is not asserted of any substratum, but rather that of which other things are asserted. But our account must not stop here, since this is not enough. The statement itself is obscure and, further, in it substance is made to be matter. For if matter is not substance, it is beyond us to say what else is. Once all other things have been removed, there is clearly nothing else left. For all the rest are affections or products or potentialities of bodies: length, breadth, and depth are quantitative attributes but not substances, for quantity is not a substance; it is, rather, the thing to which all these ultimately belong that is substance. But if we take length, breadth, and depth away, we see that there is nothing left except whatever is bounded by them; therefore, if we look at the question in this way, we inevitably find that matter is the only substance. And by matter I mean that which of itself is not said to be anything or to have any size, nor are any of the other terms used of it by which being is defined. For there is something about which each of these terms is asserted, and whose being is different from what it is in each of the categories (since all other terms are asserted of substance, and substance is asserted of matter); so that the ultimate substratum on its own is not any particular thing, nor is it any size, nor indeed anything else; it is not even the negations of these, since these will belong to it only by accident.

When we study the question with these considerations in mind, it follows that matter is substance. This, however, is impossible, since separability and individuality are both thought of as belonging particularly to substance, so that form and the product of the two would seem to be substance more than matter is. But we must reject the idea of the product of the two (by which I mean the product of matter and shape) being substance, since it is subsequent to the other two and its nature is obvious. The position of matter is, in a way, clear too. But we must examine the third possibility, which is the most difficult.

It is generally agreed that some sensible objects are substances; so we ought to begin our inquiry among them. It is useful to move towards what is more intelligible; for with everyone learning proceeds in this way, through what is by nature less intelligible to what is more so. And just as with behavior the task is to start from what is good for individuals and then to make what is good absolutely also good for individuals, so here our task is to start from what is most intelligible to a man and then to make what is naturally intelligible intelligible to him. The things that are intelligible to individuals, in the first instance, are often really only moderately so, and have little or no share in being. However, we must start with those things that, even if they are only moderately intelligible, are nonetheless intelligible to oneself, and so try to understand things that are intelligible absolutely, moving over to them, as I have said, through these others.

4. Since we distinguished at the outset the number of terms by which we define substance, and one of them was the essence, we must now study that. Let us first of all make a few remarks about it in the abstract.

The essence of each thing is what it is said to be in itself. The essence of you is not "being musical," for you are not of yourself musical. Your essence is what you are of yourself. But it is not even all of that; it is not what a thing is of itself, in the way that a surface is white, since being a surface is not being white. But the compound of the two, "being a white surface," is not the essence either, since the thing itself is present in that

phrase too. The account of the essence of anything, then,
is what does not include that thing even though it describes it; thus, if being a white surface were the same
as being a smooth surface, being white and being smooth
would be one and the same thing. But since there are
compounds corresponding to all the other categories too
(for all of them have substrata; quality does, for instance,
and so do quantity, time, place, and movement), we must
see whether there is an account of the essence of all of
them, and whether they in fact have an essence. Does
"white man" have one, for instance? Let us call "white
man" x. What is the essence of x? It may be objected
that this is not a thing that can be said to be of itself at
all. But in fact there are only two ways in which a term
is not of itself true of a subject: one is the addition of
something; the other, the opposite. In one case, the term
consists of the very thing being defined added on to
something else, as, for instance, if one were to define
"being white" by giving an account of a white man; in
the other, something else belongs to the thing, but is
omitted from the term, as, for instance, if x meant "white
man" and someone defined x as white. "White man" is
indeed white, but being white is not its essence.

  But is being x an essence at all? It is not, for the
essence is just what an individual thing is; but when one
thing is asserted of another, this is not just what an individual thing is. "White man," for instance, is not an individual thing, since individuality belongs only to
substances. So the things that have an essence are those
of which the account is a definition. We do not have a
definition every time that an account means the same
thing as a name; this would make all accounts definitions, for any account that you mention has a name, so
that even the *Iliad* will then become a definition. An
account is a definition only if it is of something primary;
and the things that are primary are those whose mention
does not involve one thing being asserted of another.
No form or species, then, that does not belong to a genus

has an essence; only those that do so belong have them.
For these do not seem to be talked of as being participated in, or as affections, or as accidents. With everything else, provided it has a name, there will be an
account of what it means, saying that this belongs to
that; or, instead of this simple account, there may be a
more accurate one. But in these cases there will be no
definition and no essence.

But perhaps definition, like essence, can be talked of
in several ways. In one sense, "essence" means substance and the individual thing: in another it means what
is in any of the other categories—quantity, quality, or
anything else that is of this kind. Just as being belongs
to everything, but not to everything in the same way,
rather primarily to one thing and only secondarily to the
rest, so too essence belongs absolutely to substance, but
in a way to everything else as well. For we could ask
what quality is, so that quality, too, is one of the things
that is; but it is not so absolutely: just as, in the case of
not-being, people say in the abstract that what is not
is—but not absolutely so, only insofar as it is not being—
so too with quality.

But although we ought to study the way in which we
should speak of each of these things, we ought not to
study this more than we study the actual facts. So, since
the way in which we talk about it is now clear, essence
(like the question "what a thing is") will belong primarily and simply to substance, and secondarily to everything else, although there not as a simple essence but as
the essence of quality or quantity. For it must be either
ambiguously that we say that these things are, or, by
adding to and taking from the meaning, in the same way
that we say that what is unknowable is knowable. But
the truth is that we do not use the term "being" ambiguously, nor always in the same sense. Rather, like the
term "medical," we use it to indicate relation to one and
the same thing, without its always meaning one and the
same thing, or yet being ambiguous. For when we call a

patient, a job, and an implement all medical, there is no
ambiguity in our use of the term, nor do we in each case
mean one and the same thing; but there is a relation to
the same thing in each case.

But it makes no difference in which of the two ways
we like to use these terms. What is clear is that definition
and essence belong primarily and simply to substances.
They do, nonetheless, belong to other things as well, but
not primarily. We are not compelled, if we make this
assumption, to say that there is a definition of every term
that has the same meaning as an account, only that there
is one of everything that has the same meaning as a
particular kind of account; and this particular kind of
account is an account of one thing; and by "one" we do
not mean what is one just by continuity, like the *Iliad*,
or by being bound together, but what is one in any of
the ways in which things are said to be really one, which
are the same as the ways in which things are said to be:
"being" in some cases indicates an individual, in others
quantity or quality. So there will be both an account and
a definition of "white man," but in a different way from
that in which there is one of "white" or of a substance.

5. There is this further problem. If we say that no
account that uses an additional term is a definition,
which of the terms that are compound as opposed to
simple will have a definition? For one must use an additional term to make them clear. The kind of thing I
mean is this. We have the terms "nose" and "curvedness"; then, there is "snubness," which is a compound
of the other two, because of the presence of the one in
the other. It is not accidentally that either "curvedness"
or "snubness" is an attribute of "nose"—they belong to
it of themselves. They do not belong to it in the way in
which "white" belongs to Callias, or to "man" because
Callias, who is accidentally a man, is white, but in the
way in which "male" belongs to "animal," "equal" to
"quantity," and everything else that is said to belong to

something of itself does so. These terms are all those in which either the account or the name of the thing of which they are attributes is present, and which cannot be explained without reference to that thing. "White" can be explained without reference to "man," but "female" cannot be explained without reference to "animal." So either there is no essence or definition of any of these terms, or, if there is, it is in another sense, as we have said before.

There is another problem about these terms. If a snub nose and a curved nose are the same thing, "snub" and "curved" will be the same thing. But they are not the same; for it is impossible to say "snub" without implying the thing of which in itself it is an attribute, "snubness" being "curvedness of the nose"; and if this is so, either it will not be possible to speak of a snub nose, or to do so will involve saying the same thing twice: one will then be saying "curved-nose nose," since the nose that is the snub nose will be the curved-nose nose. So it would be strange for such terms to have an essence; if they did, the account of them would continue to infinity, since one would still always be able to add another "nose" to "snub-nose nose."

It is, then, plain that it is only of substance that there is definition. If there is any definition of terms in the other categories, it must make use of something additional, as in the case of "odd;" for this cannot be defined without reference to "number," nor can "female" be defined without reference to "animal." (When I speak of using something additional, I am referring to cases where one finds that one is saying the same thing twice, as one does in these cases.) If this is true, there will be no definition of compound terms like "odd number" either; we fail to notice this, however, because these terms are far from rigorous. If, on the other hand, there are definitions of these terms too, either they are defined in some other way or, as we have said, "definition" and "essence" must have several different senses, so that in one sense there will be no definition or essence of anything other than substances, and in another there will. It is clear, then, that the definition is the account of the essence, and that essences belong to substances only, or at least chiefly, primarily, and simply to them.

6. We must now inquire whether the essence and the individual thing are the same or different. For this is of use to us in our inquiry into substance. The individual does not seem to be anything other than his own substance, and it is the essence that is said to be the substance of each individual. Where there are accidental attributes, the two seem to be different. "White man," for instance, is different from "being a white man." If they were the same, "being a man" and "being a white man" would be the same; for a man and a white man are the same, so they say, so that being a man and being a white man would also be the same. But perhaps it is not necessary for the essences of subjects with their accidental attributes to be the same as those of the subjects alone. For the two extreme terms in the syllogism, although they are identical with the middle term, are not both so in the same way. Perhaps, however, what would follow from the subject with its accidental attribute being the same as its essence is this: the two extreme terms that are accidental would be the same—being white and being musical, for example. We see that in fact they are not the same.

But in the case of things that are said to "be" of themselves, must the essence be the same as the thing itself? Is this the case, for instance, if there are substances to which no other substance or nature is prior, substances such as some say the ideas are? If the good itself and the essence of good are different, and the same applies to animal and the essence of animal and to being and the essence of being, there will be other substances, entities, and ideas as well as the ones that are said to be; and these others will be prior, if essence is substance.

But if the ideas and their essences are separated from each other, there will be no knowledge of the ideas, and the essences will not exist. (When I speak of these terms being "separated" from each other, I am referring to the kind of situation in which the essence of good does not belong to the good itself, and has not the property of being good.) For we have knowledge of any given thing when we know its essence; and the situation with regard to good is like that with regard to everything else, so that if the essence of good is not good, the essence of being will not be existent, nor that of unity one. Now, either all essences exist or none does, so that if the essence of being does not exist, none of the others will either. Further, anything to which the essence of good does not belong will not be good itself.

The good, then, must be one and the same thing as the essence of the good, and the beautiful as the essence of the beautiful; and the same holds of everything that is not asserted of something else but is primary and of itself. It is enough if this is the case even if these things are not forms, or perhaps I should say especially if they are forms. (At the same time, it is clear that if there are ideas of the kind that some people speak of, the substratum will not be substance. For these ideas must be substances, and yet not be asserted of a substratum; for if they are so asserted, they will exist only by virtue of its participation in them.)

The individual and the essence, then, are one and the same thing, and it is not accidentally that they are so. This is clear from the above arguments, and also from the fact that knowledge of an individual is knowledge of its essence; so that from a setting out of instances, too, it necessarily follows that both are one. With accidental terms, however, like "musical" or "white," because of their double meaning, it is not true to say that the essence and the thing itself are the same. For both the accidental attribute and the thing of which it is an accident are white, so that here the essence and the thing itself are in a way the same and in a way not. The essence of white is not the same as the man or as the white man, but it is the same as the actual attribute.

The absurdity of separating the essence from the individual becomes apparent, too, if one gives each essence a name. In that case there will be another essence besides the original one; the essence of horse will itself have a further essence. But what is there to prevent us from saying straightaway now that some things are the same as their essences, if essence is in fact substance? Not only are these two one, but the account of each is the same, too, as is clear from what has been said; for it is not accidentally that the essence of unity and the one are one and the same. Further, if the two are different, the process will go on to infinity: on the one hand, there will be the essence of unity; on the other, the one; so that in the case of these terms, too, the same principle will apply.

Clearly, then, in the case of things that are primary and are spoken of as being of themselves, each individual and its essence are one and the same. The sophistical objections to this position are clearly disposed of in the same way as that about whether "Socrates" and "being Socrates" are the same; there is no difference either in what leads one to ask these questions and in what enables one successfully to answer them. We have then made clear in what way the essence is the same as the individual, and in what way it is not.

7. Of the things that come to be, some do so by nature, others through art, still others spontaneously; but everything that comes to be does so through the agency of something, and from something, and there is something that it comes to be—and I speak of its coming to be something with reference to any of the categories: it may come to be a particular thing or a particular size or of a particular kind or in a particular place.

Natural processes of coming to be occur with things

that come to be according to nature. That from which they come into being is what we call matter; that by whose agency they come into being is something that exists by nature; and that which they come to be is a man or a plant or something else of the kind, which we say is substance more than anything else. (In fact, everything that comes to be, either by nature or by art, contains matter; for all of them are able both to be and not to be, and what has this ability is the matter in each of them.) In general, not only the thing from which but also the thing in accordance with which they come to be is nature—for what they come to be, a plant or an animal, for instance, has a nature; and the thing by whose agency they come to be is the so-called formal nature, which has the same form as the thing itself (although it is in something else), since man begets man.

This, then, is the way in which things that come to be by nature do so; the other processes of coming-to-be are described as "productions." All productions come from art or from capacity or from thought. Some of them, too, come to be spontaneously and by chance, in much the same way as do some of the things that come to be by nature—for there, too, the same things come to be both from a seed and without one. (We must look into these later.) But the things that come to be through art are those whose form is in the producer's soul; and by "form" I mean the essence and primary substance of each thing. Even contraries, in a sense, have the same form, for the substance of a privation is the substance contrary to it: health, for instance, is the substance of disease, since it is through the absence of health that disease occurs; and health is in fact the account and knowledge of disease, which is in the soul. The patient becomes healthy when the doctor has thought in the following way: "Since health is *this*, the patient, if he is to be healthy, must have *this*—say, a uniform condition; and if he is to have that, he must have heat"; and he goes on continually thinking in this way until he finally arrives at something that he himself can produce. And the process from this point onward—the process towards being healthy—is called "production." So it follows that in a way health comes into being from health, house from house, and that which has matter from that which does not have it: for the art of medicine and the art of building are the forms respectively of health and of a house; and by substance without matter I mean the essence.

In these processes, one part is called "thought," the other "production." Thought starts from the first principle and the form, production from the final stage of the thought. Each of the intermediate stages of the process occurs in the same way. What I am describing is like this: if a patient is to be healthy, he must be made to have a uniform bodily condition. What does being made to have a uniform bodily condition involve? It involves this or that, which will come about if he is made hot. And what does that involve? It involves this, which is potentially there, and thus already within the doctor's power.

The thing that does the producing and from which the process of getting to be healthy starts is, if this is being done by art, the form in the soul; but if the state of health is produced spontaneously, it comes, in the case of the producer who produced what he did by art, from what was the starting point of his production. In the treatment of a patient, for instance, perhaps the starting point of the production process is the patient's being hot, and perhaps this is produced by friction; the heat in the body is, then, either a part of health or is followed, whether immediately or through successive stages, by something such that it is a part of health; this, then, is the ultimate thing, that which produces the part of health, and is to that extent a part of it itself; it is the same with the production of a house (where the stones play a similar role), and with everything else.

So, as people say, it is impossible for anything to come

into being unless there is something there beforehand. Clearly, then, some part will of necessity be there beforehand; for matter is a part since it is present in the thing and is itself what comes to be something. But is matter also included in the account of the thing? There are two ways in which to explain what bronze circles are: one is naming their matter and saying that it is bronze; the other, naming their form and saying that it is such and such a shape; and shape is the proximate genus in which it is placed. Any account of a bronze circle, then, will include its matter.

With regard to that from which, as matter, things come to be, in some cases, when they do so, they are not said to be that thing but to be of that thing; a statue, for instance, is not said to be stone but of stone. A healthy man, on the other hand, is not at all said to be the thing from which he comes to be what he is. The reason for this is that he comes to be what he is both from the privation and from the substratum, which we call the matter (it is, for instance, both the man and the invalid that become healthy); but since it is more from the privation that he is said to come to be what he is, we say that a man comes to be healthy from being an invalid rather than from being a man. Thus, too, he who is healthy is not said to be an invalid but to be a man, and it is the man who is said to be healthy. But in cases where the privation is obscure and has no name—such as the privation of any particular shape in the case of bronze, or that of a house in the case of bricks and timber—the thing seems to come to be from these materials, just as in the other case it came to be from an invalid. Therefore, just as there the thing was not said to be that from which it came to be, so here the statue is not called "wood," but by a modification of the term, "wooden," and so, too, it would be called "brazen" rather than "bronze," or "of stone" rather than "stone"; and a house is said to be "of bricks" rather than "bricks." For upon closer examination one cannot even say without qualification that the statue comes into being from wood, or the house from bricks, since that from which a thing comes into being ought to change and not persist. That, anyway, is why we speak in this way.

8. What comes into being comes into being through the agency of something (and here I refer to the source of the process), and from something (and this, we will agree, is not the privation, but the matter; we have already distinguished the ways in which we use these terms), and there is something that it comes to be (and that is a sphere or a circle or whatever it chances to be). Now, just as the maker does not produce the substratum, the bronze, so he does not produce the sphere either— except accidentally, insofar as the bronze sphere is a sphere, and he produces that. For to produce a particular thing is to produce it out of what is fully a substratum. I mean that to make the bronze round is not to make the roundness or the sphere, but to do something different: to produce this form in something else. If somebody produces something, he produces it out of something else—this we assumed; for instance, he produces a bronze sphere, and this he does by producing out of *this* (which is bronze) *this* (which is a sphere). If, then, someone produces the substratum too, clearly he will produce it in the same way, and the process will continue to infinity.

Clearly, then, the form, or whatever one ought to call the shape in a perceptible object, does not come into being, nor does any such process apply to it; and the essence does not come into being either, for it is rather what is made to be in something else, through art or nature or capacity. But someone does make this to be a bronze sphere: he produces it out of bronze and out of the sphere; he puts the form into a particular bit of matter, and the result is a bronze sphere. But if the essence of sphere in general is to come to be, it will have to come from something to be something. For whatever comes to be will always have to be divisible, to be partly this and partly that—that is to say, partly matter and partly form. If then a sphere is a figure whose circumference is everywhere equidistant from the center, the one part will be the thing containing what is being produced, the other what is inside that thing; and the whole will be what has come into being, the bronze sphere, for instance. From what we have said, it is clear that what is spoken of as form or substance does not come to be, but that the whole, which is called after the form, does; and also that in everything that comes to be there is matter, so that part is matter and part is form.

Is there a sphere that exists apart from the particular spheres around us, or a house that exists apart from bricks? Surely if there were, no individual would ever have come to be; a form indicates being of such and such a kind, it is not a definite individual; it produces or generates what is of a particular kind out of a particular thing, and when this has been generated, it is a particular thing of a particular kind. The whole of the particular thing, Callias or Socrates, is like this particular bronze sphere; whereas "man" and "animal" are like "bronze sphere" in general. Plainly, then, the forms, when they are thought of as causes in the way in which some people are accustomed to speak of them, are of no use for explaining processes of coming-to-be or substances, even if there are forms apart from particulars; so here at least there are no grounds for regarding them as substances in themselves. In certain cases it is clear that what generates is of the same kind as what is generated by it, although the former is not the same thing as the latter; it is not one in number with it, but in form only. This happens with natural processes, where man generates man. There is an exception when something comes into being contrary to nature—when a horse, for instance, generates a mule. But even here there is a similarity. No name has been given to what there is in common between a horse and a donkey, that is, to the genus immediately above them; perhaps it would be both, as in the case of a mule.

Plainly, then, there is no need to set up the form as a model; for it would be in the case of these natural objects that they would most of all have been sought for, since they more than anything else are substances. That which generates is enough to produce something and to be the cause of the form's presence in the matter. The complete whole—a form of a particular kind, in this particular flesh or these particular bones—is already Callias or Socrates; they are different in matter, since their matter is different, but are the same in form, since the form is indivisible.

9. There might be raised the further problem of why some things, like health, come into being both by art and spontaneously, while others, like a house, do not. The reason is this: the matter, which starts the process when something is being produced or is coming to be through art, and in which some part of the final thing is already present, is of various kinds. Some is such that it can be moved by itself, some is not; and of that which can be moved by itself, some can be moved in a particular way, some cannot; for there are many cases of things being able to be moved by themselves, but not in some particular way—not able to dance, for instance. Things that have matter of this kind, such as stones, are unable to be moved in one way, except through the agency of something else; but they can be moved in another, as is also the case with fire. For this reason, some things will not exist except through someone who possesses the art, but others will; for in the case of these others, the motion will be started by things that do not possess the art but which can themselves be moved, either by other things that do not possess the art or by a part of the thing which is already there.

It is plain from what we have said that in a way everything that is produced by art comes into being from something with the same name as itself, as do natural objects; or from a part of themselves that has the same name (a house, for instance, is produced from a house, inasmuch as it is first produced by the mind, since the art is the form); or from something that contains such a part—provided that what comes into being is not just accidental. For what first of all and of itself causes the thing to be produced is a part of it. The heat involved in movement produces heat in the body, and this either is health or it is followed by health or by some part of it. That indeed is why it is said to produce health: because it produces what health follows upon as a consequence. So here, just as with the syllogisms, the starting point of everything is the substance; syllogisms start from the essence, and so do processes of production.

Things that are formed by nature are in a position similar to that of these products of art. The seed produces what it does in the same way as things that do their production by art. It possesses the form potentially, and that from which the seed comes has in a sense the same name as what is produced; I say "in a sense" only because we must not expect everything to be like man coming from man, since the female also comes from the male. But the seed does in general have the same name as what is produced, unless there is some barrenness, which is the reason why mule does not come from mule. Here, as with the products of art, the things that come into being spontaneously are those whose matter can impart to itself the motion that is usually imparted by the seed; things whose matter cannot do this cannot come into being in any other way than from ordinary parents.

It is not only with regard to substance that this argument shows that the form does not come into being, but with regard to everything else that is primary too: quality, for instance, and quantity, and all the other categories as well. We have seen that it is a bronze sphere that comes into being, but not bronze or a sphere, and that the same is true of bronze, if it comes into being, since there must always be matter and form present beforehand; the same thing holds not only in the case of substance, but also in the case of quality, of quantity, and of all the other categories. It is not a "kind" that comes into being, but "wood of a certain kind"; not "size," but "a piece of wood or an animal of a certain size." But from this we can see a peculiarity of substance—namely, that there must be present beforehand another substance, fully realized, which produces it; there must be another animal there, if one is to come into being. This is not the case with quality or quantity, except potentially.

■ ■ ■

13. Since our inquiry is into substance, let us return to it. Just as the substratum, the essence, and the product of the two are all said to be substance, so too is the universal. We have discussed two of these, the essence and the substratum, and we have pointed out that there are two ways in which the *substratum* may underlie, either in the way in which an individual—an animal, for instance—underlies its attributes or in the way in which matter underlies the realized object. But since some people regard the universal as more than anything else a cause and first principle, let us go on to discuss it. For it seems impossible that any universal term should be a substance.

Firstly, the substance of each thing is peculiar to it and does not belong to anything else, whereas the universal is shared; for what is called universal is what naturally belongs to a number of things. Of what, then, will the universal be the substance? It must be the substance either of everything or of nothing. But it cannot be the substance of everything; and if it is the substance of one thing, everything else will be that thing too, since things that have one substance and one essence are themselves one.

Then, a substance is said to be that which is not asserted of a subject, whereas a universal is always asserted of a subject.

It may be suggested that it is not possible for it to be substance in the way that essence is, but that it is present in the essence, as "animal" is present in "man" and in "horse." Then, plainly there will have to be an account of it. However, it does not make any difference if there is not an account of everything that is contained in the substance; the universal will nonetheless be the substance of something, just as "man" is the substance of the man in whom it is present; so that the same consequence will follow, for the universal—animal, for instance—will be the substance of that in which it is present as a peculiar characteristic.

Further, it is both impossible and absurd for what is an individual and a substance, if it is composed of things at all, to be composed neither of substances nor of individuals, but of quality; for in this way what is not substance but quality will be prior to what is substance and is individual, and this is impossible. Neither in definition nor in time nor in the process of coming to be can the attributes precede the substance; for if they do, they will be separable too.

Further, in this case, there will be a substance present in Socrates that will thus be the substance of two things.

And, in general, if "man" and other things that are described in this way are substances, it will follow that nothing that is contained in the accounts of them will be a substance; nor will any such thing exist, either apart from them or in anything else. I mean, for instance, that it will not be possible for "animal" to exist, apart from the particular kinds of animal, nor for anything else contained in the account to do so.

If we study the matter with these points in mind, we see clearly that no universal attribute is a substance, and that no term that is asserted of a number of things in common means a particular thing, but rather "of a particular kind"; otherwise, a number of difficulties follow, including the "third man."

There is another way in which the point becomes clear. It is impossible for a substance to be made up of substances that are present in it fully realized. For what are fully realized as two things will never be fully realized as one; they will be one only if it is just potentially that they are two. Something that is double, for instance, will be potentially made of two halves; it is their realization as two which separates them. Thus, if a substance is one, it will not be made up of substances that are present in it in this way, which Democritus describes correctly. He points out that it is impossible for two to come into being out of one, or one out of two (for he makes the atomic magnitudes his substances). It is then plain that a similar situation will hold in the case of number, if number is a combination of units, as some people say it is. Either a pair will not be one, or there will be no unit in it that is fully realized.

This conclusion does involve a difficulty. If it is neither the case that any substance can be made up of universals (since universals mean "of a particular kind," not "a particular thing"), nor that any substance can be composed of substances fully realized, every substance must be uncompounded, and in that case no account can be given of any substance. But everyone agrees upon the point that we made a short way back—that substance, if not the only, is at least the main thing of which there can be definition. Now we find that there cannot be definition even of this, so that in fact there will be no definition of anything, or perhaps there will be in one way but not in another. What we are talking about, however, will become clearer from what I say later on.

14. These very considerations make it clear what the consequences are of saying that the ideas are separable substances and at the same time making the form consist of the genus and the differentia. If there are forms, and if "animal" is present in both "man" and "horse," either it will be one and the same thing numerically or it will not. (As far as the account goes, they are clearly one; for the man who talks about animal in each case will go through the same account.) If, then, some "man himself" exists on his own as a separate individual, then the things of which he is made up, such as "animal" and "two-footed," must also indicate individuals and be both separable and substances; so that "animal" will be like this too.

If "animal" is one and the same thing in "horse" and in "man," in just the way that you are the same thing as yourself, how can this one thing that in things that are apart be one? And how is it that this "animal" is not apart from itself as well? Then, if "animal" participates in both "two-footed" and "many-footed," we have the impossible result that two opposites are present in it even though it is a single individual. If this is not the case, what kind of thing is one saying when one says that the animal is "two-footed" or "equipped with feet"? It may be said that these things are put together and make contact, or that they are mingled. But all these suggestions are absurd.

But suppose that "animal" is different in each case. Then there will be an almost infinite number of things whose substance is animal, since it is not accidentally that "man" is made up of, among other things, "animal." Also, there will be many things that will be the "animal itself," since the "animal" that is present in each species will be the substance of that species. For there is nothing else that the species is named after; if there were, man would be partly made up of it, and it would be his genus. Further, all the things of which man is made up will be ideas; but then it will not be the form of one thing and the substance of another, since this is impossible; thus, the "animal" present in each species of animal will in every case be "the animal itself." Again, from what will this "animal" in each species be derived? How can it come from the "animal itself"? Or how can the "animal," whose substance is this very thing, "animal," exist apart from the "animal itself"?

In the case of sensible objects, both these and even more absurd consequences follow.

If these consequences are impossible, clearly there are no forms of sensible things in the way in which some people say there are.

15. There are two kinds of substance, the complete thing and the account; I mean that the one is substance in the sense of being the account taken together with the matter, and the other is the account in its full extent. Substances spoken of in the first way can be destroyed, since they can also come into being; but there can be no destruction of the account in the sense of its ever being in the course of being destroyed, since there is no generation of it either; for it is not "being house" that comes into being, but "being a particular house." Whether they exist or whether they do not, accounts are exempt from generation and destruction. We have already shown that nobody generates or produces them. And the reason why there is no definition or demonstration of particular sensible substances is that they contain matter, whose nature is such that it is possible for it both to be and not to be; for this reason, all individual sensible objects are perishable. Now, demonstration is only of things that are necessarily so, and definition is possible only where there is knowledge. And, just as it is not possible for knowledge sometimes to be knowledge and sometimes to be ignorance—only opinion is of this nature—so also it is not possible for there to be demonstration or definition of what is capable of being other than it is; there can only be opinion about it. Clearly, then, there can be no definition or demonstration of sensible substances. For it is not clear to those who have knowledge what happens to perishable things when they go out of the ken of the senses; the same accounts of them may be preserved in the soul, but there will no longer be any definition or demonstration of them. So, when someone who engages in definitions defines some individual, one must realize that it is always possible for the definition to be demolished; for in these cases definition is really not possible.

Nor is it possible to define any idea; the idea, according to the Platonists, is something that is individual and separable. The account of it must consist of words; but the man who is doing the defining must not invent a name, since it will be incomprehensible; and the words already in use are common to the whole class to which they refer. If, for instance, someone were to define you, he would describe you as "a thin animal" or "a white animal" or would use some other term that applies to other things as well. Somebody might then say that these terms may belong separately to many things, but it is only to this particular thing that they belong together. To this we must first of all reply that, even taken together, they will also apply to both of their own parts: "two-footed animal," for instance, will belong both to "two-footed" and to "animal." This must hold, too, in the case of things that are eternal, since the simple terms are prior to and parts of the compound. They must be separable too, if "man" is separable, for either both must be separable or neither is; and if neither is, then the genus will not exist apart from the species; but if the genus does so exist, so will the differentia. Secondly, we must reply that the elements of the definition are prior to the definition, and are not destroyed when the compound is destroyed.

Then, if ideas are made up of ideas—they must be, since the constituents of a thing are less complex than the thing itself—we shall have to assert these constituent ideas, "animal" and "two-footed," for instance, of many things as well. Otherwise, how will the idea ever be known? There will be an idea that it is impossible to assert of more than one thing. Yet this does not seem to be the case; every idea is thought of as being such that other things can participate in it.

Thus, as we have said, people fail to realize the impossibility of definition in the case of things that are eternal, especially if they are unique, as the sun and the moon are. They go wrong in adding to the definition attributes upon whose removal the sun would still exist, "going round the earth," for instance, or "hidden at night." On this basis, the sun would no longer exist if it stood still or appeared by night. But it would be strange if this were so, since the sun denotes a particular substance. But this is not the only mistake that they make: they also go wrong in adding terms that can apply to something else—if another thing like it comes into being, for instance, clearly it will be a sun; and so the account turns out to be shared. But the sun is an individual, as is Cleon or Socrates.

Anyway, why does none of them produce a definition of an idea? If they tried, the truth of what I am saying would become apparent.

16. Clearly, most of the things that are supposed to be substances are just potencies. This is the case with parts of animals: none of them exists separately; and when any of them are separated, they then exist only as matter. It is also the case with earth, fire, and air: none of them is a unity; they are all like a heap of something until they are worked on and some one thing comes into being from them. One might very easily suppose that the parts of living creatures and the parts of the soul come into being in more or less the same way, and thus exist both potentially and in a fully realized form, since they have a source of motion at some point in their joints; and it is for this reason that some animals go on living even when they have been divided. Nonetheless, these parts will exist only potentially when they form a naturally continuous unity, as opposed to one due to violence or to their growing together; this latter kind of unity is a malformation.

Since the term "one" is used in the same way as the term "being," and the substance of one is itself one, and those things whose substance is numerically one are themselves numerically one, it is clearly not possible for either "the one" or "being" to be the substance of things, just as it is not possible for "being an element" or "being a principle" to be their substance; but we inquire what the principle is so that we can refer it to something more knowable. Among these concepts, "being" and "one" are nearer to being substance than the principle, the element, or the cause, but not even they are substance, since nothing that is common to things is. For substance belongs to nothing other than itself and the thing that contains it and whose substance it is. Further, what is one cannot be in a number of things at once; whereas what is common to things is present in a number of them. Plainly, then, no universal can exist apart from its particulars.

Those who maintain the theory of forms are right in making them separate if they are substances, but wrong in making "the one over the many" a form. Their reason for doing this is that they are unable to explain what such imperishable substances are, which exist apart from the individual and sensible ones. So they make them the same in form as perishable things (since we know them), talking of "the man himself" and "the horse itself," just adding the word "self" to the names of sensible objects.

But even if we had never seen the stars, they would still, I suppose, have been eternal substances apart from those that we did know. So now, too, even if we cannot say what these substances are, we nonetheless perhaps suppose that there must be some.

It is, then, plain that none of the things described as a universal is a substance, and that no substance is made up of substances.

17. Let us state *what* we must say substance is and *what kind* of thing we must say it is by making what amounts to another start. Perhaps in this way we shall

also become clear about the substance that is separate
from sensible substances. Since substance is a first principle and cause, let us approach the question from this
angle.

The way in which the question "Why?" is asked is
always this: "Why does one thing belong to another?"
To inquire why the musical man is a musical man is
either to ask the question that we have described, or it
is something else. But to ask why a thing is itself is to
ask nothing. When we ask why a thing is so, the fact that
it is so and the fact of its existence must be evident—the
fact, for instance, that the moon does suffer eclipses; but
in the case of a thing being itself, this alone is the single
reason and cause in every case why man is man and
what is musical is musical, unless one were to say that
everything is indivisible from itself and that this is what
being one is, which is a short answer applicable alike to
every case. One can ask, nevertheless, why man is an
animal of such and such a kind.

This much, then, is clear: one does not ask why whoever is a man is a man, one asks why one thing belongs
to another; and it must be clear that it does so belong,
otherwise one is making an empty inquiry. One may ask,
for instance, "Why does it thunder?" or, rather, "Why
is a noise produced in the clouds?" since the question
really concerns the application of one thing to another
in this way. One might ask, too, "Why are these things—
bricks and stones, for instance—a house?" Plainly, then,
one is seeking the cause, or to put it abstractly, the essence, which in some cases is the purpose for which the
thing is made—as perhaps in the case of a house or a
bed—and in others the prime mover; for this is a cause
too. We look for a cause of this kind in the case of
coming-to-be or perishing, and for the other, the purpose, in the case of being. The nature of one's inquiry
becomes particularly obscure when one term is not applied to another, when people ask, for instance, "What
is man?"; for they have put the question too simply in-

stead of asking why *these* things make up *that*. One must
articulate one's question more clearly before one asks it;
otherwise it will be equally applicable to an empty inquiry and a meaningful one. Since one must already
know of the thing's existence as a fact, one is clearly
asking a question about the matter: "Why is it something
or other?" Why, for instance, are these materials a
house? Because of the presence of the essence of house.
One might also ask, "Why is *this*, or the body containing
this, a man?" So what one is really looking for is the
cause—that is, the form—of the matter being whatever
it is; and this in fact is the substance. Evidently, then, in
the case of simple things one can neither inquire nor
give information; or rather, there is a different kind of
inquiry appropriate to such things.

Now our concern is with what is composite in such a
way that the whole is one, not in the way that a pile of
things is, but in the way that a syllable is. A syllable is
not just its elements; BA is not the same as B and A,
nor is flesh the same as fire and earth. For when the
elements have been separated, the compounds—flesh
and syllable, for instance—no longer exist, but the elements—fire and earth—do. A syllable is, then, more
than just its elements—the vowel and the consonant; it
is something else too, just as flesh is something besides
fire and earth, or hot and cold. It may be maintained
that this something else must be an element, or made
up of elements. If it is an element, the same argument
will apply: flesh will be made up of this element, of fire,
of earth, and of something else, so that the process will
continue to infinity. If it is made up of elements, plainly
it will not be made up of just one, but of several; otherwise the element will just be the thing itself, and then
the same argument will apply as in the case of flesh or
syllable. But this "something else," although it seems to
be something, seems not to be an element; it seems in
fact to be the cause of *this* being flesh, and *that* being a
syllable, and similarly with everything else; in each case

it is the thing's substance, since that is the ultimate cause of a thing's being.

Some things are not substances, but everything that is a substance comes together according to nature and by nature; and so substance would seem to be this "nature," which is not an element but a first principle. An element is that into which a thing is divided up and which is present in it as matter; in the case of the syllable, for example, A and B are its elements.

■   ■   ■

Book IX

1. We have already spoken about being in the primary sense, to which all the other categories of being refer—that is to say, about substance; for it is only by virtue of the concept of substance that we say that other things "are": quantity, quality, and the other terms of this kind, since they all contain the concept of substance, as we said in our initial discussions. But it is not with reference only to being something, or being of a particular kind of size, that we talk of being; we do so, too, with reference to potency and realization and to action. Let us, then, discuss and clarify potency and realization. Let us start with what is most properly called "potency," although it is not the potency that is most useful for our present purpose; for potency and realization cover a wider field than just those things that are said to be involved in movement. After we have talked about this kind of potency, we will explain the other kinds during our discussion of actuality.

We have shown elsewhere that there are many senses in which the words "potency" and "can" are used. Let us ignore cases where there is just an identity of term; for some things are called "potencies" or "powers" just because of a certain resemblance to them—in geometry, for instance, we say that things are or are not powers because they are or are not in a given state. But all the

things that are called potencies with reference to the
same kind are principles, and they all refer to a single
primary potency, which is a principle or source of change
in something else or in the thing itself qua something
else. On the one hand, there is the potency for being
acted upon, which is present in what is being acted upon
and is the source of passive change, which is brought
about by something else or, if by itself, by itself qua
something else; on the other hand, there is the state of
immunity from either change for the worse or corruption
being brought about, through any source of change, either by anything else or by the thing itself qua anything
else. In all these definitions the account of this primary
potency is present. Again, these potencies are spoken of
as potencies either for merely acting or being acted
upon, or for acting or being acted upon *well*; so that in
the accounts of these last potencies, too, the accounts of
the primary ones are in a way present.

Clearly, then, the potency for acting and the potency
for being acted upon are in a way one: for a thing is
"capable" both by virtue of the fact that it has a potency
for being acted upon and by virtue of the fact that something else has a potency for being acted upon by it. But
in a way they are different. For one potency is in the
thing being acted upon; it is because it possesses a source
of change in itself, and because matter is such a source,
that what is acted upon is acted upon, and one thing by
one thing, another by another: what is oily is inflammable, what is yielding in a particular way is compressible,
and similarly with everything else. But the other potency
is in the thing that acts; heat is, for instance, and so is
the capacity to build; the one is in what is capable of
heating, the other in what is capable of building. Hence,
insofar as a thing is of one nature, it is in no way acted
upon by itself; for it is one thing and nothing else. Incapacity, with the incapable, is the privation that is contrary to this kind of potency, so that every potency has
as its contrary an incapacity for the same thing in the
same conditions.

The term "privation" is used in many ways. It is used of what does not have a quality; it is used of what by nature should have a quality if it does not have it, either in general or when it naturally should; and it is used when a thing either does not have a quality in some particular way—entirely, for instance—or does not have it at all. In some cases, too, if things whose nature is to have a quality do not in fact have it because of violence, we say that they have been "deprived."

2. Some such sources of change are present in inanimate objects, others in living creatures, in the soul, and in that part of the soul that possesses reason; clearly, then, some potencies will be nonrational, others rational. Hence, all the arts and all the productive sciences are potencies, since they are sources of change in something else or in the same thing qua something else. Rational potencies admit equally of contrary results, nonrational potencies only of one; what is hot, for instance, can produce only heat, but the art of medicine can produce both disease and health. The reason for this is that science is an account of something and that the same account reveals both a thing and its privation, but it does not do so in the same way in both cases and, although in a way it is an account of both, in a way it is more an account of what positively belongs to it; so that while such sciences must be concerned with both contraries, they will be concerned with the one by virtue of themselves, and with the other not; for while the account is concerned with the one contrary by virtue of what that contrary is, its concern with the other is in a way accidental. For it reveals the second contrary by denial and removal, since this contrary is the primary privation, which is the removal of the positive term. Now, contraries do not occur in the same thing; science is a potency because it involves an account of something; and the soul possesses a source of movement. For these reasons, although what is health-giving can produce only health, and what is capable of producing heat can produce only heat, and

also what is capable of producing cold can produce only
cold, the man of science can produce both of two contrary effects. For there is an account of both (though
not in the same way in both cases), and this account is
in the soul, which possesses the source of movement; so
that the soul will start both movements, starting in each
case from the same source, and linking them both with
the same thing. Hence, things whose potency is rational
do the contrary of those whose potency is nonrational,
since they are involved with only one source, the rational
account. Plainly, too, the potency for acting well, or
being acted upon well, implies the potency just for acting
or being acted upon; but the converse is not always true.
The man who acts well must be acting, but the man who
is just acting need not necessarily be acting well.

3. Some, like the Megarians, say that it is only when
a thing is in action that it has potency, and that when it
is not in action it has no potency: a man who is not
actually building, they say, cannot build; the only man
who can build is the man who is actually doing so, and
he is able to do it only at the time that he is doing it;
and similarly with everything else.

It is not difficult to see what absurd consequences follow from this. Clearly, in that case there will not even
be such a thing as a builder, except when he is actually
building; for being a builder is in fact being able to build;
and the same will hold with all the other arts. If, then,
it is impossible to possess such arts unless one has
learned and acquired them at some stage; and if after
that it is impossible not to possess them, unless one has
at some time lost them (whether through forgetfulness,
or something happening to one, or the passage of time;
for the art itself will certainly not be destroyed, it goes
on forever); and if, whenever a man stops practicing his
art, he no longer possesses it, how will he have acquired
it again when he suddenly starts building again? It will
be the same with inanimate objects; nothing will be cold

or hot or sweet or possess any sensible quality unless people are actually perceiving it. Thus, the result is that these people are maintaining the theory of Protagoras. But nothing will have any perception either, unless it is actually perceiving. If, then, what is blind is what, although it is its nature to have it, does not have sight at the time when it is its nature to have it, although it is still in existence, the same people will be blind many times in one day, and deaf too. Further, if what is incapable is what is deprived of potency, what is not actually coming to be will be incapable of coming to be; and the man who says that what is incapable of coming to be either exists or will exist will be wrong, since that is what the impossible meant: "what does not exist and never will"; thus, these arguments do away with movement and with coming-to-be. What is standing up will always be standing up, what is sitting down always will be sitting down; for if it is sitting down, it will not stand up, since it is impossible for what cannot stand up to stand up.

If, then, it is not possible to maintain this view, clearly potency and actuality are different; these arguments make them the same, and so are seeking to do away with something considerable. But since the two are different, it is possible for something to be capable of being something and yet not actually be it, or for it to be capable of not being it and yet be it; similarly, with the other categories, it is possible for something that is capable of walking not to walk, and for something that is capable of not walking to walk. A thing is capable of doing something if there is nothing impossible involved in its having the actuality of that of which it is said to have the potency. For instance, if a thing is capable of sitting down, and it is possible for it to sit down, there will be nothing impossible in its actually sitting down. The same will hold with regard to being moved or moving, standing up or standing something up, being or coming to be, not being or not coming to be. The term "actuality," which is connected with "realization," was first applied to movements and then extended to other things. For people regard actuality as being more than anything movement, which is why they do not assign movement to things that do not exist, but make other assertions about them: they say that things that do not exist are objects of thought or of desire, but not that they are moved; this is because they do not exist in actuality now, but will do so in the future. For some of the things that do not exist, exist potentially, but yet do not exist, because they are not in a realized state.

4. If what is capable of being is what we have described and vice versa, it is clearly not possible for it to be true to say that something is capable of being but will not be; in that case, things that are incapable of being would simply disappear. I am referring to the kind of situation where someone—the kind of person who does not reckon with what is incapable of being—might say that the diagonal is capable of being measured but in fact will not be, on the grounds that there is nothing to prevent what is capable of being or coming to be from in fact not being either now or in the future. But we have laid it down that, if we supposed anything either to exist or to have come into being, which in fact did not exist but was able to, there must be nothing impossible involved; and here there will be something impossible involved, for the diagonal is incapable of being measured. The untrue and the impossible are not the same thing; it is untrue that you are standing up now, but it is not impossible that you should be.

At the same time, it is clear that if when A exists, B must exist, then when A is possible B must be possible; for if B does not have to be possible, there is nothing to prevent it from not being possible. Let us assume that A is possible. Then, whenever A is possible, if it should in fact be assumed to exist, no impossible consequence follows; in that case, B must certainly exist. But the opposite view to ours supposes B to be impossible. Let us

suppose that it is impossible: if B is impossible, then A
must be too; and since B is in fact taken by this view to
be impossible, then A is too. If A is in fact possible,
then B will be possible too, so long as the two are so
related that if A exists B must too. If, then, when A and
B are thus related, B is not possible although A is, A
and B will not in fact be related in the way that was laid
down. And if when A is possible B must be possible,
then when A exists B must too. For if B must be possible
when A is possible, that means that if A exists when
and as it is possible for it to, then B must exist at the
same time and in the same way.

5. All potencies are either innate (such as the senses)
or acquired by habit (such as the potency for playing
the flute) or by learning (such as those involved in arts);
those that are acquired by habit or by the use of reason
must be actually exercised before we possess them; but
with potencies that are not of this kind, and with potencies for being acted upon, this is not necessary. What is
capable is capable of something, at a certain time and
in a certain way, with all the other qualifications that
must be present in the definition; further, some things
can initiate movement rationally and so their potencies
are rational, whereas others are nonrational and so their
potencies are nonrational too; rational potencies must
be in a living being, whereas nonrational ones can either
be in a living being or in an inanimate one. Now, all
this being so, nonrational potencies must, when what is
capable of acting meets what is capable of being acted
upon, in the one case act and in the other be acted upon;
but with rational potencies this need not be so. For nonrational potencies produce, each of them, one result; but
rational potencies can produce contrary results, so that
if they were fully realized at each encounter they would
produce two contrary results at once, which would be
impossible. There must be some other decisive factor,
and this is in fact desire or choice. A living being will

do whichever of the two contraries it decisively desires
whenever a situation arises in which it can do so and
whenever it meets what is capable of being acted upon;
thus, everything that has a rational potency must, when
it desires that for which it has the potency and desires
it in the circumstances in which it has it, do that thing;
and the circumstances in which it has the potency are
that the thing capable of being acted upon should be
there and in a particular state: if the thing is not there,
what has the rational potency will not be able to act.
(There is no need to specify further that there must be
no external obstacle; for a thing has the potency only
insofar as it is a potency for acting, and it is not this
when things are in just any state, but when they are in
some particular state, which excludes external obstacles
as well, since these are barred by some of the terms in
the definition.) Hence, even if someone wishes or desires
to do two contrary things, he will not do them; for these
are not the conditions under which he has the potency,
which is not a potency for doing the two things at once.
A man will do what the potency allows in the way that
it allows.

6. Now that we have discussed potency as applied to
movement, let us explain what actuality is and what kind
of thing it is. For as we analyze it, it will also become
clear that we talk of potency not only with regard to
what naturally moves something else, or is moved by
something else, either straightforwardly or in some particular way, but in another way too; and it is this other
way that is really the reason for our going into all these
matters. "Actuality," then, is the presence of a thing in
some other way than just what we call "potentially." We
say that the Hermes statue is potentially in the wood,
that the half is potentially in the whole (since it could
be taken away from it), and that the man of science who
is not actually studying is potentially doing so if he is
capable of studying: and we say that these things are "in

actuality," or "actually," when they are in the states that are the counterparts of these. What we mean becomes clear by a process of induction from individual instances; we ought not to seek a definition of everything, but rather to gain a general view by analogy, and see that the actual is related to the potential in the same way that the man who is actually building is related to the man who is capable of it, or the man who is awake to the man who is asleep, or the man who is looking at something to the man who has his eyes shut although he does possess sight, or what is differentiated out of matter to the matter itself, or what is wrought to what is unwrought. In this double list, let the first-mentioned be the determinate actuality, the other the potential. But not everything is said to be "in actuality" in the same way; it is sometimes only by analogy that things are so described; the way that *this* is in or is related to *this* is like the way that *that* is in or is related to *that*; in some cases it is like movement in relation to potency, in others like substance in relation to matter. The infinite, the void, and other things of this kind are also said to exist potentially and actually in a very different way from most things—from what is seeing, for instance, or walking, or being seen. For in these cases it is possible to tell the truth quite simply; one can say on the one hand that what is being seen is being seen, and that its counterpart is capable of being seen. But the infinite does not exist potentially as something that will in actuality be separate, but potentially only for knowledge. For the fact that division never stops ensures that this activity of division is always there potentially, but not that the infinite is ever separate.

No action to which there is a limit is an end in itself, but is something conducive to an end. Take slimming, for instance: when one is slimming, the parts of the body are in movement without the aims of the movement being achieved; and so this is not an action, or at best it is an incomplete one, since it is not an end. A true

action is a movement in which the end is already present. For instance, one can at the same time see and have
seen, or know and have known, or think and have
thought; but one cannot learn and have learned, or be
getting well and have got well, at the same time; one
does, however, live well at the same time as having lived
well, and one is happy at the same time as having been
happy. If this were not the case, one would have to stop
being or doing these things at some stage, as one does
when one slims; but in fact one does not have to: one
has lived and one goes on living. Of these actions, we
may call the one kind movements, the other actualities.
For every movement is incomplete; slimming, learning,
walking, building—these are all movements, and they
are certainly all incomplete. One is not walking at the
same time as having walked, or building at the same
time as having built, or coming to be at the same
time as having come to be, or being moved at the same
time as having been moved; in each case the two are different.
But a thing does see at the same time as having seen,
and think at the same time as having thought. This latter
kind of action I call an actuality; the other I call a
movement.

7. From these and similar considerations, then, we may
take it to be clear what, and what kind of thing, exists
in actuality. We must now determine when each thing
exists potentially and when it does not; for it does not
do so at just any time. For instance, is earth potentially
a man? Or is it not, except when it has become a seed?
Or is it perhaps not so even then? For, in the same sort
of way, not everything can be made healthy by medicine
or even by chance, although there is something that is
capable of being made healthy, and that is what is potentially healthy.

The conditions under which a thing may, after existing
only potentially, come into being in fully realized form
as a result of thought are as follows: someone must wish

it to come into being; there must be no external obstacle; and as far as the thing being brought to health is concerned, there must be no obstacle inside it. Similarly, a thing is potentially a house, if there is nothing in it— that is, in the matter—to prevent it from coming to be a house and if there is nothing which has to be added, removed, or changed. And it is the same with everything else the source of whose change is external to itself.

But in cases where the source of a thing's coming-to-be is in the thing itself, that thing is potentially all those things that it will be of itself, if there is no external obstacle. A seed, for instance, is not yet potentially the fully grown animal, since it must be placed in something else and be changed; but when through the source of change within itself it is in this position, then it is potentially the fully grown animal. But what comes to be in the other way needs a different source of movement; earth, for instance, is not yet potentially a statue, for it is only after it has changed that it will be bronze. Further, anything that we describe seems not to be the particular thing that possesses the potency for itself, but rather to be *of* that particular thing; a box, for instance, is not wood but *wooden*, wood is not earth but *earthen*, and earth in its turn illustrates the point if it is in the same way not something other than itself but *of* something other than itself; everything in this list simply is potentially the one that preceded it in the list. A box, for instance, is not earth nor is it earthen, it is *wooden*; for wood is potentially a box and is its matter; wood in general is the matter of boxes in general, and this particular bit of wood is the matter of this particular box. If there is anything primary, which is no longer said to be *of* something, with reference to something else, that is primary matter. For instance, if earth is *of* air, and air is not fire but *of* fire, then fire will be prime matter and not a particular thing. For things of which something is asserted and substrata differ according to whether they are or are not particular things. Man, for instance, is the substratum for his affections, and the affections are such things as musical and white; when music is present in a man, he is not said to be music but musical; similarly, he is not whiteness but white; not a walk or a movement but walking or moving; it is just as when we describe a thing as *of* something. Whenever this is so, the ultimate thing of which assertions are made is substance; but whenever this is not so, and what is asserted is a form and a particular thing, the ultimate thing of which they are asserted will be matter and material substance. It is indeed only right that we should describe a thing as *of* this or *like* this with reference in the one case to the matter and in the other to the affections, for they are both indeterminate.

We have then explained when a thing should be said to exist potentially and when it should not.

8. We have already distinguished the number of ways in which the term "prior" can be used, and it is clear that actuality is prior to potency; and I mean not merely that it is prior to that definite potency that is described as a source or principle of change in something else or in itself qua something else, but that it is prior in general to every principle of movement and of rest. For nature, too, is in the same genus as potency, since it is a principle of movement—not, however, of movement in something else but in itself qua itself. Actuality is prior to every such principle, both in definition and in substance; in one way, too, it is prior to every such principle in time, but in another way it is not.

That it is prior in definition is evident; for it is only because there is a possibility of its being actual that what is potential in the primary sense is potential; for instance, what is capable of building is what can build, what is capable of seeing is what can see, and what is visible is what can be seen. The same argument applies to everything else, so that the definition of the actual must precede that of the potential, and knowledge of it must precede knowledge of the potential.

The actuality is prior in time in the following sense: something that is the same as it in species must be actual before any particular thing is potential, but no single thing will be actual before it is potential. I mean that in the case of a particular man who is already actually in existence, and of a particular ear of corn, and of a particular seeing man, the matter, the seed, and what is capable of seeing—which are potentially the man, the ear of corn, and the seeing man, respectively—are prior to them; but prior to these things, which are potential, are separate things that exist in actuality and from which these potential things have come into being. For what exists actually always comes into being out of what exists potentially through the agency of what exists actually, man through the agency of man, a musical man through the agency of a musical man; there is always some first mover, and this mover already exists in actuality.

We have already said in our discussions about substance that everything that comes to be comes to be something and comes from something; also that it comes to be through the agency of something that is the same in form as itself. Thus, it seems impossible that man should be a builder if he has not already built something, or a lyre player if he has not already played the lyre; for the man who learns to play the lyre learns to play it by playing it, and it is the same with everyone else. Hence arose the sophistic puzzle about someone who does not possess a skill nonetheless doing what the skill involves; for the man who is still learning does not possess it. But since when a thing is coming to be something of it must already have come to be, and when something is being moved something of it must already have been moved (as we made clear in our discussions of movement), perhaps also the man who is learning must have something of the skill that he is learning. Anyway, this argument also makes clear that actuality is prior to potency in respect to the order of coming to be and to time.

But in substance, too, actuality is prior. In the first place,

this is because things that are posterior in the order of
coming to be are prior in form and in substance; this is
so, for instance, with man and boy, or with human being
and seed, since the one in each case already possesses the
form, but the other does not. It is also because everything
moves towards a principle, which is also its end; for the
principle of a thing is the thing for whose sake it is there,
and everything that comes into being comes into being for
the sake of its end; and the end is the actuality, and it is
for its sake that the potency is acquired. Animals do not
see in order that they may possess sight, but possess sight
in order that they may see; similarly, people acquire the
art of building in order that they may build and the art
of studying in order that they may study; they do not
study in order that they may possess the art of studying,
unless they are people who are practicing, and these are
only studying in a particular sense.

Further, matter exists potentially because it may arrive
at a form; when it exists actually, it is already in the form.
It is the same with everything else, even with things whose
end is movement. Hence, just as teachers think that they
have achieved their end when they display their pupil engaged in activity, so it is with nature. Otherwise it would
not be clear whether the knowledge was inside or outside
the pupil. For the end is the action, and the action is the
actuality, which is why the word "actuality" is derived
from "action" and is connected with realization. The final
stage with some potencies is their use: seeing, for instance,
is the final stage in the case of sight, and no action occurs
as a result of sight other than seeing; but with others
something comes into being from them; from the art of
building, for instance, quite apart from the process of
building, a house comes into being. Nonetheless, we must
say that, while in the first case the actuality is the end,
even in the second it is more of an end than the potency
is; for the process of building takes place in what is being
built, and it comes into being and exists concurrently with
the house. In cases where what comes into being is sepa-

rate from the mere use of the potency, the actuality is to be found in what is being produced: the actuality of building, for instance, is to be found in what is being built, that of weaving in what is being woven, and similarly with everything else; in general, too, in these cases, the actuality of the movement is to be found in what is being moved. But where there is no result apart from the actuality, the actuality is to be found in whatever is acting: seeing is in the person who does the seeing; study is in the student; and life is in the soul, and hence happiness is there, too, since it is a particular kind of life. Plainly, then, both substance and form are actuality. This argument, thus, shows clearly that actuality is prior to potency, and, as I have said, any one actuality is always preceded by another in point of time, until one arrives at the prime mover.

But the point can be made more conclusively. Eternal things are prior in substance to perishable ones, and nothing eternal exists potentially. The reason is this: every potency is a potency for two contrary things at once; for although what cannot belong to something never will belong to it, it is possible for that which can be actual not to be so. It is possible for what can be both to be and not to be, and so the same thing is capable both of being and of not being; and if anything is capable of not being, it is possible for it not to be; but if it is possible for a thing not to be, that thing is perishable: either it is perishable absolutely or it is so in respect to that which it is possible for it not to be, in respect to place or to quantity or quality; if it is perishable absolutely, then it will be so in respect to substance. Thus, nothing imperishable absolutely can be potential absolutely, although there is nothing to keep it from being potential in some particular respect, such as quality or place. All imperishable things, then, must exist in actuality. Nor can things that are as they are of necessity be potential; and yet they are primary, since without them nothing could exist. If there is any eternal movement, it cannot be potential either; nor, if anything is eternally in motion can it be in motion potentially, except insofar that it is in motion from one place to another—there is nothing to keep it from having matter that enables it to have this done to it; hence, the sun, the stars, and the whole heaven are always in activity, and there is no risk of their standing still, as the natural scientists fear. Nor do they get tired as they do this; for movement does not involve for them, as it does for perishable things, the potency for the contrary, and thus the continuity of the movement is not laborious for them. Fatigue results from substance being matter and potency, as opposed to actuality.

Things that are in a state of change, in the way that earth and fire are, imitate imperishable things; for they too are always in activity, since they have their movement in themselves and by virtue of being themselves. But the other potencies, according to the distinctions that we have drawn, are all for two contrary things; what is able to be moved in a particular way is also able not to be moved in that way; this is so, at least with rational potencies. Nonrational potencies can only produce contrary results by being there or by not being there.

If, then, there are any entities or substances such as those who are concerned with verbal discussions say that the ideas are, there will be something more knowledgeable than knowledge itself and more mobile than movement itself, since these things will be actualities more than the ideas, which will be their potencies.

It is clear, then, that actuality is prior to potency and to every principle of change.

9. That a good actuality is better and more valuable than a good potency becomes clear in this way: anything that is said to be capable of doing anything is capable of doing two contrary things; what is said to be capable of being healthy, for instance, is also capable of being ill and has these two potencies at the same time; for the potencies for being healthy and being ill are the same, as are also those for being at rest and being in movement, for building and demolishing, for being built and being demolished. Thus, the capacity to be two contrary things belongs to a thing at the same time, but it is impossible for the two contraries themselves to belong to it at the same time or for the two actualities to do so: being healthy and being ill could not do so, for instance. Necessarily, then, one of these actualities must be the good one, whereas the potency is both alike or neither; so the actuality is better. But in the case of bad things, the end and the actuality must be worse than the potency, since the same thing is capable of being both contraries. It is plain, then, that there is no evil that exists apart from things, since evil is by nature posterior to potency. Nor is there among the things that are original and eternal anything that is evil or mistaken or corrupt, for corruption is an evil.

It is by actuality or activity, too, that geometrical constructions are discovered, for we discover them by dividing figures. If the figures had already been divided, the constructions would be evident; as it is, they are there only potentially. Why do the angles of a triangle add up to two right angles? Because the angles round a point equal two right angles. If the line parallel to one of the sides had been drawn, the answer would have been immediately evident to anyone who saw the figure. Why is the angle in a semicircle always a right angle? Because, if the three lines, the two at the base and the perpendicular in the middle, are equal, the answer becomes clear to anyone who knows the former theorem. So, plainly, things that exist potentially are discovered by being brought to actuality. The reason is that thinking is an actuality; thus, the potency comes from an actuality; and that is why people discover things by constructions, even though, of course, any particular single actuality is posterior to its potency.

■   ■   ■

Book XII

1. Our inquiry is into substance, since it is the principles and causes of substance that we are seeking. For if the universe is like some whole thing, substance is its primary part; and if it only holds together as a series, substance is still what is primary in it, being followed by quality and then by quantity. But these latter hardly exist at all in the strict sense, but are just qualifications and affections of what exists; if they do exist, "not white" and "not straight" will exist too, and we do indeed speak of these as existing, as when we speak of what is not white. Further, nothing other than substance is separable. This is in fact attested by the thinkers of antiquity; for they were seeking the principles, elements, and causes of substance. Thinkers today are more inclined to declare that universals are substances (for genera are universals, and they, because of the abstractness of their method of inquiry, say that genera are principles and substances); but the ancients regarded particular things as substances, like fire and earth, rather than what they have in common, namely, body.

There are three kinds of substance. There is sensible substance, of which some is eternal and some, as everyone agrees, is perishable (plants and animals, for instance, being in this latter class). We must grasp the elements of this sensible substance and find out if there is just one or if there are many. Another kind of substance is immovable, and some people say that it is capable of existing separately. Of these people, some divide the class into two, others put the forms and the objects of mathematics into one class, and still others say that of these only the objects of mathematics exist. The sensible substances belong to natural science, since they involve movement; but the last-named substance belongs to another science, unless there is some principle common to them all.

Sensible substance is changeable. Change is from opposite to opposite or from intermediate to opposite; but it does not occur from just any opposite—a voice, after all, is not white—but only from contrary to contrary. This being so, there must be something underlying them that changes into the contrary; for the contraries do not change.

2. Then, since something persists, but the contrary does not, there is some third thing apart from the contraries: the matter. There are four kinds of change: change of what a thing is; change of quality; change of quantity; and change of place. Change of what a thing is is simple coming-to-be and perishing; change of quantity is growth and diminution; change of affection is alteration; change of place is motion; and in each case the change is into the appropriate contrary state. The matter, then, when it changes must be capable of being in both states; and since there are two ways in which what is can be, everything changes from being potentially to being in actuality; a thing changes, for instance, from being potentially white to being actually white, and it is the same with growth and diminution. Thus, not only is it possible for a thing to come to be accidentally from what is not, but everything comes into being, too, from what is, even though it comes from what is potentially but is not in actuality. This is, in fact, the "one" of Anaxagoras; but instead of saying, as he does, that "everything was together" or talking of the "mixture" of Empedocles and Anaximander or of what Democritus talks about, it is better to say that everything existed potentially but not in actuality. These thinkers, then, must have had some conception of matter. Everything that changes contains matter, although different matter in different cases; and such eternal objects as are movable in space, although they cannot come into being, contain matter too; their matter, however, does not admit of coming-to-be, but only of movement from one place to another.

Someone might be puzzled to know from what kind of not-being things come into being; for there are three ways in which one can speak of not-being.

If a thing exists potentially, it is not by virtue of a potency for just anything; different things come from different things. Nor is it enough to say that "all things were together"; things differ in matter, otherwise why have an infinite number of things come into being, and not just one? For mind is one; so that if the matter were one, too, the only thing that could have come to be in actuality would have been what the matter was potentially.

There are, then, three causes and three principles: two are the pair of contraries, of which one is the definition and form, and the other the privation; the third is the matter.

3. We must next note that neither matter nor form comes into being—I refer to proximate matter and proximate form. For with all change, there is something that changes into something through the agency of something. The agent is the proximate mover; the thing that changes is the matter; and what it changes into is the form. The process, then, will go on to infinity if not only the bronze comes to be round but also "the round" and the bronze themselves come into being; the process must stop somewhere.

Next we must note that every substance comes into being through the agency of something that shares its name and character (substances include both natural and other objects). For they come into being either through art or by nature or by chance or spontaneously. Art is a principle present in something other than what is being moved, nature a principle present in the thing itself (for man generates man); and the other two causes are privations of the first two.

There are three kinds of substance. There is matter, which looks like an individual thing—for things that are merely joined, and have not grown together, are matter and substratum, for instance, fire, flesh, and a head; they are all matter, and the last of them is the matter of what is fully a substance. Then, there is the nature, which is the particular thing, the state into which the matter moves; and, thirdly, there is the individual product of the two, Socrates or Callias, for instance. In some cases there is no particular thing that exists apart from the composite substance; the form of house, for instance, does not exist apart, except insofar as the art of building may; nor is there any coming-to-be or perishing of forms of this kind: "house" devoid of matter, health, and all forms that have to do with art exist and do not exist, but in a quite different way. But if any particular thing does exist apart from the composite substance, it does so in the case of natural objects. Hence, Plato was not talking unreasonably when he said that there were forms of all the things that exist by nature—if indeed there are forms at all that are distinct from the things around us here.

Moving causes are causes that precede their effects; formal causes come into being simultaneously with theirs. It is when a man is healthy that health exists; and the shape of a bronze sphere exists at the same time as the bronze sphere itself. We must look into the question of whether any form persists afterwards. In some cases there is nothing to keep this from happening; the soul, for instance, may be in this position—though not the whole of the soul, just the mind, since it is perhaps impossible for the whole soul to survive. Clearly, then, there is no need, on these grounds at least, for the ideas to exist. Man generates man, and an individual generates any particular man. It is the same too with the arts; for the art of medicine is the formal cause of health.

4. In one sense different things have different causes and principles, but in another—if one speaks generally and by analogy—they all have the same. One might wonder whether substances and relations have the same principles and elements or different ones, and similarly with all the other categories.

It is strange if they all have the same elements; for relations and substances will then be made up of the same things. What would these things be? Apart from substance and what is asserted of it, there is nothing that is common to them both, and the element must be prior to that of which it is an element. But then neither is substance an element of relations, nor is any relation an element of substance. How, then, is it possible for everything to have the same elements? No element can be the same as what is made up of elements; neither B nor A, for instance, can be the same as BA. (Nor can any object of thought, like "being" or "the one," be an element; for they are attributes of everything, even of composite things.) If everything has the same elements, then, no element will be either substance or a relation; but it must be one or the other. So, in fact, everything does not have the same elements.

But perhaps, as we have said, in one sense all things have the same elements, in another they do not. Perhaps, for instance, in the case of sensible bodies, the hot is an element as the form, and in another way the cold is an element as the privation, and the matter is one as well—that which directly and by virtue of being itself is potentially both the other two. These things, then, are

all substances, as are the things that are made up of
them and of which they are principles, and as is also any
unity that comes into being from the hot and the cold,
like flesh or bone; for what comes into being from them
must be different from the hot and the cold. These things,
then, have the same elements and principles, although
these elements are different things in different cases; but
we cannot say that all things have the same elements in
this way, only that they do so by analogy. One might say,
for instance, that there are three principles, the form, the
privation, and the matter. But they are all different for
each class of objects: with colors, for instance, they are
white, black, and a surface; also, there are light, darkness,
and air, from which day and night come.

But it is not only things inherent in an object that are
its causes; some external things are too, like the moving
cause, for instance; hence, it is clear that a principle and
an element are different, even though both are causes,
and that principles are divided into these two classes—
those that are and those that are not elements; also, that
which moves a thing or sets it at rest is a principle. Thus,
by analogy there are three elements and four causes and
principles; but they are different in different cases, and
the proximate moving cause is also different for different
things. There are health, disease, and the body; the moving cause here is the art of medicine. There are a form,
disorder of a particular kind, and bricks; the moving
cause here is the art of building. Since the moving cause
of natural objects is man, for instance, in the case of
man, and since in the products of thought it is the form
or its contrary, in a way there are three causes, and in
another way four. For in a sense the art of medicine is
health, the art of building is the form of a house, and
man generates man; then, apart from these there is that
which as the first of all things moves all things.

5. Some things are separable, some things are not;
substances are. And the reason why all things have the

same causes is that without substances neither affections nor movements can exist. These causes, then, will perhaps be soul and body or else mind, desire, and body.

Then in another way, too, all things have the same principles, namely, actuality and potency. But these are different in different cases and apply to things in different ways. In some cases it is the same thing that exists at one time actually, at another potentially; this is so, for instance, with wine, flesh, or man (and potency and actuality fit in with the kinds of cause that we have described; the form exists in actuality if it is separable; so does the product of form and matter, and so does the privation—darkness, for instance, or being ill; and the matter exists potentially, since it is what can become either of the two contraries). But the distinction between what exists potentially and what exists actually is different where the two do not have the same matter; in some of these cases they do not have the same form either, but a different one: in the case of man, for instance, the causes are, firstly, his elements—earth and fire as matter, and his specific form—and, secondly, something external, his father; and then, quite apart from these, the sun and its oblique course; and these last-named causes are neither matter nor form nor privation nor anything of the same form as the product; they are moving causes.

Further, we must realize that some things can be spoken of universally, whereas others cannot. The proximate principles of everything are the proximate particular thing which exists in actuality, and something else which exists potentially. The universals, then, to which we referred do not exist; for the cause of an individual is an individual; man is the cause of man universally, but there is no such thing as universal man; it is Peleus who was the cause of Achilles, and your father who was the cause of you; this particular B is the cause of this particular BA, while B in the universal sense is the cause of BA in the absolute sense. Thus, even if the causes of substances are universals, nonetheless the causes

and elements are different in different cases; the causes
of things that are not in the same class—colors, sounds,
substances, quantities—are different except by analogy;
and even things that are of the same kind have causes
that, although they are not different from each other in
kind, do differ insofar as they are causes of different
individuals: your matter, your form, and your moving
cause are different from mine, although, as far as the
account of them as universals goes, they are the same.
And if we inquire what are the principles or elements
of substances, relations, and qualities, and whether they
are the same as one another or different, the answer
clearly is that when the word "cause" is used in a number of senses at once, they are the same for everything;
but when these senses are distinguished, they are not the
same, but different. In the following ways, however, the
same things are the causes of everything: they are the same
by analogy in being matter, form, privation, and the
moving cause; they are the same insofar as the causes
of substances are the causes of everything, since if substances were destroyed everything else would be destroyed too; they are the same also insofar as what is in
actuality the first of all things is the cause of everything.
In another sense, however, things have different first or
proximate causes, insofar as these are contraries, which
are not talked of as classes or with any more meanings
than one; the same is true of their matters as well.

We have, then, explained what are the principles of
sensible substances, how many of them there are, and
in what sense they are the same and in what sense
different.

6. There were, we agreed, three kinds of substance,
two of them natural, the third immovable; we must now
discuss the third, and point out that there must be some
eternal and immovable substance. For substances are
primary among the things that exist, and if they are all
perishable, then everything will be perishable. But it is

impossible, anyway, for movement either to come into being or to perish, since it has always existed. Nor can time do either of these things, since there could not be anything "prior" or "posterior" if there were no time; and movement is as continuous as time, since time is either the same thing as movement or is an affection of it. Movement, however, is only continuous when it is movement in place—and circular movement at that.

But even if there is something capable of moving or producing things but not actually doing so, there will not necessarily be movement; for it is possible for what possesses a potency not to actualize it. It is no help, either, for us to produce eternal substances, as those who maintain the theory of forms do, unless there is going to be some principle in them that is capable of producing change. But not even this is enough, nor is any substance that may exist apart from the forms; for unless it is actualized, there will still be no movement; and even if it does get actualized, this will still not be enough if its essence is a potency; there will still not be eternal movement, since it is possible for what exists potentially not to exist. There must, then, be a principle such that its essence is actuality. Further, these substances must be devoid of matter, since they must be eternal if anything is eternal. Such substances, then, are actuality.

And yet there is a difficulty here. Although everything that is actualized seems to have potency, not everything that has potency is actualized; thus potency seems to be prior. But if this is so, nothing that exists need exist; for it is possible for a thing to be capable of existing but not yet to exist.

Yet if we follow the theologians who generate things from night, or the natural scientists who say that everything was together, the same impossible result follows. How will anything be moved, unless there is some cause that exists in actuality? Wood, certainly, will not move itself; the art of carpentry will have to act upon it. Nor will the menstrual blood or the earth move themselves; they must be set in motion by the semen and by seeds, respectively. That is why some thinkers say that there is an eternal actuality—Leucippus and Plato, for instance, who say that there is always movement. But they do not say why there is this movement or what it is; nor do they give the reason for its being of whatever kind it is. Nothing is moved just by chance; there must always be something there to move it, just as things in fact are moved by nature in one way and by violence or through the agency of mind or something else in another. Then, what kind of movement is this primary movement? This makes a tremendous difference. But it is not possible, either, for Plato, at least, to name here what he sometimes supposes to be a first principle—namely, what moves itself; for the soul is posterior to movement, and of the same age as the heavens, as he says himself. To suppose, then, that potency is prior to actuality is in a way right and in a way wrong: we have explained in what way it is each. But Anaxagoras testifies to the priority of actuality—for mind is an actuality—and so does Empedocles with his Love and Strife, and also those who, like Leucippus, say that there is always movement. So there was not just Chaos and Night for an infinite period of time, but the same things have always existed, whether recurring in a cycle or following some other principle, if actuality is indeed prior to potency. Now, if there is a constant cycle, something must always persist that is engaged in the same activity; but if there are going to be coming-to-be and perishing, there must be something else that is always engaged in activity, now of one kind and now of another. This second thing must be active in one way by virtue of its own nature, in the other way by virtue of something else; and this "something else" must be either a third thing or the first thing, that which we described as always being engaged in the same activity; it must in fact be this first thing; otherwise the first thing will be the cause of both the others. It is, then,

better to say that it is this first thing, since it was the
cause of things always moving in the same way, whereas
the second thing is the cause of their moving in different
ways; and clearly the two together are the causes of their
always moving in different ways. This is, in fact, the way
in which movements occur. So what need is there to
seek any other principles?

7. Since it is possible for things to be as we have described, and since, if they are not, everything will come
from night, and from "everything being together," and
from what is not, these problems seem to be solved.
There is something that is always being moved in an
incessant movement, and this movement is circular (as
is evident not only from argument but also from observation); and so the first heaven will be eternal. There
must, then, be something that moves it. But since that
which is moved, as well as moving things, is intermediate, there must be something that moves things without
being moved; this will be something eternal, it will be a
substance, and it will be an actuality. Now, the object of
desire and the object of thought move things in this way:
they move things without being moved. The primary objects of desire and of thought are the same. What *appears* to be good is the object of one's appetite, and
what *is* good is the primary object of our will; and we
desire things because we believe them to be good, rather
than believing them to be good because we desire them;
for thought is the starting point. The mind is moved by
the object of its thought, and only one of the two col-
umns of opposites is in itself an object of thought. In
this column, substance is the first thing, and among substances what is first is what is simple and what exists in
actuality. (What is one and what is simple are not the
same: "one" indicates a measurement, "simple" a condition.) But what is good and what is in itself worth choosing are in the same column; and the first term in a
column is always the best or analogous to the best.

That the final cause is among the things that are immovable is clear if we distinguish between its meanings. Purpose may involve a thing's being good for somebody, or it may involve its being good for attaining some end; in the latter case it is among things that are unchangeable, in the former it is not. The final cause then moves things because it is loved, whereas all other things move because they are themselves moved. If anything is moved, it is capable of being in some other state; so that if its actuality is primary movement in space, it is possible for it to be in some other state insofar as it is moved—that is to say, with regard to place, even if not with regard to substance. But since there is something that moves things, while being itself immovable and existing in actuality, it is not possible in any way for that thing to be in any state other than that in which it is. For movement in space is the primary kind of change, and circular movement is the primary kind of movement in space; and it is this kind of movement that the unmoved mover imparts. The first mover, then, must exist; and insofar as he exists of necessity, his existence must be good; and thus he must be a first principle. For the term "necessary" can be used in all of the following ways: of what happens through violence, contrary to impulse; of what is indispensable to a thing's good; and of what cannot be in any state other than that in which it is, but only in that one.

It is upon a principle of this kind, then, that the heavens and nature depend. Its life is like the best that we can enjoy—and we can enjoy it for only a short time. It is always in this state (which we cannot be), since its actuality is also pleasure. (And that is why waking, sensation, and thought are the most pleasant of things, whereas hopes and memories are pleasant because of them.) Thought in itself is thought of what is best in itself, and what is most fully thought is thought of what is in the fullest sense best. Mind thinks of itself through its participation in the object of thought; for it becomes an object of thought through touching and thinking of its objects; and thus mind and the object of thought are the same. For what is capable of receiving the objects of thought and the essences of things is mind, and when it possesses them, it is engaged in activity; so, it is this activity rather than the potency for it that seems to be the divine element possessed by the mind, and its contemplation is of all things the most pleasant and the best. If, then, God is always in the good state which we are sometimes in, that is something to wonder at; and if he is in a better state than we are ever in, that is to be wondered at even more. This is in fact the case, however. Life belongs to him, too; for life is the actuality of mind, and God is that actuality; and his independent actuality is the best life and an eternal life. We assert, then, that God is an eternal and most excellent living being, so that continuous and eternal life and duration belong to him. For that is what God is.

Some people, like the Pythagoreans and Speusippus, suppose that what is finest and best does not exist in a first principle because, although the first principles of plants and animals are their causes, what is fine and complete exists only in the products of these causes. They are wrong: for the seed comes from other things which precede it and are complete, and the first thing is not the seed but the complete object; one would say, for instance, that man was prior to the seed, not referring to the man who has come into being from the seed, but to a different one from whom the seed has come.

That there is an eternal and immovable substance separate from sensible substances is, then, clear from what we have said. We have also shown that it is not possible for this substance to have any magnitude; it is without parts and is indivisible; for it is moving things throughout an infinite time, and nothing that is finite has an infinite potency. Every magnitude is either infinite or finite; this substance cannot have a finite magnitude for the reason that we have mentioned, and it cannot have an infinite one because there is no such thing at all as an infinite magnitude. We have also shown that nothing can happen to it, and that it is not capable of being changed; for all other kinds of movement are posterior to movement in space. It is plain, then, why these things are as they are.

∎ ∎ ∎

9. There are certain problems that arise in connection with the supreme mind. It seems to be more divine than anything else that has come to our notice, but there are some difficulties in knowing what kind of state it must be in to be like this. If it is thinking of nothing, what is there that is noble in this? It will be like someone who is asleep. If it is thinking, but there is something else that determines its thinking, its substance will not be thought but a potency for thought, and it will no longer be the best substance, since its value belongs to it by virtue of its thinking.

Further, whether its substance is mind or thought, what does it think of? It must think either of itself or of something else; and if it thinks of something else, it must either think of the same thing always or of different things at different times. Then, does it make any difference or not whether it thinks of what is good, or of just anything that turns up? Would it not be strange for it to think about some things? Plainly, it thinks of what is most divine and most valuable; and plainly it does not change; for change would be for the worse, and would anyway already be a movement. Firstly, then, if it is not actual thought but a potency for it, one would reasonably expect the continuity of its thought to be laborious for it; secondly, there would clearly be something else more valuable than mind, namely, the object of its thought. For both thinking and actual thought will belong even to what is thinking of the worst of things; so that if this is something to be avoided (and it is, for it is better not to see some things than to see them), thought will not be the best of things. The mind, then, must think of itself if it is the best of things, and its thought will be thought about thought.

But it is clear that knowledge, perception, opinion, and understanding always have some object other than themselves; they are only incidentally their own objects. Further, if thinking and being thought of are different, by virtue of which of them does goodness belong to the mind? For the essences of "thinking" and "being thought of" are not the same. Perhaps we should say that in some cases the knowledge is the object; in the productive sciences, the substance and the essence (without the matter) are the object, but in the speculative ones it is the definition and the thought that are the object. If, then, the mind and its object are not different in the case of things that have no matter, they will be the same, and thought will be one with the object of thought.

There is still left the problem of whether the object of the mind's thought is composite; if so, it would change as it moved from one part to another of the whole. But perhaps everything that does not contain matter is indivisible. The human mind, or rather the mind of any composite being, does not possess the good at this or that particular moment, but attains the best of things—which is something other than itself—over a whole period. Then, perhaps thought about thought is during the whole of eternity in the same state in which the human mind, or that of any composite being, is during a certain period.

10. We must now inquire in what way the nature of the universe possesses the good and the supreme good. Does it possess it as something separate and by itself, or as the order inherent in itself? Or does it possess it in both ways, as an army does? For the good of an army lies partly in its good order, and partly in its general; but the general is its good more than its good order; he is not there because of the good order, the good order exists because of him. All things are organized in some

way or other, but not all in the same way—this is true
of fishes, birds, and plants; and the world is not such
that one thing has nothing to do with another; things do
have something to do with one another. Everything is
organized for one end; it is as in a household; there the
freemen can to only a very limited extent act at random:
everything or nearly everything is organized for them,
but the slaves and the animals make very little contribution to the common good, and for the most part they do
act at random: this sort of principle is in fact implicit in
the nature of everything. They must all at least come in the
end to be dissolved, and there are other ways too in
which everything contributes to the good of the whole.

We must not fail to observe what impossible and
strange consequences follow for those who maintain different views, nor what views are held by the more cultivated thinkers, nor again what views involve the fewest
difficulties. All thinkers make everything come from contraries. They are wrong in saying that everything does
this, and indeed wrong in saying that anything comes
from a contrary; and they fail to say how, in cases where
contraries do belong to things, these things can come
into being from them; for contraries cannot be acted
upon by each other. We have found a reasonable solution to this problem by saying that there is some third
thing. They also make one of the contraries matter: some
of them, for instance, make the unequal the matter for
the equal, or the many the matter for the one. This difficulty we solve in the same way; matter is not a contrary
to anything. Further, on the view of these thinkers, everything except the one will participate in what is worthless, since the bad itself is one of the two elements. The
other thinkers do not even treat the good and the bad
as principles; yet in everything the good more than anything else is a principle. The first group are right in saying that the good is a principle, but they do not explain
how it is one, whether as an end or as a moving cause
or as a form.

Empedocles talks in a curious way too. He makes

Love the good; but it is a principle both by virtue of
being a moving cause, since it draws things together, and
by virtue of being matter, since it is a portion of the
mixture. But even if the same thing does turn out to be
both a material and a moving principle, their essences
will still be different. In which respect, then, is Love a
principle? It is curious, too, for Strife to be imperishable;
for it has the nature of evil itself.

Anaxagoras regarded the good as a moving cause,
since mind moves things. But it moves things for the
sake of something, which will be something different
from itself, unless one explains things in the way that
we do—for in our view the art of medicine is in a sense
the same thing as health. It is strange, too, not to make
anything contrary to the good and to mind. But all those
who speak of the contraries fail to use them, unless one
systematizes what they say. None of them tells us why
some things are perishable and others imperishable; they
derive everything that there is from the same principles.
Further, some thinkers make the things that there are
come from what is not; others, so as not to be driven to
this, make everything one.

Then, no one explains why there always will be
coming-to-be, or what is its cause. Those who assert two
first principles have to admit a third, which is more decisive, and those who maintain the theory of forms have
to do the same thing; for why have things ever participated in the forms, and why do they participate in them?
Other thinkers are compelled to assert the existence of
something contrary to wisdom and to the most valuable
kind of knowledge, but we do not have to. For there is
no contrary to what is primary; all contraries contain
matter and, since they do so, they exist potentially; the
ignorance that is contrary to knowledge leads to the contrary of the object of that knowledge; but there is no
contrary to what is primary.

Further, if nothing exists besides sensible objects,
there will be no first principle, no order, no coming-to-

be, and no heavenly bodies. Every principle will have another principle, as happens in the accounts of the theologians and all the natural scientists. But if there are to be forms or numbers, they will not be the causes of anything; or, even if they are causes of something, they will not be causes of movement. Further, how can any continuous magnitude come from things that have no magnitude? Number will not produce it, either as a moving cause or as a formal cause. Further, no contrary can be essentially a productive and moving principle; for it would then be possible for the principle not to exist. Anyway, production by a contrary would be posterior to its potency. Thus, no existing things would be eternal. But in fact some are eternal. So one of our assumptions must be done away with. We have described how this is to be done.

Then, no one says what it is that the numbers are one by virtue of, or soul or body, or in general the form and the object; nor is it possible to say how they are one, except by explaining it, as we do, by saying that it is the mover that makes them one.

Those who say that mathematical number is primary, and thus make every subsequent substance come from it, each with its own first principles, make the substance of the whole incoherent (for no one substance will have any effect on any other by its existence or nonexistence), and produce a multitude of governing principles. But the world does not wish to be governed badly. As Homer says: "To have many kings is not good; let there be one."

LOGIC

Introduction

Aristotle's conception of logic and its relation to language and the structure of the world has been outlined in the General Introduction and in the introduction to the *Metaphysics*. This introduction may therefore be confined to some of the particular topics that are dealt with in the following selections from the logical writings.

The "Categories," a work wholly Aristotelian in spirit even if not certainly of Aristotelian authorship, is a treatise on predication. The first and chief category is that of substance, for everything that can be said must be said, directly or indirectly, of something in this category, something whose existence is independent of what is predicated of it. The term "category," which means "predicate," is more suitably applied to the other nine categories. These are the result of Aristotle's attempt to list the kinds or types of predicate under which all the properties and relations that may be ascribed to substances can be classified. It has often been observed that Aristotle's list falls short of being even a plausible approximation to a canonical and exhaustive list of types of terms. It would now be generally doubted whether Aristotle was right to have the ambition of producing such a list. But when these two points have been given their due weight, it remains true that Aristotle's enterprise has an enduring interest as a bold and, within its limits, successful first attempt to codify some of the logical distinctions between terms or between concepts. These logical distinctions underlie the merely grammatical distinctions to which they do not always exactly conform; and the logical distinctions in their turn were held by Aristotle to apply to the real things in the world that are the subject matter of knowledge and inquiry.

It is in the "Categories" that we find the clearest statement of Aristotle's distinction between primary and secondary substance. A primary substance is a concrete individual thing, such as a particular man or a particular horse. The species or genus, that is to say the *kind* to which a particular individual thing belongs, is substance in a secondary sense since it does not have separate existence apart from the individuals that belong to it. Substance in this sense is a kind of quality. Not every quality is secondary substance. For example, to say that something is white is not to say what sort of substance it is. One of the most important logical distinctions between substance in general and quality is that a substance does not *have* a contrary, although it *admits of* contraries. A particular man may be now hot and then cold, but there is no contrary to the term *man*. The quality of whiteness, on the other hand, has blackness as a contrary but does not admit of contraries. Nor do substances admit of degree: Socrates may be more or less musical, but not more or less *man*.

Chapter 8 of the "Categories," on quality, is given here as a representative of Aristotle's treatment of the nonsubstantial categories. It consists of remarks on the classification of quality terms, and it stresses some of the most important distinctions between types of quality. This is best done, as Aristotle does it, by examples. Justice and injustice form a pair of contrary qualities. "Red" has no contrary, but only the *contradictory*, "notred." The color terms admit of degrees, but "square" and "triangular" do not.

The "Categories" deals with *uncombined* terms; it sets out what kinds of terms can occur in propositions. "On Interpretation" goes on to give an account of the logic of propositions, that is to say of combinations of terms that have complete meaning in that they predicate something of a substance. Aristotle does not make the mistake of supposing that only a proposition in this sense is capable of having complete significance. He recognizes that prayers and wishes, for example, are fully significant forms of utterance. But in his writings on logic he is concerned with *statements*, with what can be true or false.

"On Interpretation" introduces and treats systematically, for the first time in the history of philosophy, the concepts that are most fundamental to the study of the logical character of assertion and denial. Chief among these are the notions of necessity and contingency, possibility and impossibility. The formal study of the relations between these concepts exhibits clearly some of the ways in which fallacies and mistakes can occur in the practice of speaking, writing, and reasoning. For example, it is easy to recognize, when Aristotle explains it in general terms, that "it may be so" does not contradict, but actually follows from and implies, "it may not be so." But it is not always so easy to avoid confusions on this point in the detail of actual discussion.

Aristotle's remarks on propositions about the future provide an illustration of this point. If we misunderstand the logic of statements in the future tense we may arrive at the unpalatable and unwarranted conclusion that action and deliberation on our part cannot possibly have any effect on the future. But Aristotle rightly distinguishes between saying "necessarily either a sea fight will happen or a sea fight will not happen" and saying "either necessarily a sea fight will happen or necessarily a sea fight will not happen," and so provides a clue that leads to the exit from the maze.

Book I of the "Posterior Analytics" contains much

that is still of philosophical interest. Aristotle has rightly been criticized for his unduly restrictive conception of what constitutes fully scientific knowledge. He was misled, as many of his most famous successors have been misled, by the impressive exactness and certainty of Euclidean geometry. There are strong signs of Platonic influence here. But elsewhere in the book he insists, more in the spirit of the rest of his philosophy, on the autonomy of the separate branches of knowledge.

One of the main lessons of the book is one that will always be needed: there are limits to the scope of demonstrative proof as a means of acquiring knowledge. If all knowledge requires demonstrative proof, then nothing can be known, since demonstrative proof requires premises and if they in turn require demonstrative proof there will be an infinite regress. Nor will it do to say that all knowledge requires demonstrative proof and that such proof can be provided for every true proposition separately although not for all propositions at once since this involves a circularity that is as objectionable as the regress in the other case.

This book shows how much of Plato's teaching Aristotle retained even when he had abandoned the belief that true knowledge had independently existing forms as its objects. Although the particular individual thing is the only independently existing substance, knowing something about it is knowing something that is universal, that applies not to that one thing only but to others of the same kind. In Chapter 2 he explains his famous distinction between what is prior in nature and more knowable (the universal) and what is prior in our experience and more knowable *by us* (the particular). Aristotle's commentators have found difficulty in reconciling what he says here with his belief in the primary substance as the fundamental element in our knowledge and in the world. The difficulty is all the greater for them because it is one that Aristotle shared.

Categories

· · ·

4. Every uncombined term indicates substance or quantity or quality or relationship to something or place or time or posture or state or the doing of something or the undergoing of something. To give a rough idea, substance is something like "man" or "horse"; quantity something like "two feet long" or "three feet long"; quality something like "white" or "literate"; relationship something like "double," "half," or "greater"; place something like "in the Lyceum" or "in the marketplace"; time something like "yesterday" or "last year"; posture something like "reclining at table" or "sitting down"; state something like "having shoes on" or "being in armor"; doing something the sort of thing that "cutting" or "burning" is; and undergoing something the sort of thing that "being cut" or "being burnt" is. None of these terms is used on its own in any statement, but it is through their combination with one another that a statement comes into being. For every statement is held to be either true or false, whereas no uncombined term—such as "man," "white," "runs," or "conquers"—is either of these.

5. What is most properly, primarily, and most strictly spoken of as substance is what is neither asserted of a subject nor present in a subject—a particular man, for instance, or a particular horse. But people speak, too, of secondary substances, to which, as species, belong what are spoken of as the primary substances, and to which, as genera, the species themselves belong. For instance, a particular man belongs to the species "man," and the genus to which the species belongs is "animal." So it is these things, like "man" and "animal," that are spoken of as secondary substances.

From what has been said, it is plain that both the name and the definition of what is asserted of a subject must themselves be asserted of that subject. For instance, "man" is asserted of a particular man as a subject, and thus the name is certainly asserted, since you will be asserting the name "man" of a particular man; and the definition of man will be asserted, too, of the particular man, since he is both *a* man and "man." Thus, both the name and the definition will be asserted of the subject. But in the case of most of the things that are present in a subject, neither the name nor the definition is asserted of the subject; in some cases there is nothing to keep the name from being asserted of it, but it is impossible for the definition to be. White, for instance, is present in body as a subject, and is asserted of it, for a body is said to be white, but the definition of white will never be asserted of the body.

All things other than primary substances are either asserted of primary substances as subjects, or are in them as subjects. This becomes plain from individual cases as we look at them. "Animal," for instance, is asserted of "man," and so is asserted too of a particular man; for if it were not asserted of any particular man, it would not be asserted of "man" in general either. Again, color is present in "body," and so is also present in a particular body; for if it were not present in any of the individual bodies, it would not be present in "body" in general either. So, all other things are in fact either asserted of primary substances as subjects or are present in them as subjects. If, therefore, there were no primary substances, it would be impossible for anything else to exist.

Among secondary substances, the species is more a substance than the genus, since it is closer to the primary substance. If one is giving an account of what a primary substance is, one will give a more informative and a more appropriate account by mentioning its species than by mentioning its genus. For instance, one would give a more informative account of a particular man by calling him "man" than by calling him "animal" (for the former term is more specially applicable to a particular man; the latter is more widely shared), and one will give a more informative account of a particular tree by calling it "tree" than by calling it "plant."

Further, the reason why primary substances are said to be more fully substances than anything else is that they are subjects to everything else and that all other things are either asserted of them or are present in them. Now, the relation of species to genus is the same as that of primary substances to everything else. For the species is subject to the genus; and, although genera are asserted of species, the converse is not true—namely, species are not asserted of genera. So on these grounds too we can see that the species is more of a substance than the genus.

Among the species themselves (at least, if they are not genera as well), none is any more of a substance than any other; one will not give any more appropriate account of a particular man by calling him "man" than of a particular horse by calling it "horse." In the same way, too, with primary substances none is any more of a substance than any other; a particular man is no more of a substance than a particular ox.

It is reasonable that, primary substances apart, only species and genera should be said to be secondary substances, since they alone among things that are asserted of a subject tell of the primary substance. For if someone is giving an account of the nature of a particular man, he will give an appropriate account by mentioning the species or the genus (and the account will be more informative if he describes him as "man" than if he just describes him as "animal"). But if he mentions some other thing in his account, such as the subject's whiteness or the fact that it is running or anything like that, he will be mentioning things that are unsuitable for what he is trying to do. So, it is reasonable for species and genera to be the only things apart from primary substances that are called substances. Further, it is because primary substances are subjects of everything else that they are more properly spoken of as substances than anything else; and the relationship of primary substances to everything else is the same as that of their species and genera to all other things: it is of them that all other things are asserted. You will call a particular man literate, and so you will also call "man" and "animal" literate. And it is the same with other terms.

It is a characteristic shared by all substance that it is not present in a subject. For, although primary substance is neither asserted of a subject nor present in a subject, we can see from the following consideration that neither is secondary substance present in a subject. "Man" is asserted of a particular man as a subject, but is not present in a subject, since "man" is not present in a particular man. In the same way, "animal" is asserted of a particular man, but is not present in him. Further, in the case of things that are in a subject, there is nothing to prevent their names being asserted of the subject, but it is impossible for their definitions to be so asserted; whereas in the case of secondary substances both their definitions and their names are asserted of the subject; you will assert the definition of "man" of a particular man, and the definition of "animal" too. So substance is not among the things that are present in a subject.

This characteristic, however, is not peculiar to substance. The differentia, too, is among the things not present in a subject. "Moving on foot" and "biped" are asserted of "man" as a subject, but are not present in a subject; neither "moving on foot" nor "biped" is present in man. Moreover, the definition of the differentia is asserted of whatever the differentia itself is asserted of. For instance, if "moving on foot" is asserted of "man," so too is its definition, for man is a thing that moves on foot.

But we must not allow ourselves to get into confusion over the parts of substances, and suppose that their presence in the wholes that they compose is presence in a subject—in case we are driven to say that parts are not substances. For in fact the way in which we say that parts are present in a whole is quite different from the way in which we say that this or that is present in a subject.

It is a characteristic of substances and of differentiae that all assertions of any one of them are synonymous with one another. For whenever they are asserted of anything, they are asserted either of individuals or of species. Primary substance, indeed, is never asserted of anything, since there is no subject for it to be asserted of; in the case of secondary substances, the species is asserted of the individual, and the genus is asserted of the species and of the individual; in the same way, too, the differentiae are asserted of both species and individuals. Primary substances receive, in addition, the definition both of their species and of their genera; and the species receives too the definition of its genus; for whatever is asserted of a predicate will be asserted too of the predicate's subject. In the same way, too, both species and individuals receive the definition of the differentia. Now things that were synonymous were in fact things that shared a name and had the same definition; so every time any substance or differentia is asserted of a thing, it has this synonymous character.

All substance appears to refer to some particular thing. In the case of primary substances, it is unquestionably true that it does so, since what it refers to is a single individual. In the case of secondary substances, one would judge from the form of the appellation that a particular thing was being indicated when one said "man" or "animal." But this is not true; secondary substance, rather, indicates some quality. For the subject is not a single unit in the way in which a primary substance is; both "man" and "animal" are asserted of many things. On the other hand, it does not indicate simply a quality in the way that "white" does. For "white" indicates nothing but quality, whereas species and genus define the quality that concerns substance; they indicate what kind of a substance a thing is. Definition by genus covers a wider field than definition by species; the man who speaks of "animal" embraces more by the term than the man who speaks of "man."

It is another characteristic of substances that none of them has a contrary. For what could be contrary to a primary substance? And just as there is no contrary to a particular man, so there is none either to "man" or to "animal." This is not a peculiarity of substance, but is true of many other things, such as quantity. There is no contrary to "two feet long" or to "ten" or to any term of that kind—unless you maintain that "much" is contrary to "little," or "great" to "small." Among the definite quantities, at any rate, none is contrary to any other.

Substance does not seem to admit of degree. I do not mean to deny what has already been said: that some substances are more completely substances than others; I mean, rather, that no substance is said to be more or less whatever it is. For instance, if a particular substance is "man," it will not be any more or less of a man, either than itself or than any other man. For no man is more of a man than any other man in the way that one white thing is whiter than another, or one beautiful thing more beautiful than another. And the circumstances in which a thing is said to be more or less something than itself are like those when a white body is said to be whiter now than it was before, or when something hot is said to be now hotter, now less hot. But none of this is said

of substance. A man is not said to be any more of a
man now than he was before, nor does this happen with
anything else that is substance. Substance, then, will not
admit of degree.

But what seems to be most peculiar to substance is
this: although remaining a single, identical unit, it will
admit of contraries. This is a characteristic that one will
not find in any other term. A color, for instance, which
is a single, identical unit, will not be both black and
white, nor will one and the same action ever be both
good and bad; and it is the same with all other terms
that are not substances. But substance, though it remains
a single, identical unit, certainly will admit of contraries.
A particular man, for instance, though he remains one
and the same, sometimes becomes white, sometimes
black, sometimes hot, sometimes cold, sometimes good,
sometimes bad. This does not appear to be true of anything else, unless someone objects that statements and
opinions are of this kind. For the same statement does
appear to be both true and false. If, for instance, the
statement " 'x' is sitting down" is true, it will be false as
soon as "x" has got up. It is the same with opinion. If
someone holds the correct view that " 'x' is sitting
down," he will be holding a false opinion if he still holds
this same view when "x" has got up. But even if we
admit this point, there is nonetheless a difference in the
way that the change happens. In the case of substances,
it is actually something in them that changes and so becomes receptive to contraries. A thing becomes cold
after having been hot (for it undergoes qualitative
change), black after having been white, or good after
having been bad. In the same way with the rest, it is in
each case the thing itself that undergoes change and so
admits of contraries. But statements and opinions remain
absolutely unchanged themselves; it is, rather, through a
change in the thing to which they refer that they become
contrary to what they were. The statement " 'x' is sitting
down" remains the same; it is as a result of "x" moving

that the statement is at one moment true, at another false; and it is just the same with opinion. So it is a peculiarity of substance to admit of contraries, at least in this way, through a change in itself—even if one does accept the objection that opinions and statements also admit of contraries. In fact, the objection is not valid. For it is not by virtue of their receiving something themselves that statements and opinions are said to admit of contraries, but by virtue of something having happened to something else. It is because the thing to which it refers is or is not so that a statement is said to be true or false, not because it admits itself of these contraries. Neither statements nor opinions are changed by anything in any way at all; so, as nothing happens to them, they cannot themselves admit of contraries. On the other hand, it is by reason of receiving the contraries itself that a substance is said to admit of them—by itself receiving disease and health, whiteness and blackness, and all the other things of that kind. So, it is in fact a peculiarity of substance that, although remaining itself a single identical unit, it will admit of contraries. So much for substance.

■ ■ ■

8. When I speak of quality, I refer to that by virtue of which people or things are said to be of this or that kind; it is one of the things that can be spoken of in several senses. One kind of quality we may call that of *disposition* and *state*. A disposition differs from a state in being more stable and lasting longer. The different sorts of knowledge and of virtue are of this kind. For knowledge, even when grasped only up to a point, seems to be among the things that are stable and hard to lose, unless disease or something of that sort brings about a great change in one; and it is the same with virtue too; justice, for instance, and self-control, and other things like that do not seem to be easily lost or easily altered.

What are described as states are things that are easily
lost and quickly changed, like heat and cold, health and
sickness, and other things of that sort. For it is by virtue
of these that a man is in a particular state, and he
quickly changes from being hot to being cold or from
being in good health to being ill. It is the same with
other things of this kind, except where one of these
states has through the passage of much time become
embedded in a man's nature, being either incurable or
extremely difficult to get rid of; in such a case, one would
perhaps call it a disposition. So, a disposition differs
from a state in that the latter can easily be got rid of,
whereas the former lasts longer and is harder to lose.
All dispositions are also states, but not all states are
necessarily dispositions. For those who have a certain
disposition are thereby in a certain state; but those who
are in a certain state do not for that reason have a certain disposition as well.

A second class of qualities is those by virtue of which
we describe people as "good at boxing," "good at running," "healthy," or "sickly"—in general, all terms that
refer to a natural capacity or the lack of it. For it is not
because someone is in a particular state that one applies
any of the terms of this kind, but because he has the
natural capacity or incapacity to do something easily or
not to be affected by things. People are said to be good
at boxing or running, for instance, not because they are
in a particular state, but because they have a natural
capacity to do the thing easily; they are said to be
healthy because they have a natural capacity not to be
affected readily by things that just happen to them, and
sickly because they have an incapacity to avoid being so
affected. "Hard" and "soft" are in a similar position to
these terms; a thing is said to be hard because it has a
capacity not to be easily broken up, soft because it cannot avoid this.

A third class of qualities is that of affective qualities
and affections. This comprises such things as sweetness,

bitterness, sourness, and all the things of that sort; heat and cold, as well, and whiteness and blackness. It is clear that these are qualities, since the things that admit of them are said to be of a particular kind because of them; honey, for instance, is said to be sweet because it has sweetness, the body is called white because it has whiteness, and so on with the rest. But it is not because the things that have the qualities are affected in any way that these are called affective qualities. Honey is not said to be sweet because it has been affected in any way, nor is this the case with anything else of this kind. Similarly, it is not because the things that have the particular quality are affected in any way that heat and cold are said to be affective qualities, but rather because each of these qualities produces an affection by means of the senses. Sweetness implants an affection by means of the taste, heat by means of touch, and so on with the others.

But whiteness, blackness, and the other colors are not said to be affective qualities in the same way as those that we have mentioned; they are affective rather because they have come into being as the result of an affection. It is clear that many changes of color do in fact come about as the result of an affection. When someone is ashamed he turns red; when he is frightened he turns pale; and so on. Consequently, too, if someone has a natural tendency to undergo some such affection, it is likely that he will keep the same sort of color. For the same bodily state that in the case we have been mentioning occurred when the man was ashamed might also be the result of his natural makeup, so that he would by nature have the corresponding color. Well then, as many of such states as have their origin in affections that are hard to get rid of and last some time are said to be qualities. If paleness or swarthiness is in someone's natural makeup, it is said to be a quality, since it is by virtue of it that we are said to be of such and such a kind; and if this same paleness or swarthiness has come about through a long illness or through sunburn and does not

readily disappear, or even remains throughout one's life,
then it too is said to be a quality, since, again, we are
said to be of such and such a kind by virtue of it. But
states that are the result of things that are easily broken
up and quickly got rid of are said to be affections, since
people are not said to be of such and such a kind by
virtue of them. The man who turns red because he is
ashamed is not said to be of a ruddy complexion, nor is
the man who turns pale through fear said to be pallid;
they are said rather to have been affected in some way.
Such things, then, are said to be affections, not qualities.

Similarly, too, with regard to the soul, there are said
to be both affective qualities and affections. Things that
are the results of affections occurring immediately at
birth, such as maniacal distraction for instance, or a bad
temper, are said to be qualities, since it is by virtue of
them that people are said to be of such and such a
kind—bad-tempered, for instance, or mad. Again, in the
case of distractions that are not natural but are the result
of certain occurrences, if they are hard to get rid of or
are indeed completely incurable, then we speak of qualities, since people are said to be of a particular kind by
virtue of them. But things that are the result of quick
happenings are said to be affections. If, for instance, a
man gets rather angry at being hurt, he is not said to be
bad-tempered, he is said to have something happening
to him. So, such things are said to be affections, not
qualities.

A fourth class of quality is that of shape and the form
belonging to each thing and, besides these, straightness,
crookedness, and anything of that kind. For by virtue of
each of these a thing is said to be of such and such a
kind—by virtue of being triangular or quadrilateral, for
instance, or of being straight or crooked, or, again, by
virtue of its form. "Thin" and "thick," "rough" and
"smooth," appear to indicate that a thing is of such and
such a kind, but in fact such terms seem foreign to the
class of quality. In fact, each of these terms seems rather

to indicate the position of the parts. A thing is thick if its parts are close to each other, thin if they are far apart; a thing is smooth if its parts lie more or less in a straight line, rough if some stick out and some are further in.

Another kind of quality might come to light, but we have pretty well covered the ones that are usually spoken of.

These, then, are qualities, and the things that they qualify as of a particular kind are given names that either derive from them or have some other connection with them. In the case of most, in fact practically all, of them, the term is derived from the quality; a man is called "white," for instance, from "whiteness," "literate" from "literacy," "just" from "justice," and so on. But in some cases, since the qualities do not have names, it is not possible for the descriptive terms to be derived from them. For instance, the man who is described as good at running or good at boxing by virtue of a natural capacity is not so described by derivation from any quality; for there are no names for these capacities. But there are names for the kinds of knowledge by virtue of which people are said to be in the state of being good boxers or good wrestlers, for we do speak of a knowledge of boxing or a knowledge of wrestling and it is by derivation from them that people who are in such a state are described. Sometimes, even though there is a name for the quality, the qualifying term is not derived from it. As a result of "virtue," for instance, we call a man "good"; we call him "good" because he possesses virtue, but it is not from "virtue" that the term is derived. This sort of thing does not happen in many cases, however. Things, then, are said to be of a particular kind by derivation from the qualities that we have mentioned or through some kind of connection with them.

There can be contraries in respect to quality. Justice, for instance, is contrary to injustice, whiteness to blackness, and so on; it is the same with the things they qualify: what is unjust is contrary to what is just, what is white is contrary to what is black. But it is not like this with all qualities; there is no contrary to "red" or to "yellow," or to any colors of that kind, qualitative though they are.

Further, if one of a pair of contraries is qualitative, the other will be too. This is clear if you go through the other categories. If justice, for instance, is the contrary of injustice, and is qualitative, then injustice will be qualitative too; for injustice does not fit into any of the other categories, such as quantity, or relation, or place, or indeed any of them—except quality. It is the same with the other contraries in the category of quality.

Things qualified as of a certain kind do admit of degree. One thing is said to be more or less white or more or less just than another; and a particular thing may acquire more of a quality—a thing that is white can become still whiter. This is not true of all qualities, but of most of them. Difficulties might be raised if justice itself or any other condition were said to admit of degree. Some people, in fact, dispute this, and say that there can be no question of different degrees of justice itself or of health itself; rather, they say, one man possesses health or justice to a greater extent than another, and it is the same with literacy and other conditions. But at any rate there is no doubt that the things described as having these qualities admit of degree. One man is said to be more literate or more just or more healthy than another, and it is the same with the rest. But "triangular" and "square" do not seem to admit of degree, nor indeed do any of the other shapes. For, although things that admit of the definition of "triangle" or "circle" are all triangles or circles respectively, none of the things that do not admit of them can be said to be more or less "triangular" or "circular" than any other. A square is no more of a circle than an oblong is, since neither of them admits of the definition of a circle. And in general, if neither of two things admits the definition of what is under consideration, neither of them will be described as having its character more than the other; so that not all things that are qualified as of a particular kind admit of degree.

None of the characteristics that I have mentioned is peculiar to quality; but it is only with reference to quality that the terms "like" and "unlike" are used. For no one thing is like any other in respect to anything other than what makes it of a particular kind. So the peculiarity of quality is the use of the terms "like" and "unlike" with reference to it.

We should not be worried if someone says that in giving our account of quality we have in fact listed many relational terms, alleging that dispositions and states are relational. In practically all cases of this kind, it is true that the generic terms are used in relation to something, but not that any of the specific terms are. Knowledge, being a generic term, is said to be essentially related to something: we talk of knowledge of something, but none of the specific terms is said to be so essentially related. We do not, for instance, talk of literacy as literacy "of anything," or of music as music "of anything," except insofar as these terms are used with reference to their *genus*. Literacy, for instance, is knowledge of something, but it is not literacy "of anything"; music is knowledge of something, but not music "of anything." Thus, the specific terms are not relational. And it is by virtue of specific qualities that we are said to be of a particular kind, since these are what we possess: we are knowledgeable because we have some specific knowledge. The qualities, then, by virtue of which we are said to be of a particular kind are specific qualities, and these are not among the qualities that are relational. Furthermore, if one and the same thing is in fact both qualitative and relational, there is nothing strange about its being counted in both classes.

●   ●   ●

On Interpretation

■   ■   ■

4. A sentence is a significant sound, any of whose parts has a significance of its own, but as an expression, not as an assertion. For instance, "human" indicates something, but it does not indicate that any "human" exists or that he does not (although it will become part of an assertion or denial if something is added); a single syllable of "human," on the other hand, does not indicate anything at all, nor does the "-ouse" of "mouse"; it is just a sound. In compound words, the syllable has some significance, although not independently, as we have said. But every sentence is significant, not because it is a natural instrument, but, as we have remarked, by convention. Not every sentence, however, is a proposition; only those sentences are propositions to which truth or falsehood belongs, and these do not belong to every sentence; a prayer, for instance, is a sentence, but it is neither true nor false. But let us leave the other kinds of sentence out of consideration, since an examination of them belongs more properly to rhetoric or to poetry. Propositions are what concern our present inquiry.

5. The first kind of simple proposition is the assertion, the second the denial. All the rest are simple propositions only through conjunction.

Every proposition must contain a verb, or some inflection of one. Even the definition of "man," without the addition of "is" or "will be" or "was" or some term of that sort, is not yet a proposition. (The reason "two-footed animal that moves on foot" is a single unit and not a multitude of things—and a single unit, too, by virtue of more than the mere juxtaposition of the words—must be sought in another branch of study.)

A single proposition is one that either discloses one fact or is one by conjunction; but a multitude of propositions occurs either when many things, not just one, are disclosed or when there is no conjunction.

Nouns and verbs on their own should be regarded only as expressions; for by uttering them you cannot make any significant statement, either as a reply to a question or as a spontaneous statement of your own opinion.

Among the kinds of propositions, there is the simple one, which, for instance, asserts or denies something of something else, and there is the one that is composed of simple propositions, a statement that is already compound.

A simple proposition tells you whether something is or is not true of something else, and specifies the time. An assertion is the statement that one term does belong to another; a denial is the statement that one term does not belong to another.

■ ■ ■

9. Any assertion or denial that concerns the present or the past must be either true or false. This is the case with regard to any universal proposition that really is about a whole class and to all propositions about individuals, as we have said; it is not necessarily the case with regard to universal propositions that are not meant to apply to the whole class—but this, too, we have already mentioned.

But in the case of individual propositions that refer to the future, the situation is different.

If every assertion or denial is either true or false, then

every attribute must of necessity either belong or not
belong to a given subject. For when one man says that
a thing will be and another that this same thing will not
be, it is plainly necessary that one of them should be
telling the truth if every affirmation is either true or
false, but both cannot be, since both propositions cannot
be true at the same time in such a situation. If it is true
to say that a thing is either white or not white, then it
is necessary that it should be either white or not white,
and if it is either white or not white, then it was in fact
true either to assert or to deny that it was white. Further,
if the attribute does not belong to the subject, the man
who says that it does is speaking falsely; conversely, if a
man is speaking falsely when he says that the attribute
does belong to the subject, then in fact it does not so
belong. Thus, it is necessary that either an assertion or
the denial of what it asserts should be true.

On this basis, nothing exists or happens either by
chance or because this rather than its opposite chanced
to occur; nor will anything in the future either be or
not be by chance whatever it is; everything happens of
necessity; it cannot just be whichever of two opposites
chanced to occur, since either the man who says that a
thing is or will be so or the man who denies this is
speaking truly. Otherwise, a thing might equally well
happen or not happen; for if what occurs is just whichever of two opposites chances to occur, there is no reason for a thing either now or in the future to be in a
particular state rather than not to be in it.

Further, if a thing is white now, it was true to say in
the past that it would be white; and thus it was always
true to say of anything that has happened that it would
happen. And if it was always true to say that this was
or would be so, it is not possible for it not to be so or
not to be going to be so. If it is not possible for a thing
to happen, it is impossible for it not to happen; and if
it is impossible for it not to happen, it is necessary that
it should happen. Thus, it is necessary that everything

that is going to happen should happen; and there will be nothing that is just whichever of two opposites it chances to be, nothing that occurs by chance, since when anything occurs by chance it does not occur of necessity.

But it is not possible, either, to say that neither proposition is true, to say, for instance, that a thing neither will nor will not occur. For, in the first place, this would mean that when an assertion was false, its denial would still not be true, and that when the denial was false, the assertion would not be true. Further, if it is true to say that a thing is both black and white, both these properties must belong to it; and if it is true to say that they will both belong to it tomorrow, they both will belong to it tomorrow. But if a thing were neither going to happen nor not going to happen tomorrow, there would be no question of it being whichever of a pair it chanced to be. Take a sea battle, for instance: on this hypothesis, it would be necessary that a sea battle should neither occur nor not occur.

These, then, are the curious results that emerge, these and others like them, if, in the case of every assertion or denial that is either a universal statement really concerning a whole class, or a statement about an individual, we say that one of the two is necessarily true and the other necessarily false; and that no event is whichever of two opposites it chances to be, but rather that everything exists and happens of necessity. In that case, there would be no need for us to deliberate or to exert ourselves about anything under the supposition that if we do this, this will happen, and if we do not, it will not. There is nothing to prevent one man's saying ten thousand years in advance that this or that will take place, and another saying that it will not, with the result that what happens will of necessity be the one of the two that it was then true to say would happen. But neither does it make any difference whether people have or have not actually made these opposing statements. For clearly things are as they are irrespective of whether one man has asserted and another denied that they are. It is not because of someone's asserting or denying them that things will or will not happen; nor does it matter whether the statements are made ten thousand years ahead or at any other distance of time. So, if throughout time things were such that one of two contradictory statements was true, it was in fact necessary for the thing asserted to happen, and for everything that has happened always to be such that it of necessity does happen. For it is not possible for anything that a man has truthfully said will happen not to happen; and it was always true to say of what has happened that it would happen.

But these consequences are impossible. We can see that things in the future do have an origin in our deliberations and actions, and that in general, with things that are not always in a state of active realization, it is possible for them both to be such and such and not to be such and such; and in cases where these are both possibilities, it is possible, too, both for an event to occur and for it not to occur. There are many things that are plainly in this situation. It is possible for this cloak, for example, to be cut up; but in fact it will not be, it will be worn out first, and in the same way, it is possible for it not to be cut up, since if there were not this possibility, it would not be possible for it to be worn out first. It is the same, too, with other occurrences that are said to be possible in this way. Plainly, then, not everything is as it is or happens as it does of necessity—rather, some things are just whichever of two opposites chances to occur, and neither the assertion nor the denial is any more true than the other; in other cases, the one is more generally true, but it is still possible for the other to occur in its place.

It is necessary for what happens to happen when it does happen, and for what does not happen not to happen when it does not; but it is not of necessity either that everything that does happen happens or that everything that does not happen does not happen. For there is a difference between what happens happening of necessity *when* it does and its happening absolutely of necessity; and it is the same with what does not happen. The same argument applies, too, to contradictory statements. It is necessary that everything should either happen or not happen, and indeed that everything should either be going to happen or not going to happen, but it is not possible to choose one of the two and say that it is necessary for it to happen. What I mean is something like this. It is necessary for there either to be or not to be a sea battle tomorrow; but it is not necessary that a sea fight should occur tomorrow, nor is it necessary that it should not, only that it should either occur or not occur. So, since the truth of statements corresponds to facts, it is clear that, in all cases in which either of two opposite events may occur, this will hold true of the contradictory statements about them too. This applies to things that are either not always in some particular state, or not always not in some particular state. For in these cases it is necessary that one of the two contradictory statements should be true or false, but it is not necessary that this one or that one should be, it will be whichever of the two it chances to be; one may be more likely than the other, but this does not yet make the one of them true or the other false. So, plainly, it is not necessary, for every assertion and denial, that this one of the pair should be true and that false. For the situation of things that are not something, but are capable both of being and of not being it, is not the same as that of things that are actually something; it is, rather, as we have described it.

■   ■   ■

12. Now that these points have been cleared up, we must examine the relation to each other of assertions and denials of being possible and not possible, being contingent and not contingent, being impossible, and being necessary. For there are some difficulties involved.

We might suppose that, when these various terms are combined, there would be the same kinds of opposition as when "being something" is opposed to "not being something." For instance, the denial of the assertion that he is a man is "he is not a man," not "he is a non-man"; and the denial of "he is a white man" is "he is not a white man," not "he is a non-white man." (For if the latter were the case, and if either an assertion or its denial were still true of every subject, it would be true to say that wood was a non-white man.) But if this is the situation in cases, too, where "to be" is not added to the subject, whatever is substituted for it will behave in the same way. The denial, for instance, of "man walks" is not "a non-man walks," but "man does not walk." For there is no difference between saying "man walks" and "man is walking."

So, if this rule holds universally, the denial of "it is able to be" will be "it is able not to be" rather than "it is not able to be." But in fact the same thing seems to be able both to be and not to be. For everything that is able to be cut or to walk is also able not to be cut or not to walk. The reason is that everything that has ability in this way is sometimes failing actively to realize it; and thus (if our rule holds), the denial of it will be true as well as the assertion. What can walk is also able not to walk; what is visible is able not to be seen. But yet it is impossible for contradictory statements to be made truthfully about the same subject. So in fact this latter statement is not the denial of the other. For the consequence of all these considerations is either that the same thing is asserted and denied of the same subject, or that attributions made in some other way than by saying "to be" or "not to be" constitute assertions and denials. So if the first alternative is impossible, we must choose the second. Thus, after all, the denial of "it is able to be" is "it is not able to be." The same argument applies to "it is contingent that it should be"; its denial is "it is not contingent that it should be." The same sort of behavior occurs with the other terms, like "necessary" and "impossible." For whereas, in the cases that we considered earlier, "is" and "is not" were the additions and the substantive elements were "white" and "man," here "to be" becomes one of the substantive elements, and in the case of statements about the possibility or contingency of being, "is able" and "is not able" are the additional elements that determine the truth of the proposition in a way that "is" and "is not" do in the others.

The denial, then, of "it is able not to be" is "it is not able not to be." Thus, the propositions "it is able to be" and "it is able not to be" seem to follow from each other, since the same thing is able both to be and not to be, these propositions not being contradictory to each other. But a thing can never at the same time be able to be and not able to be; these two propositions are contradictory. Nor can a thing at the same time be able not to be and not able not to be. In the same way, the denial of "it is necessary that it should be" is not "it is necessary that it should not be," but "it is not necessary that it should be," and the denial of "it is necessary that it should not be" is "it is not necessary that it should not be." Again, the denial of "it is impossible that it should be" is not "it is impossible that it should not be," but "it is not impossible that it should be"; and the denial of "it is impossible that it should not be" is "it is not impossible that it should not be." In general, as I have said, we must regard "to be" and "not to be" as substantive elements in these propositions, whereas we regard the terms to which we have been referring as making the proposition in question into an assertion or denial by linking the subject to "to be" or "not to be." The statements that we should regard as contradictory are these:

It is possible	——	It is not possible
It is contingent	——	It is not contingent
It is impossible	——	It is not impossible
It is necessary	——	It is not necessary
It is true	——	It is not true

*   *   *

13. The consequences follow logically if we set the terms out in this way. From "it is possible for it to be" follows "it is contingent that it should be" (and here the converse is true), as do also "it is not impossible that it should be" and "it is not necessary that it should be"; from "it is possible for it not to be" and "it is contingent that it should not be," it follows that "it is not necessary that it should not be" and that "it is not impossible that it should not be"; from "it is not possible for it to be" and "it is not contingent that it should be," it follows that "it is necessary that it should not be" and that "it is impossible that it should be"; and from "it is not possible for it not to be" and "it is not contingent that it should not be," it follows that "it is necessary that it should be" and that "it is impossible that it should not be."

But let us study what I am saying by means of this diagram:

It is possible for it to be	It is not possible for it to be
It is contingent that it should be	It is not contingent that it should be
It is not impossible that it should be	It is impossible that it should be
It is not necessary that it should be	It is necessary that it should be
It is possible for it not to be	It is not possible for it not to be
It is contingent that it should not be	It is not contingent that it should not be
It is not impossible that it should not be	It is impossible that it should not be
It is not necessary that it should not be	It is necessary that it should not be

Thus, "it is impossible" and "it is not impossible" follow from "it is possible," "it is contingent," "it is not possible," and "it is not contingent" as one set of contradictories following from another; but they do so in inverted form. From the assertion that it is possible for it to be follows the denial that it is impossible, and from the denial that it is possible for it to be follows the assertion that it is impossible; for "it is impossible for it to be" is an assertion, "it is not impossible" is a denial.

We must see how propositions predicating necessity follow from these others. It is clear that they follow in a different way from those predicating impossibility: although contradictory propositions about necessity do follow from the others, the contradictions are not between propositions in the same sets as was the case with the others. The denial of "it is necessary that it should not be" is not "it is not necessary that it should be." Both statements could truthfully be made about the same thing; for if it is necessary that something should not be, it is not necessary that it should be. The reason why these propositions do not follow from the others in the same way is that "it is impossible" and "it is necessary" are used in opposite ways to express the same meaning. If it is impossible for something to be, it is necessary not that it should be, but that it should not be; but if it is impossible for a thing not to be, it is necessary that it should be. So, while propositions predicating impossibility and its opposite follow directly from those predicating possibility and its reverse, propositions predicating necessity follow from the others only when the subjects are reversed; for "it is impossible" and "it is necessary" indicate the same thing, but as I have said, in inverted form.

But perhaps it is impossible for the contradictory statements about what is necessary to be arranged as they are here. For if it is necessary that a thing should be, it is also possible that it should be. Otherwise, the denial that it is possible will follow, since one must either assert or deny that it is possible; and if it were not possible for it to be, it would be impossible for it to be; thus, further, what is necessary would be impossible—which is a curious conclusion. But, on the other hand, from "it is possible that it should be" it follows that "it is not impossible that it should be"; and from this it follows that "it is not necessary"; and so the result is that what is necessary is not necessary—which is, again, a curious conclusion.

But, further, "it is necessary that it should be" does not follow, either, from "it is possible for it to be," nor does "it is necessary that it should not be." For the proposition that "it is possible for it to be" implies that either of the two results may occur; but if one of the other two propositions is true, these possibilities are no longer so; for a thing is at one and the same time able to be and able not to be, but if it is necessary either that it should be or that it should not be, the two possibilities will no longer remain open.

The remaining possibility, then, is for "it is not necessary that it should not be" to follow from "it is possible that it should be." For this statement is also true of anything of which we say that it is necessary that it should be; further, it is the contradictory of the statement that follows from "it is not possible that it should be." For, from this latter statement it follows that "it is impossible that it should be" and that "it is necessary that it should not be"; and of this last statement "it is not necessary that it should not be" is the contradictory. So, after all, these contradictories too follow from the others in the way that we have just described, and no impossible consequence results if we arrange the propositions in this way.

Some may be puzzled about whether "it is possible that it should be" follows from "it is necessary that it should be." If it does not follow, then its contradictory, "it is not possible that it should be," will; and if anyone says that this is not the contradictory of "it is possible that it should be," then he will have to say that it is "it is possible that it should not be"; but, whichever is the contradictory, both are untrue of a thing that is necessary.

But, on the other hand, it seems that one and the same thing is able to be cut and not to be cut, to be and not to be; so that, on this basis, if it is necessary that a thing should be it will also be possible for it not to be, and this is untrue.

It is clear, in fact, that not everything that is able to walk or to be is able also to do the opposite of these things; there are cases where this is not true. It is not true in the first place of things whose ability or potency is nonrational. Fire, for instance, has an ability that is nonrational for heating things. Rational abilities are abilities to do more than one thing and to do opposite things, but not all nonrational abilities are like this. As we have said, fire is not able both to heat and not to heat, nor is anything else that is always actively realizing its ability. Even among things, however, that have a nonrational ability, there are some that are able to do two opposite things. But our reason for going into all this is to show that not every ability is an ability to do opposite things, even when the term "ability" is used unambiguously. Sometimes, too, "ability" is ambiguous; the term "able" itself is not used unequivocally. Sometimes it is used of a thing that is true because the ability is being actively realized; for instance, a thing is said to be able to walk because it is walking, and in general a thing is said to be able to be something because it already actively is what it is said to be able to be. But sometimes it is used of an ability that might be actively realized; for instance, a thing is said to be able to walk because it might walk. This second kind of ability applies only to things that are capable of motion; the former can apply also to things that are unmoving. But in both cases it is true to say that it is not impossible for it to walk or to be—both of a thing that is already walking and thus realizing its ability, and of a thing that is merely capable of walking. It is incorrect to assert this second kind of ability straightforwardly of what is necessary, but it is correct to assert of it the other kind. So, since the presence of a particular implies the presence of a universal, the presence of what is necessary implies the presence of ability to be, but not of every kind of ability to be. Perhaps, indeed, further, what is necessary and what is not necessary are the principles and causes of everything's being and not being, and perhaps everything else ought to be regarded as following from them.

It is clear from what we have said that what exists of necessity is in a state of active realization; thus, if the eternal things are the first among things, realization precedes the ability to attain it. There are things that are in a state of realization without any question of ability being involved, like the primary substances; then there are things that are actively realized, which involves an ability to be realized—here the realization precedes the ability in nature, though not in time; finally, there are things that are never realized but remain only able to be so.

.   .   .

Posterior Analytics—Book I

1. All instruction and all learning through discussion proceed from what is known already. This is apparent from an examination of all the arts and sciences, since the mathematical sciences and each of the other arts come about in this way.

The same thing holds with regard to dialectical arguments, both those that work by syllogisms and those that use induction. Both achieve their task of instruction by working from things known already. Syllogism takes a point to be known by the audience, and induction is able to point out the universal because the particular is already clear.

Orators persuade in the same way. They use either examples (induction) or enthymemes (syllogisms).

"Knowing already" is to be taken in two senses. We must assume beforehand that some things are true, whereas in other cases we must know beforehand what the term means; and in some cases both are required. For example, that everything can be either asserted or denied illustrates the first case; the meaning of the term triangle—that it indicates this particular figure—the second. In the case of "unit," we must know both; i.e., what the term means and that it is true there is such a thing, since these are not equally clear to us.

It is possible to come to know something as a result

of knowing something else already; or one can recognize the "something else" at the same moment as one comes to know the "something." This applies to things that are cases of a universal already known. A man knows already that every triangle has angles equal to two right angles; but he realizes only at the moment when the proof is concluded that this figure in the semicircle is a triangle! Some things are learned in this way, without the conclusion coming to be known through the middle term: individual, particular things, not predicated of a subject.

Perhaps we should say that before the conclusion is reached or the syllogism completed he knows in one way, though not in another. If a man does not know that a thing exists at all, how can he know that it is always equal to two right angles? Clearly, he knows in a sense, because he knows the universal proposition, but he does not know it of all cases.

If this is not allowed, we shall be faced with the problem mentioned in Plato's *Meno*. Either a man will learn nothing at all or he will learn only what he already knows. We should not use the method employed by some who attempt to solve the problem: "Do you or do you not know that every pair is even?" When the respondent says that he does know this, they introduce a pair that he did not know existed—much less could he know that it was even! They solve the problem by denying that they know that every pair is even; this is only true of what they *know* is a pair.

Yet they have knowledge where they have proof by demonstration and have had it shown to them. They have had it demonstrated, not of everything that *they know* is a triangle or number, but simply of all number or triangle. No premise is included of the type—the number "that you know," or the rectilinear figure "that you know"—no, the proposition refers to all cases. Nothing prevents it from being true that in one way a man knows and in another he does not know what he is learning. There would be a paradox not if he knows in a sense what he is learning, but if he knows it in exactly the same way and manner that he is learning it!

2. We think we know without qualification (not in the sophistical, *accidental* manner) when we think we know the cause or reason why something is the case—knowing that it is the cause of the thing, and that it is impossible for it not to be so. Clearly, knowing is something of that sort; since people who do *not* know think that they are in that condition, and those who *do* know actually are. Therefore, that which is the object of knowledge cannot be other than it is.

We shall say later whether there is another way of knowing. I say here and now that we do know by demonstration. By "demonstration" I mean a scientific syllogism, and by "scientific" I mean a syllogism such that we know by grasping it.

If knowing is as we said, scientific knowledge must be derived from true, ultimate, and immediate propositions, which are better known than, prior to, and the causes of the conclusion. In this way, the principles too will be proper to what is being demonstrated.

Without the above conditions, a syllogism is possible, but not a demonstration, since knowledge will not be produced. The facts, therefore, must be true, since it is impossible to know what is not true: you cannot talk of knowing that ng that $\sqrt{2}$ is a rational number. They must be ultimate and undemonstrable, since otherwise, if you have no demonstrative proof of them, you will not know; and to know (except accidentally) what can be proved is to have proof.

They must also be causes, better known, and also prior: causes because we know when we know the cause; and if they are causes, they must therefore be prior; and known already, not merely through understanding them but also through knowing that such is the case.

"Prior" and "better known" are used in two ways.

"Prior by nature" is different from "prior in relation to us," and "better known" is different from "better known to us." By "prior in relation to us" and "better known to us," I mean what is nearer to our sense perception, whereas absolutely prior and absolutely better known refer to what is more remote. Universals are the most remote of all, whereas particulars are the closest; these are opposed to each other.

By ultimates I mean proper starting points or principles. Starting points and ultimates mean the same thing. The starting point of demonstration is an immediate premise, which means that there is no other premise prior to it. A premise is a positive or negative statement that asserts or denies one predicate of one subject: a dialectical premise takes either positive or negative indifferently; but a demonstrative premise excludes one and takes the other, because it is true. A statement is either side of a contradiction, which is an opposition that excludes a middle. The "side" of a contradiction that asserts something of something else is an affirmation; the side that denies something of something else is a denial.

A thesis is one kind of immediate starting point in syllogism. It cannot be demonstrated, and it is not indispensable for successful study. An axiom, however, is indispensable for any study; there are such truths as axioms, and that is the name we most frequently give them. If a thesis involves either a negative or a positive statement—that is, if it either asserts or denies that something is the case—it is a hypothesis. But if there is no assumption about something being or not being the case, it is a definition. Definition is a kind of thesis: the specialist in arithmetic lays down that "unit" means that which is quantitatively indivisible. However, this is not a hypothesis, since saying what a unit is is not the same as saying that there is such a thing as a unit.

The requisite is to believe in, and know something, by virtue of having a syllogism known as demonstrative. This syllogism itself depends on the truth of its elements, i.e., the premises. Therefore, we must not only know beforehand the ultimate, or first, principles, either all or some of them, but we must know them better (than the conclusion). It is always the case that if an attribute A belongs to B because of C, it belongs more closely to C. For example, if we like A because of B, the attribute "dear" belongs more to B than A.

Therefore, since we know and believe through the first, or ultimate, principles, we know them better and believe in them more, since it is only through them that we know what is posterior to them.

If a man neither knows something nor is in a better state than if he did know, it is impossible for him to have more conviction about it than about what he does know. Yet, this occurs if we are convinced by demonstration, but do not know the causes beforehand; then, it is necessary to be more convinced of the starting points (either all or some) than of the conclusion. Complete demonstrative knowledge requires not only that we have better knowledge of the starting points and more conviction about them than about the conclusion, but also that none of the propositions opposed to the starting points (from which propositions there follows the opposite, or *false* conclusion) must be more certain or better known than the starting points. This is because true, absolute knowledge cannot be shaken.

3. Some think there is no such thing as knowledge, since we must first know the ultimates; others think that there is knowledge, but that all things are demonstrable. Neither view is true or necessary.

The former (those who say that knowledge without demonstration is impossible) assert, firstly, that there is an infinite regress. They argue—and correctly—that the posterior cannot be known through the prior, unless there is a first point or ultimate; in this, they are right, since an infinite cannot be exhausted. Secondly, if there is a terminus and there are starting points, these (they say) are unknowable if they cannot be demonstrated, demonstration being the sole form of knowledge. If it is not possible to know the ultimates, there can be no absolute or valid knowledge of what is posterior to them; that could be known only *by supposing* that the ultimates are true.

The others agree about knowledge: this can arise only through demonstration. However, they continue, there is no problem as to everything's being demonstrable, since it is possible for demonstration to be circular and for all propositions to be proved from one another.

Our view, however, is different. Not all knowledge is demonstrative; knowledge of immediate premises is nondemonstrative. (This is clearly essential: if it is necessary to know what is prior—the elements of the demonstration—and there is no infinite regress but a stop at immediate terms, these must be nondemonstrable.) That is our case; and we say not only that there is knowledge but also that there is a starting point to knowledge, whereby we recognize definitions.

It is clear that absolute demonstration in a circular form is an impossibility. Demonstration must proceed from prior terms that are better known, and it is impossible for terms to be simultaneously prior and posterior to one another. (The exception is if some terms are better known by us, whereas others are better known by nature; this is the way in which induction makes things better known. If this is true, absolute knowledge is not clearly defined, insofar that it has two senses; alternatively, the second sort of demonstration, in that it proceeds from terms better known by us, is not absolute.)

The advocates of circularity are faced with the same consequences. Besides which, what they are saying is no more than that something is the case if it is the case! Everything can be proved in that way. It is clear that this is so, if we take three terms. (It makes no difference whether the circularity occurs through many terms, as opposed to a few; but there is a difference between circularity through a few, i.e., three or more, as opposed to only two.) If A necessarily implies B and B implies C, then A necessarily implies C. If A implies B and B implies A (this being a case of circularity), let A be substituted for C (above). Then, saying that B implies A will be saying that B implies C, which in turn means that A implies C, C and A being identical. The result is that advocates of demonstration by circularity are saying only that A implies A. Anything can be demonstrated in that way.

However, even that is not possible except in the case of coextensive terms, terms peculiar to their subject. We have already shown that if only one thing is posited there is no necessary implication of another. (By "one thing," I mean positing either a single term or a single premise.) The basic requirement is two premises, as for drawing a syllogism. Now, if A is coextensive with B and with C, and B and C are coextensive with one another as well as with A, it *is possible* to prove all the assumptions from one another, in a syllogism in the first figure, as was shown in the work on syllogism. In the same place, we showed too that in the other figures there is either no syllogism at all, or not about the assumptions concerned. Propositions with terms that are not coextensive cannot be proved by circularity. Since coextensive terms seldom occur in demonstration, it is clearly foolish and absurd to say that demonstration is circular and that everything can be shown in this way.

4. The object of absolute knowledge cannot be otherwise than it is. Therefore, the object of demonstrative knowledge must be necessary. (Demonstrative knowledge is the knowledge we have as the result of having demonstration.) Demonstration, therefore, is by syllogism from necessary premises. We must see, then, what kind of thing these elements of demonstration are. To begin with, let us define what we mean by "in all cases," "essential," and "universal."

An attribute is true "in all cases" of a subject if it is not true in some cases when it is not in others, nor true at some times but not at others. If "animal" is truly predicated of "human being" in all cases, then it is true to say that if any X is correctly described as a human being it is also an animal, and if one is true now, so is the other. The same argument applies to line and point. Here is an indication that this is right: this is how we raise objections when we are asked whether something is true "in all cases"—we say either that there is a case in which it is not true or that there is a time at which it is not true.

By "essential" I mean: (1) an attribute that belongs to the definition of the subject, as line belongs to triangle and point to line (triangle and line are made up, respectively, of lines and points which are included in their definitions); and (2) subjects that are included in the definition of their attributes. For example, straight and curved are attributes of line, odd and even of number (so, too, are prime and compound, square and rectangular). All of these are included in their definitions, in the one case "line," in the other "number." Similarly, in other cases too, such terms I call "essential," whereas terms that belong to their subject in neither way are "accidents," as "musical" or "white" is accidental to "animal." (3) "Essential" also means what is not predicated of something else as subject. "That which is walking" is something else that is walking, and "white" is something else that is white. Substance, however, and individual particular things are not what they are through being something else. What is not predicated of a subject I call essential; what is so predicated I call accidental. (4) That which is connected with something else because of itself is essential; that which is not is accidental. It is accidental if there is a flash of lightning while a man is out walking: we say, "it happened like that." "Because of itself" implies "essential": if something has its throat cut and dies, it dies by virtue of the cutting, "because of" the cutting; death is not an accidental consequence of throat cutting.

The term "essential," as applied to the objects of scientific knowledge, refers to attributes that are included in their subjects, or have their subjects *necessarily* included in them. In the first case, it is not possible for the attributes not to belong to their subjects; in the second, it is not possible for the opposite attributes not to belong. Line must be straight or curved, and number must be odd or even. "Opposite" here means either privation or negation in the same genus. "Even," for instance, means that which is bound to be not odd in number. Therefore, if it is necessary to assert or deny attributes, essential attributes must be asserted of necessity.

That is how we distinguish "in all cases" and "essential." By "universal" I mean that which belongs in all cases, essentially and *as such*. Clearly, then, all universal attributes *necessarily* belong to their subjects. "Essential" and "as such" are the same; for example, point and straight are essential to line (since they belong to line as such), and having two right angles belongs to triangle as such (since triangle has angles equal to two right angles as an essential attribute). The term "universal" is used when an attribute can be demonstrated of the first random case. Having angles equal to two right angles is not a universal attribute of figure, although it can indeed be demonstrated of a given figure that it has angles equal to two right angles; but this is not a figure taken at random, nor is the demonstrator using a random figure. A square, for instance, is a figure, but is not equal to two right angles. Now, any random isosceles triangle is equal to two right angles, but it is not first, since triangle is prior to it. Therefore, the first, or random, instance that is shown to be equal to two right angles (or whatever attribute is being considered) is the first instance to which the attribute is universal. To demonstrate, essentially, is to prove that a predicate is universal to a subject; in other cases, it is not "demonstrating" essentially:

you do not demonstrate that having two right angles is universal to isosceles triangle, as it is universal to a wider subject.

5. We should realize that mistakes often occur, and that "universal," demonstrated of a first instance, may not be true in the way it appears to be. This mistake occurs when (1) it is not possible to find a higher class than the particular case taken; (2) when there is such a class, but it is a nameless class covering subclasses different in kind; or (3) the subject of which the attribute is shown is taken in part of its extent only. In this last instance, the demonstration will be true of the subject taken in part only, and true in all cases; but it will not be a demonstration of the first instance of that subject to which the attribute is universal. Demonstration of the first instance of "universal" means demonstration of the first instance as such.

If one were to show (3) that perpendiculars are parallel, it would appear, because this is true of all perpendiculars, that the demonstration applies to them as perpendiculars. This is not the case, however, since the conclusion does not depend on the angles of incidence being right angles. Any angles will do, as long as they are equal.

(1) If isosceles were the *only* sort of triangle, having angles equal to two right angles would seem to be universal to isosceles.

(2) The alternation of proportionals. The mistake here would be to demonstrate this with regard to numbers, lines, solids, and time units, as used to be the case, taking each separately, although it is possible to cover all these cases in one single proof. The reason that the proof used to be made separately is that all these—numbers, lengths, time units, and solids—have no single collective name and differ in kind from each other. But nowadays the proof is universal; the truth does not depend on lines as such, or number as such, but on this quality as such, which mathematicians posit as universal.

For this reason, if a man shows of each type of triangle (by the same proof or different ones) that it is equal to two right angles—taking separately the equilateral, the scalene, and the isosceles—he cannot yet be said to know that a triangle is equal to two right angles, except in the way that sophists know. Nor does he know this of triangle as a whole, even if there is no other kind of triangle, apart from those mentioned above. He does not know it about triangle as such, nor about all triangles—except in an enumerative sense. Knowing the kinds is not knowing the thing as a whole, even though there are no kinds unknown.

When do we not know universally? When do we know absolutely? We plainly would know if triangle (for instance) had the same essence as isosceles triangle, or if the three classes (isosceles, equilateral, scalene) had the same essence taken either separately or as a group. But if triangle is different from isosceles triangle, and the attribute belongs to triangle as such, we do not know.

Does the attribute belong to triangle as such, or to isosceles triangle as such? To what subject does it belong as the first instance? Of what can it be demonstrated as universal? Clearly, that is the first instance to which it belongs when the irrelevant has been stripped off. A bronze isosceles triangle is equal to two right angles, but the attribute will stay when "bronze" and "isosceles" have both been removed. Yet, it will not stay if you remove "figure" or "closed figure"; but these, however, are not the first instances. What, then, is first? If it is triangle, the attribute belongs to other cases through being true of triangle first. We demonstrate, then, that the attribute is universal to triangle.

6. If demonstrative knowledge comes from necessary principles (the object *known* cannot be other than it is) and if essential attributes are necessarily attributes of their subjects (some occur in the definition of the subject, whereas in other instances the subject occurs in the definition of its attributes, in which case one of a pair

of attributes *must* belong to a subject), then it is clear
that the demonstrative syllogism will draw its conclusion
from some such premises. Everything that is an attribute
is either essential or accidental; and accidental attributes
are not necessary.

We must either argue in that way or take as our starting point the fact that demonstration is of necessary
truths and that if the demonstration is complete the conclusion cannot be other than it is. Syllogism, therefore,
proceeds from necessary truths as premises. From truths
you can make a syllogism without actually making a
demonstration; but the only syllogism you can make
from necessary truths is by way of demonstrating. This
is the function of demonstration.

There is a further indication that demonstration proceeds from necessary premises; when we make an objection to people who think they are proving something,
we say "it is not necessary," if we think it possible for
the case to be different, or that it may be so as far as
the particular argument is concerned. It is clear from
this that people are foolish to suppose their principles
are valid if they take a received opinion or a truism,
as sophists do when they say that knowing is having
knowledge. Received opinion is not our starting point;
we take the first element in the class of things of which
the demonstration is made. Not all truth is of the same
family tree.

The following, too, shows that demonstration proceeds
from necessary premises. A man does not have knowledge if he does not know why something is the case,
even though demonstration is possible. Now, if A is necessarily true of C, but B, the middle term of the demonstration, is not necessary to A or C, he does not know
why A is true of C. His conclusion is not made necessary
by the middle term; it is possible for that not to be the
case, and yet the conclusion is necessary.

If someone does not have knowledge of a fact now,
although he has an explanation, and if he is still alive

(and the fact is still the case) and has not forgotten his account, a fortiori he did not have knowledge before. The middle term may cease to be the case, since it is not necessary; and therefore he will have an account, still being alive (and the fact still being the case)—but he does not have knowledge. Therefore, he did not have knowledge before. If the middle term has not altered but may cease to be the case, the consequence will be only contingent; but it is not possible for it to be in that state *and* for him to have knowledge.

When the conclusion is necessary, there is nothing to keep the middle term of the demonstration from being not necessary. It *is* possible to reach a necessary conclusion from premises that are not necessary, just as a true conclusion can be drawn from untrue premises. But when the middle term is necessary, so, too, is the conclusion, just as true premises always lead to true conclusions. If A is necessarily true of B and B of C, A must necessarily be true of C. But when the conclusion is not necessary, it is not possible for the middle term to be necessary either. Suppose that A is true of C, but not necessarily true; suppose, too, that A is necessarily true of B and B of C; then A will be necessarily true of C; but this was not what we started with.

For demonstrative knowledge, there must be necessary facts. Clearly, then, the middle term of the demonstration must be necessary too. If not, we will not know *why* something is the case, or *that* something must *necessarily* be the case. Either we will think we know when in fact we do not, if we suppose that something is necessary when it is not; or else we will not even think we know, whether we "know" the fact through middle terms or "know" the reason why through immediate premises.

There is no demonstrative knowledge of accidental attributes that are nonessential, in the sense in which we distinguished the meanings of essential. It is not possible to show that such a conclusion is necessary, since acci-

dents of things need not be true of them at all (which
is what I mean by accident here). It may be asked why,
in dialectic, if the conclusion is not necessitated by the
premises, certain questions have to be put in preference
to others; it would surely come to the same thing if just
any questions were put, and the person questioned then
stated the conclusion. However, it is necessary to put
the right questions, not because the answers to them
necessitate the conclusion, but because the person who
gives those answers must also give the conclusion. If the
answers are true, so, too, is the conclusion.

The attributes essential to a class of things are necessarily true of the class as such. Clearly, then, demonstrative knowledge is knowledge of essential attributes and
develops from premises about such attributes. Accidents
are not necessary, so that one need not know why a
conclusion (from premises about accidental attributes) is
true, even if it is always the case, though not essentially
so. (This applies to syllogisms through signs.) One will
not know that an essential conclusion is essential, or why
it is; knowing "why" is knowing the cause. Therefore,
the middle term must be in a causal relationship with
the minor, and so must the major with the middle.

7. It is not possible to use a proof applicable to one
class of things in another class: you cannot demonstrate
the truths of geometry by arithmetic. There are three
elements in demonstration: (1) the truth demonstrated,
the conclusion, which is essentially true of its class; (2)
the axioms, the premises of demonstration; (3) the subject class dealt with, of which the properties and essential attributes are proved by demonstration.

The premises of demonstration may be the same in
different classes. But where the classes are different, as
geometry and arithmetic are different, it is not possible
to make an arithmetical proof fit the properties of magnitudes, unless they are also numbers. (This is allowed
in some cases, as I shall explain below.) Demonstration

in arithmetic is always concerned with a particular class; so, too, are other sciences. For a proof to be transferable, there must be absolute or partial identity of class; otherwise, it is clearly impossible. The extreme terms and the middle terms must be taken from the same class, since otherwise they will not be essential but accidental attributes. For this reason you cannot show by geometry that opposites are dealt with by one science or that the product of two cubes is a cube. The conclusions of one science cannot be demonstrated by another, except in cases in which one science is subordinated to another, e.g., optics and geometry, harmonics and arithmetic. Nor can geometry prove a property that is true of lines, but not as such or by virtue of their peculiar class. It cannot prove that the straight line is the most beautiful of lines, or that it is the contrary of the circle. These properties are not true of lines as such, but are common to several classes.

8. It is clear that if the premises of syllogism are universal, the conclusions of demonstration, in the strict sense, must also be eternal. Demonstration, or knowledge in the strict sense, does not apply to temporal or perishable things, knowledge of which can be only accidental; the attribute shown is not universal to the subject, but is only true at some times and in some ways.

When such a demonstration is made, the minor premise must be nonuniversal and temporal. It must be temporal if the conclusion is to be about temporal things, and nonuniversal because the attribute considered will be true in some cases but not in others. You cannot, therefore, conclude that something is universally the case, only that it is the case now.

The same applies to definitions, since a definition is a premise of a demonstration, or a demonstration with the terms in different order, or a conclusion of a demonstration. Demonstration of things that are frequently, but not invariably, the case is clearly eternal so far as it

demonstrates that something is the case; but so far as it
is not eternal, it is particular. Eclipses of the moon exem-
plify this, and there are other cases where the same relation holds between subject and predicate.

9. It is clear that we cannot demonstrate except by
working from the first principles of a case. If the conclusion is true of the subject as such, we cannot *know* this
if the demonstration merely works from true, immediate
premises that do not require proof. That kind of demonstration is like Bryson's proof for squaring the circle.
Such demonstrations do their proving by virtue of a
common term, which belongs to another class as well as
the one being discussed. This is why such arguments
apply to classes that are unlike. If we know in that way,
we know only that something is accidentally the case,
not that it is true of the subject as such. Otherwise, the
argument would not have applied to another class.

We are said to know not accidentally, when we know
by virtue of what (the middle term) an attribute is true
of a subject, as syllogized from the principles of the subject as such—when, for instance, we know that "having
angles equal to two right angles" is essentially true of
its subject as the result of syllogizing from the principles
(premises) appropriate to the subject. Therefore, if the
major term is essentially true of the minor, the middle
term is of the same kind as the other two.

If this is not so, it must at least be of the type that
obtains when arithmetic is used for proof in harmonics.
Such proofs are similar in one way but different in another. Knowing *that* something is the case belongs to
one science (optics)—the class of things referred to is
different; but knowing *why* it is the case belongs to the
higher science, to which the attributes are essential. It is
clear from the above that demonstration, in the strict
sense, is not possible except by working from the basic
principles of the subject. In the case just considered the
principles of the subjects have something in common.

It is also clear that it is not possible to demonstrate the principles peculiar to each subject. If it were, the principles of these principles would be the principles of all things, and the science of those principles would be the supreme science. If a man knows by virtue of the higher causes, he knows a thing better than if he did not, since he knows the prior causes when he knows causes that have not themselves a cause. If he knows better and best, his knowledge or science is better or best. Demonstration does not transfer to another class except when the case is as stated, e.g., when geometry is used in mechanics or optics, or arithmetic in harmonics.

It is hard to decide whether one knows or not, since it is difficult to determine whether we know as a result of the right first principles or not. We think we know if we have a syllogism worked from certain true and basic premises. But that is not the case, since in addition the conclusion must be of the same kind as the premises.

10. By "principles" in a class of things I mean those premises of which it cannot be demonstrated that they are the case. We make assumptions about the meaning of ultimate terms and about the premises formed from them. We must assume too that the principles are the case, but everything else (i.e., conclusions) must be demonstrated. That is, we assume the meaning of unit, straight, and triangle; we assume, too, that there are such things as unit and magnitude; but everything else is demonstrated.

Some propositions used in the demonstrative sciences are peculiar to a given science, whereas others are common. These are common by analogy, since a science needs a common proposition only to the extent required by its class. Propositions that define the meaning of line and straight are examples of "peculiar propositions": "equals remain, if equals are taken from equals" is an example of a common proposition. It is adequate if the latter is used to the extent required by the class. The example quoted above will do the same work if it is not taken in all its instances but is confined, for example, to magnitudes, or to numbers by the arithmetician.

There are also some "special principles," of which science assumes that they are the case, and studies their essential attributes. This is what arithmetic does with unit, and geometry with point and line: an assumption is made that there are such things and that they have a particular meaning; an assumption is also made about the meaning of their essential attributes. Arithmetic, for example, assumes the meaning of odd and even, square and cube; geometry assumes the meaning of irrational, deflection, and verging. But that there are such things is demonstrated by means of common principles and by working from proofs already made. Astronomy proceeds in the same way. The point is that all demonstrative science is concerned with three things: (1) what is posited, the class whose essential attributes are studied; (2) the so-called common axioms, the ultimate premises of demonstration; (3) the attributes, the meaning of which is assumed.

However, some sciences may dispense with some of the above: the class may not be posited, for example, if there obviously is such a thing (it is not so obvious that there is such a thing as number as that there is such a thing as hot or cold). The meaning of the attributes may not be explicitly stated, if it is obvious; similarly, the meaning of an axiom like "equals taken from equals, etc." is not stated, because it is well known. Nonetheless, the nature of the case is that those things—the class, the basic premises, and the attributes demonstrated—are the elements of demonstration.

A proposition that must of itself necessarily be, and appear to be, the case is neither a hypothesis nor a supposition. The thing is that demonstration, like syllogism, is not addressed to thought actually spoken but to the dialogue of the soul with itself. It is always possible to object to the spoken word, but not to the "interior" dialogue. When we assume, without actually demonstrating, propositions that can be demonstrated, we are making a hypothesis if the assumption is accepted by the student. (It is not a hypothesis in the strict sense, since it is *ad hominem.*) But if such an assumption is made when there is no such acceptance, or when the student thinks that the opposite is the case, we are making a supposition. That is the difference between supposition and hypothesis. A supposition is the opposite of the student's opinion, when it is a demonstrable proposition that is assumed and used without being demonstrated.

Definitions are not hypotheses, since it is not asserted that anything is or is not the case. Hypotheses are stated in the premises, but definitions have only to be grasped; this is not hypothesis, unless you argue that learning something is a hypothesis. A hypothesis assumes that certain things are so, and a conclusion is obtained from that assumption. The geometrician's hypotheses are not false, as some have maintained; their critics say one should not use false assumptions, and they maintain that the geometrician does this when he calls the line he has drawn "a foot long" or "straight" when in fact it is neither. But the truth is that his conclusions are obtained, not because the line is what he says, but because of what the drawn line stands for.

A further point is that hypotheses and suppositions are universal or particular, but definitions are neither.

11. Demonstration does not necessitate Platonic Ideas, or a "one" apart from the many particular instances. It does, however, necessitate the possibility of truly predicating one thing of many cases. Without this, there will be no universal, and without the universal there will be no middle term, nor, therefore, any demonstration. There must, therefore, be a term that is one and the same in many instances.

Demonstration does not assert the law of contradiction, except when the conclusion has to be exhibited in

that form. This is obtained by a major premise of the
following type: A is C and not not-C (C being the major
term). The middle and minor terms, however, do not
have to be put in that form. Take the case where a minor
term has "man" and also "not-man" truly predicated of
it (man being the middle). If man is animal (the major)
and not not-animal, it will still be true that Callias (the
minor)—even if we add not-Callias—is animal and not
not-animal. The reason is that the major term is not only
predicated of the middle, but of other terms too, since
it has a wider reference. Therefore, even if the middle
is both itself and not itself, this makes no difference to
the conclusion.

The law of excluded middle is asserted by *reductio ad
absurdum*. This does not put the law in its universal
form, but in a form adequate for the class studied, by
which I mean the class of things of which proofs are
being made, as stated above.

All the sciences have common ground in the common
axioms; I mean the elements used as premises, not the
subjects or attributes of which demonstrations are made.
Dialectic has common ground with all the sciences, as
does any general attempt to prove the common axioms,
like the law of contradiction or the principle that equals
remain if equals are taken from equals. Dialectic does
not deal with a limited subject or a given class. Otherwise, it would not have proceeded by asking questions,
since it is not possible to use questioning in making
proofs: the same conclusion cannot be proved if the contrary of the premises is true.

12. If a question put for the purposes of syllogism
is the same thing as a premise stating either side of a
contradiction, and if the premises of a science are the
elements from which that science makes proofs, then
there must be a legitimate kind of question in science,
which can serve as a premise for the conclusion appropriate to the science. But, clearly, not every question is

appropriate to geometry, or appropriate to medicine, etc. A question is legitimate when it leads to conclusions about the class studied by geometry, or about a class studied through the same principles as geometry, e.g., optics. Similarly with other cases.

The geometrician must give an account of such propositions in the light of geometrical principles and conclusions. But, as a geometrician, he does not have to give an account of his principles. The same is true of other sciences.

A specialist should not be asked any and every question; he should answer only questions relevant to his subject. If one converses with a geometrician as such, and should one prove something on this basis, the procedure will be valid; if not, invalid; and in this case the geometrician cannot be refuted except accidentally. It is not possible to talk geometry with people who are ignorant of the subject, since bad arguing will go unnoticed. The same is true of the sciences.

Since there are geometrical questions, are there ungeometrical ones too? Are there also questions that are in a sense geometrical, but posed by ignorance? What kind of ignorance is that? Is the conclusion drawn by ignorance drawn from the premises opposed to the true ones? Is there merely formal unsoundness, even though the premises are geometrical? Or is there transference from another art: e.g., in discussing geometry, a question proper to music would be ungeometrical, whereas thinking that parallels meet would be geometrical in one sense, ungeometrical in another? Ungeometrical, like unrhythmical, has two senses: in one case there is no geometry at all, in the other the geometry is bad. The latter sort of ignorance, conclusions from that sort of premise, i.e., false, is the contrary of science.

In mathematics formal invalidity is less frequent, because the middle term always works in two ways: the major term is predicated of all of the middle, and the middle is predicated of all of the minor, whereas "all" is not added to either predicate. In mathematics this can be seen, as it were, by the intellect, but in arguments it is concealed. "Is every circle a figure?" This is clearly true, if one draws one. "Are epic poems a circle?" Clearly not (in the same sense).

Objection to a proof should not be founded on an inductive premise. If something is not true of several instances, there can be neither a premise (since it will not be true of all cases, and proof depends on universal propositions) nor an objection. Premises and objections are the same, since an objection may become a premise in demonstration or in dialectic.

Some people make errors in demonstration through including the properties of both the extreme terms. This is Caineus' mistake in maintaining that fire spreads by geometrical proportion. The argument is that fire grows rapidly, and so, too, does geometrical proportion. But this is incorrect demonstration. It would be correct if "geometrical" were predicable of the most rapid proportion, and "the most rapid proportion in movement" were predicable of fire. At times, one cannot draw a conclusion from assumptions; at other times, this is possible but not realized.

Solving problems would be easy if it were impossible to draw true conclusions from false premises. The conclusion would then be necessarily convertible with the premise. For example, let A be the case; if A is the case, so, too, is this, e.g., B, which I already know is the case. From B, therefore, I shall show that A is the case. There is a more frequent convertibility in mathematics, since mathematicians do not include accidental properties (in this respect, too, their practice differs from dialectic), but definitions.

A science develops, not by middle terms, but by extension; e.g., A is true of B, B of C, C of D, and so on ad infinitum. It develops too by extension sideways; e.g., A is true both of C and of E. Suppose that A stands for finite or infinite number, B for finite odd number, and

C for a particular odd number. A, then, is true of C. If D stands for finite even number and E for a particular even number, then A is true of E.

13. There is a difference between knowing that something is the case and knowing why it is the case. This difference obtains, firstly, within a particular science, and in two ways: (1) if the conclusion is reached not via immediate premises, for in this case the ultimate cause is not included, and knowing why means knowing the ultimate cause; (2) if the conclusion is reached via immediate premises but not via the cause, being obtained instead from the more familiar of two convertible terms. It can happen that that which is not the cause may be better known than the other convertible. In that case, it will form the basis of the demonstration. That is the case, e.g., with saying that planets are near because they do not twinkle. Let C stand for planets, B for not twinkling, and A for being near. B is truly predicated of C, since planets do not twinkle. But A, too, is truly predicated of B, since that which does not twinkle is near. (Let this be grasped either by induction or sense perception.) A, therefore, must be true of C, so that here is a proof that the planets are near. This syllogism, though, does not explain why, but that! It is not the case that the planets are near because they do not twinkle, but rather that they do not twinkle because they are near.

However, the latter can be demonstrated via the former, and this proof will exhibit the reason why. If C stands for planets, B for being near, and A for not twinkling, then B is true of C and A of B; therefore, A is true of C. This proof does show why it is the case, since the ultimate cause is included.

Another example is the proof that the moon is a sphere. This uses waxing as a middle: things that wax in this way are spherical; the moon waxes in this way; therefore, the moon is spherical. This proves only that it is the case; if the middle and the major are reversed, we can prove why. The moon is not spherical because of the way it waxes; it is because it is spherical that it waxes in this particular way. (Show this by taking C for moon, B for spherical, and A for waxing.)

Where the middle terms are not convertible, and the term that is not the cause is better known, the proof shows that, not why, something is the case. This is also true when the middle term falls outside the other two. Here, too, there is proof that but not proof why, since the cause is not expressed as a premise. Here is an example. "Why does the wall not breathe? Because it is not an animal." If this last were the cause of not breathing, being an animal would have to be the cause of breathing. If A is not true because B is not, then, if B is true, so must A; e.g., if an unbalance of hot and cold is the cause of ill health, their balance is the cause of good health. Similarly, if asserting A implies B, then denying A denies B.

But this rule is not true of the present case. A syllogism showing this kind of cause is in the second figure. Let A be animal, B breathing, and C wall. Now, A is predicable of all B (since everything that breathes is animal), but not of any C. Therefore, B is not predicable of any C. Therefore, the wall does not breathe. Such causes are like exaggerated explanations, where the middle term is made too remote. There is an example in Anacharsis' proof of why the Scythians have no flute players; his middle is "they have no vines."

These are the differences between proof that and proof why in a given science, depending on the middle term used. There is, too, another kind of difference, due to the fact that each may be studied by a different science. This happens in cases where one science is subordinated to another, as optics is to geometry, mechanics to solid geometry, harmonics to arithmetic, and observations to astronomy. Some of these sciences have almost the same name; there are mathematical and naval astronomy, and mathematical and "audience" harmony.

Here it is the function of the observing science to know that something is true, whereas it is the mathematical side that studies why. The latter knows how to demonstrate the cause, though often it does not know the fact, just as people who study the universal are often ignorant of some of the particulars through not having observed them.

This is the case with things that differ in what they are, but have the same outward forms. Mathematics studies forms, since it does not demonstrate attributes of a subject. Even though a subject has geometrical attributes, they are not studied as attributes of that subject. There is another science—that which studies the rainbow—in the same relation to optics as optics is to geometry. The natural philosopher knows the fact; the optician, *as* optician or mathematical optician, knows why. Many sciences that are not in fact subordinated in this way to others do, nevertheless, exhibit that characteristic. Take the relation between medicine and geometry: the doctor knows that circular wounds heal more slowly, but it is the geometrician who knows why.

14. The first of the figures is the most scientific. This is the method of proof in the mathematical sciences, such as arithmetic, geometry, and optics, and in all sciences that study why. Demonstration of the cause why is generally (or for the most part and in most cases) conducted by this figure. That is why it is the scientific figure above all others, since seeing why has most to do with knowing.

Secondly, this is the only figure through which we know what things are. In the second figure no affirmative conclusion is possible, and knowing what a thing is is affirmative. In the third figure an affirmation is possible, but it is not universal; and what a thing is, it is universally. Man, for example, is a two-footed animal, but not in a limited sense only.

Again, the first figure does not need the other two, but both these are filled up and developed by the first until an immediate premise is reached. Clearly, the first figure is the most valid form of knowing.

15. It is possible for A to be directly true of B; in the same way, it is possible for A to be directly deniable of B. By "directly true" or "directly deniable" I mean that there is no middle term. In this way being true or being deniable will be the case, but not by virtue of another term.

When A or B, or both, is or are part of a class, it is not possible for A to be directly deniable of B. Let A be included in class C. If B is not in C (since it is possible for A to be included and B not), there will be a proof of why A is deniable of B. If C is true of all A but not of any B, it follows that A is not true of any B.

There is the same result if B is in a class, e.g., D. In this case B is true of all D and A is not true of any D, so that the conclusion will be that A is not true of any B. There will be a similar proof if both are in a class.

From the fact that there are chains of classes that do not overlap, it is clearly possible for B not to be in the same class as A, or A as B. If nothing in the chain of classes ACD is predicable of anything in the BEF chain, and A is in G, a larger class of the same chain, it is clear that B will not be in G. If it is, the chains will overlap. The same thing holds when B is in a class and A not.

But if neither is in a class, and it is the case that A is not true of B, it must be true that A is *directly* deniable. If there is to be a middle term, one of the other two must be in a class. The syllogism will have to be either in the first or the second figure. Now, if it is the first, B will be in a class, since the premise containing it must be affirmative; if the second, either (A or B) will be in a class. The syllogism works, then, if either is negated, but not if both are negated.

It is clear that a thing may be directly deniable of another, and we have explained how and when this can happen.

*   *   *

16. Ignorance—not just "not knowing," but actually being ignorant as a positive state—is error produced by syllogism.

Where we can speak of things as "directly true" or "directly deniable," this happens in two ways. One can just simply suppose "directly true" or "directly deniable," or arrive at this belief by using a syllogism. With simple supposition, there is only one kind of error; but there are various forms of error through syllogism.

Let it be the case that A is directly deniable of B. If a man, by taking C as middle term, draws the conclusion that A is predicable of B, he will be in a state of error through syllogism. It is possible for both premises to be false or for one only. If A is not true of any C, and C is not true of any B, but the contrary has been supposed in both cases, both premises will be false. It may well be that C stands in this relation to the other two terms, viz., not included in A as class, nor universal to B. Since it was said that A is directly deniable of B, it is impossible for B to be in a class; and, also, A does not *have* to be universal to everything else (hence, not necessarily to C); thus, both premises will be false.

It is possible for one premise to be true—not either premise indifferently, but only the A–C one, the major: the C–B premise will always be false, since B is not in any class, but the A–C premise can be true. This can happen if A is directly true both of C and of B, for when the same term is directly predicated of two others, neither of these will be included in the other. But it can also happen when A is not directly true of either of the other two.

These are the only ways in which the error can be made of supposing that something *is* the case. (Only in the first figure can it be shown that something is universally the case.) But the error of thinking that something *is not* the case can be achieved in the first and the second figure as well.

Let us first state the number of ways in which it can happen in the first figure, and the nature of the premises. It is possible when both premises are false, e.g., if A is directly true of C and of B; if we now suppose that no A is C and that all B is C, both premises are false. It is also possible when only one is false, and it can be either, indifferently. It is possible for A–C to be true and C–B false: A–C may be true, because A is not an attribute of everything, and C–B false, because it is impossible for C, of which A is never true, to be true of B. Otherwise, the A–C premise will no longer be true; besides, if both premises are true, so, too, is the conclusion.

It is also possible for C–B to be true as long as the other premise is false. This happens if B is in both C and A. The latter must now be subordinate, one to the other, so that if it be supposed that no A is C, the major premise will be false. It is clear, then, that false proof is possible when both premises are false or when only one is false.

In the second figure, it is impossible for both premises to be wholly false. If it is the case that A is true of all B, there will be no middle term that can be truly asserted of all A and truly denied of all B. But in order to get a conclusion, the premises must be of this sort; i.e., the middle is asserted of one term and denied of the other. If the premises, taken in this way, are false, it is clear that their contraries will be true; and this is impossible.

But both may be partially false. Suppose that C is true of some A and some B. If it is now supposed that C is true of all A and not true of any B, both premises will be false—but partially, not wholly, so. The same is true if the major is negated instead of the minor.

Or one premise—either, indifferently—may be wholly false. Let us take a case where what is true of all A must also be true of B. If it is now supposed that C is true of all A, but universally deniable of B, the A–C premise will be true, the C–B false. Another case: what is not true of any B must, therefore, be universally deniable of A. (If it is true of A, it will be true of B, which was not our position.) Now, if it is supposed that C is true of all A, but not of any B, the C–B premise will be true, and the other, the major, false.

The same applies if the major premise is negated. What is not true of any A will not be true of any B. If it is now supposed that C is universally deniable of A, but true of all B, the C–A premise will be true and the minor false.

Again, it is false to suppose that what is true of all B is not true of any A, since, if it is true of all B, it must be true of some A. Now, if it is supposed that C is true of all B but not of any A, the C–B premise will be true, the other false. It is clear, therefore, that in the case of direct predicates syllogistic error occurs either when both premises are false or when only one is false.

17. Next, we take cases where attributes are not directly true. When a false conclusion is drawn via the right middle term, it is not possible for both premises to be false, but only for the major. By "right" here, I mean the middle term used in showing the contradictory of the false conclusion.

Let it be the case that A is true of B because of middle term C. Now, the C–B premise must be affirmative for there to be a syllogism; clearly, then, this must always be true, since it cannot be distorted. But A–C will be false, since it is distortion in this premise that produces the answer opposite of the true one.

The same happens if the middle term is taken from another "chain." Take a case where D is included in A, as part in whole, and is predicated of all B. The D–B premise must stay as it is and distortion occur in the other; the minor will always be true, the major false. This type of error is generally similar to that produced when the "right" middle is used.

If the proof is not drawn via the right middle, both premises must be false when the middle is subordinate to A and not true of any B. The contradictories of the true premises have to be taken, for a conclusion to be made; if they are taken in this way, both are false. Take the case where A is true of all D and D not true of any B. If these premises are distorted, a false conclusion will ensue, and both premises will be false.

When the middle (i.e., D) is not subordinate to A, the A–D premise will be true, the D–B false. A–B will be true, because D is not included in A, by definition; and D–B will be false, because, if it were true, so, too, would be the conclusion. That, however, is in fact false.

When there is error through use of the *second figure,* it is not possible for both premises to be wholly false. When B is subordinate to A, it is not possible for something to be true of all one *and* not true of any of the other. One premise, however, is false; it can be either, indifferently. Let us take a case where C is true of A and of B. If it is supposed that C is true of A but not of B, the C–A premise will be true and the other false. Conversely, if we suppose that C is true of B but not of A, C–B will be true and the other false.

We have now explained when and how it happens that false negative conclusions are drawn. In the case of a false affirmative conclusion, if the "right" middle term is used, it is not possible for both premises to be false. The C–B premise must stay as it is if there is to be a conclusion at all, as was said before. Therefore, the A–C premise will always be false, since the distortion occurs in this one.

The same applies if the middle term is taken from another "chain," as was stated to be true of false negative conclusions too. The D–B premise must remain as is, the A–D suffer distortion; and the error resembles the one above.

Where there is a false conclusion *not* via the right middle, if D is subordinate to A, that premise will be true and the other false; it is possible for A to be true of many things, which are not subordinate to one another. If D is not subordinate to A, clearly this premise (D–A) will always be false (it is put affirmatively), whereas D–B˘ may be either true or false. There is nothing to prevent A not being true of any D and D being true of all B. As an example, no science is animal and all music is science. Equally, A may be true of no D and D of no B.

We have now explained the various ways in which false conclusions are drawn, whether the extreme terms are related by a middle or not.

18. Clearly, if there is a loss of any of the senses, there must also be a failure in knowledge, which cannot now be acquired. We learn either by induction or demonstration. Demonstration works from universals and induction from particulars, and it is impossible to see the universal except by induction. (Induction can be used to make known to a student even so-called abstracted properties. It can show that they are true of a class as such, even though they have no separate existence of their own.) To resume: finally, induction is impossible without the senses. Individual, particular, things are the sphere of the senses, since they cannot be known scientifically. They cannot be known from universals without induction; and they cannot be known by induction without sense perception.

19. Every syllogism has three terms. The affirmative type can show that A is true of C because A is true of B and B of C. In the negative type, one premise asserts that something is true of something else, the other negates the "something else" of the other extreme.

It is clear that these are the principles, the so-called hypotheses, of proof. If these are assumed, a conclusion must follow—e.g., that A is true of C through B as middle term, and A of B through some other middle, and B of C in the same way.

If our proof is merely dialectical, based on popular opinion, clearly we need only ensure that the premises of the conclusion should be the most plausible there are.

As a result, even if A and B do not in fact have a middle term, but are thought to have, a proof on this assumption is dialectically sound. But for the purpose of truth, we must use what really is the case; and there are in fact things that are predicated of others not accidentally. Here is an example. We say "that white thing is a man," which is different from saying "the man is white." In the former, the white thing is a man because white is accidental to man; in the latter, the man is white not because he is something else but because he is man. Therefore, there are such things as attributes essential to subjects.

Let there be a term C which is not attributable to anything else but has B directly true of it, without a middle. Again, let E be true of F directly, and F of B. Does this series have to stop, or can it proceed to infinity?

(i) Again, if a term A has no essential predicate, but is directly true of T, T of F, and F of B, does this series, too, have to stop, or can it also proceed to infinity? There is this much difference between the two cases. In the former case, is it possible, after starting from a term that is not attributable to another but has a term attributed to it, to proceed upwards to infinity? In the latter, is it possible to investigate downwards, seeing whether there is a procession to infinity, after starting with a term that is attributed to another but has no other attributed to it?

(ii) Another question is whether there can be an infinity of middle terms, if the extremes are fixed. An example is where A is true of C through B as middle, and there are other terms middle to B and to A, and still others middle to these. Can this continue ad infinitum, or is it impossible? This is the same question as whether demonstration proceeds to infinity—whether everything is demonstrable; or are there terms that touch directly?

(iii) The same question arises with regard to negative conclusions and premises. If A is not true of any B, this will either be so directly or because there is a prior term of which A is not true. (For instance, C, which is true of all B.) There may be still another prior term D, true of all C. In this case, too, either there is an infinite series of prior terms or there is a stop.

The problem does not occur where the terms are mutually predicable, since there is no first or last subject. All the terms are on the same footing with each other, whether the subject has an infinite number of attributes, or both subjects and attributes are infinite in number. (Both were raised in i and ii above.) The exception occurs when the terms are convertible in different ways, by accident in one case and by true predication in the other.

20. It is clear that there cannot be an infinite number of middle terms if there is an upper and a lower limit to predication. By "upper" I mean that which is more universal; by "lower," that which is more particular. If, when A is predicated of C, there is an infinite number of middle B's, it is clear that predication, starting with A, can proceed indefinitely toward the lower limit, since there is an infinite number of middles before you reach C. There is also predication ad infinitum, starting from C, toward the upper limit, before arriving at A. If that is impossible, it is impossible for there to be an infinite number of middles between A and C.

It comes to the same thing even if it is maintained that some of the terms in the series A–B–C are touching, so that they are not middles, and that others cannot be found. Whatever B–term I take, there will either be or not be an infinite number of middles in the direction of A or C. It does not matter where the infinite number first starts, whether immediately (at A or C) or not, since the succeeding terms form an infinite series.

21. It is clear that there will be a limit in the case of negative demonstration, if there is an upper and a lower limit to affirmative demonstration. Let it be impossible

to proceed upwards ad infinitum from the last term (by
"last" I mean a term that is not itself attributable to
another, but has another term attributed to it); or downwards ad infinitum from the first to the last (and by
"first" I mean a term that is attributable to others, but
has no others attributed to it). If this view is right, there
will be limits to negative premises as well.

There are three ways of showing that something is not
the case. In the first case, the premises are that all C is
B and no B is A. With regard to C–B (and this is always
the case with the minor premise), we must be dealing
with immediates, since this premise is affirmative. In the
other premise, if there is another term (e.g., D prior to
B) of which A is not true, it must be the case that all B
is D. And if there is another term prior to D, this must
be true of all D. Therefore, since there is a limit in the
upper direction, there will also be a limit in the direction
of A (i.e., a limit to negative premises). There will be a
first term to which A is not attributable.

Next (in the second figure), the conclusion "no C is A"
depends on the premises "all A is B" and "no C is B."
If the negative premise is to be demonstrated, it is clear
that it may be shown in the first figure or in this one or
the third. The first has already been given, and we shall
now give the second. The proof will run like this: all B
is D, no C is D; therefore, no C is B, if B must have a
term attributed. Again, if it is to be the case that no C
is D, there is another term true of D that is itself not
true of C. Therefore, since there is a limit to predicating
affirmatively of a higher class, there will also be a limit
to the predicates denied.

This is the third figure: all B is A, some B is not C,
and, therefore, some C is not A. The negative premise
will be demonstrated either in the first two figures or in
this same figure. In the first two, there is a limit; in this
one, we shall take a case where E is B and some E is
not C. The conclusion, some B is not C, can be proved
in the same way. Since our assumption is that downward

predication also has a limit, there will be a limit to the number of premises with C as negative predicate.

It is clear that there will still be a limit, if we use not only one method of proof but all, taking now the first figure, now the second, now the third. The methods are limited in number, and limited things combined in limited ways must be limited.

It is clear that there is a limit to negative premises, if there is a limit in the case of affirmative premises. That this is the case can be shown by the following dialectical proof.

22. It is clear, in the case of predicates included in the essence of subjects, that if it is possible to give a definition or know the essence (and yet impossible to exhaust an infinite series), predicates included in the essence must be limited.

In general I put the case in this way. We can say (and be right in saying) "the white thing is walking," "that big thing is a piece of wood;" and, again, "the piece of wood is big," "the man is walking." There is a difference between the first two ways of speaking and the last two. When I say that "the white thing is a piece of wood," I am saying that something to which white is accidental is a piece of wood, *not* that whiteness is the thing underlying wood. It did not become wood through being essentially white or a particular kind of white, so that it is not white except accidentally.

But when I say "the piece of wood is white," I do not mean that there is something else white that has the accidental property of being wood. That would be the case if I said "the musical thing is white"; for in this example I mean that "man, who has the accidental property of being musical, is white." No, the wood is, here, the underlying thing, the subject of change (i.e., to white), either as wood essentially, or as a particular piece of wood.

If we are to make rules, the latter way of speaking is

predication, whereas the former either is not predication
at all, or is predication not strictly but accidentally.
"White," then, is the predicate, and "wood" the subject
of which white is predicated. Let us take for granted
that a predicate is always predicated strictly, not accidentally, of its subject (this is required in demonstration).
Therefore, when a term is predicated of something, it is
an element included in the essence of the thing, or asserts of the thing quality, quantity, relation, doing, being-
done-to, place, or time.

Terms that indicate substance indicate what the thing
is (essence), or what particular thing it is. Terms that do
not indicate essence, but are asserted of a subject not
identical with themselves or a particular case of themselves, are "accidental attributes." This is the case when
"white" is asserted of "man." The point is that man is
not identical with white or an example of white, but with
animal, since man is a particular animal.

Terms that do not indicate substance must be predicated of another term as subject. There cannot be
"something white," which is not "something else" of
which white is predicated. The Platonic Ideas can be
dismissed: they are just sounds and noises; and even if
there are such things, they are irrelevant, since demonstration deals with such predicates as I have mentioned
above.

A cannot be a quality of B and B of A: there cannot
be a quality of a quality. Counterpredication is impossible; we can correctly assert one term of the other, but
true counterpredication is not possible.

One possibility is that a counterpredicated term will
be asserted as essence—i.e., either genus or differentia—
of its predicate. It has been shown that such predications
are not infinite, neither to the upper nor to the lower
limit. I mean, in series such as man is biped, biped is
animal, animal is, etc., and also in the series predicating
animal of man, man of Callias, and Callias of something
else. All such essence can be defined; but it is not possi-

ble for thought to exhaust an infinite series. Therefore, there is no infinite series, neither up nor down, since it is impossible to define an essence that has an infinite number of predicates. Terms, then, will not be counter-predicated as the genera of each other. If they are, we shall end with the essence being identical with a case of the essence.

Nor is it possible for a quality to be predicated of a quality (or any other category to be predicated of itself), except accidentally. All such things are accidents and are predicated of essences. Nor will there be an infinite number of terms in the upward direction. The predicate of a thing indicates a quality, quantity, etc., or the elements in the essence. These last are finite, and so, too, are the kinds of categories, which indicate quality, quantity, relation, doing, being-done-to, place, or time.

It is our assumption that, in predication, one term is predicated of another and that predicates that do not indicate an essence are not predicated of each other. All such are attributes, some essential and some not; we say that all these are predicated of some underlying thing, and that an attribute is not an underlying thing. We do not count as an attribute anything that gets its name without being something else first; an attribute is predicated of another term and this of another.

Therefore, there will be neither an upward nor a downward infinite series of single predications. The terms of which attributes are predicated are the elements of what a thing is, and these are finite; and, in the upward direction, there are these elements and their attributes, both of which are finite. Therefore, there must be a term A of which B_1 is directly predicated, and B_2 of B_1; this series must have a limit: there must be a term C, which is not predicated of anything prior to B_2 and which has nothing prior predicated of it.

This is one way of proof; I now give another. Predications that depend on prior predications can be demonstrated. Where things can be demonstrated, we cannot

be in a better relation to those things than if we know
them; and we cannot know them without demonstration.
If A is known to us via terms BCD, and if we neither
know BCD nor are in a better relation to them than if
we did know, a fortiori we shall not know A, knowledge
of which is mediated by BCD. Therefore, if it is possible
to know by demonstration in the strict sense, not merely
as a result of a set of premises or hypothetically, there
must be a limit to intermediate predication. If there is
no limit, but there is always a higher term than the one
taken, everything will be demonstrable; and, since it is
impossible to exhaust an infinite, we shall not know by
demonstration what is demonstrable. And if we are not
in a better relation to things than if we knew them, it
will not be possible to know by demonstration in the
strict sense, but only hypothetically.

These arguments would do as dialectical proofs of our
view. The following will show more briefly and analyti-
cally that it is not possible for there to be an upward or
downward infinite series of predicates in the demonstrative sciences, with which our inquiry is concerned. Demonstration deals with attributes that are essential to
things. "Essential" has two senses: essential attributes
are (1) those that are included in the definition of the
subject and (2) those that have their subjects included
in their definition. Odd (or even) in relation to number
is an example of (2). Odd belongs to number, and number itself belongs in the definition of odd. Again, (1)
plurality or divisibility is included in the definition of
number.

Neither kind of essential attribute can be infinite. The
terms cannot be infinite when they are related as odd is
to number. This would mean that something else, to
which odd belonged, would be included in odd. If this
is the case, then number will be the ultimate thing, included in all the terms that belong to it. Therefore, since
it is not possible for there to be an infinite number of
attributes included in a single subject, there will also be
no infinity in the upward series. Besides, in the ultimate

subjects—e.g., number—all the attributes must be included, and number must be included in them. The terms, therefore, will be convertible, not wider than their predecessors.

Nor is there an infinite series of attributes that are included in the definition of their subjects; in that case, definition would be impossible. Therefore, if all predicates are essential and there is not an infinite number of them, there will be a limit in the upward series and also in the downward series.

If this is the case, then the intermediates between two extremes must always be limited. If so, it is now clear that there must be principles of demonstration and that not everything is demonstrable. (See Chapter 3 where we quoted this view.) The point is that if there are principles, it is not the case that everything is demonstrable, or that it is possible to proceed ad infinitum. If either of these alternatives were true, it would mean that there would never be an immediate, indivisible relation between terms; everything would be divisible. But conclusions are proved not by adding a term, but by interposing a term between two others; if this can go on to infinity, it will be possible for there to be an infinite number of middles between two terms. Yet, this is impossible if there is a limit both to upward and to downward predication; and that there is a limit we have shown, first by dialectical methods and second by analytic proof.

23. It follows from what has been said that if the same term (A) is true of two others (e.g., C and D), when these terms can be predicated of each other either not at all or not in all instances, then A will not always be true of them by virtue of a common term. The isosceles and the scalene triangle have the property of "angles equal to two right angles" by virtue of a common term. (They have this attribute by virtue of their having the same kind of figure, not by virtue of their difference.)

This, however, is not always the case. Let us suppose

that B is the term by virtue of which A is true of C and of D. Now (if there is always a common middle), B will be true of C and D by virtue of another common term, and so on; the result would be an infinity of terms between two extremes, which is impossible. It is not the case that there must always be a common term by virtue of which a term is true of two others, since there are immediate premises. But if a common term is to be an essential attribute, the terms must be in the same class and derived from the same premises; it is not possible to transfer conclusions from one class to another.

Clearly, too, if A is true of B and there is a middle term, it is possible to demonstrate that A is true of B. The elements of the proof are identical with the middle terms, and of the same number. By elements we mean the immediate premises, either all of them or those that are universal.

If there is no middle, there is no demonstration possible. This is the path to the first principles.

Similarly, if A is not true of B, demonstration is possible when there is either a middle term or a term, prior to B, of which A is not true. If not, there is no demonstration; we have, instead, a principle. The elements are identical with the middle terms, since the premises containing these are the principles of the demonstration. There are some indemonstrable principles of the type A is B or A is true of B; similarly, there are others of the type A is not B or A is not true of B. Some principles will affirm, and some deny, that something is the case.

When we have to demonstrate, we must take a term directly true of B. Let us call this C, and say that A is directly true of C. So, as we continue, no premise or attribute "outside" A is included in the proof. What happens is that the interval is constantly being filled, until an indivisible premise is reached, a unit. A unit is obtained when we reach an immediate premise; a single premise, in the strict sense, means an immediate premise. As in other matters, a principle is simple, but not the same in all cases:

in weight the principle is the mina, in music the quarter tone, and so on. Similarly, in syllogism the unit is an immediate premise, and in demonstrative science it is the mind (which grasps an immediate truth). Therefore, in affirmative syllogisms, nothing falls "outside" the major term.

In negative syllogisms also there is a case where nothing falls "outside" the major term. An example is if A (the major) is denied of B through a middle C. The required premises are "all B is C" and "no C is A." (If we have to show that no C is A, a middle term must be taken, and this procedure will always be the same.)

If we have to show that D is not predicable of E by the premises "all D is C" and "no E is C," the middle will never fall "outside" E. E is that (the minor) of which the attribute D is to be denied in the conclusion.

In the third case, the middle will never be "outside" the subject or the attribute denied.

24. Demonstration is universal or particular, affirmative or negative. The question is, which kind is better? A similar question can be put about proof by demonstration and proof by *reductio ad absurdum*. First, let us consider universal and particular demonstration; after answering that, we can go on to proof by demonstration and proof by *reductio ad absurdum*.

It may appear to some that particular demonstration is superior, if we look at things in the following way. A superior proof is that which gives us superior knowledge, which is the proper function of demonstration. We have superior knowledge when we know something through itself, rather than through something else. Take the case of the musician Coriscus; knowing that "Coriscus is musical" is superior to knowing just that "man is musical." (The same applies in other cases.) But universal demonstration shows that something else, not that thing itself, is the case. It shows that an isosceles triangle has an attribute, not as isosceles triangle, but because it is true of triangle. If knowing something directly is superior, and this is produced by particular rather than by universal demonstration, particular proof will be superior.

Secondly, there is no universal as a thing apart from particular cases. Universal demonstration, however, leads people to suppose that there actually is something—viz., the universal—by virtue of which a particular is shown to be the case. People are led to think that some such body does exist, a substantial thing: e.g., that there are such things as "triangle," "shape," and "number," apart from particular triangles, shapes, and numbers. Now demonstration about what really is is superior to demonstration about that which has no reality; and demonstration that does not lead to error is superior to that that does. But this last is the characteristic of universal demonstration, which is alleged to make "proofs" like the following, with regard to proportions: "Everything of a certain kind will be proportional; this is a kind that is neither line nor number nor solid nor plane surface, but something apart from all these." If this is universal demonstration, it is less concerned with what really is, and it makes people have false opinions; it will, therefore, be inferior to particular proof.

Our answer is, to begin with, that the first objection above is no more true of universal than of particular demonstration. An isosceles triangle has angles equal to two right angles, but this is not true of isosceles as such, but of triangle as such. Knowing that an isosceles triangle has this attribute, as compared with knowing that triangle has it, is inferior; there is less knowledge of what the attribute belongs to as such. In general, if an attribute is not true of triangle as such, but is "shown" to be, that will not be proof; but if it is true, the man who knows that the attribute is true of the subject as such has superior knowledge. Triangle is the wider term; it has a single definition, and it is not ambiguous. Since "having angles equal to two right angles" is true of all triangles, it is not triangle as isosceles, but isosceles as triangle, that has this attribute. Therefore, the man who knows the universal has superior knowledge as compared with the man who knows the particular: superior knowledge of how an attribute is true of a subject as such. Universal proof is, therefore, superior to particular.

If the universal is a single definition and nonambiguous, it will be even more real than some of the particulars. Universals include things that do not perish, whereas particulars do tend to perish.

We are not forced to suppose that there actually is one thing, apart from the particulars, merely because the term has one meaning; any more than in cases where the term indicates quality, relation, or doing, and not substance. If such a supposition is made, it is not the fault of the proof but of the student!

Proof is a syllogism that demonstrates the cause, the reason why; and the universal has more to do than the particular with the cause. Where an attribute belongs essentially to a subject, the latter is a cause to itself; the universal is primary and essential and is, therefore, the cause. Universal proof is, therefore, superior, since it has more to do with the cause and the reason why.

Besides, our search for the reason why goes to the point when we think we know; i.e., when it is no longer the case that there is some further thing responsible for the process or fact studied. The ultimate reached in this way is the limit and end of the problem. An example is the question "Why did he come?" In order to get some money, which, in turn, was to pay a debt, which was to avoid breaking the law. If we proceed in this way, we come to a point at which there is no further cause or reason why. We say then that the point so reached is the final reason why he came (or was, or came into being), and at that stage we know par excellence why the man came.

This is true of all causes and reasons why, and this is how we come to have complete knowledge in the case of final causes. And therefore, in other cases too, we have full knowledge at the stage when there is no further reason for something being the case. When we know that "the interior angles are equal to two right angles because it is an isosceles triangle," there is still to be supplied the reason for isosceles, viz., triangle, and the reason for triangle, viz., figure with straight lines. But if there is no further reason for this, that is when we have full knowledge; the very point when the universal is reached. Universal proof is, therefore, superior.

The more particular proof becomes, the more it tends toward things unlimited, whereas universal proof tends to what is simple and limited. Things are not objects of knowledge so far as they are unlimited, but only so far as they are limited; therefore, things tend to be objects of knowledge so far as they are universal, rather than so far as they are particular. Universals, then, are more demonstrable than particulars; and demonstration is fuller when things are more demonstrable, since correlatives increase together. Universal proof is, therefore, superior, since it is fuller.

Proof that gives knowledge of A and B is preferable to that which leads to knowledge of A alone. Knowing the universal also gives knowledge of the particular, but knowing the particular does not involve knowing the universal. That is another reason why universal proof is superior.

Another argument is this: there is an ever higher degree of universal proof as the middle term of a demonstration draws nearer to the first principle. The nearest point is the immediate premises, which is the principle. Proof from the principle is more exact than proof that is not; and, therefore, the more connection there is with the principle, the more exact the proof. Universal proof will thus be superior. Take the case where one has to show that A is true of D by the middle terms B and C. Since B is the higher term, proof by B as middle will be more universal.

Some of the above arguments are dialectical. The fullest proof that universal demonstration is best is as follows. When we have the prior of two premises, there is a sense in which we also know the posterior one: we have knowledge of it potentially. If we know that every triangle has angles equal to two right angles, we also know in a sense—potentially—that this is true of the isosceles, even if we do not know that the isosceles is a triangle. But knowing the posterior premise does not mean knowing the universal, either potentially or actually. The universal is known by mind, but the particular ends up as sense perception.

25. This is enough to show that universal proof is superior to particular. The following arguments will show that affirmative proof is superior to negative.

Where there are several ways of demonstrating the same thing, the best is that which depends on the fewest suppositions, hypotheses, or premises. If these are all equally well known, using fewer premises will give knowledge more quickly, which is preferable.

The reason for saying that demonstration from fewer premises is superior can be put in this universal form. Let us take two cases, assuming that the middle terms are equally well known and that the prior middles in the proof are better known than the posterior. Let us assume that in (1) A is true of E by the middle terms B, C, and D, and that in (2) A is true of E by the middles F and G. Then, knowing that A is true of D in (1) is of the same standing as knowing that A is true of E in (2). The reason is that, in (1) "A is true of D" is prior to, and better known than, "A is true of E." This conclusion is demonstrated by means of the former as premise, which is, therefore, more certain than the result. Demonstration by fewer premises is, therefore, superior. Both kinds (affirmative and negative) of demonstration use three terms and two premises. But affirmative proof assumes that something is the case, whereas negative proof assumes both that something is the case and that something is not. Therefore, it makes use of more elements and is inferior.

It has already been shown that it is not possible for there to be a syllogism if both premises are negative; if one is negative, the other must be affirmative. The following observation should also be made. When a syllogism is developed, there must be an increase in the number of affirmative premises. However, there cannot be more than one *negative* premise in a "total syllogism." Let us take a case where no B is A and all B is C. If we have to "develop" both premises, we must insert a middle. Let D be the middle term to A and B, and E the middle to B and C. E, then, will be affirmed of both terms, but D will stand affirmatively to B and negatively to A. D is affirmed of all B, but it must be the case that no D is A. There is therefore only one negative premise: A–D.

The same is true of the other syllogisms. It is always the case, with regard to the terms of an affirmative syllogism, that the middle is affirmative in relation to both. But in the negative syllogism the middle must be negative only in relation to one of the terms, so that this is the only negative premise, the rest being affirmative. Now, the ground of a conclusion is better known and more certain than the conclusion. Since the negative premise is shown by the affirmative, *not* the affirmative by the negative, the affirmative premise, being prior, better known, and more certain, will be superior.

The principle of a syllogism is a universal, immediate premise. In affirmative proof, this is affirmative; in negative proof, the universal premise denies. The affirmative is prior to and better known than the negative, since the negative is made known by the affirmative, and the affirmative is prior in the same way that "that which is" is prior to "that which is not." Therefore, the principle of affirmative proof is superior to the principle of negative proof; and the method that uses superior principles is itself superior. Also, the affirmative has more resemblance to the principle, since a negative proof is impossible without it.

26. Since affirmative demonstration is superior to negative, it is clearly superior to *reductio ad absurdum* as well. One must be sure about the difference between negative proof and *reductio*. Let us suppose that no B is A and that all C is B; it must follow that no C is A. When these assumptions are made, there is a negative proof, which *shows* that A is not true of C.

But *reductio* works in the following way. If we have to prove that A is not true of B, we must assume that it is true, and that B is true of C, from which it follows that A is true of C. But this, we must suppose, is known and agreed to be impossible. Therefore, it is not possible for A to be true of B. If it is agreed that B is true of C, it is impossible for A to be true of B.

The order of the terms is the same in both kinds. The difference is, which negative proposition is better known? That is, is it better known that A is not true of B or that A is not true of C? When the conclusion is the better known—that A is not true of C—we have *reductio;* but when the premise—no B is A—is better known, we have negative demonstration. The A–B premise (negative) is prior to the negative conclusion—no C is A. The point is that the elements of the conclusion are prior to the conclusion. In our example "A is not true of C" is the conclusion, whereas "A is not true of B" is a premise that leads to the conclusion. (It is not the case that a negative result by *reductio* is a conclusion, nor that the steps to the result are premises. The truth is that the premises of a syllogism are related as whole to part or part to whole; and this relationship is not exhibited by the A–C and A–B premises in the case of *reductio* above.)

To sum up, the superior form is the one that proceeds from the prior and the better known. Both kinds (negative proof and *reductio*) obtain their conclusion as a result of something not being the case; but the former develops from what is prior, whereas *reductio* works from what is posterior. Therefore, negative proof will be absolutely superior to *reductio;* and it follows that the superior to negative proof—i.e., affirmative—will be better than *reductio.*

27. A science is more exact than, and prior to, another when it studies the fact and the reason, not just the fact apart from the reason.

A science that studies properties not as contained in a subject is prior to one that treats them in that relationship. Arithmetic is prior to harmonics.

A science that works with fewer principles is prior to one that requires additional principles: arithmetic is prior to geometry. By "additional" I mean that, while in arithmetic a unit is a substance without position, in geometry a point is a substance *with* position. This is an addition.

28. A single science is one concerned with a single class of things, the compounds made up of the basic elements of the class, and the parts or essential properties of these. Sciences differ when their principles are derived from different things, or when the principles of one are not derived from the principles of the other. It becomes plain that we are dealing with a single science when we arrive at indemonstrable premises, since these must be of the same class as the conclusions. And if the conclusions developed from the first premises are homogeneous, this in turn shows that the first premises are in the same class.

29. There can be several proofs of the same conclusion. This happens when we take a nonadjacent middle from the same series, e.g., if we prove A–B by taking C, D, and F; but this can also be achieved by taking a middle from another series. Let A stand for changing, D for being moved, B for feeling pleasure, and C for coming to a gentle state. Now, we can truly predicate D of B and A of D, since a man who feels pleasure is being moved and that which is being moved is changing. Again, A can be predicated of C and C of B, since a man who feels pleasure comes to a gentle state and coming to a gentle state is changing. The proofs, therefore, use different middles, not from the same series. However, neither middle can be universally deniable of the other, since there must be something of which both are true. (One should also consider in how many ways the same result can be proved in the other figures.)

30. There cannot be a demonstrative science of what happens by chance. A chance result is neither necessarily nor generally so. It is neither of these, something apart; whereas demonstration deals with one or the other. Every conclusion is proved by premises that are either necessarily or generally so. If the premises are necessary, so is the conclusion; if they are general, then the conclusion has the same character. Therefore, since a chance result is neither necessary nor general, it cannot be demonstrated.

31. We cannot obtain true knowledge by perception. Even if perception (as a faculty) is of qualities, not just of particular things, still, when we perceive, we must perceive a particular thing in a particular place now. But the universal, what is true in all cases, cannot be perceived, since it is not a particular thing now. If it were, it would not be universal. We mean by universal that which is always and everywhere the case. Since demonstrations are universal, and universals cannot be perceived, it is clear that scientific knowledge cannot be obtained by perceiving. And, clearly, if we could perceive that triangles have angles equal to two right angles, we would still look for proof. We would not have knowledge, though some people say so. Perception must be perception of particular things, but knowledge is getting to know the universal.

Even if we were on the moon and saw the earth cut-

ting off the sun's light, we would not know the cause of
the eclipse. We would have a perception—"there is an
eclipse now"—but we would not know the reason why.
Perceiving does not have to do with the universal.

It is, of course, true that as a result of seeing the same
thing happen many times we would look for the universal
and have a proof; the universal becomes clear from a number of particular instances. The universal is highly esteemed because it makes the cause obvious. In the case of
things that have a cause other than themselves, the universal is more highly esteemed than perceptions and intuitional
grasp. (The account of the ultimate premises is different.)

Clearly, then, it is impossible to have knowledge of a
demonstrable truth just by perceiving, unless one were
to say that perceiving means knowing by demonstration.
But there are some cases in which our not knowing can
be referred to a failure in perception. There are cases
where we would not have to inquire, if we had seen the
phenomenon; not that we have knowledge by the mere
act of seeing, but that we would have come to the universal as the result of seeing. If we saw the pores in the
glass and the light traversing them, the reason for the
thing being set on fire would be plain. We would see
each case separately, and grasp at the same time that it
must be true in all cases.

32. It is impossible for there to be the same first principles for all syllogisms. Here is a dialectical proof. Some
conclusions are true and others false. Even though we
can draw a true conclusion from false premises, this can
happen only once. Suppose that A is truly predicated of
C and that the middle term B is false—that is, A is not
true of B nor B of C. If we take middle terms and premises to prove those premises (A–B, B–C), they will be
false, because every false conclusion is drawn from false
premises, whereas true conclusions are drawn from true
premises; and true and false are different.

Secondly, even false conclusions do not come from the

same first principles. There are false conclusions that are contraries and incompatible, as the following pairs show: "justice is injustice, justice is cowardice"; "man is horse, man is cow"; "equality is more, equality is less."

However, in the light of what we have established, consider the following. Not even all true conclusions have the same principles. Many of them have principles that differ in class and do not apply to other things. Units, for instance, are nonapplicable to points, since units have no position but points do. They would have to be applied as middle terms or as related to the major or minor terms; or they would have some of the other terms between them and others outside.

Nor can it be the case that any of the common principles will be the premises for all conclusions. I mean, for instance, a principle like the law of excluded middle. There are different classes of things, and some are quantities and some qualities only; conclusions are shown by means of the common principles working *in conjunction with* such things.

The principles are not much fewer than the conclusions. The principles are the premises, and the premises are formed either by adding or interposing a term.

Also, conclusions are not limited in number, but terms are; and some principles are necessary, whereas others are contingent.

On this line of thought, there cannot be a limited number of the same principles, since the conclusions are unlimited. But suppose it is said that "the same principles" means something else. If this means that "geometry has the same, or identical, principles" (and similarly with arithmetic and medicine), what else is being said except that the sciences do have principles? It is ridiculous to say that they are the same just because they are self-identical. Everything can be made identical in that way.

Nor can the attempt to make all conclusions have the same principles mean that any conclusion requires all the premises together. That is too simpleminded. It is not so in the mathematical sciences, which are plain to see, nor is it possible in analysis. The immediate premises are the principles, and a fresh conclusion is reached only by adding a new immediate premise.

If it be argued that the primary, immediate premises are the principles, there is one of these to each class.

But if it is not true that any conclusion requires all the premises, nor that different sciences have different principles, the only possibility is for the principles of all things to be of the same class, though different conclusions will require different premises. But, clearly, this too is impossible: we have already shown that different classes have different principles. There are two kinds of principle, the premises and the subject matter. The premises are common but the subject matter is peculiar to itself (I mean things like number and magnitude).

33. There is a difference between the objects of science and science itself on the one hand, and the objects of opinion and opinion itself, on the other. Science is universal, being attained through necessary premises, and what is necessary does not admit of being other than it is. There are some things that, admittedly, are true and real, but it is possible for them to be different. Now, clearly, science is not concerned with such objects; if it were, that which can be different would be incapable of being different! Nor is intellectual grasp (which I call the starting point of science), or indemonstrable science, which takes up the immediate premise. The word "true" is used of "grasp," science, opinion, and the conclusions that these produce. The only possibility, therefore, is that opinion deals with what is true or false, and can be different.

Opinion amounts to taking an immediate premise, which is not necessary. This statement agrees with the facts, since opinion is a shifting thing, and so, too, is the object with which it deals. Besides, when we think that something cannot be different, we do not think that we have an opinion, we think that we have knowledge. But when we think that a fact may well vary, then we think that we have opinion;

for that is the kind of thing with which opinion deals, whereas it is science that deals with the necessary.

How does it come about that the same thing can be the object both of opinion and of knowledge? If we say that any object of knowledge can be an object of opinion, why will opinion not then be knowledge? A man who knows and a man who has opinion will work right through the middle terms to the immediate premises; thus, if the former knows, so does the man who has opinion. One can have opinion about the reason why, just as one can about the fact; and the reason why is the middle term.

That is the argument; we may answer as follows. If a man grasps the necessary truths in the same way that he grasps the definitions that mediate proof, he will have knowledge, not opinion. But if he takes them as true without thinking that they are essentially so, he will have opinion, not true knowledge. If he gets to his opinion through immediate premises, he will have opinion about the fact *and* the reason why; otherwise—that is, if he does not get to his opinion through immediate premises—he will have opinion about the fact only.

Opinion and knowledge do not have altogether the same object. It is the same object only in the sense in which true opinion and false opinion are about the same object. (The meaning that some people give to "true and false opinion have the same object" leads to very many absurdities, such as that the man who has false opinion does not have opinion at all.) "Same" has many meanings: there is one sense in which true and false opinion have the same object, whereas in another they do not. It is absurd to say that "the square root of 2 is a rational number" is a true opinion; but because it is with the same square root that both opinions deal, they are about the same object. Yet the essential meaning of the object, in respect to definition, is not the same in both cases.

Similarly, knowledge and opinion have the same object. Knowledge that something is "animal," say, means knowing that it cannot not be animal. Opinion, however, admits the possibility of its not being animal. Knowledge has it that "animal" is essentially predicable of "man," whereas opinion has it that "animal" is predicable of "man" but not essential. There is "the same object"— man—in both cases; but the manner of considering it is not the same.

It is clear from what we have said that the same thing cannot *simultaneously* be the object of opinion and of knowledge; for in that case, one would have to suppose that the same thing was both necessary and variable, which is impossible. Two different people can have knowledge and opinion about the same object in the sense outlined above; but the same person cannot. If he could, he would be supposing two things at once: (1) that man is *essentially* animal (the case where it is not possible for man not to be animal); and (2) that man is animal, but not essentially (the case where the attribute may or may not be true).

How everything else should be distributed among mind, intellectual grasp, science, art, practical sense and wisdom is more properly discussed under physics and ethics.

34. Quick-wittedness is a knack of seeing the middle term without taking time to think. If a man sees that the moon always has its bright side towards the sun, he shows quick-wittedness when he realizes at once the reason for this—namely, that the moon gets its light from the sun. Another example is if, upon seeing someone talking to a rich man, he realizes that he is borrowing money, or realizes that the reason why two people are friends, is that they have a common enemy. In these cases, that person has seen the extreme terms and immediately recognized the causes, the middle terms.

Let A stand for "the bright side towards the sun," B for "light from the sun," and C for moon; then, B is true of C and A of B, and it follows that A is true of C through B as the middle term.

PHYSICS

Introduction

"Physics" is the most misleading of the traditional titles of Aristotle's works and topics. Metaphysics, ethics, politics, the soul, the art of poetry, the parts of animals—all these are immediately intelligible in senses very close to those that Aristotle himself had in mind when he wrote about them. But many of the topics that are covered by Aristotle's conception of physics have ceased to be of interest to us, and those that retain their importance would now be treated as philosophical rather than as scientific questions.

The Greek word *phusike* means "science of nature," and Aristotle's treatise on this subject deals with those substances that are intermediate between the pure forms that are studied by "theology" or "first philosophy" and the abstractions that are the subject matter of mathematics. The former are separately existing substances that are not susceptible to change; the latter are also exempt from change, but they have no existence independent from that of the substances from whose properties they are abstracted. Physics is concerned with things that are both separately existing and susceptible to change, and that means primarily what are still called *physical* bodies. If we speak of physics as the science of matter and motion, we come as near as is possible to finding a description that will fit both Aristotle's conception and that of the physicists of our own time.

In its fullest sense, the science of nature covers the topics dealt with in the biological works as well as in the *Physics*, but in this latter work Aristotle treats of the subject matter of physics in its most general terms. It is in the mode of treatment rather than in the sphere of operation that Aristotle's physics differs from work that would now be called by the same name. It is in this treatise that he derives the categories according to which we are to understand and arrange the things and processes that our experience of the natural world presents to us. Since knowledge is primarily of causes, a very important section of the work is Book II, in which we find the fullest continuous account of Aristotle's doctrine of the four causes. The present selection is confined to Book II.

Before we go on to consider the doctrine of the causes, it will be advisable to mention some points that Aristotle makes in the first book and that are necessary as background for the understanding of what he says in Book II. Physics is concerned with change and the changeable. What Aristotle shows in Book I is that the description of the occurrence of any change requires the specification of three elements. There must be a particular form *into which* there is a change, and a corresponding privation or lack that is supplied by the change to the new form: that which changes its color to red must hitherto have been not-red. But Aristotle's most important point is that change requires an underlying *something* that is the *subject* of the change and that is characterized first by the absence, then by the presence, of that form that, in the process of change, the subject comes to have. The word "subject" is a Latin form of the Greek word *hypokeimenon* (underlying), which Aristotle uses in the *Physics* for the stable element that persists through change. Here again we recognize the power of the subject-predicate form of assertion over the formulation of the categories within which Aristotle interprets the world; and here again, because the subject-predicate form is so natural and fundamental in our language, the resulting doctrine turns out to be an illuminating systematization of the concepts with which we habitually order our experience.

It was suggested in the General Introduction that Aristotle's four causes constitute the framework within which we ask and answer questions about the character, the origin, and the structure of the substances we find in the world. Aristotle's account of them is much clearer than is his exposition of some of his other doctrines, but a general summary may be helpful. The doctrine can most simply and clearly be explained by describing the causes of a particular example of each of the two main types of substance in whose causation Aristotle is especially interested—natural substances, such as plants and animals, and products of human skill, such as houses and statues. It will be convenient to take a human artifact first, because the whole language of causation is so well adapted to the description of human skill and its operation that it was very probably derived from that context, and extended to natural processes by a kind of metaphor.

Consider, then, a house, a typical product of human skill. It is *made of* bricks and mortar, wood and stone, which constitute its matter, or *material cause.* (Aristotle's word for "matter" literally means "timber," one of the most familiar building materials in both ancient and modern times: unless we remember this, we may not appreciate how concrete and familiar are the concepts with which he is working here.) These materials are arranged according to a definite plan and put into a definite order, which is the form or shape or *formal cause;* it is this that distinguishes the finished house from the casual aggregation of raw materials with which the builder starts. The operations of the builder are the *efficient cause,* or "moving cause," by which the form is imposed on the relatively unformed materials. (The materials are only *relatively* unformed. For example, a brick is the finished product of a brickmaker. Pure, unformed "prime" matter is an abstraction, not found in the actual world.) The end or *final cause* is the purpose aimed at by the whole operation—namely, that of protecting men and their possessions from the effects of weather conditions.

It may easily be seen in this example that the formal, final, and efficient causes are closely connected in the way that has been explained in the General Introduction. The form in which the building materials are arranged is determined by the purpose that the finished house is to serve. Although we usually speak of the builder as the efficient cause of the house, it is the builder qua builder—that is to say, the *art* of building—that is the cause; and to possess the art of building is to have in mind the *form* that must be imposed on the given materials if a house is to be produced.

The coalescence of the three nonmaterial causes is even clearer in the case of a natural substance, say, a particular man. The *end* is the condition of being a mature specimen of the human species—that is to say, having the specific *form* of humanity. This form can be imposed on the matter provided by the female parent only by a father who has himself reached that maturity and who therefore himself instantiates that form.

The account of chance and spontaneity serves to emphasize further the primacy of this teleological framework in Aristotle's understanding of the structure of our knowledge and of the world that is its object. Events that are said to happen by chance (as in Aristotle's example of the man who goes to the marketplace to buy something and happens to meet somebody who owes him money) or spontaneously (as in the example of the generation of small organisms in mud or in decaying flesh) are explained by the privation of the modes of causation that *normally* bring about events of the types in question. The generation of organisms is normally the result of natural purposive action. The collecting of debts is normally the result of deliberate human action; the exceptional cases serve to stress the generality of the rule.

It is fashionable to criticize Aristotle for carrying the teleological account of nature too far, and it is true that teleological explanation was overworked and misapplied by many of his successors in the investigation of nature. But it is undeniable that the teleological framework is useful as a means of ordering and arranging a wide diversity of natural phenomena, especially in biology. Biologists still have difficulty with the notions of form and adaptation. They have not so far succeeded, even if they ever can succeed, in making their science conform to the quantitative paradigm of physics. It is one thing to say that we must now make an effort to achieve this liberation, and quite another to blame Aristotle for all the failures of his successors.

Sir David Ross has rebuked Aristotle for using the notion of an *unconscious* purpose in nature. But it is surely unduly restrictive to deny the use of this concept outside the sphere of the conscious purposes of persons. Although teleology can indeed be carried too far, it remains true that many natural phenomena are easily and plausibly described in teleological terms; and this is a sufficient justification for Aristotle's attempt to produce a single framework of explanation within which both human life and the natural world could be understood.

Book II

.   .   .

1. Of the things that exist, some exist by nature, others through other causes. Those that exist by nature include animals and their parts, plants, and simple bodies like earth, fire, air, and water—for of these and suchlike things we do say that they exist by nature. All these obviously differ from things that have not come together by nature; for each of them has in itself a source of movement and rest. This movement is in some cases movement from place to place, in others it takes the form of growth and decay, in still others of qualitative change. But a bed or a garment or any other such kind of thing has no natural impulse for change—at least, not insofar as it belongs to its own particular category and is the product of art; these things do, however, have such an impulse accidentally, through being made of stone or earth or some mixture of these materials, and insofar as nature is the principle and cause of the motion or rest of the thing in which it is present primarily and by virtue of itself, as opposed to accidentally. (When I say "as opposed to accidentally," I am thinking of the kind of case in which a man might be the cause of his own good health because he was a doctor. It could still be true that it was not his own good health that showed him to be a doctor, but that it was an accident that he was at one and the same time a doctor and in good health; which is why these attributes are sometimes found independently of each other.) It is the same with everything that is produced: none of them has the source, or principle, of its production in itself. Some of them have it in other, external things, as houses do and all manufactured objects; others have the source in themselves, but not by virtue of their being themselves, which is the case with all things that are accidentally their own causes. "Nature," then, is what we have said; and all those things are "natural" that have a source of that kind.

Each of these things is substance; for each is a substratum, and nature is always present in a substratum. Again, both they and the attributes that belong to them by virtue of their being themselves (such as upward motion, in the case of fire) exist "according to nature." For the upward motion of fire is not nature, nor has it a nature; but it exists "by nature" and "according to nature."

We have explained, then, what nature is, and what things exist by nature and according to nature. It would be absurd to try to show that nature exists; for, clearly, there are many things of the kind that we have been describing; and to demonstrate the evident by means of the obscure is the mark of a man who cannot judge what is and what is not in itself knowable. (It is, however, clear that it is possible for this to happen to a man; a man who was blind from birth might still argue about colors.) The result of such a procedure is that one is talking about mere names, without there being any object for one's thought.

Some people regard the nature and substance of things that exist by nature as being in each case the proximate element inherent in the thing, this being in itself unshaped; thus, the nature of a bed, for instance, would be wood, and that of a statue bronze. Antiphon produces as evidence of this the fact that if you were to bury a bed, and the moisture that got into it as it rotted gained enough force to throw up a shoot, it would be wood and not a bed that came into being. For his view is that its arrangement, according to the rules of an art, is an accidental attribute, whereas its substance is what remains permanently, and undergoes all these changes. Further, if each of these materials stands in this same relation to something else (as bronze and gold do to water, or bones and wood to earth, or as any of them that you could mention does to something), it is this something that will be their nature and substance. That is why some people say that the nature of things is fire, others that it is earth, still others that it is air or water; and it is also why some regard two or three of these as the nature of things, and others say that it is all of them. For whatever element or elements men have chosen, they have regarded it or them as constituting the whole of substance, all other things being just their qualities, dispositions, or states. Everything that is substance they regard as eternal, since it never changes from being what it is; all other things come into being and perish innumerable times.

That, then, is one way in which the term "nature" is used, as the proximate underlying matter of things that possess in themselves a principle of movement and change. But it is spoken of in another way too, as the shape of a thing, and the form that accords with its formula. Just as the term "art" is used of what is done according to an art and of what is artistic, so, too, the term "nature" is used of what accords with nature and is natural. In the one case, we would never say that what was merely a potential bed, but had not yet got the form of bed, conformed with art, nor would we admit that there was art there. It is the same with things that come together by nature; what is potentially flesh or bone does not yet have its own nature until it acquires the form that accords with the formula, by means of which we define flesh and bone; nor can it be said at this stage to exist by nature. So, in another way, nature is the shape and form of things that have a principle of movement in themselves—the form being only theoretically separable from the object in question. (The product of matter and form—man, for instance—is not nature, but does exist by nature.)

And, in fact, it is this form that is nature, rather than matter. A thing is always described as being itself at the time of its realization, rather than when it merely exists potentially. Further, man comes into being from man, even though a bed does not come into being from a bed. It is this latter fact that leads people to say that it is not the shape but the wood that is the bed's nature, since, so they say, if the bed were to put forth a shoot, it would be wood and not a bed that would appear. But even if the wood is in fact the thing's nature, nonetheless the shape is a thing's nature too: for man does come into being from man. Again, when the term "nature" is used to describe a process of coming into being, it is really the path to nature that is being referred to. For this process of nature is not analogous to the processes of medicine; there the process takes the art of medicine as its starting point, yet it is not a path to medicine, but is rather the path to health. The relation of the process of nature to nature itself is different from this. What comes into being naturally from something follows a natural course to something else; and what it becomes by nature is not what it started from, but the final state toward which it is moving. And, so, the shape is the real nature of the thing.

But shape and nature can be talked of in two senses, since in a way the privation is itself a form. But whether we can talk of privation as a contrary, where simple coming into being is concerned, is a question that we must look into later.

2. Now that we have defined the number of ways in which nature can be spoken of, we must look into the difference between the mathematician and the natural scientist. For natural bodies have plane surfaces, volumes, lengths, and points, although these are subjects of mathematical inquiry. We must also see whether astronomy is different from natural science or is a part of it. For it would be odd if it were the natural scientist's business to know what the sun and the moon are, and yet not to know anything of their essential attributes—the more so since all natural scientists plainly do inquire into the shape of the sun and moon, and into whether the earth and the universe are spherical or not.

Such attributes as these are studied by mathematicians as well as by natural scientists, but not by virtue of their being limits of natural bodies. The mathematician is not interested in them as attributes of whatever they are attributes of, and so he separates them. For these attributes can be conceptually separated from movement, without this separation making any difference or involving any false statement. This is what those who hold the theory of forms do too, although they do not realize what they are doing; for they separate natural things. These, however, are less susceptible to separation than the objects of mathematics, as becomes clear if one tries to define each of these two classes of objects together with their attributes. The odd, the even, the curved, the straight, or, again, number, line, and shape are all definable without reference to movement; but flesh, bone, and man are not; these latter terms are more like "snub-nosed" than like "curved." This is well illustrated by the more physical or natural of the mathematical sciences, such as optics, harmonics, or astronomy, which are in a way the converse of geometry. Whereas geometry is concerned with the physical line, but not qua physical, optics studies the mathematical line, but qua physical rather than qua mathematical.

Since the term "nature" is used in two ways, both of form and of matter, we must investigate it in the way in which we would investigate "snubness"—not ignoring matter, but not confining ourselves to it either. Here

another difficulty might be raised: there being two kinds
of nature, which is the natural scientist to study? Should
he study the product of both? If he does this, he must
study each of the two on its own as well. But is it or is
it not the business of the same science to study both? If
we look at the men of the past, we get the impression
that matter is what the natural scientist should study;
Empedocles and Democritus touched only very lightly
on form and essence. But it might be said that art imitates nature; and in art it is the business of one and the
same science to know the form as well as the matter, up
to a certain point. A doctor has to know about health,
and about the bile and phlegm in which health will be
present; a builder has to know the form of the house
that he is building, and also that its matter will be bricks
and wood; and it is the same with the other arts. Thus,
if art imitates nature, it will be the business of natural
science to study both kinds of nature.

Further, the end and purpose of a thing must be studied by the same science as studies the means to their
attainment. Nature is an end and purpose; for in the case
of things that are in continuous motion and have an end,
this end is their purpose. (It was this point that led the
poet to say, rather absurdly, that "he has met the end
for which he came to be." The absurdity of this lies in
the fact that it is not just any end that one seeks as a
purpose, but the best.) The arts, too, make their own
matter—some of them making it in the absolute sense,
others merely making it serviceable; and we make use
of all things on the assumption that all of them are there
to serve our purposes. (For we are in a way an end in
ourselves, too; the term "purpose" can be used in two
ways, as I have explained in my dialogue on philosophy.)
There are, in fact, two arts that control the matter and
possess knowledge: that of the man who uses the product and that of the man who directs its production. The
art of the user in a way involves the giving of directions
too; but there is this difference between the two: that

the art of the user involves knowledge of the form, whereas that of the director, concerned as it is with production, involves knowledge of the matter. The pilot knows the form of the rudder that he wants, and orders it; the producer knows what kind of wood it should be made of, and what movements are necessary for the process. Thus, in what has to do with art, we make our matter for the purpose of the job; in what has to do with nature, it is already there. Further, matter is a relative term; different forms have different kinds of matter.

How far, then, ought the natural scientist to know the form and the essence? Should it not be in the way that the doctor knows the sinew, or the smith his bronze? That is to say, he should know the purpose of each thing: and his knowledge has to do with things whose forms can be separated conceptually, but are in fact embedded in matter. For man generates man—but the sun does so, too. As to the state and nature of what can be separated, it is the task of first philosophy to determine that.

3. Now that we have drawn these distinctions, we must inquire further into causes, and see what the various kinds of cause are and how many they are. Since our treatment of the subject aims at knowledge, and since we believe ourselves to know anything only when we can say why it is as it is—which in fact means grasping its primary cause—plainly we must try to achieve this with regard to coming-to-be and perishing and all natural change, so that we may know what their principles are and may refer to them everything into which we inquire.

In one sense, what is described as a cause is that out of which a thing comes into being and that which remains present in it. Such, for instance, is bronze in the case of a statue, or silver in the case of a cup, as well as the genera to which these materials belong.

In another sense, the form and pattern are a cause, that is to say the account of the essence and the genera to which the essence belongs; such, for instance, in the case of the octave, are the ratio of two to one and, in general, number. The parts of the account are a cause in this sense, too.

Then there is the proximate source of change or rest: the adviser, for instance, is a cause; the father is the cause of his child; and, in general, what produces is the cause of what is produced, what does the changing is the cause of what is changed.

Then there is what is a cause insofar as it is an end; this is the purpose of a thing; in this sense, health, for instance, is the cause of a man's going for a walk. "Why," someone asks, "is he going for a walk?" "For the good of his health," we reply, and when we say this we think that we have given the cause of his doing so. All the intermediate things, too, that come into being through the agency of something else for this same end have this as their cause: slimming, purging, drugs, and surgical instruments—all have the same purpose, health, as their cause, although they differ from each other in that some of them are activities, others instruments.

These are pretty well all the senses in which we talk of causes; the consequence of our using the term in all these senses is that there are many causes of the same thing, without any of them being accidental causes. Both the art of sculpture and the bronze, for instance, are causes of the statue, without either of them being its cause in respect to its being anything other than a statue; they are, however, causes in different ways, the one being its matter, the other the source of the movement that produced it. There are some things that are even each other's causes; working hard, for instance, is a cause of one's good condition, and one's good condition is a cause of one's working hard; but, again, they are not causes in the same way; the one is an end, the other is a source of movement. Then, the same thing will be the cause of two contraries; for we will sometimes describe what is, by its presence, the cause of one thing as being, by its absence, the cause of that thing's contrary: for instance, we describe the absence of the pilot as the cause of the ship's being sunk, whereas his presence would have been the cause of its preservation. But all the causes that we have just mentioned fall into the four most obvious groups. The letters of a syllable, the raw material of a manufactured article, fire and such things in bodies, the parts of a whole, and the premises of a syllogism—all these are causes in the sense of being what a thing comes from; but whereas some are causes in the sense of being a substratum (the parts of a whole are, for instance), others are causes by virtue of being a thing's essence: the whole, the combination, and the form. The seed, the doctor, the adviser, and the producer, in general, are all sources of change or rest. Other things are causes by virtue of being the end and the good of everything else. For being the purpose means being the best of things and the end of everything else—and let us take it that it makes no difference whether we speak of the real or of the apparent good.

These, then, are the different kinds of cause that there are; but there are a great many different classes of these, though they, too, can be reduced by being classified. For there are many ways in which we can talk of causes: even with those that are of the same form, one thing can be the cause of another in a more remote or a more immediate sense. Both the doctor and the professional man, for instance, are causes of health; both double and number are causes of the octave; and general terms are always causes of the more particular ones contained in them. Then, one can describe as causes what are accidents, or the genera to which these accidents belong; in one sense Polyclitus is the cause of a statue, for instance; in another sense, the sculptor is; for it is an accident of the sculptor that he is Polyclitus. The classes in which the accident is included, too, are causes; one could say, for instance, that man or animal in general was the cause of the statue; and other accidents, whether closer or more remote, could be described as causes; both "the white man" and "the musical man," for instance, could be described as causes of the statue. Then, all causes, whether they properly belong to a thing or are accidental to it, may be talked of either as potential or as actual: we could say, for instance, that the cause of the house being built was either a builder or a builder who is actually building. Similarly, all the things of which these causes are said to be causes can be described in as many ways as the causes themselves; one can talk, for instance, of the cause of this statue, or of statue in general, or of image in general; or one can name the cause of this bit of bronze, or of bronze in general, or of matter in general; and it is the same with their accidents. Then, we may, too, combine both proper and accidental causes; we may, for instance, say neither that Polyclitus is the cause, nor that the sculptor is, but, rather, that Polyclitus the sculptor is.

Even so, all these kinds of cause are only six in number, although each may be talked of in two senses. One can describe as a cause either the individual or the genus to which he belongs, and also the accident or the genus of the accident; then, we can describe as causes either those terms taken in combination or one of them on its own; and then, in all these cases, we can talk of them as causes either potentially or actually. There is, however, this difference—things that are actualized and individual exist and cease to exist simultaneously with the things of which they are causes: the doctor who is practicing his art exists as such for the same length of time as the man who is being healed exists as such, and it is the same with regard to the man building and the house being built; but this is not always the case with things that are potential: the house and the builder do not perish at the same time.

Here, as in every other subject, we must always seek the most precise cause: a man, we must say, builds because he is a builder, and he is a builder because of his building art; this latter, here as in every other case, is the prior cause. Then, we should properly describe genera as the causes of genera, and individuals as the causes of individuals: sculptor is the cause of statue, and this sculptor the cause of this statue; and we should, also, describe potencies as the causes of things that are potential, and things that are active as causes of things that are actualized. Let us take it, then, that we have discriminated adequately between the different causes and their different ways of operating.

4. Chance and spontaneity are also said to be causes; many things are said to exist or to come into being by chance or spontaneously. We must now see in what way chance and spontaneity take their place among the causes that we have mentioned, and whether they are the same as each other or not; in general, too, we must see what chance and spontaneity are. Some people are uncertain even whether they exist or not; they say that nothing comes to be by chance and that all the things that we say come to be spontaneously or by chance have, in fact, some definite cause: if, for instance, a man goes by chance to the marketplace and finds someone there whom he wanted to see but did not expect to see, they say that the cause was his wish to go and buy things in the market; similarly, with everything else that is said to happen by chance, they say that it is always possible to find the cause and that it is not chance; if it were, that really would seem odd, for one might wonder why none of the ancient philosophers, when describing the causes of coming-to-be and perishing made no mention of chance, and why they all, instead, thought, as it seems, that nothing at all happens by chance. But it is surprising, too, if this is the case; for many things do exist and come to be by chance and spontaneously; and although everyone is aware that it is possible to assign a cause to everything that comes to be, as is maintained by the ancient argument that does away with chance, nonetheless they all say that some of these things happen by chance and that some do not; so that these thinkers should at least have made some mention of chance. Certainly they did not think that any of the causes that they named was chance; they did not think that Love, or Strife, or Mind, or fire, or anything else of that kind was. What they did was odd, then, whether they supposed that there was no such thing as chance, or whether they thought that there was and ignored it; and it is all the odder since they sometimes made use of it: Empedocles, for instance, says that air is not always separated upwards, but sometimes moves in whatever direction it chances to. He certainly says in his *Cosmogony*: "This is the way that it happened to run then, but it often ran in other ways." He says, too, that most of the parts of animals came into being by chance.

Some people, too, explain this heaven and all worlds by spontaneity; they say that the whirl and movement that separated out the universe and set it into its present order came into being spontaneously. This is a very remarkable view; on the one hand, they say that animals and plants do not exist or come into being by chance, but that nature or mind or some other such thing is their cause (for it is not just what chances to come into being that comes into being from any particular seed, but an olive tree will come from one kind of seed, and a man from another); and yet on the other hand they maintain that the heavens and the most divine of visible objects came into being spontaneously, and that they have no such cause as animals and plants have. If this is so, it is worthy of attention and something ought to be said about it. Besides being odd in other respects, it is even odder to say this when we see that in the heavens nothing comes into being spontaneously, but that among the things that they say do not come to be by chance many things do in fact come to be by chance; we might expect the exact opposite to happen, on the basis of their theory.

There are some people, too, who think that chance is a cause, but that it is hidden from the human intellect, as something divine and rather miraculous.

Thus, we must see what each of these two, chance and spontaneity, is, whether they are different from one another, and how they fit into the causes that we have already distinguished.

5. Firstly, then, since we see that some things always come to be in the same way, and that others usually do, clearly neither chance nor what happens by chance can be described as the cause of either of these classes of things; they cannot be the causes, that is to say, either of what happens always and of necessity or of what usually happens. But since there are things that come to be, apart from these, and since everyone says that these other things come to be as they are by chance, plainly there is such a thing as chance and such a thing as spontaneity: for we know that things of this kind happen by chance, and that things that happen by chance are of this kind.

Of things that come to be, some serve a purpose, others do not; of those that do, some come to be in accordance with an intention, others do not, although in both cases they serve a purpose. Plainly, then, even apart from things that happen according to necessity, or to what is usual, there are some things that can have a purpose. Things that serve a purpose include everything that might have been done intentionally, and everything that proceeds from nature. When such things come to be accidentally, we say that they are as they are by chance. For just as a thing may be what it is in itself or may be so accidentally, so it is possible for its cause to be a cause in either way; with a house, for instance, what is in itself its cause is what is capable of building, what is accidentally so is what is white and what is musical; so that what is in itself the cause is determinate, whereas the accidental cause is indeterminate; for there will be an infinite number of accidental causes for any one thing. As we were saying, then, when among things that serve a purpose something comes to be accidentally, that thing is said to come to be spontaneously and by chance (we must define the difference between these two terms later; there is only one point on which we need to be clear now, that both occur among things that serve a purpose). For instance, a man may go somewhere and find that a debtor of his is collecting some interest that he is owed; and thus he can collect what he is owed by the debtor. Now, if he had known that the debtor was going to be there, he would have come with the purpose of collecting the money; but in fact he did not come for this purpose, rather, it was just an accident that he came. Yet what he did served the purpose of collecting the money; and he did this although he did not usually or necessarily go to this place; and the end—the collection of the money—was not the kind of cause that is present in oneself, but the kind of cause that is the result of a deliberate choice. In fact, he is said to have gone there by chance; but if he had gone there deliberately and with this purpose, or if he had always or usually gone there, he would not be said to have gone there by chance. Clearly, then, chance is an accidental cause in the case of things that serve a purpose and are normally deliberate; hence, mind and chance are concerned with the same thing, since there is no intention without mind.

The causes, then, of what happens by chance must be indeterminate; hence, chance, too, seems to be part of what is indeterminate, and to be obscure to man; and in a sense nothing would seem to come to be by chance. All these views are correct and are backed by good reasons. For in one sense things do come to be by chance; they come to be accidentally, and chance is a cause insofar as it is an accident; but in the absolute sense, chance is not the cause of anything. The cause of a house, for instance, is its builder, but accidentally it may be a flute player; and the causes of the man's coming and collect-

ing his money when he did not come with that purpose
will be infinite in number; he might have come wanting
to see someone, or because he was following someone,
or because he was avoiding someone, or to look at a
spectacle.

It is right, too, to say that chance is something that is
contrary to one's calculations; for calculation is concerned with things that are as they are either always or
usually, whereas chance is to be found in things that do
not happen in this way; and since things that are causes
in this way are indeterminate, chance must be indeterminate too. Nonetheless, in some cases one might wonder
whether things that happen by chance are the causes of
another chance event; one could say, for instance, that
the cause of a man's good health was the wind or the
sun's heat, but not that it was the fact of his having had
his hair cut: some accidental causes are closer to the
effect than others.

Chance or fortune is said to be good when something
good results from it, bad when something bad does; and
we talk of good fortune or ill fortune when these attain
a certain magnitude; hence, to miss some great good or
some great evil too narrowly is bad fortune in the one
case and good fortune in the other, since the mind thinks
of what has just been missed as being no distance off.

Further, good fortune is with good reason regarded as
something insecure, since chance is insecure; for nothing
that happens by chance can happen either always or
usually.

Both chance and spontaneity, then, are, as we have
said, accidental causes in the case of things that do not
happen either always or usually; and among these they
are causes of things that might have a purpose.

6. The difference between chance and spontaneity is
that spontaneity covers a wider field: everything that
happens by chance happens spontaneously, but not everything that happens spontaneously happens by chance.

Chance and what happens by chance apply to those objects to which good fortune and activity in general might
belong. Hence, chance must be applicable to things that
have to be done; there is evidence of this in the fact that
good fortune seems to be either the same as happiness
or nearly so, and that happiness is an activity, since it is
nothing other than doing well; so that beings that are
not able to act cannot do anything by chance either.
Hence, nothing inanimate, no beast, no child can do anything by chance, since none of them has the faculty of
choice; nor does good fortune or ill fortune apply to
them except by analogy—as for instance when Protar-
chus said that the stones of which altars are made are
fortunate because they are honored, whereas their fel-
lows are trampled upon. Even these things, however, will
be able to have something done to them by chance, in
a sense, if someone is affecting them by his actions and
is doing so by chance; but they cannot have anything
done to them by chance in any other sense. Spontaneity,
on the other hand, can apply to the animals other than
man and to many inanimate objects; we talk, for instance, of the horse having come spontaneously because
he was saved by coming but did not come with the purpose of being saved; we say, too, that the tripod fell
down on its feet spontaneously, for it was originally set
up with the purpose of someone's sitting down on it, but
it did not fall back on its feet with that purpose. Clearly,
then, in the case of things that normally occur for a
purpose, when something whose cause is external does
not occur for the purpose of what actually follows from
it, we say that that thing has occurred spontaneously; we
say that things happen by chance when, with beings that
have the power of choice, things that are normally the
objects of choice occur spontaneously.

There is evidence of this in the use of the phrase "in
vain," which is used when something that occurs for a
purpose does not achieve that purpose: if, for instance,
someone goes for a walk with the purpose of evacuating

his bowels, and this does not happen after his walk, he is said to have walked in vain, and the walk is said to have been vain; we clearly assume that what is "vain" is what has a natural purpose and fails to achieve it; for if someone said that he had washed himself in vain, since there had not been an eclipse of the sun, he would be a laughingstock, since the purpose of his washing himself was not to produce an eclipse of the sun. And so, as the name implies, there is spontaneity when the thing itself comes to be in vain; the stone, for instance, did not fall with the purpose of hitting somebody, and so it fell spontaneously, since it would normally have fallen through someone's agency and with the purpose of hitting someone.

What happens spontaneously is particularly distinct from what happens by chance in the case of those things that come to be by nature: when something comes into being contrary to nature, we do not say that it has come into being by chance, but spontaneously; and yet even this is different from the spontaneity of which we have been speaking; for in that previous case, the cause was external, whereas here it is internal.

We have, then, explained what spontaneity and chance are, and how they differ from each other. As for the kind of cause that they are, each of them belongs to that class of cause that contains the source of movement; for they are always either natural causes or causes of the kind that come from intention; the number of these is indeterminate.

Since spontaneity and chance are causes of things of which mind and nature would normally be causes, and since they are only causes when their effects are caused accidentally, and since, further, nothing accidental is prior to what exists in itself, plainly no accidental cause can be prior to what is of itself a cause. Spontaneity and chance, then, are posterior to mind and nature; thus, however much spontaneity may be a cause of the heavens, mind and nature must in a prior sense be the cause both of many particular things and of the world as a whole.

7. It is clear, then, that there are causes, and that they are as many in number as we say; for they correspond to the different ways in which we can answer the question "why?" The ultimate answer to that question can be reduced to saying what the thing is (as, for instance, in mathematics, where any question ultimately leads to the definition of the straight or the commensurate or something else); or to saying what the first mover was (if, for instance, one is asked why certain people went to war, one replies, "Because they were raided"); or to naming the purpose ("so that they could rule," for instance); or, in the case of things that come into being, to naming the matter.

Plainly, then, these are the causes, and this is the number of them. Since there are these four causes, it is the business of the natural scientist to know about them all, and he will give his answer to the question "why?" in the manner of a natural scientist if he refers what he is being asked about to them all—to the matter, the form, the mover, and the purpose. Three of these often come together into one; for the essence and the purpose are one; and the proximate source of movement is of the same kind—for man generates man, and this is so in general with things that move other things in being moved themselves. Things that are not moved themselves are not the concern of natural science: for such things, without having any movement or any source of movement in themselves, cause movement although remaining unmoved themselves; so it is that there are three branches of study: one is concerned with immovable objects, the second with things that are in movement but are imperishable and the third with perishable things. Thus, the answer to the question "why?" is to be given by referring to the matter, to the essence, and to the proximate mover. In cases of coming-to-be it is

mostly in this last way that people examine the causes;
they ask what comes to be after what, what was the
immediate thing that acted or was acted upon, and so
on in order. The causes that move things in a natural
way are twofold; but of these, one is not a natural cause,
since it does not contain the source of its movement in
itself. A thing is in this position if it moves something
else without being moved itself; this is the case with what
is absolutely immovable and the first of all things, and
it is also the case with the essence and shape, since this
is at the same time the end and purpose; thus, since
nature has a purpose, we must know this cause too, and
we must give our answer to the question "why?" in all
these ways. We must say that from this, that must follow
(which will be either universally or usually true); that if
this is going to be so, there must also be that (just as
there must be premises for a conclusion to come from):
that this is the thing's essence; and that it is so because
it is better so—not in any absolute sense, but relatively
to the substance of whatever is in question.

8. Now, we must first explain why nature is said to be
one of the causes that are purposes, and then we must
discuss necessity, and how it appears in natural objects.
For necessity is a cause to which everyone refers things;
they say that since the hot and the cold and all other
such things are of a particular kind, particular things of
necessity exist and come into being; even if they mention
another cause, they merely touch upon it and then take
leave of it: one will mention Love and Strife in this way,
another, Mind.

There is the problem of knowing what there is to keep
nature from acting without a purpose, and not because
things are best as she does them; Zeus does not send
the rain in order to make the corn grow; he sends it of
necessity; for what is drawn up and evaporated must get
cold, and what gets cold must come down again as water;
and it is an accident that, when this has happened, the

corn grows; similarly, if someone's corn is lost on the threshing floor, the rain did not fall with the purpose of destroying the corn; it was an accident that this happened. What is to keep this from being so with the parts in nature too? What is to keep it from being of necessity, for instance, that one's front teeth come up sharp and suitable for cutting things up, and that the molars are flat and useful for grinding the food? One would then say that these things did not happen purposely, but came about by accident. It is the same with all the other parts in which purpose seems to be present. On this view, all things that accidentally turned out to be what they would have become if they had had a purpose were preserved spontaneously, once they had come together in a suitable fashion; beings that did not turn out in this way perished, and continue to do so, as Empedocles says happened with his "man-faced oxen."

This argument, and others like it, are the ones that might make one at a loss to know whether there is a purpose in nature; but it is in fact impossible for things to be like that. For these and all natural objects either always or usually come into being in a given way, and that is not the case with anything that comes to be by chance or spontaneously. We do not think that it is by chance or by accident that it often rains in the winter, but we do think that it is if it rains in the dog days; nor do we think that it is by accident or by chance that it is hot in the dog days, although if it is hot in the winter we do think so. If, then, we think that things happen either by accident or for a purpose, and if it is not possible for them to happen by accident or spontaneously, then they must happen for a purpose. But all things of this kind happen by nature, as even those who maintain the view that we are criticizing would admit. Thus, there is purpose in things that come to be and exist by nature.

Further, in all cases where there is an end, the first and all the subsequent actions are carried out with that end as their purpose. Now, the course of nature corresponds to the course of action, and the course of any action corresponds to the course of nature—unless there is some obstacle in the way. But actions have a purpose; so nature must have one too. For instance, if a house were one of the things that come into being by nature, it would come into being in the same way that it now does through art; and if natural objects came into being not only by nature but also through art, they too would come into being in the same way that they do by nature. We may say, then, that one thing does have the next as its purpose. In general, art in some cases finishes what nature is unable to accomplish; in others, it imitates nature. If, then, things that happen in accordance with art have a purpose, plainly things that happen in accordance with nature will too. For the relation of the earlier and later stages to each other is the same in nature as it is in art.

This becomes particularly clear in the case of the other animals: they do not do things by art or after any inquiry or deliberation. This has led some people to wonder whether spiders and ants and things of that kind act through mind or by some other means. If one gradually goes on in this direction, one sees that in plants, too, things come into being that are conducive to their end: the leaves, for instance, come into being for the purpose of protecting the fruit. Thus, if it is both by nature and to fulfill a purpose that the swallow makes its nest and the spider spins its web, and if plants put forth their leaves for the sake of their fruit and send their roots down rather than up for the purpose of getting food, plainly a cause of this kind is present in things that come to be and exist by nature. And since nature is twofold—in one sense being matter, and in another shape, which is the end—and since everything else has the end as its purpose, it is in fact the shape or form that will be the cause, in the sense of its being the purpose.

Mistakes occur in things that are done according to art: the literate man will write incorrectly, the doctor will give the wrong dose; so it is clearly possible, too, for mistakes to happen in things that are in accordance with nature. Now, just as in the case of art, if things are done correctly, they serve a purpose, whereas if they go wrong, the attempt is made to serve a purpose, but it fails; so the situation must be with natural objects, and monsters must be failures to achieve a purpose. And in the original combinations, the oxlike creatures, since they were unable to come to a defined end, must have come into being through the corruption of some principle in them, just as it is now through the corruption of the seed that monsters are produced. Further, there must have been a seed first; the animals cannot have come into being straightaway; and the "primal generator of all" must have been such a seed.

Purpose is present in plants, too, but it has been less clearly articulated in them. Did what is supposed to have happened with animals also happen with them? Did there come into being, corresponding to the oxen with men's faces, vines with the appearance of olives? This is absurd; but some such thing would have to happen, if it happened too among animals.

Further, on this theory, things would have had to come into being from the seeds just as they chanced to; but the man who holds this kind of view does away with natural objects and with nature. For natural things are things that are continuously moved by some principle within themselves and attain some end; it is not the same thing that comes to be from each principle in each case, nor is it just what it chances to be; but it always tends toward the same thing if there is nothing to prevent it. The purpose for which a thing is done, and what is done for that purpose, may come to be by chance: we say, for instance, that the stranger came by chance and went off after ransoming the man when he acts as though he had come for this purpose but had in fact not come for it. This is accidental, for, as we said earlier, chance is an accidental cause; but when it happens always or usually, it is not accidental, and does not happen by chance. And in natural occurrences, things always are like this, unless there is some impediment.

It is strange to suppose that things do not happen for a purpose simply because one does not see the mover deliberate. Art does not deliberate; and if the art of ship-building were present in the wood, it would act in the same way by nature; so that if purpose is present in art, it is present in nature too. This becomes most clear when someone heals himself, for that is just what nature is like.

It is clear, then, that nature is a cause, and is a cause in the sense of being a purpose.

9. Does necessity apply in nature absolutely, or only on the basis of certain assumptions? For at the moment people suppose that the necessity occurs in the process of coming-to-be; it is as if one thought that a wall had come into being of necessity because the heavy parts naturally moved downwards and the light parts up to the surface, so that the stones and foundations were therefore at the bottom, the earth above them because of its lightness, and the wood right at the top because it is the lightest of them all. But, in fact, although the wall has not come into being without these, it has not come into being because of them, except insofar as they are matter; it has, rather, come into being for the purpose of concealing and preserving various things. Similarly with all other things in which purpose is present, they do not come into being without the things that possess the necessary nature, but they do not come into being because of them, except insofar as these things are mat-ter; they, rather, come into being for a purpose. Why, someone asks, is the saw like *this*? So that it can do *this*, we say, and with *this* purpose. But this purpose cannot come to be unless the saw is of iron; and so there must be iron if the saw and its activity are going to exist. The necessary, then, is present only on the basis of some

assumption, it is not there as an end; for the necessity
is present in the matter, whereas the purpose is present
in the form or account.

Necessity in mathematics is in a way very similar to
necessity in things that come into being by nature; because the straight is what it is, the triangle must contain
angles equal to two right angles; but it does not follow
from the fact that the latter is true that the straight is
what it is; if, however, the latter proposition is not true,
the straight will not be what it is said to be either. In
the case of things that come into being for a purpose, it
is the other way around: if the end is to exist either now
or in the future, what leads up to it must do so too; but
if what leads up to the end does not exist, the end and
purpose will not exist either, just as there will be no
premise if the conclusion does not hold. For it is the
purpose is the starting point, not, indeed, of the activity,
but of the calculation leading to it; and in the case of
mathematics, too, the premise is the starting point of the
calculation, since there is no activity involved. Thus, if
there is going to be a house, particular things must come
into being or be there: matter must necessarily exist for
the achievement of any purpose—bricks and stones must
be there, for instance, for a house. But it is not because
of these things that the end exists, except insofar as they
are matter, nor will it do so in the future because of
them. In general, if these things do not exist, neither the
house nor the saw will exist: the house will not exist if
there are no stones, the saw will not exist if there is no
iron; for in the other case the premises will not be true
unless the triangle contains two right angles.

Clearly, then, necessity in natural objects is what is
described as matter together with its affections. Both
causes must be named by the natural scientist, but more
especially the purpose; for it is the cause of the matter,
but the matter is not the cause of the end. The end is
the purpose, and the starting point is the definition and
account, as it is too in things that have to do with art:

since, we say, the house is to be of a particular kind,
these particular things must come into being and be
present of necessity; since health is like this, particular
things must come into being and be present of necessity;
similarly, since man is a particular thing, other particular
things must be there; and if these other things are to be
there, still others must be, too. But perhaps there is necessity present in the definition as well. For if one defines the activity of sawing as a particular kind of
dividing, this activity will not take place unless the saw
has teeth of a particular kind; and these will not be there
unless the saw is made of iron. For in the definition, too,
there are some parts that are, as it were, the matter of
the definition.

PSYCHOLOGY

Introduction

What we misleadingly call Aristotle's psychology is
not confined to the study of the human mind or soul,
but is concerned with all forms of *psyche,* which means
to Aristotle all that distinguishes living creatures, including man, from inanimate objects. What is sometimes
quaintly called Aristotle's distinction between "types of
soul" takes on a different and more immediately intelligible aspect if we recognize it as a classification of the
kinds of living organism—plants, animals, and man. But
we must guard against a misunderstanding to which the
alternative way of putting it may give rise. Aristotle's
classification is designed to mark the connections as well
as the distinctions between the fundamental categories
of living beings. The functions of feeding, growing, and
reproducing, which are the sole functions of plants, are
found in animals, which are capable of the further activities of feeling, sensation, and locomotion. Man has all
these attributes in common with the lower creatures, but
he is distinguished from them by his faculty of reason.
All organisms have souls, just as all bodies have shapes;
there are different kinds of soul, systematically related
to each other, as there are distinct shapes between which
the geometrician can perceive the formal relations.

The psychology is in effect a study of the fundamental

principles of biology, a philosophical synthesis that forms
the background for the detailed researches into the nature and properties of plants, animals, and men that are
pursued in the more specialized biological writings. Here
it must be noticed that Aristotle's contribution to biology was not confined to systematic observation and classification into species and genera, important as his work
in these fields may be. His largest and most permanent
biological achievement was the perception of a greater
and more comprehensive order in animate nature. Although he had no inkling of the conception of the evolu-
tion of species, the descending order of complexity and
of value in which he placed the animal and plant
species—ranging from man down through the other
mammals, birds, reptiles, and fishes to the most lowly
organisms known to him—corresponds closely to the as-
cending order of evolutionary development as understood by later biologists. Aristotle did not apply to
species, or to the animal and plant worlds as a whole,
the concept of development that was so important in his
account of the individual organism; but he prepared the
way for this extension of his work by exhibiting the relationships between one species and another, one order
and another, which are the basis on which evolutionary
biology has been built.

Nevertheless, the interest of his psychology for the
modern philosophical reader is naturally centered on its
treatment of those problems in the philosophy of psychology that are still debated in very much the form in
which they presented themselves to Aristotle. Chief
among these is the perennial problem of formulating the
relationship between the human mind or soul and the
human body, and the kindred questions that arise about
the relation between the senses and the intellect, between sensation, perception, and thought.

Aristotle's distinction between form and matter is nowhere more effectively applied than in his account of
the relation between soul and body. Plato, like Des-

cartes, was an extreme dualist. Soul and body were, for
Plato, two enemies locked together against the inclina-
tions of both. Each was a separate substance that lacked
all the most characteristic properties of the other. Their
separation, far from being a merely theoretical possibility, was something that was inevitably achieved at death
and that the philosopher would earnestly strive for even
during his lifetime.

Aristotle's theory of soul places him, with Spinoza, in
the other tradition of philosophical reflection on the
mind-body problem, according to which the mind or soul
and the physical body are not totally independent substances, but aspects, separable only in thought, of one
and the same substance.

These two types of theory will be placed in their
proper context, and will thus help us to understand Aristotle's contribution to this unending debate if we pause
to look at the mind-body problem itself. The problem
soon presents itself to one who reflects on the nature
and powers of man. The difference between a living
human being and a corpse is so striking that even the
earliest speculation has some account to offer of the
spirit that is naturally supposed to inhabit the body and
to depart at death; in some primitive works of art it is
portrayed as a bird or a little man, and the etymology
of the word "spirit" and of the corresponding words in
many other languages is a reminder of its connection
with air or breath. At a later and more sophisticated
stage, when it is realized that there is no separate, physically detectable element in a man's body that constitutes
the life principle, it is natural to suppose that there must
be an invisible, intangible substance in every living body.
This tendency is reinforced by the idioms in which ordinary language, both Greek and English, speaks of the
mind and the body as quite separate and distinct. But a
problem arises: how are the mind and body connected?
If they are utterly distinct in kind, how is it possible for
them to be conjoined? The mind, if it lacks all spatial

and material properties, cannot be literally *in* the body.
Descartes and his successors were forced to choose, as
strict dualists must always choose, between two equally
unpalatable possibilities: that the union of mind and
body is mysterious and unaccountable or that, contrary
to all experience and common sense, there is no real
connection between the mind and the body.

Aristotle's theory of causation was very helpful to him
in facing this problem, and here especially he reaps the
benefit of his conception of form, moving cause, and end
as related aspects of one and the same principle, jointly
contrasted to the material cause. For Aristotle, the individual organism is a single, unified, and independent substance whose matter is its body and whose form, moving
cause, and end are its soul. Soul and body are separable
only as the matter of a physical object is separable from
its shape. Aristotle himself uses this illustration, which
is in any case implicit in his terminology of form and
matter; but it is his examples of the ax and the eye that
most clearly explain his doctrine, because they introduce
the all-important notions of function and purpose. The
sharpness of the ax is not something separable from the
iron or bronze; it is the form and function of the metal.
Similarly, if the eye were a complete living creature, its
sight would be its soul: if we compare a living and func-
tioning eye with a dead or painted eye (which is an eye
only "by equivocation"), we have a small-scale model
of the relation between the soul as the properties and
capacities of the organism, and the body as the material
constituent, the instruments or organs by means of which
the soul fulfills its functions of growing, breeding, seeing,
feeling, and thinking.

This pervasive distinction between form and matter
unifies Aristotle's detailed discussions of the particular
functions and activities of living creatures. But a full
understanding of his psychological theory also requires
attention to two other points that are familiar from other
departments of his philosophy but that have a special
relevance to the study of the nature of living things.

In Book II, Aristotle defines the soul as "the *first* actuality of a natural body that is potentially alive." The distinction between the first and second grades of actuality is often explained by Aristotle's example of the two senses in which a man may be said to have knowledge. Even a sleeping man may be said to know Greek, but it is only the man who is actually reading or writing or speaking Greek who is knowing it in the fullest sense, who is exercising or using his knowledge. A babe in arms potentially knows Greek, but in a sense that puts him two stages away from the exercise of such knowledge. Again, we may say of a schoolboy or of a colonel that he is a potential general, but the sense of potentiality is different in the two cases.

So it is with life or soul. A natural body is alive if it reaches the first grade of actualization, but it is fully living only when it actually engages in the activities of feeling, seeing, growing, or thinking or uses one or more of the other capacities that distinguish animals, plants, and men from their inanimate environment. Similarly, an ax may be sharp, but may not actually be engaged in cutting; an eye may have the power of sight, but it will be fully actualizing that capacity only when it is actually seeing something.

Aristotle's theory of "coupled terms" also has an important application in the study of living beings. A coupled term is one that specifies form and matter at the same time by implying a particular form in a particular type of matter. Aristotle's favorite example is the snub nose. The word "snub" means "curved," but it is used only of noses. Such terms are useful to us because in the study of nature we are interested in the union of form with matter; and Aristotle emphasizes that all natural substances, not only those for which we have special coupled terms, have an important feature in common with snub noses. Just as there is nothing that is snub unless there is a nose that has a certain form, so with other natural substances and, indeed, with human artifacts there is an intimate connection between the form and the matter appropriate to each kind. Flesh and bone, ax and house, must *both* be made of particular kinds of materials *and* have the materials arranged in particular *forms*. The fulfillment of the particular purposes of particular species of living creatures requires the specially appropriate instruments, just as each craft has its own special tools. The Pythagorean theory of transmigration is absurd because the soul of a man can no more be joined with the body of a dog than a flute can be used for carpentry.

Aristotle's treatment of sensation and perception has a special interest for students of modern philosophy. In insisting that the senses as such are infallible when they are dealing with their own proper objects, he gives the first clear exposition of a conception of the distinction between sense experience and the interpretation of sense experience that has been important at all later stages of the history of philosophy. His discussion of these topics is also notable for the care with which he draws two other fundamental distinctions: (1) between the proper objects of the particular senses (sounds, colors, odors, etc.) and the external objects that are the sources of these affections; and (2) between color, sound, smell, etc., as activities of the external objects and color, sound, smell, etc., as passivities, or states of being acted upon, of the individual sense organs.

It should also be remarked that the conceptions of form and matter and of potentiality and actuality are prominent in Aristotle's account of sensation, perception, and thought. For example, when sensation occurs, there is an actualization of capacities both of the sense organ and of the object sensed; and perception is described as the process by which the mind receives the form of an external object without its matter.

It is clear from the main tenor of Aristotle's account of the human mind and soul that his conception allows no room for individual immortality; and yet, in the account of the distinction between the active and the passive reason in Book III and in the aspirations toward a life of pure thought that we find in Book XIII of the *Metaphysics* and in Book X of the *Ethics,* there are signs that Aristotle never wholly freed himself from the Platonic dualism about the world and man from which he took his starting point.

When Aristotle became the official metaphysician of the Christian Church, his doctrine on this point had to be eked out with much commentary and interpretation, and it is difficult now to separate his own meaning from what has been laid over it by the theological tradition. But in the judgment of most recent scholars, there is little doubt that individual immortality is not a doctrine to which the mature Aristotle continued to subscribe; and there is good reason to accept Jaeger's view that Book III of this treatise preserves some ideas from Aristotle's earlier Platonism. Elsewhere in the same work he is as critical of Plato's dualism and of the doctrine of the tripartite soul as the logic of his own developed theory requires him to be.

Book I

1. We regard knowledge as something fine and precious; and our reasons for valuing any one branch of it more than any other are either that it is more accurate or that the objects of its study are better and more remarkable; these are both good reasons for giving high importance to an inquiry into the soul. The knowledge of the soul seems to be a great help for the understanding of truth as a whole, but particularly for the understanding of nature; for the soul is a sort of first principle in animals. Our aim is to study and understand, first its nature and essence, and then its attributes; of these latter, some seem to be affections peculiar to the soul, others through the soul to belong to animals as well.

But to gain any trustworthy view of it is very difficult in every way. Our inquiry here is the same as in many other subjects, insofar as it is an inquiry into the essence of a thing and what the thing is; and so we might suppose that there was a single method applicable to everything whose essence we wish to discover, just as there is a single method of demonstrating attributes that are implicit in a thing's nature; and we might consequently suppose, too, that it was this method that we had to seek. But if there is no single common method by which we may discover what a thing is, the treatment of the subject becomes still more difficult; for we shall have to find the

appropriate method for each subject. And even if it is
clear whether this method is demonstration, division, or
some other, there will still be many difficulties and
sources of error involved in finding out from what premises we ought to start our inquiry; for different things
have different principles: numbers and plane surfaces
have different ones, for instance.

But perhaps the first thing to do is to determine what
genus the soul is in, and what it is: is it, I mean, an
individual and a substance, or a quality, or a quantity;
or is it in any other of the categories that we have distinguished? Further, is it something that exists potentially,
or is it fully realized? For that makes a considerable
difference. Then we must see whether it is divisible into
parts or has none; and whether every soul is of the same
species or not; and, if not, whether souls differ only in
species, or in genus too. Till now, those who have discussed and inquired about the soul seem to have considered only the human soul; but we must take care not to
forget the question of whether one single definition can
be given of soul in the way that it can of animal, or
whether there is a different one in each case—for horse,
dog, man, and god, for instance; in that case there would
be no such thing as a universal animal, or, if there were,
it would be something posterior to the particular species.
(This same question could be raised about any term that
is asserted of things in common.) Further, if there are
not many kinds of soul, but different parts of it, we must
decide whether we ought to look into the soul as a whole
first, or into its parts. With these parts, too, it is difficult
to define the nature of their different kinds, and to determine whether we ought to look into the parts themselves
or their activities first; should we, for instance, consider
thinking or the mind first, perceiving or the faculty of
perception? The same question arises as to all the other
parts. If we ought to examine their activities first, we
might, again, be at a loss to know whether we should
not consider before them the objects that are their

counterparts—the object of perception, for instance, before the faculty of perception, and the object of thought before the mind. Knowledge of what substances are is, of course, useful in studying the causes of their attributes: in mathematics, for instance, knowing what straightness and curvedness are, or a line and a plane surface, is useful for seeing how many right angles the angles of a triangle are equal to; but, conversely, knowledge of a thing's attributes is a great help to knowing what the thing is. For it is when we can give an account of either most or all of the attributes of a thing as we see them that we shall be in a position to talk most effectively about its substance. For in all demonstration, knowing what the thing is is the starting point; thus, any definitions that do not enable us to discover the thing's properties or even to guess at them fairly easily have clearly been framed in a dialectical and futile fashion.

The affections of the soul present a further problem: are they all shared by that which possesses the soul, or is there any one that is peculiar to the soul itself? This is something that we must discover, but it is difficult to do so. For the most part, the soul seems unable to have anything done to it, or to do anything, without the body; this is so, for instance, with regard to feeling anger, confidence, or desire, and with sensation in general. What seems most likely to be peculiar to the soul is thought; but, if even this is a kind of imagination, or at least does not occur without imagination, then not even it can occur independently of the body. If, then, any of the activities or affections of the soul are peculiar to it, it will be possible for the soul to exist separately; but if it has no such peculiar activity or affection, it will not be separable but will be like the straight: for the straight qua straight has many properties, such as touching a bronze sphere at a point; but it never will so touch a sphere if it is separate; yet, it is inseparable, if it is always linked with a body. The affections of the soul, too, seem all to be linked with the body: anger, gentleness, fear, pity, confidence, and also joy, love, and hatred; for all these involve affections of the body too. There is evidence of this in the fact that sometimes, despite the unmistakable force of what is happening to one, one is not excited or frightened; whereas at other times one is stirred by insignificant and obscure events, and one's body becomes tense and gets into the same state as when one is angry. There is even clearer evidence of this in the fact that, when nothing terrible is happening, one can nevertheless have all the reactions of a man who is terrified. If this is so, plainly the affections of the soul are forms embedded in matter. Their definitions, then, must be of the following kind: "anger is a movement of a particular kind of body (or part or faculty of body) brought about by the agency of a particular thing for a particular purpose." For this reason, it is the business of the natural scientist to study the soul—either all of it, or at least this kind of soul. The natural scientist and the logician would define all these affections in different ways; if they were asked what anger is, the one would say that it was a desire to hurt someone in return, or something like that, the other that it was a boiling of the blood and the heat around the heart. Of these, one is describing the matter, the other the form and the definition; for the latter is indeed the definition of the thing, but it must be in matter of a particular kind if the thing is going to exist. With a house, for instance, the definition will be something like "a shelter that prevents one from being harmed by wind, rain, or heat," but the other will say that the house is "stones, bricks, and wood"; and someone else will say that it is the form present in these materials for a particular purpose. Which of these is really the natural scientist? The one who concerns himself with the matter alone, and knows nothing of the definition, or the one who is solely concerned with the definition? Or is it, rather, the man who is a combination of the two? In that case, what are the other two? Perhaps there is no one who is concerned with the insepara-

ble affections of matter, except insofar as they are
separable; perhaps the natural scientist is concerned with
all the activities and affections of a particular kind of
body and a particular kind of matter, whereas its other
attributes are dealt with by someone else: some may be
dealt with by a man who possesses an art—a carpenter
or a doctor, for instance; the mathematician will perhaps
deal with attributes that are not separable, insofar as
they are abstract and not affections of any particular
kind of body; insofar as the attributes are separable, they
will be dealt with by whoever studies first philosophy.
But we must return to where this discussion started
from. We were saying that the affections of the soul are
inseparable from the natural matter of animals, insofar
as such things as anger and fear belong to the soul, but
they are inseparable in a different way from line and
plane surface.

■ ■ ■

4. Another view about the soul has come down to us
that many think as plausible as any of those that we
have mentioned, and which has rendered a sort of public
account of itself in general discussions. This view is that
the soul is a harmony: for a harmony is a mixture, or
combination, of contraries, and the body is composed
of contraries.

But a harmony is either the proportion in which the
ingredients are mixed or a combination of them, and the
soul can be neither of these. Further, it is no function
of a harmony to move things, and yet everyone assigns
this function more than almost any other to soul. Then,
it seems more fitting to apply the term "harmony" to
health, and to the excellences of the body in general,
than to the soul. This becomes very clear if one tries to
give an account of the affections and activities of the
soul in terms of a harmony; it is difficult to make any
such account fit. Further, we talk of harmony with two

ideas in mind: most properly, we mean the combination
of magnitudes in things that move and have position,
when they are so fitted together that they can admit
nothing else of the same kind; the second idea is derived
from this, that harmony is the proportion in which the
ingredients are mixed. Neither of these ideas can be
plausibly applied to the soul. It is only too easy to refute
the view that it is just a combination of the parts of the
body; for there are many combinations of parts, and they
are formed in many ways. Of what are we to suppose
that the mind or the faculty of sensation or of desire is
a combination? In what way can any of them come to
be a combination? It is equally absurd to regard the soul
as the proportion of the mixture; for the elements are
not mixed in the same proportion in the case of flesh as
they are in the case of bone. It will follow, then, that
one has many souls throughout the body, if every part
of the body is made up of a mixture of elements, and
the proportion of this mixture in every case is a harmony
and a soul. (One might question Empedocles about this,
too; he says that each part is as it is because of a certain
proportion. Is this proportion, then, the soul, or is the
soul something separate, which comes to be present in
the parts? Further, is Love the cause of just any mixture,
or only of the one that is in the right proportion? And
is Love itself this proportion, or something else separate
from it?) Such, then, are the difficulties that these
views involve.

On the other hand, if the soul is separate from the
mixture, why is it destroyed at the same time as the flesh
and the other parts of the animal? Also, if it is not the
case that each of the parts possesses a soul, and the soul
is not the proportion of the mixture, what is it that perishes when the soul disappears?

That the soul cannot be a harmony or be in circular
motion is plain from what has been said. It is, however,
possible, as we have remarked, for it to be moved and
to move itself accidentally; it is possible, for instance, for

the thing that it is inside to be moved—and to be moved by the soul.

There are other considerations that might more reasonably make one puzzled about whether the soul is moved. We say that the soul feels pain and pleasure, is confident, is afraid; also, that it gets angry, that it perceives, that it thinks. All these activities give the impression of being movements, so that one might infer from this that the soul is moved. That does not necessarily follow, however. Let us fully admit that feeling pain, feeling pleasure, and thinking are movements, and that each of them in fact involves being moved; let us also admit that the movement is imparted by the soul, that being angry, for instance, or being frightened involves the heart being moved in a particular way, and that thinking involves perhaps the heart, perhaps something else being moved (some of these consequences follow when things are moved in respect to place, others when the movement takes the form of alteration; the kinds of things that are moved and the way in which they are moved are separate issues). Even if we admit all this, to say that the soul is angry is like saying that the soul weaves or builds. It is probably better to say not that the soul feels pity or learns or thinks, but that man does these things with his soul; for we should not suppose that the movement is actually in the soul, but rather that in some cases it penetrates as far as the soul, in others it starts from it; sensation, for instance, starts from the particular objects, whereas recollection starts from the soul and proceeds to the movements or their residues in the sense organs.

It seems, however, that the mind comes to be present in things as a substance, and that it does not decay. If it did decay, it would be more than anything the dulling influence of old age that would make it do so. But, in fact, what happens with the mind is like what happens with the senses: if an old man were to obtain an eye of a particular kind, he would see as well as a young man.

Old age does not involve anything happening to the soul,
but to what the soul is in, as is also the case with drunk-
enness and disease. Thought and speculation waste away
because something else inside the body is decaying;
nothing happens to the thought itself. Thinking, loving,
and hating are not affections of the mind, but of what
possesses the mind, insofar as it does possess it; it is
when this possessor fails that remembering and loving
stop; for they did not belong to the mind, but to the
compound that has perished. The mind is perhaps something more divine, and so nothing happens to it.

These considerations, then, make it clear that the soul
cannot be moved; and if it cannot be moved at all,
clearly it cannot be moved by itself. . . .

5. . . . There are three ways of defining the soul that
have come down to us: some have declared it to be,
more than anything else, a source of movement because
it moves itself; others have regarded it as being made
up of finer parts, or as being more incorporeal, than
anything else. We have given a pretty full account of the
difficulties and inconsistencies that these views involve.
It remains to examine the view that it is made up of the
elements. This theory is maintained to account for the
soul's perceiving and recognizing everything that there
is; but many impossible consequences inevitably follow
from it. The holders of this theory assume that one recognizes like by like, so that it is as if they identified soul
with things in general. But the elements are not the only
things that there are; there are many others too—or perhaps we should, rather, say that the products of the elements are infinite in number. Let us grant that the soul
recognizes and perceives the elements of which all these
things are composed; but with what will it perceive or
recognize a whole thing, like a god, a man, a piece of
flesh, or a bone? Similarly with anything else that is composite, it will not be the same as its elements in just
any state, for these will be arranged according to some

proportion or principle; it will be like what even Empedocles says about bone: "The pleasing earth took in its
full-breasted molds two of the eight parts of gleaming
moisture, and four of Hephaestus; and white bones came
into being."

It is no help, then, for the elements to be present in
the soul unless the proportions and principles of combination are going to be there too; for everything will recognize what is like itself, but nothing will recognize the
bone or the man unless these are present in the soul
too. And there is no need to point out that this is impossible; who could begin to wonder whether stone or man
is present in the soul? The same argument applies to the
good and to the not-good and, indeed, to everything
else.

Then, there are many ways in which the term "being"
is used: on the one hand, it may be used with reference
to an individual thing; on the other, with reference to
quantity, quality, or any of the other categories that have
been distinguished. Will the soul be made up of all these,
or not? There do not seem to be any elements common
to them all. Is it, then, made up only of the elements of
substances? In that case, how does it recognize all the
things other than substances? Or are these people going
to say that there are elements and principles peculiar to
each class, and that the soul is made up of all of them?
In that case, the soul will be quantity and quality and
substance. But it is impossible for what is made up of
the elements of quantity to be substance and not quantity. These consequences, then, and others like them follow from saying that the soul is made up of all the
elements.

It is curious, too, to say, on the one hand, that like
cannot be acted upon by like, and on the other, that like
perceives like, and that one recognizes like by means of
the like; for the holders of this view do regard perception
as an affection and a movement, and similarly with
thinking and knowing.

There are many problems and difficulties involved in saying, as Empedocles does, that everything is recognized by the bodily elements by virtue of its likeness to them, as this next point shows. All the parts of the bodies of animals that are made up simply of earth—such as bones, sinews, and hairs—seem not to perceive anything, and so not to perceive anything that is like themselves either; yet on the basis of this theory they should do so. Further, each principle will have more ignorance than knowledge; for each principle will know one thing and be ignorant of many, since it will be ignorant of everything other than this one thing. And with Empedocles, at least, the consequence is that God is very foolish; for he alone will not recognize one of the elements, Strife, whereas every mortal being will recognize them all, since each is made up of them all. In general, too, why do not all the things that exist have souls, since each of them either is an element or is made up of one or more, if not all, of them? For they must all, according to this theory, know one thing, or a number of things, or everything. Then one might be at a loss to know what it is that unifies them. For the elements are like matter, and the most important thing is what holds them together, whatever it is; but it is impossible for there to be anything stronger than the soul controlling it, and even more impossible for there to be anything stronger than the mind. For it is reasonable to assume that mind is prior both in age and in importance to everything else, whereas they maintain that the elements are the first among the things that exist.

But neither those who say that the soul is made up of the elements because it recognizes and perceives the things that exist, nor those who say that it is more than anything else, a source of movement, are taking into account every soul. For not everything that has perception is a source of movement: some animals seem to be stationary, as far as movement in place is concerned, and yet this seems to be the only kind of movement that the soul imparts to the animal. Similar difficulties confront those who make the mind and the faculty of perception come from the elements: plants seem to live without any share in perception, and many animals seem to be without intelligence. But even if one were to let these points pass, and admit that the mind is a part of the soul, and the faculty of perception likewise, even so these people would not be talking universally about every soul, nor indeed about any soul in its entirety. There is the same defect in the theory in what are called the Orphic poems, according to which the soul enters animals from the universe when they breathe, being carried along by the winds; this cannot happen with plants, nor indeed with some animals, if not all of them do in fact breathe; this point has eluded those who hold this view. Further, even if we must construct the soul out of the elements, there is no need to construct it out of all of them. For one of a pair of contraries is sufficient to discern both itself and its opposite. By means of the straight, we can know both it and the curved: the carpenter's rule is a criterion for both; but what is curved is no criterion either for itself or for what is straight.

Some think that the soul is intermingled throughout the whole universe, which was perhaps what led Thales to suppose that everything was full of gods. This view, however, involves certain difficulties. What is the cause of the soul not producing an animal when it is present in fire or in air, whereas it does so when it is present in compounds, and that too although it seems to be better when it is present in the former class of objects? (One might ask in addition what is the cause of the soul in the air being better and more immortal than that in animals.) Either way the consequences are absurd and unreasonable. To say that fire or air is an animal is more than unreasonable, and to say that they have souls but are not animals is absurd. But these people seem to have supposed that the soul is in these things on the grounds that the whole is of the same kind as its parts; and thus they are compelled to say that the soul, too, is of the same kind as its parts, if animals come to have souls by cutting off a portion of what surrounds them and taking it inside themselves. But if the air cut off is all of the same kind, whereas the soul is made up of dissimilar parts, clearly some of the soul will be present in the air, and some will not. Then, either the soul must be made up of parts that are alike, or it cannot be present in just any part of the universe.

It is clear, then, from what has been said, that it is not because of the soul's being made up of elements that knowledge belongs to it; it is also clear that to say that the soul is moved is neither sound nor true.

Now, knowledge is an activity of the soul, and so are perception and belief; so, too, are desires, wishes, and appetites in general; further, movement in space is imparted to animals by the soul, as are also growth, maturity, and decay; all this being so, do all these activities belong to the whole soul, and is it with the whole soul that we think, perceive, become moved, and do and have done to us all the other things that I have mentioned, or do we do different things with different parts? And is life dependent on any one of these parts, or on a number of them, or on all of them? Or has life some other cause? Some say that the soul is divisible into parts, and that one thinks with one part and desires with another. What, then, holds it together, if it is naturally so divisible? Certainly the body does not. On the contrary, it seems rather that the soul holds the body together; at any rate, when the soul leaves it, the body disintegrates into the air and decays. But if there is some other thing that unifies it, this other thing will have more right than anything to be called the soul. Then, one will have to inquire about it, in its turn, whether it is one thing or has many parts. If it is one, why do we not straightaway say that the soul is one? If it is divisible into parts, the argument will lead us to inquire again what holds it together, and thus the process will go on to infinity.

People might be puzzled, too, about the parts of the

soul, and the function that each of them has in the body.
If the whole soul holds the whole body together, each
of the soul's parts should hold a part of the body together. But this seems impossible; it is difficult even to
imagine what kind of part the mind will hold together,
or how it will do it. Plants seem to live even when they
are divided, as do some insects, for the segments have
what is in species the same soul, even though it is not
the same individual one in each case: each of the two
parts retains sensation and moves in space for some
time. And if they do not continue to do so there is nothing strange in this: for they do not have the organs necessary for retaining their nature. Nonetheless, all the
parts of the soul are present in each of the two portions,
and they are of the same form both as each other and
as the whole soul; they are of the same form as each
other since they are not separable from each other, and
of the same form as the whole soul since it is not divisible. The first principle in plants, too, seems to be a soul:
for this is the only thing that both animals and plants
share; it is separate from the principle of sensation, but
nothing has sensation without it.

Book II

1. So much for the views about the soul that have come down to us from our predecessors. Let us now start again, as it were, from the beginning, and try to define what the soul is, and see what is the most general account that we can give of it.

We maintain that one class of the things that exist is substance; of this, one part is matter, which is not in itself a particular thing; a second part is the shape and the form, by virtue of which a thing is described as a particular thing; and the third is the product of the two. The matter is potency, the form realization; and realization can be spoken of in two ways, in the way in which knowledge is realization and in the way in which actual studying is. Bodies more than anything else seem to be substances, and particularly natural bodies, since they are the first principles of everything else. Some natural bodies have life, some do not; by life we mean self-nutrition, growth, and decay. Every natural body, then, that possesses life will be a substance, and a composite substance, too. Since body is of this kind—that is, possessing life—the soul will not be a body, for the body is not one of the things asserted of a substratum; it is, rather, substratum or matter itself. The soul, then, must be a substance inasmuch as it is the form of a natural body that potentially possesses life; and such substance is in fact realization, so that the soul is the realization of a body of this kind. Now, since there are two kinds of realization—realization in the sense in which knowledge is realization, and realization in the sense in which actual studying is—plainly the soul is realization in the sense in which knowledge is; for where the soul is present, both sleeping and waking can be present; and waking is analogous to actual studying, sleeping to the possession of knowledge without its active exercise; and with any given person, in the order of coming-to-be, the possession of knowledge is prior to its exercise. Hence, the soul is the primary realization of a natural body that possesses life. Also, the body must be such that it possesses organs. (Even the parts of plants are organs, although they are quite simple ones: the leaf, for instance, is the cover of the pod, and the pod the cover of the fruit; the roots are analogous to the mouth, since they both absorb food.) If, then, there is any common term that we ought to apply to every soul, it will be "the primary realization of a natural body that possesses organs." We do not, therefore, have to inquire whether the soul and the body are one, just as we do not have to inquire whether the wax and its shape, or in general the matter of any given thing and that of which it is the matter, are one. "Unity" and "being" are used in many senses, but the dominant sense is that of actuality.

We have, then, said in general what the soul is: it is a formal substance. That means that it is the essence of a body of a particular kind. Suppose that some instrument were in fact a natural body—an ax, for instance. Its formal substance would be "being an ax," and that is what its soul would be; if its soul were separated from it, it would no longer be an ax, except insofar as it had the same name as one. In fact, however, without a soul it is still an ax, because the soul is not the essence or form of a body of that kind, but of a natural body such as possesses within itself the source of its movement or rest. But we must also consider what we have said with reference to the parts of the body. If the eye were an animal, its soul would be sight; for sight is the formal substance of the eye. The eye is the matter of sight, and if sight leaves it, it is no longer an eye, except insofar as it has the same name as one, like an eye that is carved in stone or painted. Now, we must apply what we have said of the part to the whole of the living body; for the relation of a part of sensation to a part of the body is analogous to that of sensation as a whole to the sensitive body as a whole—insofar as it is sensitive. It is not the body that has lost its soul, but the body that possesses one, that exists potentially in such a way that it could live; but the seed and the fruit are potentially bodies of this kind. It is the same sense as that in which the seeing of the eye and the cutting of the ax are their realizations that waking is the realization of the body; but it is in the sense in which the power of sight and the power of the instrument are the realizations of the first two that the soul is the realization of the body. The body is what exists potentially; but just as the eye consists both of the pupil and of the power of sight, so the animal consists both of soul and of body. Clearly, then, the soul is not separable from the body; or, if it is divisible into parts, some of the parts are not separable, for in some cases the realization is just the realization of the parts. However, there is nothing to prevent some parts being separated, insofar as they are not realizations of any body. Further, it is not clear whether the soul activates the body in the same way as the sailor activates the ship. So much by way of an outline definition and sketch of the soul.

2. Since what is clear and in principle more knowable emerges from what is obscure but immediately more evident, we must try to review the subject again with this in mind. For a definition ought not merely to show that something is so, as most definitions do, but also to have the cause clearly present in it. At present, the terms of our definitions are like the conclusions of syllogisms. For instance, what is squaring? It is the construction of a square equal in area to a rectangle. Such a definition is an account of the conclusion. But the man who says that squaring is the discovering of a mean proportional line is naming the cause of the thing. Going back, then, to the beginning of our inquiry, we say that that which distinguishes what has a soul from what has not is life. The word "life" is used in many senses, but if it is present in a thing in any one of these senses, we say that that thing lives: for life may indicate the presence of mind, of sensation, of movement or rest in space, or finally of the movement involved in nutrition, together with growth and decay. Hence, all plants seem to live too; for clearly they have within themselves a faculty and principle such that through it they can grow or decay in opposite directions. For they do not just grow upwards without growing downwards; they grow in both directions alike, and indeed in every direction—provided they are always nourished and, so, continuously living—for as long as they can receive nourishment. This nutritive faculty can be separated from the other faculties, but the other faculties cannot exist apart from it in mortal creatures. This is clear in the case of plants, since they have none of the other faculties of the soul. It is because of this primary principle that life belongs to living beings; but a thing is an animal primarily through sensation. For we describe things that do not move or change their position, but do possess sensation, as animals; we do not say that they are merely alive. The primary kind of sensation that is shared by all animals is touch; and, just as the nutritive faculty can be separated from touch and from all sensation, so, too, can touch be separated from the other senses. But we describe as nutritive that part of the soul that is such that even plants share in it; all animals manifestly possess the sense of touch. We shall explain later why both these things are so.

For the time being, it is enough to say that the soul

is the source of these functions, and is defined by them—
that is to say, by the faculties of nutrition, sensation,
thought, and movement. But is each of these a soul, or
only part of a soul? And if each is just a part, is it such
as to be only theoretically separable, or is it physically
separable too? In some cases, it is easy to see the answer
to these questions; in some, there is some difficulty involved. In the case of plants, we see that some of them
live when they are divided and separated from each
other, since, although there is only one soul present in
fully realized form in each plant, there are several potentially present; in the same way, with regard to other varieties of soul, we see this happening with insects, in their
divided segments: each of the two segments retains sensation and local movement; and if each has sensation, it
must have imagination and appetite; for where there is
sensation, pain and pleasure are also present; and where
these are present, there is necessarily desire, too. But in
the case of mind and the faculty of thought, nothing is
yet clear; this seems, however, to be a separate class of
soul, and to be the only class that is capable of being
separated, in the way in which what is eternal can be
separated from what is perishable. But from all this, it
is quite clear that the remaining parts of the soul are
not separable as some people say that they are, although
obviously they are theoretically distinguishable. There
must be a difference between the faculty of sensation
and that of belief, if feeling and believing are different;
and it is the same with all the other faculties that we
have mentioned. Some animals possess all these faculties, others only some of them, still others only one (it
is this that distinguishes different animals from each
other). The reason for all this we must look into later,
but something very similar occurs in the case of the
senses: some animals possess all of them, some have only
some of them, and some have only the one that is most
necessary—namely, touch.

There are two ways in which we talk of that through

which we live and have sensation, just as there are two ways in which we talk of that through which we know; for here in one sense we mean knowledge, in the other the soul, since we say that we know through both of these; similarly, we are healthy in one sense through our good health, in another through some part or even the whole of our bodies. In these cases, knowledge and health will be the shape, form, or definition, and in a way the actuality of what is capable of receiving: in the one case, the actuality of what can have knowledge, in the other the actuality of what can be healthy. For it is in what is being acted upon and being brought into a certain state that the actuality of what is capable of producing an effect seems to be present. Now, the soul is the thing through which we live, have sensation, and think in the primary sense; so it will be the definition and form, not the matter or substratum. We have already pointed out that there are three ways of talking of substance: it can be talked of as form, as matter, or as the product of the two; and of these the matter is the potency, and the form the realization. Now, since the product of the two is what has soul in it, the body will not be the realization of soul, but the soul will be the realization of some body. For this reason, those people are right in their view who maintain that neither can the soul exist without the body nor is it a body; it is not a body, but has something to do with a body, and for this reason it is present in body, and in body of a particular kind; this is not as our predecessors maintained who fitted the soul into a body without specifying in addition what or what kind of body—and who did this although they cannot have thought that one thing receives another just by chance. It is, rather, as we have described, and it is reasonable that it should be. For the realization of each thing naturally occurs in what potentially is that thing and in its own proper matter. It is, then, clear from all this that the soul is a realization and is the form of what possesses a potency for having a soul.

*   *   *

3. Some animals have all of the faculties of the soul
that we have mentioned, others have only some of them,
and still others have only one. The faculties that we have
mentioned are those for nutrition; for sensation; for appetite; for movement in space, or locomotion; and for
thought. Plants possess only the nutritive faculty, but other
beings possess both it and the sensitive faculty; and if they
possess the sensitive faculty, they must also possess the
appetitive; for appetite consists of desire, anger, and will.
All animals possess at least one sense, that of touch; anything that has a sense is acquainted with pleasure and
pain, with what is pleasant and what is painful; and anything that is acquainted with these has desire, since desire
is an appetite for the pleasant. Further, all animals have
a sense for their food. For the sense with which one apprehends food is touch; all animals are nourished by dry and
moist and by hot and cold things, and touch is the sense
that apprehends these; other sensible objects are apprehended by touch only accidentally. For neither noise nor
color nor smell makes any contribution to food, but flavor
is one of the things that can be apprehended by touch.
Hunger and thirst are kinds of desire; hunger is a desire
for what is dry and warm, thirst for what is moist and
cold; and flavor is a sort of seasoning of these. We must
clarify these points later on; but for the time being it is
enough to say that animals that have the sense of touch
also have appetite. Whether they have imagination is not
clear, but we must look into that later. Some animals
have in addition to these faculties, the faculty for locomotion; others have mind and the faculty for thought—
man does, for instance, and so must any other being that
is like him or superior to him.

Plainly, then, there is one definition of soul in the
same way that there is one definition of shape: in the
one case, there is no shape apart from triangle and those
figures that follow it; in the other, there is no soul other
than those that we have mentioned. A common account

can be given of shapes that will fit them all but will not be peculiar to any; and the situation is similar with the kinds of soul that we have mentioned. Hence, it would be absurd in either the one case or the other to seek a common account; for this will not be peculiar to anything that exists, nor will it refer to any indivisible species of its own; further, it is equally absurd to abandon the search for such an indivisible species. There is a close resemblance between what is true of shapes and what is true of the soul: in the case both of shapes and of things that have souls, the one thing is potentially present in what follows it; the triangle is potentially present in the quadrilateral, for instance, and the nutritive soul in the sensitive. We must, then, inquire, species by species, what is the soul of each living thing—what is the soul of a plant, for instance, or what is that of a man or of a beast. We must also ask for what reason they are thus in order. For the sensitive faculty does not exist without the nutritive, but the nutritive faculty is separated from the sensitive in plants; again, without the faculty of touch, none of the other senses is present, but touch may be present without any of the others; there are many animals that possess neither sight nor hearing nor a sense of smell. Again, among animals which are sensitive, some have the faculty of locomotion, others do not; very few, finally, possess the power of reasoning and thinking. Such perishable beings as possess reasoning power also possess all the other faculties; but not all those that possess all the other faculties possess reasoning power; some do not possess even imagination, others live just with that. The subject of the speculative mind is a separate issue. It is then clear that the account of each of these faculties is also the most appropriate account that can be given of the soul.

4. Anyone who is going to examine these faculties of the soul must first of all grasp what each of them is, go on to consider the questions that follow next, and then consider those that remain. But if one is to say what each of them is—what the thinking or the sensitive or the nutritive faculty is, for instance—one must also beforehand say what thinking and feeling are; for in any account the actualities and activities precede the potencies. And if this is so, and if even before these one ought to consider the objects that are their counterparts, we ought, for this same reason, first of all to give a precise account of these objects—of food, and the objects of sense, and the objects of thought. Thus, first of all we must discuss food and generation; for the nutritive soul is found where any of the other faculties are present, it being the primary and most universal faculty of the soul, by virtue of which life belongs to everything that has it. The functions of this faculty are to generate and to make use of food; for the most natural function of any living being that is complete, is not deformed, and is not born spontaneously is to produce another being like itself—in the case of an animal, an animal and in the case of a plant, a plant—so that it may share, as far as it can, in eternity and divinity; that is what they all desire, and it is the purpose of all their natural activities. ("Purpose," however, is ambiguous: it can have reference to an end one is trying to achieve or it can have reference to a person one is trying to benefit.) They cannot, however, share in eternity and divinity continuously, since it is not possible for any perishable thing to remain forever numerically one and the same thing; so they participate in it in the only way in which they can, some to a greater, some to a lesser degree; and what persists is not the thing itself but something like it, what is not numerically, but only in species, one with it.

The soul is the cause and first principle of the living body. These terms are used in several senses; but the soul is a cause in each of the three senses that we have distinguished. It is the source of the body's movement, it is its purpose, and it is the substance of all bodies that contain souls.

That the soul is the cause of the body in the sense of being its substance is evident. The substance is the cause of the being of everything; life is the being of living things; and the cause and first principle of life is the soul. Further, the realization of what exists potentially is its form.

It is clear, too, that the soul is the cause of the body in the sense of being its purpose. Just as a mind produces things for a purpose, so does nature; and this purpose is its end. For all natural bodies are the instruments of the soul, and it is as true of the bodies of plants as it is of those of animals that they exist for the sake of the soul. Purpose, however, as we have said, is ambiguous: it can be used with reference to what one is trying to achieve and also with reference to the person that one is trying to benefit.

The soul is also the original source of locomotion, although the faculty for this does not belong to all living beings. Qualitative change and growth, however, are also due to the soul; for sensation appears to be a kind of qualitative change, and nothing has sensation that does not have soul. Similarly with growth and decay: nothing decays or grows naturally without being fed, and nothing is fed without a share in life.

Empedocles is wrong in the account that he adds of the way in which growth takes place in plants; he says that they grow downwards with their roots uniting because earth naturally moves in this direction, and that they grow upwards because fire, in the same way, naturally moves upwards. His view of "upwards" and "downwards" is unsound; these terms are not the same for everything as they are for the whole universe; rather, if we are to describe organs as the same or different by virtue of their functions, the head is to animals what the roots are to plants. Further, what holds the fire and the earth together when they are moving in opposite directions? They will be torn apart unless there is something to prevent it; and if there is something to prevent it, that something will be the soul, and it will be the cause of their growth and nourishment. Some think, however, that the nature of fire is of itself the cause of nourishment and growth; for it is the only body or element that is obviously nourished by itself and obviously grows of itself; hence, one might suppose that it was what produced these effects in plants and animals. But in fact, although it is in a way a contributory cause, it is not the cause in the absolute sense; it is, rather, the soul that is that. For the growth of fire goes on indefinitely, so long as there is something to be burned; but there is a form and limit imposed on the size and growth of all things that come together by nature, and these (form and limit) are appropriate to soul but not to fire, to form rather than to matter.

Since the same faculty of the soul is both nutritive and generative, we must first of all define food; for it is by the activity of feeding that this faculty is distinguished from the others. One contrary is generally considered to be food for the other; this, however, is not so in every case, only where the contraries do not merely come into being from each other but also derive their growth from one another, for there are many contraries that come into being from each other, but without being quantities—health, for instance, comes into being from illness. But not even all the contraries of the sort mentioned are food for each other, both in the same way: water is food for fire; but fire does not feed water. In simple bodies, then, it generally seems to be the case that one contrary is the food and the other is what is fed. But there is a difficulty here: some say that like is fed by like, just as it is increased by like; others, as we have said, hold the opposite view, that contrary is fed by contrary, since like cannot be acted upon by like, and that food changes by being digested; further, they say, change in every case is into what is contrary or intermediate. Then, food is acted upon by what is fed, but what is fed is not acted upon by food, just as the carpenter is not acted upon by the wood, even though the wood is acted upon by him—he merely changes from idleness to activity. Then, it makes a difference whether food is what is added finally or initially to what is fed. If it is both, but in the one case it is undigested, whereas in the other it is digested, it would be possible to speak of food in both the ways that we have mentioned. Insofar as the food is undigested, contrary is fed by contrary; insofar as it is digested, like is fed by like. So, plainly, in a way both views are right and both are wrong.

Now, nothing is fed that does not share in life; so it will be the body that has a soul that is fed, by virtue of its having a soul; so, too, food is for what possesses a soul, and not accidentally either. But being food is different from being a cause of growth: what causes growth causes it insofar as the being that has a soul is of some size or other; but food feeds insofar as the being is an individual and a substance. Thus, what is fed preserves its substance, and it exists as long as it is fed; further, it is capable of producing the birth, not of what is being fed, but of something like what is being fed; for its own substance already exists, and nothing generates itself, but only preserves itself. Thus, this kind of principle in the soul is a faculty capable of preserving the being that possesses it as such; and food prepares this being for activity. Hence, if it is deprived of food, it cannot exist.

There are three factors in the situation. There is what is fed; there is that by which what is fed is fed; and there is what does the feeding. What does the feeding is the primary soul; what is fed is the body that contains this soul; and the thing by which it is fed is the food. Now, since it is right to name everything with reference to its end, and the end of this kind of soul is the generation of something like itself, the primary soul may be said to be that which is capable of generating something like itself. But "the thing by which what is fed is fed" is ambiguous, just as "the thing by which one steers" is ambiguous: the latter can be the hand, or it can be the rudder, the one moving things as well as being moved, the other just being moved. All food must be capable of being digested, and it is heat that brings about digestion; hence, every being that has a soul in it possesses heat.

We have, then, given an outline account of what food is; we must give a more thorough account of it later on, in writings that are specifically concerned with it.

5. Now that we have drawn these distinctions, let us engage in a general discussion of sensation as a whole. Sensation consists, as we have said, of being moved and acted upon; for it seems to be a kind of qualitative change. Some people say that like is acted upon by like; we have already explained, in our discussions of acting and being acted upon in general, in what way this is possible and in what way it is impossible. But there is a problem as to why there is no sensation of the senses themselves, and why the senses do not produce sensations without the aid of external objects, despite the fact that fire, earth, and the other elements are all present in them, and that there is sensation of all of these by virtue either of themselves or of their attributes. Plainly, then, the sensitive faculty does not exist in actuality, but only potentially, and for that reason sometimes it does not have sensation, just as what is inflammable does not burn of itself, without what is capable of burning it being there; otherwise it would burn of itself, and there would be no need for fire to be present in actuality. Now, there are two ways in which we can talk of having sensation: we say that what is potentially hearing and seeing has hearing and sight even if it happens to be asleep, and also, of course, that what is actually engaged in these activities has these faculties; so, also, there are two ways in which we can talk of sensation: there is what is potentially sensation, and there is what is sensation in actuality; and the same is true of the objects of sense: there is what is potentially such an object and what actually is one. Firstly, then, let us take it that being acted upon and being moved are the same as being in activity; for movement is an actuality or activity, as we have said elsewhere. Everything is acted upon or moved by what is capable of producing an effect and exists in actuality. Thus, in a way things are acted upon by what is like them, in a way by what is unlike them, as we have said: for when a thing is being acted upon, it is unlike what is acting upon it; when it has been acted upon, it is like it.

But we must draw some distinctions with regard to potency and actuality; just now we were talking about them indiscriminately. We can call a man knowledgeable because man is one of the beings that are knowledgeable and that possess knowledge; but in another way we call that man knowledgeable who possesses a knowledge of grammar. Each of these two is capable, but each in a different way from the other: the one is capable because his genus is of a particular kind, and because his matter is what it is; the other is capable because he can study when he wishes to, provided he is not prevented by anything external. Then, there is the man who is already studying; he is knowledgeable in actuality because he knows absolutely a particular A. The first two are knowledgeable only potentially, but become so in actuality: the one does so after a series of qualitative changes from a contrary state, by means of learning; the other does so by changing from the mere possession of the knowledge of arithmetic or grammar to their actual exercise; and, so, the two kinds of change are different. But not even the term "being acted upon" is unambiguous: in one sense it means some sort of destruction of one contrary, brought about by the other; in another sense it means the preservation of what exists only potentially by what exists in actuality and is like it in the same way as the potency is like the realization. In this second sense, what possesses knowledge becomes something that is actually studying; and this process either is not qualitative change at all (since it is a growth of the thing into itself and its

realization) or is a different kind of qualitative change.
So it is not right to say that what thinks changes qualitatively when it thinks, just as it is not right to say that
the builder changes when he builds. The process, then,
of bringing what thinks and is intelligent out of potential
existence into realization ought not to be called teaching;
it ought to have some other name. And, as for the process of learning and acquiring knowledge, starting from
its merely potential presence, and taking place through
the agency of what exists in actuality and is capable of
teaching, either this ought not to be called "being acted
upon" at all, as we have said, or else there must be two
kinds of qualitative change: the one being change into a
condition in which one is deprived of a quality, the other
change into what is one's proper state and nature.

In the case of the faculty of sense, the first kind of
change is brought about by the creature's father; it possesses sense at birth in the same way that it possesses
knowledge; then, actually having sensation corresponds
to studying. There is this difference, however: in the case
of sense, what can produce the actuality is external—
what is visible, what is audible, and so on with all the
other objects of sense. The reason for this is that actual
sensation is sensation of individual things, whereas
knowledge is knowledge of universals, which in a sense
exist in the soul itself. For this reason it is in a man's
power to think whenever he wishes, but having sensation
is not in his power; there must be an object of sensation
there. It is the same, too, with those branches of knowledge that deal with sensible objects; and the reason is
the same: that sensible objects are individual things and
are external.

But we shall have an opportunity to clarify these
points later. For the time being, it is enough to have
shown that the term "potential" is not unambiguous:
there is one sense in which one describes a boy as potentially a general; there is another in which one so describes an adult. It is in this latter way that we talk of

the faculty of sense as potential. Since there are no terms to express this difference of meaning, and since we have shown that these meanings are different, and in what way they are different, we must continue to use the terms "being acted upon" and "qualitative change" as though they were valid terms. The faculty of sense, as we have said, is potentially like what the object of sense is in actuality: when it is being acted upon, it is not like it; but when it has been acted upon, it has been made like it and is of the same kind as it.

6. We must first of all discuss the objects of sense with reference to each sense. There are three ways in which we can talk of the objects of sense: in the first two of these ways, we are talking of things that we perceive in themselves; in the third we are talking of things that we perceive accidentally. Of the first two kinds of object, one is peculiar to each sense, the other is common to them all. By a peculiar object I mean one that it is not possible to perceive with any other sense, and about which it is not possible to be deceived—color in the case of sight, sound in the case of hearing, flavor in the case of taste, and several different objects in the case of touch. A different sense judges about each of these, and it is not deceived about its being a color in one case or a sound in another, although it may be deceived about what or where the thing is that is colored, or what or where the thing is that is making a noise. Such objects are said to be peculiar to a given sense; the common objects of sense are movement, rest, number, shape, and magnitude, which are peculiar to no one sense but are common to them all. For movement can be perceived either by touch or by sight. But we talk of an incidental object of sense where, for instance, a particular white object is the son of Diares; one perceives him incidentally, since he is incidental to the whiteness that one perceives; hence, one is not acted upon by the object of sense insofar as it is incidental. But of the things that

are of themselves the objects of sense, it is the peculiar
objects that are most properly so, and it is toward them
that each sense is essentially and naturally directed.

. . .

12. But about all sensation in general we must grasp
that a sense is what is capable of receiving the forms of
sensible objects without their matter, just as the wax receives the impression of the ring without the iron or the
gold, and indeed receives an impression from what is gold
or bronze even though it does not receive it by virtue of
the thing's being gold or bronze. Similarly, each person's
sense is acted upon by what possesses color or flavor or
sound, not by virtue of what each of these things is said
to be, but by virtue of its being of a particular kind, and
having a form. And "sense organ" primarily means that
in which a faculty of this kind is present. The sense organ
is, in fact, the same as the faculty, but their essences are
different. What perceives is a magnitude, but neither the
capacity for sensation nor sensation itself is a magnitude;
they are, rather, the form and faculty of what perceives.

From this it is clear why an excess of sensible objects destroys the sense organs. If the movement imparted to the
sense organ is too strong, the form (which we agreed to be
the sensation) is destroyed, just as the harmony and pitch
may be destroyed if the strings are plucked too hard. It
is also clear from this why plants have no sensation, even
though they do possess a portion of the soul and are acted
upon by the objects of the sense of touch (they do get
hot and cold, for instance). The reason is that they have
no intermediate element nor any principle of such a kind
that it can receive the forms of sensible objects; instead,
they are acted upon by matter at the same time as form.

One might be at a loss to know whether what cannot
smell is acted upon by smell; or what cannot see, by
color; and so on with the other senses. If smell is just
what can be smelled, anything that it acts upon must be

the sense of smell; and, thus, nothing that cannot smell
can be acted upon by smell; and the same argument
applies to the other senses. Nothing can be acted upon
by an object of sense except insofar as it has the relevant
faculty of sensation. This point becomes clear in another
way, too. Neither light nor darkness nor noise nor smell
affects bodies at all; it is what these things are *in* that
affects bodies; it is, for instance, the air that accompanies
the thunder that splits the wood. But, it may be said,
the objects of the sense of touch and flavors do affect
bodies; otherwise, what are things that do not possess
souls acted upon and changed by? Perhaps, then, the
other objects of sense do affect things, too; or, perhaps
not every body can be acted upon by smell and sound,
but those that are so acted upon are indeterminate and
do not persist; this would seem to be so with air, for
instance, since it gives off a smell as though it had been
acted upon. What, then, is smelling apart from being
acted upon? Perhaps, whereas smelling involves sensation, what happens to the air when it is acted upon is
that it momentarily becomes an object of sense.

Book III

1. We may be sure that there is no sense apart from the five that we have mentioned—sight, hearing, smell, taste, and touch—on the basis of the following arguments.

We may take it that we have sensation of everything for which touch is the appropriate sense, since all the qualities of what is tangible insofar as it is tangible are perceptible to us by touch; also that if any sense is lacking to us, some sense organ must be lacking too. We may take it in addition that such things as we perceive by touching them are perceptible by means of the touch that we in fact possess, whereas such things as we perceive through media without touching the things themselves are perceptible by means of the simple bodies like air and water. (The situation with regard to perception of this kind is like this: if objects of sense that are different from each other in kind are perceptible through one medium, the man who possesses the sense organ appropriate to this medium must be capable of perceiving both kinds of objects; this will be so, for instance, if the sense organ is made of air, and air is a medium both for sound and for color; if, on the other hand, several bodies are media for the same object, as air and water both are for color, both of them being transparent, the man who possesses just one of these media will perceive what

283

passes through both.) We may take it too that the sense organs are made up of only these two of the simple bodies, air and water; the pupil of the eye is made of water, the hearing organ of air, and the organ of smell of one or other of the two; fire is either found in none of them, or is common to them all (since nothing is capable of sensation without heat), and earth is found in none, or, if it is found in any, it is found exclusively and specially in the sense of touch. Hence it would seem that no sense organ is made of anything but water and air, and some animals do possess sense organs made of these. If we accept all these facts, it seems that all the senses are possessed by animals that are not incomplete or maimed, for we observe that even the mole has eyes beneath its skin; and thus, if there is no body other than those that we know and no quality other than those that belong to the bodies that we know, there can be no sense that we have omitted.

Further, there cannot be any special sense organ for the common objects of sense, which we perceive accidentally with every sense—things like movement, rest, shape, magnitude, number, and unity. We perceive all of these through movement; it is through movement that we perceive magnitude, for instance, and hence also shape, since shape is a kind of magnitude; we perceive what is at rest through its lack of movement; and number we perceive through the negation of continuity, and through the special objects of sense, since each sense perceives a single thing. Clearly, then, it is impossible for there to be a special sense for any of these things like movement; if it were possible, it would happen in the way in which we now perceive what is sweet by means of sight; this happens because we possess a sense for both these qualities of sweetness and color, by means of which we recognize them together when the two coincide. If this were not so, our perception in such cases would always be accidental, as it is in the case of Cleon's son, where we perceive not that this is Cleon's son, but

that this is white and that it is an accidental attribute of
it that it is Cleon's son. But we do have a common sense
for the common objects of sense that is not accidental;
and this is not a special sense. Otherwise we should
never perceive these objects in any way other than that
in which we have said that we see Cleon's son. The
senses perceive each other's special objects accidentally,
not by virtue of their being themselves, but in virtue of
their all being a unity when there is a simultaneous sensation with regard to one and the same thing; in the case
of bile, for instance, there is the simultaneous sensation
that it is both bitter and yellow, for to say that this one
thing is both cannot be the act of either sense on its
own. Thus a sense can in this kind of case be deceived,
and if a thing is yellow, it may suppose it to be bile.

Someone might ask why we have several senses and
not just one. Perhaps it is so that we may lose sight less
of the common objects of sense that accompany the special objects, things like movement, magnitude, and number. For if we had only had sight, and sight only of what
was white, we would have failed far more to notice the
common objects of sense, and we would have thought
that all things were identical because color and magnitude always accompany each other. But in fact, since the
common objects of sense appear too in a second object
of sense, it is made clear to us that each of them is
separate.

2. Since we do perceive that we are seeing or hearing,
we must perceive that we are seeing either by means of
sight, or by some other sense. If we do it by means of
sight, the same sense will perceive both sight and the
color that is its object. Thus, either there will be two
senses with the same object or one sense will be its own
object. Further, if the sense that perceives sight is separate from sight, either the process will go on to infinity
or a sense will again be its own object, in which case we
might as well have accepted this consequence in the first

instance. This involves a problem. If perceiving by means
of the sight is just seeing, and if what is seen is color or
what possesses color, then if somebody sees the activity
of seeing, the original activity will possess color too.
Plainly, then, perceiving with the sight is not just one
thing, for we observe both darkness and light by means
of sight, but in different ways. Furthermore, even what
sees is in a way colored; for each sense organ is capable
of receiving an object of sense without its matter. Hence
even when the objects of sense have departed, sensations
and images remain in the sense organs.

The actuality of the object of sense and that of the
sense are one and the same, but their essences are not
the same. Take for instance an actual sound and actual
hearing. It is possible for what possesses hearing not to
hear, and what possesses a sound is not always making
a sound. But when what is capable of hearing is engaged
in its activity, and when what is capable of making a
sound is making one, then the actualized hearing occurs
at the same time as the actualized sound; one might call
the one of them "audition," the other "sounding."

If movement, action, and affection are all to be found
in what is being acted upon, both the sound and the
hearing when actualized must be in what is potentially
the hearing. For the actualization of what can act and
impart movement occurs in what is being acted upon;
this is why it is not necessary for what imparts movement
to be moved itself. The actuality, then, of what can produce sound is sound or sounding, and that of what can
hear is hearing or audition; for both "hearing" and
"sound" are ambiguous terms. The same argument applies to the other senses and their objects. For just as
acting and being acted upon occur in what is being acted
upon and not in what is acting, so too the actuality of
the sensible object and that of what is capable of perceiving occur in what is capable of perceiving. In some
cases both these actualities have names, as with sounding
and audition, but in some cases one of the two has none:

the actuality of sight is called seeing, but that of color
has no name; the actuality of what can taste is tasting,
but that of flavor has no name either. Since the actualities of the sensible object and of what is capable of perceiving it are one, although their essences are different,
hearing and sound (these terms being used in the sense
of the actualities) must perish simultaneously with and
be preserved for the same length of time as each other,
as also must flavor and tasting, and similarly with the
others. But when these terms are used of what is potential, this is no longer necessarily true. Previous inquirers
into nature made a mistake here. They thought that
white and black could not exist without sight, nor flavor
without taste. In a way they were right, in a way they
were wrong; for both the sense and its object are talked
about in two different ways according to whether they
are potential or actual; in the latter case what they say
is true, in the former it is not. Their mistake was to
use ambiguous terms in their statements as though they
were unambiguous.

If voice is a kind of harmony, and if the voice and the
hearing are in a way one, and if the harmony is a ratio,
hearing too must be a ratio; it is for this reason that any
excess, whether of the high or of the low, destroys the
hearing; the same thing happens to the taste with flavors;
in the case of colors, what is too bright or too dark
destroys the sight, and a strong smell, whether sweet or
bitter, does the same to the sense of smell. This is all
because sensation itself is a kind of ratio. This is also
why, although things are pleasant when they are brought
into the ratio pure and unmixed (things like the pungent,
the sweet, and the salty, for they *are* pleasant then), in
general what is mixed is more pleasant; a harmony, for
instance, is more pleasant than the high or the low on
its own. The sensation is the ratio, and any excess pains
or destroys it.

Every sensation, then, is related to the object that corresponds to it, being present in the sense organ by virtue

of its being a sense organ, and it judges of the differences in its object; sight, for instance, judges of white
and black, taste of sweet and bitter, and it is the same
with the others. But since we also distinguish the white
from the sweet, and every sensible object from every
other, by means of what do we perceive that these are
different? It must be by sense, since these are the objects
of sense. It is thus also clear that flesh is not the ultimate
sense organ; if it were, anything that made a judgment
would have to do so by actually touching its object. It
is not possible, either, for separate senses to judge that
white is different from sweet; both must be plain to some
one sense; if they did not have to be, whenever you
perceived one thing and I another, it would be apparent
that they were different, but it must be one sense that
says that they are different; for the sweet is different
from the white. What asserts the difference, then, must
be one, and consequently it must think and perceive as
one just as it speaks as one. It is clear, then, that it is
not possible for senses that are separate to judge objects
that are separate. They cannot judge them at separate
times either, as is clear from the following arguments.
Just as it is the same faculty that says that the good is
different from the bad, so too the time at which it says
that the one is different from the other is not accidental
to the assertion, as it would be if it were just a question
of saying now that it is different as opposed to saying
that it is different now; it is in fact the latter that it is
doing; it is not only talking now but is also saying that
it is different now; so the objects must be being talked
of together. Thus what makes the assertion must be indivisible, and it must make it in an indivisible moment of
time. But then it is impossible for the same thing insofar
as it is indivisible to be moved in opposite directions at
the same time, and in an indivisible moment of time. If
a thing is sweet, it moves the sense or thought in one
way, while the bitter moves it in the opposite way, and
the white in a different way from both. Is what distin-

guishes between them, then, indivisible and inseparable
from itself in the numerical sense while being separated
in essence? In one way it is what is divided that perceives divided objects; in another way what does so does
so by virtue of its being indivisible: it is divided in essence, but not numerically or spatially. But perhaps this
is not possible. What is the same indivisible thing can
be two opposites potentially, but not in essence; when it
is actualized, it must become divided. It is not possible
for a thing to be both white and black at the same time,
and so it is not possible either for it to be acted upon
by the forms of both, if indeed sensation and thought
do involve being acted upon by forms. The situation is
in fact the same as with what some people call a point;
insofar as it is both one and two, it is both indivisible
and divisible. Insofar as it is indivisible, what judges is
one and judges at one and the same time; insofar as it
is divisible, it uses the same symbol twice at once. Insofar, then, as it uses the symbol or limit twice, it is judging
two things and is in a way judging them separately; but
insofar as it is using one limit, it is a single thing making
the judgment.

So much, then, by way of discussion of the principle
by virtue of which we call the animal sensitive.

3. There are two distinguishing characteristics by
which people generally define the soul: movement in
space, or locomotion; and thinking, understanding, and
perceiving. Thinking and understanding give the impression of being forms of perceiving; in both cases the soul
is judging and recognizing something that exists. The ancients, too, certainly say that understanding and perceiving are the same; Empedocles, for instance, has said that
it is in the light of what is before him that man's wisdom
is increased, and in another passage that this is why it
happens to them that they always think different things;
the same idea is indicated in Homer's phrase "Such is
the mind." All these people regard thinking as some-

thing corporeal like perceiving; they say, as we showed in our discussions at the beginning, that one perceives and understands like by means of like. Yet they ought at the same time to have discussed error; for this is a more natural state for animals than being right, and one in which the soul remains for a longer period of time. On the basis of this view, either, as some say, everything that appears must be true, or error must consist in contact with what is unlike, for this is the contrary process to recognizing like by like; but it is generally held that as with knowledge, so with error; error about one contrary is the same as error about the other. It is then plain that perceiving and understanding are not the same. All animals share in the former, few in the latter. Thinking is not the same as perceiving either; thinking contains both what is correct and what is incorrect, what is correct being wisdom, knowledge, and true opinion, what is incorrect being the contraries of these. Thinking, then, I say, is not the same as perceiving, since perception of the special objects of sense is always true and belongs to all animals, while it is possible to think falsely as well as truly; also, thinking does not belong to any being that does not possess reason. For imagination is different both from sensation and from thought; it does not occur without sensation, and without it there can be no belief. But it is clear that it is not the same thing as belief. Imagining is within our power whenever we want to exercise it: we can produce something before our eyes as people do who call up images in mnemonics; opinion is not within our power: one's opinions must be either true or false. Further, whenever we believe something to be terrible or frightening, we are at once affected by it, and it is the same if we believe something to be heartening; but in the case of imagination, we are in the same state as if we were looking at what was frightening or heartening in a picture. There are different kinds of belief: knowledge, opinion, understanding, and their contraries; about the differences between these I must speak elsewhere.

Thinking, then, is different from perceiving, and it seems to include both imagination and belief. Let us first of all thoroughly define imagination, and then go on to the other. If imagination is that by virtue of which we say that there is an image present in us in a real as opposed to a metaphorical sense, is it, then, one of those faculties or states by virtue of which we make judgments and are either right or wrong? The faculties and states of this kind are sensation, opinion, knowledge, and mind.

The following considerations make it clear that imagination is not sensation. Sensation is either a faculty or an activity (as with sight or seeing, for instance); but something can be imagined when neither of these is present—the things that are imagined in dreams are an example. Then, sensation is always present, whereas imagination is not. If they were the same in their actualities, it would be possible for all the beasts to possess imagination; in fact, however, this does not seem to be the case; it does not seem that ants, bees, or earthworms can possess imagination. Further, sensations are always true, whereas most imaginings are false. Also, it is not when our sense is being precise and active about its object that we imagine something to be a man, but rather when we do not perceive clearly whether this is true or false. And, as we were saying earlier, we imagine sights even when we have our eyes shut.

Nor can imagination be any of the faculties that are always right, like knowledge or intelligence, for it can be false as well as true.

It remains, then, to see whether imagination is opinion, since opinion can be both true and false. But opinion is accompanied by belief, since it is not possible to hold opinions that one does not believe; and no beast is capable of belief, although many of them possess imagination. Further, although every opinion is accompanied by belief, belief is also accompanied by conviction; and conviction is accompanied by reason; and although some beasts possess imagination, none possesses reason. Plainly, then, imagination is not opinion accompanied by

sensation, nor is it opinion formed through sensation,
nor is it a combination of the two. This is so both for
the reasons that I have mentioned and also because the
object of opinion will in that case be nothing other than
the object of sensation. I mean, for instance, that imagination will be a combination of the opinion about and
the sensation of what is white; for it will not be a combination of the opinion about what is good and the sensation of what is white. This will mean that imagining
something will be holding an opinion about what one
perceives, and not about what one perceives accidentally
either. But what we imagine can be false even in the
case of things about which we have a true belief; for
instance, we imagine the sun to be one foot in diameter,
but we are convinced that it is larger than the inhabited
earth. Consequently, then, in such a case one must either
have rejected the true opinion that one had, without the
facts having changed and without one having either forgotten one's true opinion or been converted from it, or
if one still retains the same opinion, the same opinion
must be both true and false. But in fact, of course, the
time when an opinion becomes false is when the facts
do change without one's noticing it. Imagination, then,
is not any of these faculties, nor is it made up of them.

But when something has been moved, it is possible
for something else to be moved by it; and imagination
seems to be a movement and seems not to occur independently of sensation; it seems to occur only in beings
that have sensation, and its objects seem to be the same
as the objects of sensation. Further, it is possible for this
movement to be brought about by the activity of the
sense, and it must be like sensation. For all these reasons, this movement that is imagination cannot occur
without sensation, nor can it be possessed by beings that
do not have sensation; by virtue of it, what possesses it
may act and be acted upon in a number of ways; and
the imagination itself may be true or false. The reasons
are these. Perception of the special objects of sense is

true or at least contains the minimum of falsehood. But perception is secondarily of the fact that the attributes of its objects are their attributes; and here there is already a possibility of error. One cannot be wrong in perceiving whiteness, but one can be wrong in supposing that the white thing is this or that. Thirdly, perception is of the common objects that accompany the things to which the special objects of sense are attached; I mean things like movement and magnitude. These are the things about which it is most possible to be deceived in perception. Now there will be a difference between the movements imparted by the activities of these three different kinds of sense. The first kind is always true, so long as the sensation is present; the other two can be wrong whether the sensation is present or not, and they are particularly likely to be so if the object of sense is some way off.

If, then, nothing else possesses the characteristics that we have named except imagination, and imagination is in fact what we have described, imagination will be a movement imparted by the sense when the sense is in a state of actuality. And since sight is more of a sense than any of the others, imagination has gained its name from light, since it is not possible to see without light.

Because imaginings persist and resemble sensations, animals do a great deal by virtue of them, some, like beasts, because they possess no mind, others because their minds are clouded by some affection or by disease or by sleep, as happens, for instance, with mankind.

So much, then, by way of an account of what imagination is and why it is as it is.

4. We must now turn to the part of the soul with which it knows and thinks, and (whether it is physically separable or only theoretically so) we must see what its distinguishing characteristics are and how thinking ever occurs. If thinking is like perceiving, it must either be a process of being acted upon by the object of thought or something else of the same kind. Strictly, this part of the soul must not be capable of being acted upon, but capable of receiving the form of its object; and it must be potentially like its object, without ever being its object; and indeed the relation of the mind to the objects of thought must be like that of the faculty of sense to the objects of sense. It is necessary, then, since it thinks of everything, for the mind to be unmixed with anything, so that, as Anaxagoras says, it may have control, that is, so that it may recognize things. For any alien element that appears in it is a hindrance and impediment; it follows that it cannot have any nature other than that of being capable of doing what it does. That part of the soul that is called the mind (and by the mind I mean that with which the soul thinks and believes) is not a thing that exists in actuality at all before it thinks. So it is not plausible to suppose that it is mingled with the body; if it were, it would come to be of a particular kind—hot or cold—or it would have some organ as the faculty of sense does; but as it is, it has none. These people speak well who describe the soul as the place where the forms are, except that this is not true of the whole soul, but only of the part that is capable of thinking; nor are the forms there in a realized state, but only potentially. That the incapacity of the faculty of sense to be acted upon is not like this same incapacity in the faculty of thought is plain from a consideration of the sense organs and of sensation. After encountering a too-violent object of sense, the sense cannot perceive; it cannot hear after hearing very loud sounds, it cannot see or smell after having seen very bright colors or smelled very pungent smells. But when the mind thinks of what is in the most extreme sense an object of thought, it does not think any the less of what are objects of thought to a lesser degree; rather it thinks of them even more. For the faculty of sensation does not exist independently of the body, but the mind is separable from it. But when the mind becomes each of its objects in the way that the man who is knowledgeable in actuality is said to (and

this happens when he is able to be active on his own),
even then the mind is still in a way in a potential state,
though not in the same way as it was before it learned
or discovered what it did learn; the mind is now able to
think on its own.

Now, magnitude and the essence of magnitude are different; so are water and the essence of water; and it is
the same in many other cases, though not in all—in some
the two are the same. Since this is all so, either one will
judge of flesh and of the essence of flesh with different
faculties, or one will do so with the same faculty when
it is in different states. For flesh is not devoid of matter;
like "snub," it is one definite thing contained in another
definite thing. It is with the faculty of sense that one
judges the hot and the cold and all the things of which
flesh is a proportion; but it is with some other faculty,
which is either separate from the faculty of sense or
bears the same relation to it as a crooked line does to
itself when it is straightened out, that one judges the
essence of flesh. Again, in the case of things that exist
only abstractly, the straight is like the snub in that it is
always accompanied by what is continuous. But its essence, if there is a difference between straight and the
essence of straight, will be something different. Let us
take this essence to be duality. This must be judged by
a different faculty, or by the same faculty when it is in
a different state. In general, then, the activities of the
mind are separable in the same way as objects are separable from their matter.

If the mind is as Anaxagoras says it is, simple, incapable of being acted upon, and having nothing in common
with anything, one might be at a loss to know how it
will think if thinking is having something done to one;
for it is only insofar as there is something in common
between two things that the one of them seems to act,
the other to be acted upon; one might also wonder if
the mind is an object of thought itself. For if the mind
is an object of thought in itself, and not by virtue of

anything else, and if all objects of thought are one in kind, either mind will be present in everything else as well or it will contain something mixed in with it that makes it an object of thought in the way that everything else is. But perhaps we have already settled the question of something being acted upon by virtue of a common element by saying that in a way the mind is potentially the objects of its thought, but that it is not any of them in a realized form until it is actually thinking; it is potentially those objects in the same way that a writing tablet on which nothing is actually written is potentially something written upon: exactly the same thing happens with the mind. It is itself an object of thought in the same way as the things that are the objects of its thought. In the case of things that are devoid of matter, what thinks and what is thought are identical, for speculative knowledge and its object are identical. We must inquire later why the mind is not always thinking. In the case of things that contain matter, each object of thought is only present potentially. It follows that although mind will not be present in them (since the mind is only a potency for being such things insofar as they are separable from matter), the object of thought will be present in the mind.

5. Now, in nature as a whole, every class of objects has its matter, which is what potentially is those objects; then, as a second factor, there is the productive cause, so called since it produces everything, which is related to matter in general in the same way that art is related to its material. This being so, these distinctions must be present in the soul as well. There is the mind that is such as we have just described by virtue of the fact that it becomes everything; then, there is another mind, which is what it is by virtue of the fact that it makes everything; it is a sort of condition like light. For in a way light makes what are potentially colors become colors in actuality. This second mind is separable, incapable of being acted upon, mixed with nothing, and in essence an actuality. For what acts is always more to be valued than what is acted upon, and the first principle more than the matter.

Knowledge that exists in actuality is identical with its object; potential knowledge is prior to it in time in any one individual, although in general it is not even prior to it in time. There is no question of the mind sometimes thinking and sometimes not doing so. But it is only when it is separated that it is fully itself; it alone is immortal and eternal; we do not remember this because, although this mind is incapable of being acted upon, the other kind of mind, which is capable of being acted upon, is perishable. But without this kind of mind nothing thinks.

6. Thought of indivisible objects occurs when there is no question of falsehood; where there can be either falsehood or truth, there is already a combination of thoughts treated as though they were one. Just as, according to Empedocles, "where the heads of many grew without necks," they were then combined through Love, so these separate thoughts are combined—incommensurability and the diagonal, for instance; and if one is concerned with things in the past or the future, one thinks of time as well and puts it into the combination. It is always in a combination that falsehood appears; if anyone says that what is white is not white, he has combined the white with the not-white. It is possible, too, to describe all these statements as divisions. Anyway, it is not only the statement that Cleon is white that is false or true, but also the statements that he was or will be white. Now, what unifies each of these statements is the mind.

Since there are two senses in which we can talk of what is indivisible, according to whether it is incapable of being divided or just not actually divided, there is nothing to stop the mind thinking of what is indivisible when it thinks of length (since the length is actually undivided) or to stop it thinking of it in an indivisible time;

for the time will be divisible and indivisible in the same
sense as the length. It is not possible to say in this kind
of case what the mind is thinking of in each half of the
time, for if the whole is not divided, the half does not
exist other than potentially. But the man who thinks of
the two halves separately is also at the same time dividing the time; and he is treating the two halves as though
they were both lengths. But if the mind thinks of the
length as made up of two halves, it will do so in a time
that is made up of two halves. But it thinks of them in
this way accidentally; it does not think of the length or
of the time in which it thinks of the length by virtue of
their being divisible, but by virtue of their being indivisible; for even in them there is something indivisible,
though perhaps not separable, that makes the time and
the length one. This is true of everything that is continuous, whether a time or a length.

What is not quantitatively but only qualitatively indivisible is thought of in an indivisible time and by an
indivisible activity of the soul.

Points, all kinds of divisions, and all other things that
are in this way indivisible, are revealed in the same way
as privation. A similar principle applies elsewhere to the
way in which one recognizes the bad or the black, for
instance; one recognizes each in a way by its contrary;
but what does the recognizing must potentially be the
contrary, and the contrary must potentially be present
in it. But if anything has no contrary, it recognizes itself,
it is an actuality, and it is separable. Assertion involves
applying one term to another, as does also denial; hence
every assertion and every denial must be true or false;
but this is not always the case with the mind. The
thought of what a thing is and of its essence is always
right and does not involve the application of one term
to another. Just as the sight of a special object of sense
is true but the perception that what is white is a man
is not always true, so it is with things that are devoid
of matter.

*   *   *

7. Actualized knowledge is the same as its object; potential knowledge is prior to it in time in the case of a single individual, but in general it is not prior to it even in time, for everything that comes into being comes from what exists in a realized state. Clearly the object of sense makes the sensitive faculty actual after it has just been potential, for the faculty is not acted upon nor is it changed qualitatively. Hence this process must be some other kind of thing than movement, for movement is the activity of what is imperfect; but unqualified activity, that of what is perfect, is different.

Perceiving, then, is like just asserting or thinking; but when the object is pleasant or painful, the sense makes what amounts to an assertion or a denial and pursues or avoids the object. Both feeling pleasure and feeling pain involve being actively concerned through the sensitive mean with the good and the bad as such. Avoidance and appetite, when they are fully actualized, are in fact this same thing; the faculty of appetite and that of avoidance are no different either from each other or from the faculty of sense. Only their essences are different.

For the thinking soul, images are like objects of sensation. Whenever the soul asserts or denies that something is good or bad, it avoids or pursues it. Hence the soul never thinks without an image. This is like what happens when the air has a particular effect upon the pupil of the eye, and the pupil then has one on something else, and it is also like what happens with hearing. The last thing affected is a single thing and a single mean, but it has several essences.

We have explained before the means by which one judges how the sweet differs from the hot; but we must add this explanation too. The thing by means of which one judges is a single thing, and thus is like a limit; and these means which form a unity both by analogy and in actual number are related the one to the other as the sweet and the hot are related to one another. Indeed, what is the difference between being puzzled about how one distinguishes between things that are not in the same class and about how one distinguishes between contraries like white and black? Suppose that A (white) is related to B (black) as C is to D, so that C then is to A as D is to B. If C and A belong to the same thing, it will be the same as if D and B did. The two will be one and the same thing though their essences will be different, and the same will be true of the other pair. The same argument will apply if A is sweet and B is white.

The thinking faculty, then, thinks of its forms in images; and what is to be pursued and what avoided is defined for it in the same way as with the objects of sense; and quite apart from sensation, whenever the thinking faculty is involved with images, it is moved. For instance, when a man perceives a beacon, he knows that it is fire; but when he sees it moving, he recognizes by the common sense that it is an enemy beacon. But sometimes he calculates on the basis of images and thoughts in his soul as though he were seeing them, and deliberates, weighing the future against the present. And just as with sense, so here, too, whenever he declares something to be pleasant or painful, he avoids or pursues it, and this indeed is what he does in action in general. But quite apart from action, the true and the false are in the same class as the good and the bad; they differ in that the one pair is used generally, the other with reference to some particular.

In the case of abstract terms, it is as if one were thinking of the snub, not insofar as it is snub but separately, as being in actuality curved, independently of the flesh in which the curve is present. Similarly, with the objects of mathematics, one thinks of them as separate, although they are not, when one thinks of them as themselves. In general, mind when actualized is the same as the things that it is thinking of. Whether it is possible for it to think of any of the things that are separate from magnitude when it is not separate from magnitude itself, we must inquire later.

• • •

9. Now, the soul in animals has been defined with reference to two faculties, the faculty of judgment (which is the function of intellect and sensation) and that of movement in place. Let what we have said about mind and sensation suffice; we must now consider what imparts movement; we must see what it is, whether it is a single part either physically or theoretically separable from the soul, or whether it is the whole soul; and if it is a part, we must see whether it is a special one in addition to the ones that are usually mentioned and that we have mentioned, or whether it is just one of the latter. We meet a difficulty straightaway about how we can talk of parts of the soul and of how many of them there are. In one way there seems to be an infinite number of them, and not just the ones that some people name when they define the soul—the reasoning, the spirited, and the desiring, or, as others say, the rational and the irrational. For if we follow the principles of differentiation according to which these people divide the soul up, other parts will emerge as well, more different from each other than these are; we have in fact already mentioned them: there is the nutritive faculty, which is present both in plants and in all animals; and there is the sensitive faculty, which cannot be easily classed either as rational or irrational; then there is the imaginative faculty, which is distinct from the others in its essence, though it is very difficult to know which of the others it is the same as or different from, if one assumes that there are separate parts of the soul; and in addition to these, there is the appetitive part, which would appear to be distinct from all the others, both in definition and in capacity. It is certainly absurd to split this part up; yet this is implicit in the view of some thinkers, since the will is in the rational part and desire and anger are in the irrational; if the soul is in fact three parts, appetite will be present in each.

Then, to turn to the subject of our present discussion, what is it that makes animals move from place to place?

The movement involved in growth and decay, which belongs to all living beings, seems to be imparted by the faculty that they all possess—the generative and nutritive faculty. Inhalation and exhalation, sleep and wakefulness, we must look into later, since they involve a great many difficulties. But in the case of movement in place, we must see what it is that moves an animal in such a way that it travels. It is clear that it is not the nutritive faculty, for this movement always has a purpose and is accompanied by imagination and appetite, for nothing moves except when it is wanting or avoiding something or unless it is compelled to. Also, if it were the nutritive faculty, plants would be capable of moving as well and would have the organs necessary for this movement. Similarly, it is not the sensitive faculty, for there are many animals that possess sensation but are continually stationary and immovable. If, then, nature does nothing in vain and omits nothing that is necessary, except in the case of deformities and beings that are incomplete, and if the animals of the kind that I have been mentioning are complete and not deformed (as is shown by their being capable of generation and having a peak beyond which they decay), these animals, if the sensitive faculty had been the cause of movement in place, would have possessed the necessary organs for it. But it is not the rational part of the soul either or what is called mind that does the moving; for the speculative mind does not speculate on anything that is practical, nor does it discuss at all what is worth avoiding or pursuing; and movement is always movement of something that is pursuing or avoiding something else. Even when the mind does speculate on something of this kind, it does not tell us to avoid or to pursue it; for instance, it often thinks of something frightening or pleasant, but the mind does not tell us to be frightened; it is the heart that is moved, or, if the thing is pleasant, some other part. Further, even when the mind does give us instructions and the intellect does tell us to avoid or to pursue something, the soul may not be moved; the man may act according to his desire, as the uncontrolled man does. In general, too, we see that the man who possesses the art of medicine does not necessarily practice his art, since there is something else, which is not his knowledge, that determines whether he shall act in accordance with his knowledge. But it is not appetite either that is the decisive factor with this kind of movement; people who have self-control, although they may have an appetite and desire for something, do not do what they have the appetite for, but follow their minds.

10. But there are clearly two things that cause movement, appetite and mind, if, that is, one can regard imagination as a kind of thought; for many men follow their imaginations in defiance of their knowledge, and in the other animals there is no thought or calculation, there is only imagination. These two things, then, are capable of causing movement in place—mind and appetite; the mind is the kind that calculates for a purpose, the practical mind; it differs from the speculative mind in the end at which it aims. All appetite has a purpose, for the object of the appetite is the starting point of the practical mind, and the finishing point of the practical mind is the starting point for action. It is, then, reasonable for these two to be regarded as the producers of movement, appetite, and the practical intellect; for the object of appetite produces movement, and so the intellect does too since the object of appetite is its starting point. And when the imagination produces movement, it does not do so independently of the appetite. There is, then, one thing which really moves things—the object of appetite; even if there were two things that were doing so, mind and appetite, they would still be doing so by virtue of a common form. But in fact the mind clearly does not cause movement independently of appetite; for will is a kind of appetite, and when one moves according to one's reasoned calculations, one is moving according to one's will;

but appetite can cause movement that is in defiance of
rational calculation, since desire is an appetite too. Mind
is always right; but appetite and imagination can be right
or wrong. Hence, while it is always the object of appetite
that causes movement, this may be what really is good,
or it may be what just appears to be good; and it is not
just any kind of good, but only the kind of good that is
practicable; and a thing is practicable if it is possible for
it to be other than it is.

Clearly, then, it is a faculty of this kind in the soul,
what is called appetite, that causes movement. People
who divide the soul into parts, if they divide and separate it according to faculties, find that there are a great
number of them: the nutritive, the sensitive, the intellectual, the deliberative, and then the appetitive; for these
are far more different from each other than the desiring
and spirited parts are. Now, there are appetites that are
opposed to each other; this happens when the reason
and the desires are contrary, and it occurs with beings
that have a sense of time; for the mind bids us resist the
desire for the sake of the future, and the desire bids us
act for the present; for what is immediately pleasant appears absolutely pleasant and absolutely good because
one does not see the future. Hence what causes movement is one in kind; it is the faculty of appetite qua
appetite; and the primary mover of all is the object of
appetite, for this causes movement without being moved
itself through just being thought of or imagined; but the
causes of movement are more than one in number.
There are three factors involved: one is what causes the
movement; the second is what it causes the movement
with; and the third is what is moved. What causes the
movement may be two things: it may be something that
is unmoved; it may be something that is moved itself as
well as causing movement. The unmoved cause is the
practicable good; the cause that is also itself moved is
the faculty of appetite (for what is moved is moved insofar as it has appetite, and appetite, when it is actualized,

is a kind of movement); what is moved is the animal; and the instrument with which the movement is caused is the appetite—and this is already corporeal; hence it must be studied among the joint functions of body and soul.

Now to summarize: what causes movement as an organ or instrument is at the point at which the end and the beginning are the same; it is like a ball-and-socket joint, for here what is convex and what is concave are, the one, the end, and the other, the beginning, which is why the one is at rest and the other moves. They are distinct in principle, but physically inseparable. Everything is moved by pushing and pulling; and so here, just as in a wheel, something must be at rest, and movement must start from it.

In general, then, as has been said, the animal has the faculty of moving itself insofar as it has the faculty of appetite; it does not possess the faculty of appetite without having imagination; and imagination has to do either with the reason or with sensation. And in sensation all the other animals share as well as man.

▪ ▪ ▪

ETHICS

Introduction

The *Ethics* is one of the most immediately accessible of Aristotle's writings and is almost entirely lacking in that flavor of quaintness that sometimes strikes the modern reader of the *Physics* or the *Metaphysics*. But there are several misunderstandings against which we must be on our guard, and one or two points at which a recollection of some of Aristotle's nonethical doctrines will add to the appreciation of his ethical theory.

If it is judged by the standards appropriate to Plato's *Republic,* the *Ethics* cannot but be misjudged. Although Aristotle sincerely insists that the aim of ethical philosophy is practical—to make us better men—it is clear that he has a strong theoretical interest in human motive, character, and behavior and in the logical problems that cluster around the concepts of ethics. These are the aspects of ethical inquiry that have most preoccupied the philosophers of the present day, and for that reason most contemporary philosophers are more interested in Aristotle than in Plato or in many of the later classics of moral philosophy. His discussion of the nature of voluntary action is a striking but typical case in point. Like many who have written on this topic in recent years, Aristotle almost takes it for granted that we have the power of choosing between alternative courses of action;

he sets himself to give a coherent account of the tests by which we can distinguish the cases in which this power is exercised from those in which a man acts under compulsion or duress. He shows a characteristic mistrust of paradox and a characteristic acuteness in the discussion of an important general question by means of a detailed particular case in his treatment of the example of the traveler who jettisons his cargo in order to save his ship and his life. The sailor performs an action that is in itself involuntary but that is freely chosen in preference to the disastrous alternative.

Recent writers also share Aristotle's concern with received opinions and ways of speaking, which is nowhere more fundamental to his thought than in his writings on morals. Plato was influenced by the conviction of Socrates that the road to moral knowledge was narrow and steep; and he was led ultimately to an exaggerated form of the Socratic view that goodness is a special skill or branch of knowledge, accessible only to the gifted and highly trained philosopher. Aristotle held fast to the common-sense view that the good life is within the reach of ordinary men. At each stage of his inquiry, he appeals to common experience and common opinion, and he will abandon these *endoxa* for some philosopher's paradox only if the reasons are very strong indeed. In particular, he makes clear that some of the main features of Plato's ethical philosophy are quite unacceptable to him.

The nature of Plato's ethical theory was determined by his conception of mathematics as the paradigm case of knowledge combined with the influence of the Socratic search for definitions and the Pythagorean-Orphic belief that the immortal and immaterial human soul is imprisoned in the earthly body. Socrates was in the habit of complaining that although men turn to specialized experts when they need shoes, ships, or medical treatment, they reserve to themselves much more important and difficult matters, such as the settlement of political questions concerning peace and war and, above all, the choice of their own mode of life and existence. Socrates thought that we should seek for the skilled expert in ethics and politics, which were for him the medicine of the soul, just as we seek out the qualified doctor when we are physically sick. It is unlikely that Socrates thought of moral knowledge as knowledge of a transcendent metaphysical realm of being; but when Plato developed this conception, and added to it his religious convictions about the nature and fate of the soul, and his mathematical conception of knowledge as universal and hierarchical, the result was the conception of the Form of the Good expounded in the central books of the *Republic*.

Aristotle is fundamentally opposed to this approach. The Form of the Good is useless in the making of moral choices because moral action is concerned with concrete particular circumstances. The identification of virtue with knowledge, and the consequential paradox that men's crimes and sins are the result of ignorance and are therefore involuntary, is dismissed by Aristotle as contrary to received opinion and common experience. Plato's mistake was to fail to distinguish between one type of inquiry and another. The exact definitions and rigorous proofs of the mathematician are out of place in practical affairs. We do not expect demonstration from an orator any more than we allow a mathematician to support his propositions by rhetoric. We must deal with men and things as we find them. We must ask what is the right condition, the appropriate activity for human beings; and we must answer these questions in *human* terms, just as we must understand the oak tree or the jellyfish *as such*, and not as an attempt and a manifest failure to be something it was never meant to be.

The first line of the *Ethics* makes clear that Aristotle's own approach is fixed by his biological, teleological standpoint. Every human activity has some good as its end or object; but different human activities have different ends. Although Plato was right when he related these ends together as forming a hierarchy, he was wrong in supposing that knowledge of the highest end was sufficient for virtue. We must start at the other end of the scale: just as the doctor treats *individual* patients, so must the moralist remember that human actions are particular responses to particular situations. Even though Aristotle accepts the traditional view that happiness is the highest good for man, he insists that that proposition is too vague to guide us in our detailed choices.

The *Ethics* is a portrait of the good and happy man— an exploration of human nature. Just as the nature of a plant or animal is conceived as equivalent to the form or qualities of a mature, perfected, complete, finished specimen of the species to which it belongs, so in our study of humanity we must seek for an understanding of the complete man. If we see what the best man is like, we are seeing at the same time what man's true nature is: we understand the species by understanding the perfect individual. Here, as in all Aristotle's biological work, the form of the individual is the form of the species; it is identical with the form of every other individual of the species when fully realized and developed. The nature of a man, like the nature of any other substance, is identical with the end and the purpose of the creature.

If we bear this in mind, we shall cease to be puzzled by some features of Aristotle's ethical thought that are disturbing to those who see Platonism as the ideal or only possible form of moral philosophy. In particular, it will no longer surprise us to find in the *Ethics* so much *descriptive* writing—portraits and character sketches, almost in the manner of Theophrastus—in which Aristotle sums up the types and traits of human nature and personality. These observations of actual specimens are as essential to ethics, as Aristotle understands the subject, as the examination of plants and animals is to botany and zoology, the study of particular plays to the theory of tragedy, or the study of existing constitutions to the study of politics.

This also explains why Aristotle sets such store by received opinions. He studies man as he is and judges human nature by human standards; the recorded moral views of men are important evidence of man's moral nature. So too with Aristotle's preoccupation with moral training and habituation, with pleasure and pain and reward and punishment. Sometimes he seems to be thinking of men as if they were rose trees or racehorses, to be conditioned and shaped by the statesman or the philosopher; nevertheless, the condition into which he wishes them to be molded is a specifically *human* perfection. A man differs, of course, from a horse or a tree; yet all creatures are alike in that each must fulfill its *own* nature, and is not to be shaped or judged by standards appropriate to some other creature. Aristotle places man firmly between bestiality and divinity, between animal and god: specifically human virtue—both moral and intellectual—is to be seen in its own terms. We must not depress man to the level of a *mere* animal, but neither must we, in Plato's manner, elevate him to a divinity that is foreign to his composite nature.

Aristotle does indeed urge men to "aspire after divinity as far as a man may," and he firmly rejects the traditional maxim that men must "think mortal thoughts." But this is quite consistent with his general view of the nature and purpose of man as we find it in the earlier books of the *Ethics*. For him, as for Plato, the reason in man is divine, and its fulfillment transcends the limits of the rest of man's nature; but the rest of our nature is not to be denied or neglected. Even the most accomplished sage can achieve divine contemplation only rarely and briefly; at most times he is a man like the rest of us. We must not allow Aristotle's special remarks about the contemplative life to blind us to the importance he attaches to the state of moral and intellectual virtue that is the highest to which most men can aspire and that even the sage is rarely able to transcend.

It is a shock to strict moralists, who take Plato as their

patron, to find that Aristotle gives an important place in
the good man's life to such external goods as riches,
honor, good looks, good fortune, and worldly success.
Plato's program for the reform of humanity, his religious
mission to convert men to "higher things," led him to
condemn such trivialities. But when ethics is conceived
as the attempt to understand human nature, not to
change it, when we are concerned to see man at his
human best, we must consider the habitat of the creature, his proper environment in a flourishing community,
and we may also consider his appearance and bearing,
his voice and demeanor, his manners as well as his morals in the narrower sense. Aristotle paints man entire,
not just man as intellect or man as moral hero. He prizes
all that is good in and for man: chiefly his intellectual
and moral capacities, but also the proper fulfillment of
his physical and social nature. We still speak of "the
good things of life" as naturally as we speak of "the
good life," but we feel a contrast between these two
phrases which Aristotle, freeing himself from Plato's authority and not yet subject to Christian influence, would
have used in the same breath and the same tone of
voice.

All this is summed up in the figure of the *megalo-
psychus,* the great-souled man, who has often been made
into a figure of fun, with his deep voice, his steady gait,
and his self-importance. He will appear in a new light if
we remember Aristotle's purpose and do not confuse it
with Plato's. The great-souled man is to be set beside
Castiglione's Courtier, Lord Chesterfield's Gentleman,
and perhaps Machiavelli's Prince; but certainly not in
the same company as the Platonic philosopher-king, the
Stoic sage, or the Christian saint. He must inevitably be
defeated in a competition that he has neither the will
nor the qualifications to enter; in his own class he puts
up a notable performance. What is too often forgotten
by those who ridicule his voice and gait is that he is
explicitly said to possess all the virtues, intellectual and

moral: in his great soul are found wisdom and knowledge and courage and liberality and temperance. His
portrait extends over the whole of the *Ethics,* and is
not confined to the few pages in which he is mentioned
by name.

A word must also be said about the *phronimos* or *spoudaios,* the "man of prudence," who is so often cited by
Aristotle as a standard and authority for correct judgment
in the details of moral choice and action. One's first impulse is to complain that this ubiquitous character is
merely a device for evading concrete issues. We feel that
we have been told nothing when we have been told simply
that we must do something "at the right time, in the right
way, to the right extent, or as the *phronimos* or *spoudaios*
would do it." Here let us remember Aristotle's warning
that moral philosophy is not for the young and inexperienced. His book, like most books on cookery, golf, chess,
gardening, and other human skills, is addressed to those
who already know something, perhaps a great deal, about
the matter at hand and who wish to know still more. To
the complete novice the notion of a "moderate" oven or
a "pinch" of salt may be mystifying and unhelpful. Aristotle's recipes are addressed to those who are capable of
understanding them and acting on them; and if they are
read in that spirit, they are not the empty formulas that
they at first appear to be.

This is the answer, by implication, to those who complain of the triviality of the doctrine of the mean. The
doctrine is not to be read as an abstract and empty formula, but as a principle unifying and clarifying what we
shall recognize to be right conduct in each of the separate concrete spheres of feeling, choice, and action.
Throughout the *Ethics* it is the same: the general formula kills; but for the spirit that gives life and understanding, we must look to the detail that Aristotle
supplies in such abundance and that we can find, in rich
plenty, in reflecting on our own observation and experience of human life, human nature, and human conduct.

Book I

1. Every skill and every inquiry, and similarly, every action and choice of action, is thought to have some good as its object. This is why the good has rightly been defined as the object of all endeavor.

However, there appears to be some difference among the ends: some of them are activities, whereas others are products, apart from the activities. Where there are ends apart from the activities, in these cases the product is by nature better than the activity.

Just as there are many activities, crafts, and sciences, so too, there are many ends. For example, health is the end of medicine, the vessel of shipbuilding, victory of generalship, and wealth of estate management. Many of these fall under some one craft: making bridles and all other skills concerned with riding equipment come under the art of riding; and this art and all actions that have to do with war come under the art of generalship; and so with others. But in all these the ends or objects of the highest competences are to be preferred to all the ends of the arts that they include. The lesser is pursued for the sake of the greater. It makes no difference whether the end of action is the activity itself, or something else apart from that, as we said above.

*   *   *

2. Now, if there is some object of activities that we want for its own sake (and others only because of that), and if it is not true that everything is chosen for something else—in which case there will be an infinite regress, that will nullify all our striving—it is plain that this must be the good, the highest good. Would not knowing it have a great influence on our way of living? Would we not be better at doing what we should, like archers with a target to aim at? If so, we must try to get a general idea of what the good is and to which science or competence it belongs.

This would seem to be the supreme and most authoritative art; and that appears to be politics. Politics decides what arts should be given a place in states, which should be learned by each class of persons, and how far their study should go. We observe that the most esteemed skills come under politics, such as generalship, estate management, and persuasive speaking, i.e., oratory. Politics, then, employs the other arts and legislates as to what we should and should not do; therefore, the end of politics will embrace the objects of the other arts, so that this will be the good for man. Even if it is the same for individual and for state, the good of the state is greater and more complete, both to attain and to keep. It is desirable for one individual to obtain, but finer and more godlike for countries and whole states.

3. Our treatment will be adequate if we make it as precise as the subject matter allows. The same degree of accuracy should not be demanded in all inquiries any more than in all the products of craftsmen. Virtue and justice—the subject matter of politics—admit of plenty of differences and uncertainty, so that some have thought them to be matters of convention rather than natural and absolute. The "goods," too, admit of some such variation, for many people have suffered injury from them. There have been cases where money or courage was the death of a man.

Then, since our discussion is about, and proceeds from, matters of this sort, we must be content with indicating the truth in broad, general outline. Since our statements are about things that are generally such and such, and that is also the character of our starting point, we must be content with conclusions of the same sort. This is how we should also estimate every statement made here. The educated man looks for as much precision in each subject as the nature of the subject allows. It is, for example, much the same to allow a mathematician to argue persuasively as to demand rigorous proof from an orator.

Now, each man judges correctly those things he knows about; it is of these that he is a good judge. In every subject it is the man educated in it who judges correctly, and the man of good general education is the good judge in general. This is why young people are not proper students of morals and politics: they are inexperienced in the practical side of living, whereas our arguments derive from and are about precisely that. Also, since young people are ruled by their emotions, their study will be in vain and profitless, for the ultimate object of the study is not knowing but doing. Young in years or young in character makes no difference: the weakness is not in the time lived, but in living by the emotions and choosing pursuits accordingly. For such people knowledge is useless, just as it is for those without self-control; but for those who choose and act by reason, knowing these things will be a tremendous help. This is enough about the type of student, the kind of belief, and the object of this inquiry.

4. Let us go back. We said that all knowledge and choice aim at some good. What then does politics aim at? What is the highest good in all matters of action? As to the name, there is almost complete agreement; for uneducated and educated alike call it happiness, and make happiness identical with the good life and success-ful living. They disagree, however, about the meaning of

happiness: uneducated people give a different answer
from that of the theoreticians. The former say it is something plain and obvious, like pleasure, wealth, or honor,
and so on. Quite often, the same man gives different
answers—when he falls ill, he says it is good health;
when he is poor, wealth. They are aware of their own
ignorance, and therefore respect those who say it is
something marvelous, something beyond them. Some
have thought that, quite apart from all these many
"goods," there is something else, which is good of itself,
and the reason for all these other things being good too.

Perhaps there is little point in examining all opinions;
it is sufficient to take the most current and those with
some plausibility. We must remember that there is a
difference between arguments *from* principles and arguments *to* principles. Plato was quite right to consider and
question whether the path should be from or to principles, just as in the stadium the race can be away from
the judges to the turning point, or back to them. We
have to start with the known, and "known" has two
meanings: there are things known to us, and things
known absolutely. Perhaps, since we are making the inquiry, we should start with what is known to us. That is
why the student who is going to profit from hearing
about the fine, the just, and politics in general, should
have had a sound moral upbringing. The principle here
is the fact that something is the case; if this is shown
adequately, there will be no need to show why it is the
case. The person with a sound moral upbringing already
has, or can easily acquire, "principles." Let us quote the
words of Hesiod about the man to whom neither
applies—"He is far the best who solves everything himself. He too is good who can take good advice. But he
who cannot solve things himself or take the point from
someone else is a useless fellow."

5. Let us go back to where we digressed. The uneducated majority appear to think that pleasure is the good

or happiness. This view, like those below, is not unreasonable in view of how they live. That is why they admire the life of enjoyment. There are three kinds of life that stand out: this one; the life spent in public affairs; and the life of contemplation. Now, the vast majority show themselves to be absolute slaves in choosing the kind of life lived by cattle. But they get a hearing because many people in high places feel the same as Sardanapallus.

Clever people and men of affairs say that honor is the good, since, roughly, that is the objective of political life. But it seems to be more superficial than what we are looking for, since it rests in the man who gives the honor rather than in him who receives it, whereas our thought is that the good is something proper to the person, and cannot be taken away from him. Also, people seem to pursue honor to prove that they are good; they want to be honored for their excellence by people of good sense and by their acquaintances. So, it is clear from these that excellence is higher than honor, and perhaps one may be more inclined to take this as the objective of political life. But this, too, seems to be incomplete. It is possible, even when you have excellence, to sleep or to be inactive throughout your life, and also to suffer great hardship and extreme failure. No one would call such a man happy, unless he were arguing for a paradox. But no more about that; there is enough on the subject elsewhere.

The third life is the life of contemplation. We shall examine it later on. A life of making money is contrary to nature; it is clear that wealth is not the good: it is merely useful, acquired with a view to something else. That is why one might prefer the "goods" mentioned before, since they are admired for their own sake. Yet, not even they will do, although much argument has been made to establish their claim.

6. Let us pass on. Perhaps it is better to investigate and decide what is meant by "the universal good." This is a difficult subject because our friends introduced the Ideas. But it may seem better (and, indeed, essential to preserve the truth) to demolish our nearest and dearest, especially since we are philosophers: for although both are dear to us, it is our duty to give first place to truth.

Those who introduced this view did not posit Ideas in cases where they spoke of "prior" and "posterior," which is why they did not establish an Idea of numbers. But good is called such in the categories of substance, quality, and relation; and substance, or that which is by itself, is prior by nature to relation, which is like an offshoot or accident of substance. Therefore, there could not be any Idea common to these.

Secondly, "good" is used in as many ways as "is." It is used in the category of substance, e.g., god and mind. The virtues show its use in the category of quality; measure, in that of quantity; usefulness, in relation; opportunity, in time; environment, in place; and so on. Therefore, there cannot be a single universal entity common to all; otherwise, "good" could not have been predicated in all the categories, but in one only.

Thirdly, things that come under one Idea are studied by one science. Therefore, there ought to have been a single science applying to all things called good; as it is, even for things in one category, there are many sciences. Take opportunity: opportunity in war is studied by generalship; in disease, by medicine. Or take right measure: medicine studies it in the case of nourishment; athletic training, in the case of exercise.

One might well ask what they mean by "the thing itself," if in both cases—both "man himself" and some particular man—there is one and the same definition, namely, that of man. For as man, they will not differ from one another; and the same will be true of some particular good and "the good itself."

Good will be no more good through being eternal, just as degree of whiteness does not depend on the length or the shortness of its duration.

The Pythagoreans seem to have a more persuasive argument about the good, for they put unity in the column of the good things. Indeed, Speusippus appears to follow them.

However, let us leave these objections now. There is a glimmer of an objection to what we have said. They may say that their arguments were not about good in every sense, but that there is one class of goods pursued and admired for their own sake, whereas another class of goods makes for or preserves the former and guards against their opposites, thus existing as a means in another sense. Good, then, would be used in two senses: good as an end in itself, and good as a means. Let us separate the ends in themselves from the means, and see if they are spoken of under one idea. What would one count as goods that are ends in themselves? Are they the things that are pursued even in isolation from others, such as wisdom, sight, and certain pleasures and honors? Even should we pursue these things as means, they would be counted as ends. Or is it the Idea only? In that case, the Idea will be pointless. But if the above-mentioned things also belong to the class of goods that are ends in themselves, the definition of good must appear the same in all cases, like the definition of whiteness in the case of snow and of white paint. Yet, the definitions of honor and wisdom and pleasure, as being good, are distinct from one another. Good, therefore, is not a common term corresponding to a single Idea.

How is it used then? It does not seem like a chance ambiguity. Is it perhaps that things are good through deriving from one single good, or through all contributing to one single good? Or is it perhaps a matter of analogy? As sight to the body, so mind to soul, and so on. But perhaps we should leave this now, since going into detail on this is more appropriate to another branch of philosophy. Let us do similarly with the Idea: for if good, as a common predicate, actually is a single thing or something separate by itself, it is clear that it could

not be an object of human action or aspiration. But it is
something of that kind that we are seeking.

However, it may seem advantageous to know this
Idea, with a view to the good ends that *are* objects of
action and aspiration. With that as an example, we shall
know better those things that are good relative to us;
and, by so knowing, we shall obtain them. This argument
is plausible, but it is at variance with what happens in
the arts and sciences. In all of these, people aim at some
good and try to find where they fall short; yet they leave
aside knowing this Idea! It would be unreasonable for
all craftsmen to be unaware of it, if it is so useful, and
not even try to find it. It is hard to see *how* a weaver
or builder will benefit in his art, by knowing this Idea
of the good. How will a man who has seen the Idea be
a better general or doctor? Doctors do not study health
in this way; they study the health of man or, better, the
health of this individual. Doctors practice on individuals,
not on the species. Enough on this subject.

7. Let us return to the good we are looking for and
ask what it is. It appears to vary according to the activity
or craft: it is different in medicine from what it is in
generalship, and so with the rest. Then, what is meant
by "the good" in each and every art? It is that toward
which all other activities are means. In medicine, this is
health; it is victory in generalship, a house in architec-
ture, and so on. In every activity and choice of action,
it is the end: everything else that people do, they do
because that is their object. If there is an ultimate end
in all matters of action, that will be the good in matters
of action; or if there is more than one, then the sum of
these. By a different approach, then, the argument has
reached the same result. But we must try to be still
clearer about this.

There seem to be a number of ends. Some of these
we choose on behalf of yet another end—like wealth,
flutes, and instruments in general. Not all ends, there-

fore, are ultimate ends, whereas the supreme good is something final. So if there is some one thing that is alone ultimate, this is what we are looking for; and if there are more than one, it will be the most complete or final among these. That which is sought for its own sake is more complete than that which is sought as a means to something else. That which is never sought as a means to something else is more complete than things sought both on their own account and on account of the former. By absolutely final, we mean that which is sought for its own sake, and never as a means to something else. Happiness seems to be something of that sort. We always pursue that for its intrinsic value, never as a means; whereas we pursue honor, pleasure, wisdom, and all the virtues, both for their own sakes (we would want them even if they led to nothing further) and for the sake of happiness, since we think we shall attain happiness by means of them. But no one wants happiness as a means to these other things, or indeed as a means to anything else at all.

The same conclusion is reached from the notion of the self-sufficient. The final good is thought to be something self-sufficient. The term "self-sufficient" does not refer to an individual living a hermit's life; it embraces parents, children, wife, friends, and citizens, since man is naturally a social animal. But there should be a limit to these; if we extend the term to ancestors, descendants, and friends of friends, there will be an infinite series. However, we must look into that at another time. We regard as self-sufficient that which, just by itself, makes life worth choosing, and lacking in nothing. We think that happiness has that character. Also, we think it the object of choice par excellence, even when other things are not taken into account. For when other goods are reckoned in, happiness *and* the least of them is superior to happiness by itself. The extra makes an increment of good, and the greater good is always preferable to the lesser. Happiness, therefore, seems to be something final and self-sufficient, the ultimate object of matters of action.

It may be that in calling happiness the highest good, we are only stating a platitude. It needs to be defined more clearly still. We might achieve this by ascertaining the specific function of man. In the case of flute players, sculptors, and all craftsmen—indeed, of all who have some function and activity—"good" and "excellent" reside in their function. Now, the same will be true of man, if he has a function peculiar to himself. Do builders and cobblers have functions and activities, but man not, being by nature idle? Or, just as the eye, hand, foot, and every part of the body has a function, similarly, is one to attribute a function to man over and above these? In that case, what will it be? Living is something shared by man even with plants, whereas we are after something specific. Therefore, we must rule out nutritive living, life as growth. Next comes perception; but this too is shared—in this case by horses, cows, and all animals. We are left with a life concerned with action, belonging to the rational part of man. This has two parts: that which obeys reason, and that which has reason and thinks. This kind of life, concerned with action, is itself twofold; and we must take the part that is actually operative, as this is the more correct sense.

The function of man is activity of soul in accordance with reason, or at least not without reason. Now, we say that function is generically the same when we speak of an individual and of an individual good at his job, as in the case of a lyre player and a good lyre player. This is generally true in all cases. Function comes first, and superiority in excellence is superadded. As an example, playing the lyre is the function of the lyre player, playing it well belongs to the good lyre player. If this is so, the good for man proves to be activity of soul in conformity with excellence; and if there is more than one excellence, it will be the best and most complete of these. Also, it requires a complete lifetime: one swallow does not make a spring, nor does a single fine day; similarly, one day or a short time does not make a man blessed or happy.

This is our outline of the good. I say outline advisedly, since perhaps we should make a sketch first and put in the details later. Anyone can then develop the outline and fill in what is appropriate to it; time itself seems to be a discoverer and a good workmate. This is how progress has been made in the arts and crafts, since anyone can fill in what is missing. We should also recall our earlier remarks, and not look for the same degree of accuracy in everything, but only according to the subject matter and as far as is appropriate to the inquiry. Both builders and geometricians look into the right angle, but in different ways: the former does so, so far as it is useful for the job in hand; but the latter studies what it is, or what kind of thing, as he studies truth. We must behave in the same way in other things too, so that side issues do not overshadow the main ones.

Not even the cause should always be precisely accounted for. In some cases, it is enough if we show clearly that something is so, as with principles. That something is so is itself a starting point and principle. Some principles are gathered by induction, some by perception, some by a sort of habituation, and so on. We should inquire into each in the way natural to it, and be serious about distinguishing them rightly, since they have a great bearing on what follows. The principle or beginning is thought to be more than half of the whole, and to provide solutions to many of our questions.

8. We should examine happiness not only on the basis of the conclusion and the parts of the definition but also by what is said about it. All the available facts are in harmony with the truth; whereas, when something is false, the discord between it and the facts is soon apparent.

Goods are divided into three groups. Some are called external, others goods of the soul, and others goods of the body. Goods of the soul are the ones we call goods proper, and we take it that acts and activities of the soul are of the soul. So, according to this view, which is of some antiquity and meets with agreement among philosophers, we are right to define happiness as we do.

It is correct, too, that certain acts and activities are asserted to be the end. In that way they belong to goods of the soul, not to external goods.

The view about the good life and "successful living" of the happy man agrees with our definition. For we have really spoken of a sort of good life and "successful living."

It seems as though everything that people look for in connection with happiness resides in our definition. Some think it to be excellence or virtue; others wisdom; others special skill; whereas still others think it all these, or some of these together with pleasure, or at least not without pleasure. Others incorporate external goods as well. Some of these views are held by numerous venerable authorities, others by a few distinguished men. It is likely that neither group will be totally wrong, but rather that they will get some part or most of it right. Our definition agrees with those who call it virtue or a virtue; for activity in conformity with virtue shows that virtue is present.

There is probably a big difference between treating the supreme good as possession and as use, between the state and the activity. It is possible for the state to be there but achieve nothing, as when one is asleep or inactive for some other reason. But this is not possible for the activity of good: it will necessarily act, and act well. At the Olympic games, it is not the handsomest and strongest who are crowned, but actual competitors, some of whom are the winners. Similarly, it is those who act rightly who get the rewards and the good things in life.

Also, their life is in itself pleasant. The feeling of pleasure belongs to the soul, and pleasure for each individual consists of what he is said to be a lover of—horses for horse lovers and plays for theater lovers. In the same way, justice is pleasant for the man who loves justice; and in general, things that conform to virtue are pleasant for him who loves virtue. The things thought pleasant by the vast majority of people are always in conflict with one another, because it is not by nature that they are pleasant; but those who love goodness take pleasure in what is by nature pleasant. This is the characteristic of actions in conformity with virtue, so that they are in themselves pleasant to those who love goodness. Their life has no extra need of pleasure as a kind of wrapper; it contains pleasure in itself. In addition, the man who takes no pleasure in fine acts is not even good. No one would regard as just the man who takes no pleasure in just acts, nor as liberal the man who takes no pleasure in liberal acts, and so with the rest. If this is true, acts in conformity with virtue are pleasant in themselves.

However, they are also good and fine, and each of them especially so, if the judgment of the good man, which I have described, is correct. Happiness, therefore, is at once the best and finest and most pleasant thing, and there is no separating out of these attributes, as the epigram at Delos would have it: "The most just is the finest; health is the best; and the most pleasant is getting what you desire." All these belong to the best activities, and we say that these or one of them are or is happiness.

However, it seems also to require external goods, as we have said. It is impossible (or at least not easy) to do fine acts without a supply of "goods." Many acts are done through friends, or by means of wealth and political power, which are all, as it were, instruments. When people are without some of these, that ruins their blessed condition—for example, noble birth, fine children, or beauty. The man who is quite hideous to look at or ignoble or a hermit or childless cannot be entirely happy. Perhaps this is even more so if a man has really vicious children or friends or if they are good but have died. So, as we have said, happiness does seem to require this external bounty. Hence, some people identify happiness with good fortune, although others identify it with virtue.

9. For this reason, the question is raised whether happiness is to be learned or got by habit or by some other kind of training, or whether it comes about through some divine providence or even by chance.

If the gods give any bounty at all to mankind, it is likely that happiness is a gift of the gods, especially since it is the best thing in the world for man. But perhaps this subject is more suitable for a different inquiry. Even if happiness is not sent from heaven, but comes about through virtue and learning or training, it seems that it is one of the most godlike things. The prize and end of virtue appears to be the best thing, something godlike and blessed. Happiness will also be within the reach of everyone, since, through learning and exercise, it can be obtained by all who are not totally corrupted as regards virtue.

This is better than happiness by chance. The nature (i.e., tendency) of natural things is to be as fine and good as possible; the same, therefore, is likely to be true of things in the crafts and all sciences, and especially of things in the best of these. It is too unfitting to hand over the most important and finest thing to chance.

We can get some light on this question from our definition, too. We have said that happiness is an activity of the soul in conformity with virtue, an activity of a certain kind. Some of the other goods must necessarily be there, with others, which are by nature like tools, cooperating and of use toward other ends. This agrees with what we said at the start. We considered the objective of politics to be the best, and politics takes very great care about making citizens have a certain character; that is, good people who will be able to do fine actions.

Reasonably enough, therefore, we do not speak of oxen, horses, or any other animals being happy. None of them can participate in this activity. For this reason, not even children are happy; for, because of their age, they cannot yet act in the way required. Those who are called such are thought to be so because of the expectation we have of them. What is needed, as we have said, is complete virtue and a complete lifetime. There are many changes and all kinds of chances throughout a lifetime, and it is possible for a man who is really flourishing to meet with great disaster in old age, like Priam at Troy. No one gives the name happy to a man who meets with misfortune like that and dies miserably.

10. Should we not give the name to anyone in his lifetime, but look at the end, as Solon advised? If so, is a man happy when he has died? Surely that is quite absurd, especially since we say that happiness is an activity. If we do not speak of the dead as happy (and that was not Solon's meaning), perhaps what he meant was that at that time one could safely call man blessed as being now out of reach of evils and misfortunes. This, too, gives us something to discuss. It is thought that good and evil do in some way affect the dead, just as they do a man who is alive but does not notice them—I mean things like the honor and dishonor of one's children, the successes and failures of descendants in general. This, too, creates a problem. It is possible for many changes to occur among the descendants of a man who has lived happily and died accordingly: some of them may be good and get the life they deserve, for some it may be the opposite; also, it is obvious that their descendants may stand in the most varied degrees of relationship to their forebears. It would be absurd for the dead man to change with the living and become at times happy, at other times wretched; but it is also absurd if the condition of the descendants does not for a moment affect the ancestors at all.

However, let us go back to the former problem, for we may be able to deal with the present one in the light

of that. If one must look at the end of a man's life, and
only *then* use the word happy—not because he is so, but
because he was so before—surely it is absurd not to give
him this attribute when he *is* happy, just because we do
not wish to use that word about the living because of
chances and changes, and because we assume that happiness is something permanent, not easily changed, whereas
good and ill fortune often revolve about the same people. If we use our language according to the standards
of fortune, we shall frequently have to call the same
man both happy and, conversely, miserable, making the
happy man a chameleon, without stability. Going by
chance and change cannot be right: good and bad do
not consist in them. Life needs them as extras, as we
have said; but it is activities in conformity with virtue
that control happiness, and so with the opposite.

The present question is evidence in favor of our definition. Nothing else in the world of man has the steadi-
ness that goes with activities conforming to virtue. They
seem to be even more permanent than the sciences. And
the most valuable among them are more lasting because
the blessed continuously and by preference spend their
life in them—which seems to be the reason why there is
no forgetting them.

This element will be present in the happy man, and
he will be like that throughout his life. He will always,
or more than all others, do and consider what is virtuous;
he will bear changes of fortune most nobly and quite
moderately in every way, that is, the man who is truly
good, the all-round, blameless man.

Many things happen by chance, varying greatly in their
importance. It is clear that petty luck, whether good or
ill, has no influence on life; but important good luck,
occurring often, will render a man's life happier, since it
is the nature of luck in this way to be an additional
grace, and one can use it finely and virtuously. But when
there is bad luck on the grand scale it reduces and dam-
ages the condition of happiness, for it introduces pain

and impedes some activities. But even here nobility shines through, when a man puts up patiently with great bad fortune, not through insensitivity to pain but because he is of a strong and noble character. If activities determine life, no blessed man can ever be wretched, since he will never do mean or hateful things. We think that the man who is truly good and controlled bears graciously with fortune and acts as nobly as the existing situation allows; in the same way a good general makes the most warlike use of the serving army, and a cobbler makes the best shoes that the given material allows. And so with all the other arts.

If so, the happy man will never be miserable, although he will not be blessed if he meets with misfortune like Priam's. Nor is he a mercurial character, always changing: it will not be easy to move him from his happiness, either by minor misfortune or by bad luck on the grand scale; if that does happen, he will not become happy again in a short time but, if at all, after a long period, and after obtaining great distinctions.

May we say that the happy man is active in conformity with complete virtue, and adequately supplied with external goods, not just for any length of time but for a complete lifetime? Must we add that he is to live like that and to die accordingly? The future is out of our sight, but we are quite positive about making happiness an end, something complete. If so, we shall say that living people, to whom the above conditions do and will apply, are blessed, blessed as human beings. Let that be enough on the subject.

11. It seems too unfriendly an idea, that the fortunes of our descendants and of all our friends should not make the least contribution to our own. It would be contrary to received opinions, too. Now, there are many events and they admit of great degrees of difference, and some have more effect than others. Detailed accounting of their division would be tedious, indeed end-

less; it will be sufficient to give a rough general idea.
Take, first, misfortunes concerning oneself: some of
these have weight and influence on our life; others are
lighter; the same division must apply to misfortunes affecting our friends. The great thing is whether disasters
happen to them in life or after death. There is more
involved here than whether the awful and criminal act
of a tragedy has occurred before it starts or is committed
during its course. We must take this difference into account, though perhaps we ought even more to consider
whether the dead do share in good and evil. On this
basis, it seems that if anything does penetrate to them,
good or bad, it must be dim or petty, either absolutely
or relatively to them; and if it is not just dim or petty,
it can be only so great and of such a kind as not to make
happy those who are not, nor to deprive those who are
of their happiness. The success of friends, then, contributes something to the happiness of the dead, but only
to the extent that it does not make the happy unhappy
or produce any other similar result.

12. After these distinctions, let us see whether happiness belongs to things praiseworthy or to things precious
and valuable. It is clear that it is not a potentiality.
Everything that is praiseworthy appears to be praised
because it has a certain quality and stands in a certain
relation to something else. We praise the just man, the
brave man, the good man, and virtue generally, because
of acts and achievements. We praise the strong, the good
runner, and so on, because they have a certain quality
by nature, and stand in a certain relation to something
good and fine. This is clear from praises given to the
gods. It is absurd to measure the gods by our standard;
yet, this is what happens, since praising involves comparison. If praise is like that, it is clear that there cannot
be *praise* of the best, but something higher and better,
as also appears from our language: we call the gods
blessed and count them happy, and so with those men

who are most godlike. Similarly, too, with good things. No one praises happiness as he praises justice, but counts it as blessed, as something more divine and better. Eudoxus is a good advocate when he tries to get first place for pleasure. Since it is good but is not praised, he thought it better than things that are praised, for such a thing could be only good and the good—standards to which other things are referred. Praise is of virtue, since it is by virtue that people do fine acts; encomia, however, are of bodily and mental achievements alike.

Accuracy about this is more suitable for people who are occupied with encomia; to us it is clear that happiness is something precious and complete. It appears to be so because it is a principle. It is with that in view that we all do all other acts; we assume that the principle and reason for good things is something valuable and divine.

13. Since happiness is an activity of the soul in conformity with complete virtue, we must investigate excellence, or virtue. In that way we can take a better look at happiness.

The man who is truly a statesman is thought to be chiefly occupied with virtue: he wants to make the citizens good and obedient to the laws. We have an example of this in the Cretan and Spartan lawgivers, and any others of the same sort. If this inquiry belongs to politics, it is clear that our search will be in accord with what we decided at the beginning. Plainly, we must investigate human virtue; after all, we *were* looking for human good and human happiness. By human virtue, we mean virtue not of the body but of the soul; and we say that happiness is an activity of soul. If this is true, it is clear that the politician must have *some* knowledge of things to do with the soul, just as the man who is to heal eyes must know about the whole body; indeed, the more so, as politics is more valuable than medicine. The better doctors take a lot of trouble studying the body. Similarly, then, the politician must study the soul, study for the sake of knowing about virtue, but only so far as is sufficient for his purpose. Greater precision than necessary is too laborious in view of the objective.

There are some remarks about the soul in my public lectures; those remarks should be used. For example, that part of the soul is irrational, part rational. Are these divided and marked off like the parts of the body and everything else that is divisible? Or are they two in definition, being by nature inseparable, like the concave and convex sides of a curve? The answer makes no difference to our present inquiry. Part of the irrational part resembles something shared by others, by plants; I mean here the cause of nourishment and growth. One must assume a like faculty of soul among all things that develop by nourishment, all embryos, as well as all adult creatures. That is more reasonable than supposing some other faculty.

The excellence or virtue of this faculty is shared by others, and is not confined to humans. This faculty seems to be especially active during sleep, whereas good and bad men make their natures plain least of all in sleep. (This is why people say that happy men are no different from the wretched for a good half of their lives—which is reasonable enough, since sleep is an inactivity of the soul, so far as good and bad can be predicated of it.) The only exception is so far as some motions actually come through, and in this respect the dreams of the good are better than those of the ordinary man.

But enough of this. Let us leave the nutritive part, since by nature it does not participate in human virtue. There seems to be another part of the soul that is irrational, although it participates in reason to some extent. In the case of the restrained and unrestrained man alike, we praise the reason, that part of their soul that has reason: it exhorts them in the right way, and towards the best ends. There is in them something else too, which is by nature contrary to reason and resists reason. When parts of the body are paralyzed, and people decide to move them to the right, they move off to the left; just the same happens in the case of the soul: the impulses of uncontrolled people are in the wrong direction. Of course, in the case of bodies, we can see what makes the wrong movement, but not in the case of the soul; yet, perhaps we must still think that there is something in the soul, too, that is contrary to reason and that resists and opposes it. It does not matter in what way it is different from the rest of the soul.

Yet, even this appears to participate in reason, as we have said: for in the restrained man this part is obedient to reason, and perhaps the obedience is still more marked in the cases of the moderate and brave man, since with him everything is in harmony with reason.

So the irrational part appears to be twofold. The "plant part" has no share in reason at all, but the part concerned with desiring and appetite does have a share, insofar as it listens to reason and obeys it. This is the way in which we say that we "attend to" our father and our friends, not the way in which we "attend to" the principles of mathematics. That the irrational is in some way persuaded by the rational part is shown also by rebukes and by all reproofs and exhortations.

But if we must say that this part, too (i.e., the appetite), is rational, then the rational part will also be twofold: one part of it definitely and in itself, the other like something that listens to its father. Virtue, too, is divided along the lines of this difference. We say that some virtues are intellectual, others moral: wisdom, understanding, and prudence are intellectual ones; liberality and moderation are moral. For when we speak of moral character, we do not say that a man is wise or intelligent, but that he is good-tempered or moderate; but we praise the wise man also in respect to his disposition, and we say that praiseworthy dispositions are virtues.

Book II

1. There are, then, two sorts of virtue: intellectual and moral. Intellectual virtue is mostly originated and promoted by teaching, which is why it needs experience and time. Moral virtue is produced by habit, which is why it is called "moral," a word only slightly different from our word for habit.

It is quite plain that none of the moral virtues is produced in us by nature, since none of the things with natural properties can be trained to acquire a different property. For example, the stone, which has a natural downward motion, cannot be trained to move upwards, not even if one "trains" it by countless upward throws. Similarly, fire cannot be trained to move downwards. In general, none of the things with a given natural property can be trained to acquire another.

The virtues, then, are neither innate nor contrary to nature. They come to be because we are fitted by nature to receive them; but we perfect them by training or habit.

Further, in the case of all our natural faculties, we have them first potentially, but it is only later on that we make them fully active. This is clear in the case of the senses: we do not acquire our senses as a result of innumerable acts of seeing or hearing, but the opposite is the case. We have them, and then make use of them;

we do not come to get them by making use of them. However, we do acquire the virtues by first making use of them in acts, as is also the case with techniques. Where doing or making is dependent on knowing how, we acquire the know-how by actually doing. For example, people become builders by actually building, and the same applies to lyre players. In the same way, we become just by doing just acts; and similarly with "temperate" and "brave." There is further evidence in contemporary institutions: legislators make citizens good by training them. Indeed, all legislators aim at that, and those who do it incorrectly miss their objective. That is the point of difference between the institutions of a good and of a bad community.

Further, the very things that make virtue can also unmake it. Compare the techniques, where both good and bad players alike are produced by actually practicing. The same is true of building and all the skills: good building will make good builders, and so with bad. If this were not the case, there would be no need for an instructor, for all men alike would be born good or bad at their craft. Now, the same applies to the virtues. By acting in affairs that involve a contract with others, some of us become just, some unjust. By acting in dangerous situations, and being trained to show fear or confidence, we become brave or cowardly. The same can be said of desire and temper: some become moderate and controlled, others immoderate and bad-tempered, from actually behaving in such or such a way in cases where desire or temper is involved. In short, like practices produce like dispositions. For this reason activities should be qualified, since they qualify the disposition. Therefore, training from an early age for good or bad makes no little difference. Indeed, the difference is considerable; in fact, it makes all the difference.

2. Since the present inquiry is not "theoretical" like the rest—we are not studying in order to know what

virtue is, but to become good, for otherwise there would
be no profit in it—we must consider the question of how
we ought to act. Action is lord and master of the kind
of resulting disposition, as we said. Action should be in
accordance with right reason; that is true of all actions,
and it will serve as our basis. (We shall define right reason later on, and state its relation to the other virtues.)
Before going on, it must be agreed that all our statements about action have to be general, not exact. The
point is, as we said at the start, that the type of answer
turns upon the kind of subject matter, and matters dealing with action and questions of expediency are always
changing like the circumstances that promote health.
Since this is true in general, it is still truer to say that
answers about particular issues cannot be exact. These
issues cannot be dealt with by a single technique or a
set of rules; those who are engaged in action must study
the special circumstances, as in the case of medicine
and navigation.

But although the present discussion is of this type, we
must try to help. Let us consider this first: it is in the
nature of things for the virtues to be destroyed by excess
and deficiency, as we see in the case of health and
strength—a good example, for we must use clear cases
when discussing abstruse matters. Excessive or insufficient
training destroys strength, just as too much or too little
food and drink ruins health. The right amount, however,
brings health and preserves it. So this applies to moderation, bravery, and the other virtues. The man who runs
away from everything in fear, and faces up to nothing,
becomes a coward; the man who is absolutely fearless, and
will walk into anything, becomes rash. It is the same with
the man who gets enjoyment from all pleasures, abstaining
from none: he is immoderate; whereas he who avoids all
pleasures, like a boor, is a man of no sensitivity. Moderation and bravery are destroyed by excess and deficiency,
but are kept flourishing by the mean.

However, the virtues are actively concerned with the

same things by reason of which they originate, are promoted, and also decline. This applies to more straightforward examples like strength. Strength is acquired by taking plenty of food and exercise, and it is the strong man in turn who is best able to take food and exercise. That is the case with the virtues. We become moderate through abstaining from pleasure, and when we are moderate we are best able to abstain. The same is true of bravery. Through being trained to despise and accept danger, we become brave; we shall be best able to accept danger once we are brave.

3. The pleasure or pain, supervening upon the activity, should be taken as a pointer to the disposition. The man who abstains from pleasures of the body and gets pleasure in doing just that, is moderate; but he who is vexed by abstention is immoderate. He who accepts danger, and is pleased or not vexed, is brave; whereas the man who is vexed is a coward. The point is that moral virtue is concerned with pleasures and pains. We do bad actions because of the pleasure going with them, and abstain from good actions because they are hard and painful. Therefore, there should be some direction from a very early age, as Plato says, with a view to taking pleasure in, and being pained by, the right things. This is correct upbringing.

Further, the virtues are concerned with actions and emotions. Both are accompanied by pleasure and pain, and that is another reason why virtue is concerned with pleasures and pains. The fact that punishment is administered by means of pleasure and pain is further evidence. Punishment is a kind of healing, which in the nature of things is effected by opposites.

Further, as we said earlier, every disposition is naturally engaged in, and concerned with, those things that by nature make it better or worse. Men become bad through pleasure and pain, by pursuing or avoiding those things that they should not, or perhaps doing so at the wrong time or in the wrong way, and so on. For this reason, people define the virtues as a sort of unmoved state, or calm. They are wrong in not qualifying this with provisos as to "how one should or should not," or "when," and all the rest.

Our basis, therefore, is that moral virtue is the art of doing what is best, concerned with pleasures and pains, and that vice is the opposite. (From what follows, it is also plain that both are concerned with pleasure and pain.) There are three factors relating to choice and avoidance, the honorable, the expedient, and the pleasant on the one side; on the opposite, the dishonorable, the harmful, and the painful. Now, the good man acts correctly with respect to all these, and the bad man wrongly, and especially as regards pleasure. Pleasure is common to animals as well, and is a factor in all questions of choice, since the honorable and expedient appear pleasant. Also, we grow up with it from childhood, which makes it hard to remove something so well ingrained. And we measure action, some of us more than others, by pleasure and pain. Because of this, they are the center of the whole inquiry. Right or wrong pleasure or pain makes no small difference to action. Also, it is harder to fight pleasure than anger, as Heraclitus says, and techniques and excellence in general go with what is harder, since this provides a higher standard.

Therefore, the whole business of moral virtue is about pleasure and pain. He who makes correct use of them will be good, and wrong usage makes bad men. That is enough on these subjects—namely, that virtue is concerned with pleasures and pains; that it is promoted by the very same things from which it originates (and also is destroyed by them when they are done differently); and that it is active in relation to the same things from which it originates.

4. Perhaps there is a question about our saying that we must become just by doing just acts, and moderate by doing acts of moderation. It may be argued that if people do just or moderate acts, they are already just or moderate, just as, if they get something right in grammar or music, they are grammarians or musicians. But this does not apply even to the arts. One can get something right in grammar by chance, or at someone else's prompting. The man will himself be a grammarian only when he gets something right as a grammarian would— in accordance with the art of grammar, which is in him.

Also, there is no analogy here between the arts and the virtues. The products of techniques have an internal standard of excellence. It is enough for them to have a certain arrangement or disposition. But the products of the virtues—i.e., actions—are not just or moderate according to the nature of the actions, but according to the disposition of the doer. Firstly, he must know; secondly, he must act from choice, choosing what he does for its own sake; and thirdly, he must act from a firm and unshakable disposition.

These factors, apart from knowledge, are not included when we consider whether someone has the other arts. But knowing contributes little or no strength toward having the virtues, whereas the other factors make no little difference. On the contrary, they make all the difference, since justice and temperance come about through frequent just and temperate acts.

Acts are called just and temperate when they are such as the just or temperate man would perform. The temperate and just man is not he who does these acts, but he who does them in the way in which just and temperate men do them. People are right when they say that the just man is formed by doing just acts, the temperate man by doing temperate acts: without doing them, no one would even be likely to become good.

However, the great majority do not act on this principle. Instead, they take refuge in argument, thinking that they are being philosophers and will become morally good in that way. They are like invalids who listen attentively to their doctor, but carry out none of his instructions. These will never be made fit by that sort of regime; nor will people become healthy in soul by philosophizing like that.

5. Now, we must consider what virtue is. There are three things in the soul: emotions, capacities, and dispositions. Virtue must be one of these.

By emotions I mean appetite, anger, fear, confidence, envy, joy, friendliness, hatred, desire, emulation, pity—in short, everything that is accompanied by pleasure and pain.

By capacities I mean our ability to experience the emotions—for instance, the capacity of feeling anger, pain, and pity.

Disposition describes how we react—well or badly—toward the emotions, e.g., feeling anger. If the reaction is either excessive or insufficient, we are bad; if moderate, good; and so with other feelings.

Neither the virtues nor the vices are emotions. It is not our emotions that decide whether we are called good or bad, but our virtues and vices. We are not praised or blamed for our emotions (men are not praised for feeling fear or anger, nor does feeling anger as such get blamed, but feeling anger in a certain way), whereas we are for our virtues and vices. Another point: we feel anger and fear without choosing to, whereas the virtues are a sort of choice, or at least not possible without choice. In addition, the emotions are said to "move" us whereas in respect to the virtues and vices, we are said not to be moved, but to be in a certain state.

For this reason, the virtues are not capacities either. We are not called good or bad merely because we have a capacity for feeling, nor are we praised or blamed for that reason. Also, we have capacities by nature, but we are not good or bad by nature. (We have spoken of this earlier.) If, therefore, virtue is neither emotion nor capacity, it must, by elimination, be disposition. This is a statement as to the generic meaning of virtue.

*   *   *

6. We must not leave it at that—just "disposition"; we must also say what kind. It should be said that all virtue, whatever it belongs to, renders that thing good and makes it function well. The virtue of the eye makes the eye good and makes it function well, since it is by the virtue of the eye that we have good sight. Similarly, the virtue or excellence of a horse makes the horse good, good at running and at carrying its rider and at facing the enemy. Now, if this is always the case, the virtue of man will be the disposition through which he becomes a good man and through which he will do his job well. How that will come about, we have already said, but it will be still clearer if we examine the nature of this virtue.

Of every continuous—that is, divisible thing—one can take more or less or the equal amount; and these divisions can be made either by reference to the thing itself as standard, or relatively to us. Equal is the mean between excess and deficiency. What is the mean relative to the thing? It is that which is equidistant from each end, which is one and the same for all. The mean relative to us is that which is neither too much nor too little; and this is not one and the same for all. If ten is a lot and two a little, then six is the mean relative to the thing: six exceeds two by the same amount that it is exceeded by ten; it is the mean by proportion. The mean relative to us should not be interpreted like that. If ten pounds are a lot for a man to eat, whereas two are too little, the trainer will not order six. Perhaps that will be too much or too little for the particular man: too little for Milo, but too much for the man who is just starting to train. Similarly with running and wrestling.

In this same way, everyone who knows, in any field, avoids excess and deficiency; he looks for the mean and chooses the mean, not the mean according to the thing, but the mean relative to us. Every art does its job well in this way, by looking to the mean and leading its products toward it—which is why people say of things well done that you cannot add anything or take anything away, since "well done" is ruined by excess and deficiency and achieved by the mean; and good craftsmen, as we were saying, work with their eye on the mean. To resume: if virtue, like nature, requires more accuracy and is better than any art, then it will aim at the mean. I speak here of moral virtue, since that is concerned with emotions and actions; and excess, deficiency, and the mean occur in these. In feeling fear, confidence, desire, anger, pity, and in general pleasure and pain, one can feel too much or too little; and both extremes are wrong. The mean and the good is feeling at the right time, about the right things, in relation to the right people, and for the right reason; and the mean and the good are the task of virtue. Similarly, in regard to actions, there are excess, deficiency, and the mean.

Virtue is concerned with emotions and actions, where excess is wrong, as is deficiency, but the mean is praised and is right. Both being praised and being right belong to virtue. So virtue is a kind of mean, since it does at least aim at the mean. Also, going wrong happens in many ways (for bad belongs to the unlimited, as the Pythagoreans conjectured, and good to the limited), whereas doing right happens in one way only. That is why one is easy, the other difficult: missing the target is easy, but hitting it is hard. For these reasons, excess and deficiency belong to evil, the mean to good:

"There is only one kind of good man, but many kinds of bad."

Virtue, then, is a disposition involving choice. It consists in a mean, relative to us, defined by reason and as the reasonable man would define it. It is a mean between two vices—one of excess, the other of deficiency. Also, virtue discovers and chooses the mean, whereas the vices exceed or fall short of the essential, in the spheres of both emotions and acts.

Therefore, as regards its essence and the definition of what it really is, virtue is a mean; but seen from the viewpoint of the supreme good and the best, it is an extreme. Not every act or emotion admits of the mean. The very names of some things imply evil—for example, the emotions of spite, shamelessness, and envy and such actions as adultery, theft, and murder. All these and their like get their name because they are evil in themselves, and not through excess or deficiency in them. In their case (i.e., in doing them), you can never be right; you must always be wrong. In such matters there is no good or bad in the sense of committing adultery with the right woman, at the right time, and in the right way. Quite absolutely, doing any of these things is wrong. One might in the same way claim that there is a mean, excess, and deficiency with regard to being unjust or cowardly or profligate. If so, there would be a mean of excess and of deficiency, an excess of excess, and a deficiency of deficiency. Now, there is no excess or deficiency of temperance or courage, since the mean is in a sense an extreme: similarly, there is no mean of the above vices (nor any excess or deficiency). They are wrong, however performed. In general, there is no mean of an excess or a deficiency, nor is there an excess or a deficiency of a mean.

7. We must not only put this in general terms but also apply it to particular cases. In statements concerning acts, general statements cover more ground, but statements on a specified point are more accurate. Acts are concerned with particulars, after all; and theory should agree with particular facts. Let us, then, take these particular virtues from our table.

Now, courage is the mean in matters of fearing and feeling brave. The man who exceeds in fearlessness has no special name (there are many vices and virtues that have no names). He who exceeds in confidence is over-confident, whereas the man who exceeds in feeling fear and falls short in confidence is a coward.

Concerning pleasures and pains (not all are involved, and indeed pains are less so), the mean is temperance, and the excess profligacy. As for falling short in connection with pleasures, there are hardly any such people, and that is why they, too (compare the instances above), do not have a name. But let us call them "insensible."

As regards giving and taking money, the mean is liberality, whereas the excess and the deficiency are, in order, spendthriftness and illiberality. In this case, excess and deficiency work in opposite ways. The spendthrift exceeds in spending and falls short in taking, whereas the illiberal man exceeds in taking and falls short in spending.

For the moment, we are giving a rough summary, resting content with just that; later, a more accurate distinction will be made. With money, there are other dispositions too, magnificence being the mean. The magnificent man differs from the liberal by his scale of operations, large as opposed to small. The excess is lack of taste and vulgarity, whereas the deficiency is meanness. These, too, differ from the vices related to liberality, but the nature of the difference will be explained later.

As for honor and dishonor, the mean is grandeur of soul, whereas the excess is a sort of vanity, and the deficiency meanness of soul. We said above that liberality differs from magnificence in the minor scale of its operation. Similarly, there is a minor virtue related to grandeur of soul; whereas the latter has great honor as its object, this one is concerned with small honors. It is possible to strive for honor in the right way, and also more or less than one should: he who strives too much is called ambitious, he who falls short unambitious, and the man in the middle has no name. There are no names for the dispositions, except for ambition—which is why the extremes lay claim to the middle territory, so that there are times when we call the mean "ambitious" and other times when we call it "unambitious"; and sometimes we praise the one, at other times the other. Why we do this will be explained later; but now let us speak about the rest of the dispositions in the manner indicated.

In connection with anger also, there are excess, deficiency, and the mean, although they have no established names. But let us call the middle man good-tempered and speak of the mean as good temper. Now for the extremes: he who exceeds is quick tempered, and the corresponding vice is quick temper; but the man who falls short is without temper, and the deficiency is an absence of temper.

There are also three other means. They have a certain resemblance to one another, but they do differ. All are concerned with human relations in word and action. The difference, however, is that one is concerned with truth, the others with pleasure, pleasure being here of two sorts, one in the sphere of amusement, the other in all matters that have to do with life.

We must discuss these, too, to see more clearly that the mean is always praiseworthy, and the extremes neither praiseworthy nor right, but blameworthy. Most of these, too, have no name, but we must try to coin names for them, as we did before, for the sake of clarity and ease of understanding.

Let us take truth. The man who exemplifies the mean is the truthful man, and the mean should be called truthfulness; pretence of this virtue by way of excess is boastfulness, and the corresponding man boastful; but pretence by way of deficiency is false modesty.

Now, for pleasure by way of amusement. The middle man is the wit, and his disposition wittiness; the excess is buffoonery, and the man a buffoon; the deficiency is boorishness, and the man a boor. As for the other sorts of pleasure in life, the man who pleases in the right way is a friend, and the mean is friendship. The man who exceeds this, if he does so for no ulterior motive, is obsequious, but if it is for his own advantage, he is a flatterer. He who falls short and never gives pleasure is quarrelsome and a surly fellow.

There are means, too, in the sphere of the feelings. Shame is not a virtue, but the man who is modest is praised. In this case, too, we speak of the mean (the

man mentioned above) and of the excess: the man who
feels shame about everything is cowed, whereas the man
who falls short, or feels no shame at all, is shameless.
The mean, again, is the man who is modest.

Indignation is the mean between envy and malice.
These concern the pleasure and pain experienced over
what happens to neighbors. The indignant man feels pain
when people prosper without deserving to; the envious
man, who exceeds the former, feels pain at all good fortune; whereas the malicious man, so far from feeling
pain, actually feels pleasure. However, there will be time
to return to this again. Since justice is ambiguous, we
shall distinguish the two senses and say in what way each
is a mean. (And so on with intellectual virtues.)

8. There are, therefore, three conditions: two are
vices—one of excess, the other of deficiency—and there
is one virtue, the mean. All are opposite to one another,
in a sense: the extremes are opposite to the mean and
to one another, and the mean is opposite to the extremes; equal is greater than less and less than greater;
in the same way, the means are greater than the defi-
ciencies and deficient by comparison with the excesses,
both in feelings and in actions. The brave man, by comparison with the coward, seems overconfident, but cowardly compared with the overconfident. Similarly, the
temperate man seems profligate when compared with
the insensitive man, and insensitive compared with the
profligate. The liberal man is a spendthrift compared
with the illiberal, but illiberal compared with the
spendthrift.

That is why both extremes push the mean away from
its place toward each other: the coward calls the brave
man overconfident; the overconfident man calls him a
coward; and so throughout.

Since this is so, there is more opposition between the
extremes than between the extremes and the mean. They
are further away from each other than from the mean,

just as great is more remote from small (and vice versa) than either is from equal. Again, some extremes have an apparent resemblance to the mean, as overconfidence has to courage and spendthriftness to liberality; but the greatest difference is between the two extremes. People mark off as opposites things that are very remote from one another; the more remote, the more opposite. In some cases, the deficiency is more the opposite of the mean; in others, the excess. Overconfidence, the excess, is not the opposite of courage; but cowardice, the deficiency, is. With temperance, however, the opposite is not the deficiency, insensitivity, but profligacy, the excess. This happens for two reasons, one of them being the objective facts themselves. Where one extreme is more like and closer to the mean, we treat its contrary as counter to the mean. Since overconfidence is closer to and more like courage, whereas cowardice is less like it, we take cowardice as opposite of the mean. That which is further away from the mean or middle is thought to be more opposite. That is the objective reason. The other has to do with human nature, those things toward which we have a greater natural inclination appear as opposites of the mean. We have a greater inclination toward pleasures, and so we are more prone to profligacy than to decent behavior. So we call extreme the side we tend to, rather than the other; therefore, profligacy, the excess, is more opposite to temperance.

9. We have said enough about moral virtue being a mean, and in what way it is a mean—i.e., between two vices, one of excess and one of deficiency. It is what it is because it aims at the mean both in feelings and in actions.

This is why it is a hard job to be good. It is hard to get to the mean in each thing. It is the expert, not just anybody, who finds the center of the circle. In the same way, having a fit of temper is easy for anyone; so is giving money and spending it. But this is not so when it comes to questions of "for whom?" "how much?" "when?" "why?" and "how?" This is why goodness is rare, and is praiseworthy and fine.

The man aiming at the mean should first keep clear of that extreme that is more the opposite of the mean. As Calypso says: "Keep your ship outside the spray and the waves." One of the extremes has more wrong in it than the other. Since hitting the mean just right is hard, we must take the least of the evils by way of second-best. This will happen in the following way.

We should see what we ourselves are most prone to (each of us has different natural tendencies). Now, this will be clear from the pleasure and pain we get. We should then drag ourselves off in the opposite direction. By moving to a long way from going wrong, we shall come to the mean, which is what people do who are straightening warped timber.

Above all, we should keep a sharp eye on pleasure and what is pleasant. The point is that we are not impartial judges of it. We should feel about pleasure as the old men in Homer felt about Helen, and say what they said all the time.* In this way, as we send pleasure away, we shall go less wrong. In so doing, to put it briefly, we shall best be able to attain the mean. But it is certainly hard, and above all in particulars. It is not easy to decide how and with whom and about what and for how long one should be angry. At times we praise those who fall short and call them good-tempered; at other times we call those who are harsh real men. However, a slight deviation from the good is not blamed, either in the direction of excess or of deficiency; yet, the larger deviation is blamed, since it gets noticed. It is not easy to determine about blame, i.e., to what point and how far it should be applied. Nor is it easy to determine anything else that has to do with the senses; and such things as these depend on particulars, which are decided by per-

---

Iliad, iii, 156–160.

ception. However, it is clear that the mean is always praiseworthy, but at times we should lean toward the excess, at other times to the deficiency. In this way, we shall most readily attain the mean, i.e., the good.

Book III

1. Virtue, as we have said, is concerned with feelings and actions. Praise and blame are accorded to voluntary acts; but involuntary acts are accorded pardon, and at times pity. Perhaps, since we are examining virtue, we should define voluntary and involuntary; this is useful also for those who are laying down laws about rewards and punishments.

Involuntary acts are performed under compulsion or through ignorance. Compulsion here means that the principle of action is external, and that the doer (or the person to whom things are done) contributes nothing of his own—as when the wind carries one off somewhere, or other human beings who have power over one do this.

Some acts are performed out of fear of greater evils or for some good thing. A tyrant may order one to commit a dishonorable act because he has control over one's parents and children. If one does it, they are saved; if not, they die. It is debatable whether these acts are voluntary or involuntary. This is the case with throwing cargo overboard in storms. In general, no one willingly throws things overboard; but all people of sense do so to save their own lives and those of other people. These actions are mixed, but they are more like voluntary acts. We choose or decide to do them at the time they are carried out, and the end or goal of the act is fitted to the occasion. "Voluntary" and "involuntary" should be referred to the time of action. Now, the action is voluntary, since the principle of moving the instrumental parts in such acts resides in the doer himself; and where the principle resides in the man himself, the doing or not doing is also in his power. Such acts, then, are voluntary; but perhaps in a general way they are involuntary, since no one would choose any such act of itself.

For such acts, there are times when people are actually praised, whenever they endure shame or dishonor on behalf of some great end. But if the situation is the opposite, they are blamed; for enduring shame for no good or reasonable end is the mark of a low man. In some cases, the acts are not praised, but pardoned; as when a man does what he should not because of something that is too much for human nature, something unendurable. But in some cases, such compulsion is impossible, and one should suffer the worst and die rather than give in. What "compelled" Euripides' Alcmaeon to kill his mother was just ridiculous.

There are times when it is hard to decide what should be chosen at what price, and what endured in return for what reward. Perhaps it is still harder to stick to the decision. For the most part the pain lies in what is expected, the dishonor in what people are compelled to do; hence, praise and blame are allotted to those who were compelled or not compelled.

What, then, is an act "by compulsion"? In general, it means that the cause is external and that the doer contributes nothing of his own. But there are acts that, though in themselves involuntary, at a given time are to be chosen over others; the principle of acting resides in the doer; and, therefore, although these actions are essentially involuntary, at such a juncture, and in the face of such alternatives, they are voluntary. They resemble voluntary acts more; for conduct consists of particular actions, and in this case, the particular actions are voluntary.

It is not easy to say if one course should be chosen rather than another, since there is great variation in particular circumstances. If anyone argues that pleasure and good work on us by compulsion (the point being that they are external and force us), then everything will be done by compulsion, in that view. Everything done by everybody is done for the sake of pleasure and the good. Those who act under compulsion and involuntarily do so with pain, whereas people who act because of pleasure and the good do so to the accompaniment of pleasure. It is absurd to blame external things and not oneself for being an easy prey to such things, to hold oneself responsible for good, and pleasure responsible for dishonor. Compulsion, then, appears to occur where the principle of action is external, and the man compelled has no part that is properly his own.

No act committed through ignorance is voluntary; but some are involuntary, such as those that bring pain and repentance. The man who does any act through ignorance, and without then regretting the act, has not acted voluntarily—after all, he did not know; but neither has he acted involuntarily, since he feels no pain about it. To divide acts committed through ignorance: the man who repents is thought to have acted involuntarily, but the man who does not repent, since he is different from the former, let him be "nonvoluntary." Since he is different, it is better for him to have a special name.

There appears to be a difference between acting *through* ignorance and acting *in* ignorance. The man who is drunk or raging with anger does not seem to act through ignorance, but because of one of the above; he does not know, and is *in* ignorance. All wicked men are in ignorance of what they should and should not do, and it is because of this fault that men become unjust and wicked in general. But by involuntary we do not mean the case where someone is in ignorance of what is for his own good. Ignorance in the choice of an end does not produce an involuntary act, it produces wickedness. Nor does ignorance in general, for men are blamed because of that. But ignorance in particular circumstances does—that is, ignorance concerning the sphere and scope of the action—since this is the case where pardon and pity apply. It is the man who is ignorant in one of a number of particular respects who acts involuntarily. So perhaps it would be a good thing to say what the particular respects are and how many: there is the man who acts, what he does, what the act is concerned with or the sphere in which it occurs, and sometimes also the thing with which (e.g., an instrument), and the reason why (e.g., safety), and the manner (e.g., quietly or vehemently). No one who is not a lunatic could be ignorant of all these; nor, plainly, of the doer: how can he be in ignorance of himself? A man may be ignorant of *what* he is doing: e.g., when people say that "it slipped out in the course of conversation"; or that they did not know these things were secret (like Aeschylus on the mysteries); or like the man with the catapult, who wanted "only to demonstrate it," but fired it instead. Someone, as Merope does, might think his son an enemy; or mistake a sharp spear for one with a button; or think the stone was pumice. One might give a man something to drink, with a view to saving his life, and kill him instead; one might want merely to touch, like wrestlers skirmishing, but strike a hard blow instead.

Ignorance relates to all these things—namely, the sphere in which the act happens. The man who was ignorant of any of these is thought to have acted involuntarily, especially if his ignorance is of the crucial things, these being the sphere and purpose of the act. The term "involuntary" is applied to acts committed through that kind of ignorance, but there should also be a feeling of pain and repentance.

"Involuntary," then, applies to acts committed under compulsion or through ignorance. "Voluntary" would appear to apply to acts in which the principle of acting resides in the individual who also *knows* the particular circumstances of the action.

Perhaps it is wrong to use "involuntary" of acts done

through anger or desire. In that case, firstly, no animal other than man will act voluntarily, not even children. Secondly, is none of the acts we do through anger or desire done voluntarily, or do we restrict voluntary to the good ones and involuntary to the bad? Is that not ridiculous, when the cause is one and the same? It is absurd to call things involuntary when they are things we should strive for. Besides, there are some things we should be angry about, and some we should strive for, such as health and learning. It seems, too, that involuntary acts bring pain, whereas acts done through desire are pleasant. Again, what is the difference between errors of judgment and errors committed through anger, as regards their involuntary character? Both are to be avoided. Irrational feelings are as much a part of man as reason, and the same is true of the acts of man committed through anger and desire. It is absurd, then, to say they are involuntary.

2. Since we have distinguished between voluntary and involuntary, the next thing is to discuss choice. This is thought to be very closely connected with virtue, and to distinguish character still more than our actions do.

Choice appears to be voluntary; but they are not identical, for voluntary is a wider term. Children and the other animals have a share in the voluntary, but not in choice. We say that acts done on the spur of the moment are voluntary, but they are not acts of choice.

Those who say that choice is desire or spirit or wish or a sort of opinion seem to be incorrect, for choice is not found among irrational creatures, whereas desire and spirit are. Also, the unrestrained man acts from desire but not from choice, whereas the restrained man is the opposite, acting from choice, not from desire. Choice is the contrary of desire, but one desire is not the contrary of another. Desire is desire for the pleasant or the painful, but this is not true of choice.

Still less is choice anger. Acts committed through anger are, least of all, acts of choice.

Nor is it wish, although that is closely related. You cannot choose the impossible, and anyone who said he did would be a fool; but you can wish for the impossible (as well as the possible), e.g., immortality. Secondly, you can wish for things you could never bring about on your own, like the success of a particular actor or athlete. No one *chooses* things like that, only the things that can be effected by oneself. Thirdly, whereas we wish for the ultimate end, what we choose is the means to the end. For example, we wish for good health, but we choose what will make us healthy. We wish for happiness, and say so; but to say that we choose to be happy is wrong. For, in general, choice is concerned with things that are in our power.

Nor can it be opinion. Opinion is about everything, the eternal and the impossible no less than what is in our power. Besides, it is distinguished according to true and false, not according to bad and good, as is the case with choice. Perhaps no one says that choice is identical with opinion in general. But it is not a kind of opinion, either. We are men of a certain moral type through choosing good or bad, not through having opinions. We choose to get or to avoid something good or bad; but we have opinions about what a thing is, or whom it benefits, or in what way it does. We do not have opinions about getting or avoiding.

Choice, too, is praised for being choice of the right thing and for being right, whereas opinion is praised for being true. We choose what we really know is good, but we have opinions on subjects about which we do not really know. It seems that it is not the same people who make the best choice that are best at opinions: some people are rather good at opinions, but choose the wrong things because of vice. It makes no difference whether opinion precedes choice or follows after; we are not studying that, but whether choice is identical with opinion.

What is it then, what kind of thing, since it is none of the above? It appears to be voluntary, but not all volun-

tary acts are acts of choice. Is it what has been deliber-
ated about beforehand? Choice is certainly accompanied
by reason and thought. Indeed, the term itself (in Greek)
appears to indicate that it is something chosen before
(in preference to) other things.

3. Do men deliberate about everything? Is everything
a matter for deliberation, or are there some things where
deliberation is impossible? We should not speak of "a
matter for deliberation" in cases where a fool or a lunatic might be the deliberator, but in cases where the man
of sense might be. No one deliberates about eternal
things, e.g., about the universe or the incommensurability of the diagonal and the side of the square. Nor about
things that are in motion but always happen in the same
way—whether from compulsion or by nature or some
other reason—like solstices and the sunrise. Nor about
things that happen differently at different times, like
droughts and rain. Nor about chance events, like finding
treasure. Nor even about everything in the world of man;
no Lacedaemonian deliberates about the best constitution for the Scythians! For none of these things could
be brought about through our efforts.

We deliberate about things that are in our power and
are matters of action; this is what remains. Nature and
compulsion and chance are thought to be causes; but so,
too, are mind and everything that involves man. Each
group of men deliberates about what can be done by
them.

There is no deliberation about those arts and sciences
that are accurate and complete. We do not disagree, for
example, about how we should write the letters of the
alphabet. We deliberate about things that take place
through our efforts, although not always in the same
way. Examples are things that have to do with medicine
and business; and about piloting ships more than about
physical training, since in the former there is less accuracy of detail. The same applies to other cases: we delib-

erate more about the arts than the sciences, since we disagree more about the arts.

Deliberation occurs in matters that are for the most part such and such, but where the result is uncertain and indefinite. We turn to advisers for important matters, since we distrust ourselves, thinking that we are not adequate for a decision. We deliberate about the means to ends, not about the ends: a doctor does not deliberate on the question whether he shall cure the patient; an orator does not deliberate on whether he shall persuade the audience; nor a politician on whether he shall produce law and order; nor does anyone else deliberate about the end. No, people assume the end, and consider how they can get it, by what means. Where it seems that the end can be produced by several means, they consider which means does it most easily and best. Where the end is produced by one single means, they examine how that comes about, and what will produce it, until eventually they arrive at the first cause, which in fact is last in the process of discovery. The man who deliberates appears to inquire and to solve in this way, just as in solving a problem. (Of course, not all inquiry is deliberation: mathematics is an example; but all deliberation is inquiry.) The last point in the solution is the first point in the actual process. If people come upon an impossibility, they let it go—e.g., if one needs money but this cannot be found; whereas if the thing seems possible, they start on the course of action. What is possible is what can happen through our agency. Even things done through the agency of friends happen in a sense through us, since the starting point of the action is within us.

Sometimes we investigate the instruments of action; at other times how to use them. Similarly in other matters: sometimes we consider the agency, sometimes how and by what means it will work. It seems, as we have said, that man is the principle of action, and deliberation is about the courses of action to be pursued by man. Acts themselves are done with a view to other things. Only the means, not the end, can be the subject of deliberation. Nor are particular things the subject of deliberation; e.g., is this bread? Has it been baked properly? The answer to these questions is given by the senses. If deliberation is always possible, there will be no stopping.

Deliberation and choice have the same object, except for the element of determinacy that is implied in choice. What is chosen is what has been decided on after deliberation, since everyone stops investigating how he is to act when he has got back to himself as principle (and, furthermore, to that element in himself that decides, since this is what chooses). This is plain from the old kinds of constitution seen in Homer: there the kings report to the general assembly what they themselves have decided. Therefore, what is chosen is something within our power, a matter for deliberation and striving; and choosing is a deliberative striving for things that are within our power. After deliberation, we decide; and then we strive, in accordance with our deliberation. Let this stand as a rough account of deliberation, of its objects, and of the fact that it has to do with the *means*.

4. We said that wishing referred to the end. But some people think that wishing applies to the good, others to the apparent good. Now, those who say that the good is what is wished for have to say, too, that the wish of the man who chooses incorrectly is not a proper wish. If it is a proper wish, it will be good; whereas in fact it was bad, if it was as they say. Those who say that the apparent good is what is wished for have, as a consequence, the view that there is no absolute object of wishing, only one relative to each individual. Different men have different ideas about the good, and, it may be, views that are mutually exclusive.

If this is insufficient, should we say that, in general and in truth, it is the good that is wished for but that, relative to the individual, it is the apparent good? The good man has the true good as his object of wishing; the bad man has anything. This is similar to what happens with the body. For healthy people, the truly wholesome is wholesome, whereas for diseased people something different is wholesome. The same is true of bitter, sweet, hot, heavy, and so on. The good man judges each correctly, and in every case the true good is apparent to him. For every disposition there are certain particular good things and pleasures; but the good man is really outstanding at seeing the true good in each case, being a kind of measure and a norm. In most cases, deception comes about through pleasure; for although it is not the good, it appears to be. So, people choose pleasure as being the good and avoid pain on the grounds that it is evil.

5. The end, then, is what is wished for, and the means are the objects of deliberation and choice. And so, actions concerned with these will be voluntary, acts of choice. The activities of the virtues are concerned with these things. Virtue is within our power, and so, too, is vice. The point is that where we can act, we can also refrain, and vice versa. So if acting, in a case where acting is good, is within our power, so, too, is refraining, which in this case is bad. And if refraining, when refraining is good, is in our power, so, too, is acting, which in this case is bad. If doing and not doing good and evil actions are within our power, and if this is what constitutes being good or bad, then being good or bad is something within our power.

To say that "no one is willingly bad or happy against his will" seems to be partly false and partly true. No one is happy against his will; but vice is voluntary. (Or else we must contradict our statements above and deny that man is a principle of action, begetting acts as he begets children.) If this is evident and we are unable to refer our actions to other principles apart from those in ourselves, things of which the principles are in us are themselves also within our power and voluntary. Individ-

uals and lawgivers alike speak in favor of the truth of
this view. Men punish and condemn those who do bad
acts—all, that is, who do so not under compulsion, nor
through an ignorance for which they are themselves not
responsible. But they honor people who do fine things,
their purpose being to encourage these latter and to prevent the former. Yet, no one is encouraged to do what
is neither voluntary nor within the power of man, since
there is no point in being *persuaded* not to get hot or
cold or be hungry, etc. We shall experience them just
the same.

We punish men too, for the very fact of being in ignorance, if a man seems responsible for his own ignorance.
Hence, the fine for offenses committed by drunks is double, since the principle of acting resides in the offender:
after all, he can decide *not* to get drunk, and it is this
that causes his ignorance. There is punishment, too,
when people are in ignorance of a point of law that
should be known and is not difficult to know. The same
is true in other cases, when men appear to be in ignorance through carelessness; for not being in ignorance is
equally within their power: they can decide to take care.

But perhaps the man's character is such that he cannot
take care. Well, people themselves are responsible for
getting like that, through living disorderly lives: they are
responsible for being unjust or profligate, the former
through evildoing, the latter through spending their time
drinking, and so on. Activity in a certain thing gives a
man that character; this is clear from those who are practicing for any contest or action, since that is what they
spend their time doing. Not knowing that dispositions
are attained through actually doing things is the sign of
a complete ignoramus.

Also, it is absurd to say that the man who acts unjustly
does not wish to be unjust (or profligate, when it is a
case of his doing profligate acts). If a man does acts,
not in ignorance, that will make him unjust, he will be
voluntarily unjust. However, he will not stop being un-

just and become just merely by wanting to. Nor does the sick man suddenly become healthy. It may happen that his illness is voluntary because his way of life is unrestrained and he disobeys his doctors. At the start, it was possible for him not to be ill; but this is no longer so, once he has let things go. It is like the man who has let a stone go and cannot recover it. However, letting it go was in his power, since the principle of action was in him. Similarly with the unjust and the profligate: at the start, it was possible for them not to become like that; that is why they are *voluntarily* so. Once they have become that, however, it is impossible for them not to be so.

Not only vices of the soul are voluntary; with some people vices of the body are too, and those people we criticize. No one blames people who are ugly by nature, but we do blame those who do not exercise or who neglect themselves. Similarly with weakness and defects. No one would blame a man who was blind from birth, or as a result of disease or a blow; rather, he would meet with pity. But everyone would blame a man who was blind from drink or some other excess. In the case of the bodily defects, those within our power are blamed; those that are not are not. If this is so, then moral vices that are blamed must be within our power.

Suppose someone says that all people aim at the apparent good, but are not responsible for what its appearance is: the end in its appearance corresponds to what each man is like himself. Well, if each man is in a way responsible for his own state, he will also be responsible for how things appear to him. Or, if this is not so, then no one is responsible for his own evil acts; a man acts that way through ignorance of the end because he thinks he will attain the good that way. The search for the good is not a matter of one's own choosing; you must be born with, as it were, a kind of sight whereby you judge rightly and pick the absolute, true good. Good character will mean having that gift in good measure. A man will have the most important and finest thing, which cannot be got from another or learned, to the degree he had it at birth. True and complete good nature will mean having that gift of nature in fine good measure.

But if this is true, why should virtue be voluntary any more than vice? In this view, to both men alike (both the good and the bad), the end is apparent by nature, or some way or another; there it is, and they act however they do by referring to that standard.

If, then, the end, whatever it is, is not apparent by nature to each man, but there is a factor apart from itself; or if the end is nature-given, but virtue is voluntary because the intermediate acts of the good man are voluntary; then vice, too, will be voluntary. The bad man, just like the good, acts on his own initiative, if not in the matter of the end. If, then, the virtues are voluntary (and in a way we *are* ourselves responsible for our characters, and our views of the end depend on the sort of people we are), the vices, too, will be voluntary; the cases are analogous.

We have given an outline account of what is common to the virtues, and have shown their genus. They are the mean, and they are states of character. We have explained that, essentially, they make us do the things by which they are acquired in the first place; they are within our power and voluntary; they need to be performed as right reason demands.

But actions and states are not voluntary in the same way. We control our acts from the beginning right up to the end, with full knowledge of each stage. But we control only the start of our states; we do not know about each bit of addition to the state, any more than we notice the detailed progress of diseases. And yet, they are voluntary because it was within our power to use our capacities in this way or not.

Let us take each virtue in turn and say what it is, what it is concerned with, and how. At the same time their number will become clear.

*   *   *

6. Let us take courage first. It is already clear that it is a mean with regard to fear and confidence. Plainly, we fear what is fearful, this being generally bad. (So, people define fear as expectation of bad or evil.) We fear all that is bad, like ignominy, poverty, disease, friendlessness, and death. But the term brave does not apply to all these. Some things it is right and proper to fear and base not to fear—e.g., ignominy. The man who fears that is good and has a sense of shame; but the man who does not is shameless. Some people call him brave by transference of terms, since he does resemble the brave man a bit: the brave man is himself a kind of fearless man. Perhaps one should not fear poverty or disease or anything that does not come about through vice or entirely at one's own doing. But even people who are fearless about such things are not brave, although we do say so because of similiarity; e.g., some people who are cowards when faced with the dangers of war are liberal and do not panic at the thought of losing money.

Fear of injury to one's children or wife, or fear of envy or of anything like that, does not mean cowardice; nor is a man brave, because he shows confidence when he is about to be whipped.

Then, about what fearful things is the brave man brave? Surely about the greatest. No one endures dangers more than the brave man; and the most fearful thing is death, for death is a limit, and as far as the dead are concerned, there appears to be neither good nor evil left. However, not every kind of death is relevant here, not, for example, death at sea or by sickness. What death then? Surely it is death in the noblest circumstances, which is to be found in war, that being the greatest and most noble danger.

The rewards granted in republics and in kingdoms confirm this. The proper meaning of brave, then, is fearless in the face of noble death, and of everything that brings sudden death; and this is found in the perils of war. However, the brave man is fearless at sea and in sickness, but not in the same way as sailors are. The brave man and his like have despaired of surviving, and complain against the indignity of this sort of death, whereas seamen are cheerful even in the teeth of their experience. Also, men behave bravely in cases where one can fight back, or where dying is honorable; but neither of these applies to disasters like death at sea.

7. The fearful is not the same for all people: some of it is beyond the capacity of man, and this is fearful to every man of sense; but the fearful things that lie in the human range vary in size and degree, as do those things that make for confidence.

The brave man cannot be fearstruck, as far as this is possible for man. Now, he will fear such things as are not beyond human capacity, but he will face them as he should and as reason dictates: for the sake of the good, this being the end of virtue.

One can fear these things more or less, and one can also fear things that are not fearful, as though they were. One error occurs when a man fears what he should not, another when he fears in the wrong way, yet another when he fears at the wrong time or some such thing. And all these apply to that which gives confidence.

The man who endures and fears what he should and for the right reason, in the right way and at the right time, and who is confident in the same way, is brave; for the brave man is he who suffers and acts as things demand and as reason prescribes. Every activity has as its end the state to which it corresponds. Bravery is good for the brave man; and so the goal of his activity will be that, since everything is defined by its end. So, the brave man endures and acts bravely for the sake of the noble and good.

Now, as to those who go to excess. The man who is excessive in fearlessness has no name—as we said before, there are numerous cases of this; but he would be a kind of madman, someone who simply felt no pain, if he feared nothing at all, "neither earthquake nor waves," as they say of the Celts. But the man with excessive confidence in respect to what is fearful is rash. The rash man appears to be boastful, a pretender to the title "brave," since he wishes to appear what the brave man is in relation to the fearful and, therefore, imitates him where possible. Most of them are a mixture of confidence and cowardice, since they put on a bold face, but do not face up to the fearful.

He who exceeds in fearing is a coward. He fears what he should not, and in the wrong way; and all such things are true of him. He also falls short in confidence; but what is more obvious is that he exceeds in feeling fear. The coward is a hopeless sort of man, since he is afraid of everything; the opposite is true of the brave man, since confidence is the mark of the hopeful.

This is what the coward, the bold man, and the brave man are concerned with, though in different ways. Some of them exceed and some fall short, whereas the brave man has the mean position, and the right attitude. The overconfident are rash: they want to fight before the danger comes; but in the actual danger they abdicate, whereas brave men are sharp in actions but quiet beforehand.

As we said, bravery is a mean concerned with what inspires fear or confidence. The circumstances have been explained: the end chosen is noble, and bravery faces up to things because it is noble to do so, and not to do so is dishonorable.

Dying so as to escape from poverty or passion or something painful is not the mark of the brave man; rather, it characterizes the coward, since avoiding hardship is softness, and death is here faced, not because it is good to do so, but as an escape from evil.

8. That, then, is what bravery is. There are other sorts, however—five in number. First, there is patriotic courage, since that most closely resembles courage proper.

Citizens face danger because of the penalties and the dishonor imposed by the laws, and because of the rewards, too. For this reason the bravest people seem to be those among whom cowards are dishonored and the brave honored. Homer writes of people like that, Diomede and Hector for instance: "Polydamas will be first to rebuke me"; and "Hector will say, as he holds forth among the Trojans, 'Diomede was driven back by me. . . .' "

This is most like courage proper, because it comes through virtue—through shame, desire for the good (i.e., honor), and avoidance of dishonor, which is bad. One might put in the same rank those who are forced or compelled by their rulers; but these are inferior, since they act not through shame but fear, avoiding not dishonor but pain. Their masters do the compelling, as did Hector: "The man I see skulking down away from the fight, he will not be able to avoid the scavenging dogs." Commanders, too, do the same when they beat their men if they retreat; so do those people who draw up a line of men with ditches or some such obstacle behind them. All these compel; but one should be brave not because one is compelled, but because it is noble.

Experience of some particular form of danger seems to be courage—which is why Socrates thought that courage was knowledge. There are various cases of this, e.g., mercenaries in war: there are many vain threats in war, which these soldiers, above all, have seen; they appear to be the brave ones because the others do not *know* what the things mean. Again, because of their experience, they, above all, can inflict losses without suffering them, being able to use their weapons, and having the weapons best disposed, to inflict wounds without suffering them themselves. They fight, therefore, like armed men against unarmed, or like trained men against amateurs; and in that sort of contest, it is not the bravest who fight best, but those who are strongest and in the best physical condition. Yet these same soldiers turn cowards when danger overwhelms them, and they are inferior in numbers and equipment: they are the first to run away, whereas the citizen-soldier stays and dies, as happened at the Hermaeum. For the citizen-troops, flight was a disgrace, and death preferable to survival on those terms; but the mercenaries from the start faced danger with the thought that their side was stronger, and when they realized the facts, they ran away, for they feared death more than dishonor. The brave man is not like that.

People relate spirit or anger to courage. Those who act from anger appear to be brave, like beasts that turn on their attackers, because brave men, too, are spirited, and spirit has a tremendous drive for coping with dangers. Hence, Homer says: "He put might in his spirit," and "He roused his might and spirit," and "He breathed fierce might," and "His blood boiled." All such are evidences of the spirit rising and working. Well, the brave act because of the good, and spirit cooperates with them; but beasts act because of pain after being hit or alarmed, although if they are in a wood they do not approach. It is not courage, when, because of pain and anger, things are driven out and rush to face the danger, with no foresight for terrors; in that case, asses too will be brave when they are hungry; even though they are beaten, they still stick to their grazing! Adulterers, too, commit many acts of daring because of their desire. Bravery through anger seems to be most natural; it becomes bravery proper when it acquires choice and purpose. Men feel pain when they are angry; and pleasure when they take revenge; now, people who fight for these reasons are good fighters, but they are not brave. They do not fight because of the good, or as reason prescribes, but because of their feelings. Yet, they somewhat resemble the brave.

Hopeful people, too, are not brave. They are confident in danger because they have won many victories. They are like the brave in that both they and the brave are confident. Nevertheless the brave are confident for the reasons given above, whereas these are because they think they are supreme and will suffer nothing. People who are getting drunk do much the same: they become hopeful. But when things do not turn out like that, they run away; whereas it was the mark of the brave man to face what inspires fear in man because it is noble to do so and dishonorable not to. And so, being fearless and calm in sudden danger is more the mark of a brave man than remaining calm when the danger is plain to see: the action here proceeds more from the state of being, and less from preparation. One might choose obvious danger out of calculation and reason; but one would choose to face sudden danger only if one possesses the disposition of bravery.

Those who are ignorant also seem brave. They are not far from the hopeful, but they are inferior in that they have no proper awareness of the position. Hence, the hopeful stick it out, at least for a time. But those who have been deceived, if they realize or suspect that things are different from what they thought, run away. This is what happened to the Argives who attacked the Spartans, thinking that they were Sicyonians.

This is an account of those who are brave and of those who seem to be brave.

9. Bravery is concerned with the fearful and with that which inspires confidence, but not with both to the same degree. It is more concerned with the fearful. The man who keeps calm and has the right attitude to the fearful is braver than the man who does the same thing with regard to what inspires confidence. People get to be called brave, as we said, through facing painful things; bravery, therefore, brings pain, and it is rightly praised, since it is more difficult to endure pain than to abstain from pleasure.

However, the end appropriate to bravery seems pleasant, but it is lost to sight because of the surroundings, as happens at athletic competitions. The end that boxers

have in view is pleasant—that is, the crown and honor—
but getting hit hurts men of flesh and blood, and their
whole occupation is painful. Because there are many
such trials, the purpose, which is insignificant, appears
to have no pleasure in it at all.

Now, if something like this is true of bravery, death
and wounds will be painful to the brave man and will
come to him against his will. But he will stand up to
them because it is good to do so and dishonorable not
to. The more complete his virtue and the happier he is,
the more will he be pained by death. Such a person has
the best claim on life; when he is deprived of very great
blessings he knows it, and that is painful. However, he
is nonetheless brave, perhaps more so, for choosing
honor in war instead of the other good things.

Not all the virtues are pleasant to exercise; except insofar as the activity achieves its end.

Perhaps such people are not the best soldiers; perhaps
the best will be those who are less brave and have no
other advantage. These people are ready for dangers,
and give their lives in return for small gains. Let this be
enough about courage. It is not hard to grasp what it is
in outline on the basis of what we have said.

10. Next, let us discuss temperance; for courage and
temperance seem to be the virtues of the irrational parts
of men.

We have said that temperance is a mean that has to
do with pleasures. (It is less concerned with pains, and
not in the same way; and profligacy appears to have to
do with the same.) Now let us define what pleasures
they have to do with.

We distinguish between pleasures of the body and
pleasures of the soul, such as ambition and love of learning. The lover of each of these (of honor or of learning)
takes pleasure in that of which he is a lover, without the
body being affected, although the mind is. Now, concerning such pleasures the expressions "temperate" and

"profligate" are not used; and this applies to all other pleasures that do not involve the body. People who like hearing or telling stories, or who spend their time on just anything, we call gossips, not profligates. Nor do we call profligate those who feel pain about money or about their friends.

Temperance, then, is concerned with pleasures of the body, though not even all of these. People who take pleasure in things seen, such as colors, shapes, and painting, are not called temperate or profligate; yet, even in this case, there would appear to be a right way of taking pleasure, and also ways of excess and of deficiency. Similarly with things heard. No one says that people who take excessive pleasure in songs or in acting are profligate, or that people who do so in the right way are temperate. Nor does this apply to smell, except incidentally. We do not use "profligate" of people who take pleasure in the smell of apples, roses, or incense; we do so, rather, of people who take pleasure in the smells of perfumes and food, since the reason why profligate people take pleasure in these is that by so doing they are reminded of their desires. Other people, too, take pleasure in the smell of food when they are hungry; but to be always doing so is profligacy, since that is where the desires of the profligate are.

Also, among animals other than man, there is not any pleasure in these senses, except incidentally. Dogs do not take pleasure in scenting hares, but in eating them; the smell, however, is what brings them to their notice. Nor do lions take pleasure in the lowing of oxen, but in eating them; yet they perceive that the ox is near by means of the lowing, and that is why they appear to take pleasure in this. Similarly, they do not take pleasure just "on seeing a deer or a wild goat"; they are pleased because they will have food.

Temperance and profligacy are concerned with those pleasures that are shared with other animals, and thus appear servile and bestial. These are the pleasures of touch and taste; and even taste is not of great importance in this field.

To taste belongs the task of distinguishing flavors, which is what wine tasters do and people who are preparing meat. However, their pleasure is not exactly in that, or at any rate the pleasure of the profligate is not; it is in enjoying them, which happens entirely through touch, in food, drink, and sex alike. That is why one great glutton prayed for a neck longer than a crane's—because his pleasure came from the sense of touch.

The sense with which profligacy is concerned is the most common of the senses, and it would seem rightly to be a matter of scorn since it is something we have, not as human beings but as animals. Taking pleasure in such things and enjoying them is brutish. For the most elegant of the touch pleasures are neglected, such as the pleasures of massage and warm baths in the gymnasia; they are not included because the "touch" of the profligate is confined to certain parts of the body, and does not extend to the whole of it.

11. Some desires are common to all men, whereas others are special, acquired tastes. The desire for food is natural: everyone who needs it has a desire for liquid or solid nourishment, and at times for both. The vigorous young male, as Homer put it, has a desire for sex. But not everyone desires this or that particular kind of food, or even the same things; that is why the taste for food seems to be an individual thing. However, it does seem to have something natural, since different people take pleasure in different things, and some luxuries are more pleasant to everyone than just a normal diet. Now, in the case of natural desires, few people go wrong, and always in one direction, that of excess. Eating "everything" or drinking to repletion is exceeding what is natural, in terms of the amount: natural desire is the desire to fill the want, but no more. These people are called "stomach fiends" because they fill it up beyond where they should. It is people of slavish character who are prone to this excess.

But many people go wrong and in many ways concerning the individual pleasures. People who are "fanciers" of anything get the name because they take pleasure in things they should not, or more than the majority do, or in the wrong way. Now, the profligates are excessive in all these respects: they enjoy some things that they should not (things that are hateful), and if there are some things one should take pleasure in, they do so more than is right or more than the majority. It is clear, then, that excess concerning pleasures is profligacy and something blameworthy. There is no parallel here to the position of pains in the case of courage; people are not called temperate for enduring them, nor are they called profligate for not enduring them. No, the profligate gets his name for feeling more pain than he should at not getting his pleasure, so that pleasure actually causes pain for him. But the temperate man is so called because he is not pained by the absence of the pleasant, nor by his own abstaining from it.

The profligate has desires for all pleasant things or for the most pleasant. He is led by his desires to choose the pleasant rather than anything else. That is why he feels pain both when he fails to get his desire and while desiring; desire is accompanied by pain. But to speak of feeling pain because of pleasure sounds paradoxical.

There are hardly any people who fall short in relation to pleasures and take less pleasure than they should. This sort of insensitivity is hardly human. Even other animals make distinctions, and enjoy some foods, while not enjoying others. If there is anyone to whom nothing gives pleasure, for whom one thing gives no more pleasure than another, he is a long way from being human. This sort of man does not even have a name, because there really is not anyone quite like that.

The temperate man takes the mean position: he does not take pleasure in the things that give most pleasure to the profligate, but is, rather, revolted by such things; in general, he does not take pleasure in the wrong things, nor does he take any extreme pleasure in anything. He feels neither pain nor desire for what he has not (or if he does, it is only moderately, not more than is right), nor at the wrong time, nor with any other such qualification. He will have a moderate and correct appetite for all things that are pleasant and that have to do with good health and good physical condition. Similar, too, will be his appetite for any other pleasure that does not impede these ends, and is not against the good or beyond his income. The man who does go too far admires such pleasures more than they are worth; the temperate man does not behave like that, but as right reason orders.

12. Profligacy, more than cowardice, appears to be something voluntary, since it occurs through pleasure, whereas the latter occurs through pain. Pleasure is what we deliberately choose, but we try to avoid pain. Indeed, pain undoes a man and corrupts his nature; but pleasure does nothing so violent.

Profligacy, then, is more voluntary. That is why it is more blameworthy than cowardice. It is easier to get accustomed to pleasure: there are many things in life like that, and getting accustomed to them is not dangerous; whereas there *is* danger in the case of the fearful, and in getting used to that.

Cowardice as such, however, would seem to be more voluntary than particular cases of it. In itself it is not painful, but particular instances may unman a person through pain, so that he throws away his weapons and behaves disgracefully. This is why there appears to be an element of compulsion in it. However, the reverse is true of the profligate; particular cases are voluntary, since the man has the desire and the appetite; but the general case is less so, since no one desires to be profligate.

In Greek, we use the same word for profligacy and for the naughtiness of children, which resembles adult profligacy. There is no importance in deciding which got the name from which, although it is clearly a case of the later state getting the name from the earlier. The use of the word is really apposite, for in Greek it means "unchecked" and it is that which craves for disgraceful things that ought to be checked if it is not to become inordinate. Both desire and children are notable for these characteristics. Children too live by desire, and the appetite for pleasure is particularly noteworthy in them. If the appetite is not made obedient and subject to rule, it will become inordinate, since appetite for pleasure is insatiable; the fool's appetite turns to all sources of pleasure; and desire, through being active, increases its innate power. If the desires are great and violent, they drive reason out. Hence, they ought to be few and moderate, not opposing reason—which is what we mean by obedient and chastened—and, just as children live in obedience to their tutors, similarly the appetitive part of the soul should live ruled by reason. That is why, in the temperate man, appetite and reason must be in harmony: both aim at the good; the temperate man desires the right thing, in the right way, and at the right time, and the directives given by reason are similar. This finishes our account of temperance.

Book IV

∎ ∎ ∎

2. It would seem to be appropriate to take magnificence next. This virtue, too (just like liberality), has to do with money. But its scope does not consist of all actions that have to do with money, but only of those that involve spending. It is on a larger scale than generosity; as the name signifies, it stands for the appropriate spending of large sums. The size of the sums is relative, since there is not the same expenditure involved in equipping a trireme as in leading a delegation. What is appropriate is also relative to the individual, and refers also to the occasion and object of the spending. The term "magnificent" is not applied to people who spend appropriately on petty or only average objects like Odysseus saying "I have often given to beggars." But it is applied to the man who spends in that way on important things. The magnificent man is liberal, but the liberal man is not ipso facto magnificent.

The deficiency that corresponds to this disposition is called meanness, and the excess is called vulgarity and lack of taste, etc.; the excess consists not of spending too much on the right things, but of spending on the wrong things and in the wrong manner. We shall explain this later.

The magnificent man is like an artist. He can see what is appropriate and can spend large sums in the proper way. As we said at the outset, a disposition is defined by its activities and by the sphere in which it is exercised. The magnificent man's spending is both immense and proportioned; the same is true of his results. In this way, an immense expenditure will also be appropriate to the result. The result must be suited to the expenditure, and the expenditure either suited to the result, or, alternatively, bigger than need be.

The expenditure of the magnificent man will aim at what is fine and good, since that is the goal common to all the virtues. Also, he will take pleasure in spending, and will do it lavishly; counting it out exactly is petty. The questions he asks are not "how much?" and "how cheaply?" but "how can it be done best and most fittingly?"

The magnificent man is, necessarily, liberal as well; for the liberal man, too, will spend the right amount in the right way. This is where the true greatness of the magnificent man appears, and where liberality too is displayed. However, given the same amount to spend, the magnificent man will achieve a more magnificent result. Achievements have a different standard of what is good from that for possessions. With the latter, value depends directly on price, as in the case of gold; but the value of achievements depends on how splendid and fine they are. Seeing a fine and grand result makes one marvel, and magnificence makes one marvel. And the standard of excellence of an achievement—its magnificence—consists of its size and scale.

Spending on the gods, in the way of offerings, buildings, and sacrifices, is an example of valued and respected expenditure. So, too, is spending that has to do with the gods in any form, and spending on matters that are the subject of laudable rivalry for public favor: as when, for example, people think that they must spend lavishly on training a chorus, having a ship built for the state, or giving a public feast. In all these cases, as we said, we judge a man's benefaction according to who he is, and what his means are. The expense must be proportionate to his means, and suited not only to the result but also to the person. That is why a poor man cannot be magnificent: he does not have the resources for extensive spending on the proper scale, and the poor man who tried to do so would be stupid. He would be acting contrary to what is suitable and requisite, whereas moral excellence means acting rightly.

Such spending is appropriate for people who have enough resources, whether earned by their own efforts or inherited; and such people as are wellborn or famous; and so on. All these are persons of substance and reputation. That is what the magnificent man will be like; and his magnificence will operate through the kinds of spending mentioned above, which are the most splendid and most highly valued. We should also include particular private occasions, such as marriages and so on, or any object dear to the whole state or to the ruling classes, as well as receptions and farewell parties for distinguished foreigners and gifts and presentations. The magnificent man does not spend on himself but on public concerns, and his gifts are rather like dedications. It is also a sign of magnificence if a rich man furnishes his house in a manner appropriate to his wealth, since this too is a public adornment; so, too, is spending on things that are permanent, since these things are the finest of all. And what is fitting has to be observed in each case: the same is not appropriate for gods and for men, for a sacrifice and for a funeral.

The greatness of an expenditure depends on the kind of thing; and what is most magnificent, in the absolute sense, is a great expenditure on something important. However, in a particular case, magnificent means a great amount spent in that case, and the greatness of the result obtained is different from the amount expended: for example, a ball or oil flask is magnificent as a present for a child, even though the price of even the finest one is trivial and does not need great liberality. The mark of the magnificent man is that, whatever the kind of thing he spends on, he procures a magnificent effect (a standard that cannot easily be surpassed), an effect proportionate to the expense.

That is the character of the magnificent man. The man who errs to excess is a vulgarian, since his spending does not fit the occasion; as we said, this is what constitutes his excess. He spends a great deal and makes an extravagant show on minor things: he gives a club dinner as though it were a wedding reception. When he is in charge of the chorus for a comedy, he makes them wear purple at their first entrance, as the Megarians do. He does these things, not with a view to what is right, but in order to show off his wealth. He thinks that this brings him respect and admiration; where he ought to spend a lot he is mean and sparing, and vice versa.

On the other hand, the mean man falls short in every respect. Even when he spends a lot, he will ruin the chance of perfection for a trifle. Whatever he does, he shilly-shallies and tries to see how he can spend the minimum. He complains about everything, thinking it all to be on a bigger scale than is strictly necessary. These dispositions are both vices, but they incur no reproach because they do not injure one's neighbor and are not too unseemly.

3. Now we come to greatness of soul. The name itself shows that it is concerned with great things; let us, first, decide what they are. (It does not matter whether we take the disposition or the man who exhibits the disposition.)

A person is thought to be great-souled if he deserves much and claims his deserts. The man who makes the claim without being deserving of it is a fool; and no person who displays virtue is foolish or stupid. And so, the great-souled man is as described above. It is true that the man who deserves little and claims just that is temperate; but he is not great-souled. Greatness of soul has to do with grandeur. There is a parallel with physical beauty, which requires a fine, tall figure; small people can be smart and well-proportioned, but not beautiful. If a man is undeserving but claims a great deal, he is vain; though not all people who claim more than their worth are vain. If a man claims less than his true deserts he is mean-spirited, whether his deserts are great or moderate; this applies even if they are small, so long as he puts his value still lower. "Mean-spirited" par excellence fits the first case: the man who deserves a lot but claims less. What would he do if he deserved less?

With respect to scale, the great-souled man is at the extreme, but by virtue of behaving in the right way, he is at the "mean" position; after all, he claims his due, whereas the others either go to excess or fall short. If his deserts are great and he claims much, and if the term properly belongs to the man whose claims are greatest, he will be mainly concerned with one thing. "Being deserving" refers to external goods; and the greatest of these, we can say, is what we offer the gods, what people in high places strive for, above all—the reward of the finest actions. That is honor, which is the greatest external good. Therefore, the great-souled man is he who behaves in the right way about honor and disgrace. It does not seem that any argument is needed to show that great-souled men are occupied with honor. It is honor that they claim above all else—the honor that they deserve.

The mean-spirited man falls short, whether you take his own deserts as a standard, or the claims of the great-souled man. The vain man, however, is guilty of excess with regard to his own value, although not so when measured against the great-souled man. The latter, since his deserts are very great, will be the best of men. Better men deserve more than good men; and so, he who is the best will deserve the most. The man who is truly

great-souled is necessarily good; greatness in every virtue
would appear to be the mark of the great-souled man.
It would never be right for the great-souled man to run
away in a panic or to commit an injustice. What would
be the point of a man behaving disgracefully when nothing, in his eyes, is really great? If we look at all the
virtues, it will seem quite absurd for the great-souled
man *not* to be good. If he is bad, he will not deserve
honor, since honor is the reward of virtue and is a trib-
ute paid to good men.

It seems, then, that greatness of soul is a sort of
crowning grace of the virtues. It enhances them, and it
is impossible without them. This is why it is difficult to
be really great-souled, since it is impossible without
being really good.

The great-souled man is mainly concerned with honor
and disgrace. When he receives great honor from good
men, he will be moderately pleased, since he will be
getting his due or even somewhat less. The point is that
no honor is adequate to complete virtue. He will, however, accept the reward, simply because they have nothing more to offer him. He will despise honor offered by
just anybody and for insufficient reasons, since it is beneath his deserts. Similarly, he will take no notice of
dishonor, since it cannot rightly have any relevance to
him.

As we said, the great-souled man is, above all, concerned with honor. It is also true that he will react moderately to wealth, to power, and to all good or bad
fortune, whenever they happen. When he has good fortune, he will not show excessive pleasure; nor will he be
greatly pained by bad fortune. Even honor he does not
treat as of the greatest importance. Power and wealth
are desirable because of the honor they bring; at any
rate, people who have them want to be honored for their
sake. But the man who looks on honor as insignificant
will also have the same attitude to other things; that is
why such men are thought to be arrogant.

Good fortune, too, is thought to help with greatness of soul. People of good family and men of power and wealth are thought to deserve honor. They are in a superior position, and everything that is superior in any good quality is more deserving of honor. Such things make people even greater-souled, because they are honored by other people. In the strict sense, only the good man should be honored, although the man who has both—goodness *and* good fortune—is thought to be more deserving of honor. Those who have such "goods" without being good cannot rightly claim to deserve much; nor can they properly be called great-souled, since this is not possible without complete virtue. People with these advantages become arrogant and insulting. Without virtue, it is not easy to manage these blessings in the proper way; and as they are unable to manage them and think they are better than other people, they despise others, and their own behavior is quite casual. The great-souled man is their model, but they are not like him. They copy him where they can: although they do not act in conformity with virtue, they despise other people, as he does. The great-souled man has right on his side when he despises, for his opinions are correct; but most such people spread their contempt at random.

He does not go in for petty risks, and he does not love danger, simply because there are so few things that he thinks important. He is a man for great dangers and, when he does incur danger, he is unsparing of his life; for he does not think that life must be preserved at all costs. He is able to confer benefits, but is ashamed of having good turns done to him: the former is the sign of a superior, the latter of an inferior. He returns favors with interest, since after this the man who started it will be in his debt and will himself be the person favored. The common opinion is that people remember the good turns they do to others but not the favors they receive. (The beneficiary is inferior to the benefactor, but wants to be his superior.) People like hearing about their benefactions, but not about the favors they have received: that is why Thetis did not mention to Zeus the services she had done him; and why the Spartans did not tell the Athenians of their services to Athens, but spoke of Athens' services to Sparta.

It is also a sign of the great-souled man that he seldom or never needs help, but comes readily to help others. He is mighty toward men in power and wealthy men, but moderate toward average people. To be superior to the former is difficult and lends dignity, but it is quite easy to be superior to the latter. In the first case, it is not ignoble to adopt an air of dignity; but it is vulgar to be pleased at triumphing over insignificant people. That is like showing off one's strength on the physically weak. He does not compete for the things that are valued by most people, nor in cases where others are supreme. He is restrained and slow, except where the honor or the event is great. He acts seldom, and then only where the acts are great and glorious. Necessarily, he shows his hatred and love quite openly, for not to show them would indicate fear, and more care for reputation than for sincerity. He also speaks and acts openly: he speaks his mind because he does not care what other people think, and he tells the truth—except with common people, when he sometimes makes understatements about himself. He cannot live as someone else wants him to, unless the man is a friend. To do so would be servile, which is why all flatterers humble themselves and all humble men are flatterers.

He is not given to showing admiration, since nothing is great in his eyes. He does not harbor grudges: great-souled men do not carry memories of what others have done, especially if they are wrongs; rather, they just overlook them. He does not talk of personalities, being disinclined to speak either of himself or of anyone else. He is not concerned with getting praise for himself, or with seeing that others are blamed. He does not praise people; nor does he speak evil of others, even of his enemies, except as a direct insult. Where things cannot be helped, or are only petty, he is not querulous or importunate, for that would indicate that he took them seriously. He has a greater gift for acquiring fine but useless things than for acquiring those that are useful and advantageous, since this shows a greater self-sufficiency.

A calm and steady manner of walking is thought suitable for him, and also a deep voice and a stately manner of speaking. Since he does not think many things important, he will not hurry; the man who thinks nothing great is not vehement, for quickness of speech and action occur just because people do think things important.

That is the character of the great-souled man. The man who falls short is mean-spirited, whereas he who goes to excess is vain. The common opinion is that these sorts are not bad—after all, they do no evil—but that they have missed the mark. The mean-spirited man deprives himself of his true deserts and appears to have something bad about him, in that he does not claim good for himself. Also, he does not know himself; if he did, he would reach for his deserts, which are good. Opinion has it that he is not stupid, but hesitant. But this seems to make him still worse, since all men reach for their deserts, and draw back from fine acts and pursuits (and external goods too) only if they do not deserve them.

But vain people *are* stupid; they do not know themselves, and that is really noticeable. They are not deserving people, but try to win honors, only to be found out. They wear fine clothes and walk about like fine persons, and so on. They want their successes to be well known, and they talk about them with the idea that they will be respected for them. It is smallness of soul, rather than vanity, that is the opposite of greatness of soul. It happens more frequently, and is worse. As we said, then, greatness of soul has to do with great honor.

■   ■   ■

Book VI

1. We have already explained that we ought to choose the mean, not the excess or the deficiency. Since we also said that the mean is prescribed by right reason, we must now analyze this idea. In all the dispositions we have described (as in other things too), there is a sort of mark, or target. The man who has right reason keeps his eye on that when he increases or relaxes his effort. There is a standard limiting all the mean positions, which, in our theory, are (1) between an excess and a deficiency, and (2) in accordance with right reason.

Put like that, it is indeed correct, but not clear. In all other concerns that can be treated scientifically, it is true to say that effort or relaxation ought to be neither too much nor too little, but the mean amount, as right reason dictates. But if this were all one had, one would not be better off. If someone said "Use what medicine prescribes, and in the way the doctor orders," we would not know what treatment to apply to the body. This is why it is not enough just to have this truism about the dispositions of the soul; we must decide what right reason is and what is its determining character.

When we divided the virtues of the soul, we said that some were moral and some intellectual. We have already dealt with the moral virtues; before dealing with the others, let us first make some observations about the soul.

Earlier it was said that the soul has the two parts, the rational and the irrational. Now we must make a similar division of the rational part. We take for granted that there are two rational elements: one we use to study those things the principles of which cannot be other than they are; with the other, we study things whose principles do admit of variation. For things different in kind there are parts of the soul, different in kind from other parts and naturally related to the appropriate things; the parts come to have knowledge by virtue of their similarity to and relationship with the objects known.

Let us give them names, calling the former the "scientific" and the latter the "deliberative" part. Deliberation and calculation are the same; no one deliberates about things that *must* be as they are. The deliberative part is therefore one element of the rational part. We must next decide what is the best disposition of each of these; that will show us the special excellence in each case, and the excellence of each part is related to its proper function.

2. There are three factors in the soul that determine action and truth. They are perception, intellect, and desire. Of these, perception is not a principle of action; this is plain from the fact that animals have perceptions, but do not share in action.

There is an analogy between pursuit and avoidance in the matter of desire, and affirmation and denial in the sphere of the intellect. Since moral virtue is a disposition involving choice, and choice is deliberative desire, it must therefore be the case, if the choice is good, that the reason is true and the desire right. What reason assents to is what desire pursues.

This sort of intellect and truth has to do with moral action. When we are speaking of intellect, not with regard to action or production but in its scientific aspect, then good or bad means true or false. Truth, after all, is the objective of every intellectual operation; but when we speak of the part that deals both with action and intellect, truth and right desire are in agreement.

The starting point of action is choice—in the sense of the efficient, not the final cause; and the starting point

of choice is desire and "the reason why." There is, therefore, no choice without intellect or thought or moral
disposition, since there is no such thing as successful action (or its opposite) without thought and character.

By itself, thought does not start anything; that is done
only by thought that involves conduct and that aims at
an end. This kind of thought is also at the start of production: everyone who makes something makes it with
an end in view. The article made is not, strictly, the
purpose or end, since it is subordinate to something else
to which it properly belongs; but moral action is an end,
since successful action is the ultimate good at which desire aims.

Choice, therefore, is thought along with desire, or desire along with thought; and a starting point of action of
this sort is found in man. No past event can be an object
of choice; e.g., no one chooses "to have sacked Troy."
Nor do people deliberate about the past, but about future contingencies; whereas it is not possible now for the
past not to have happened. Agathon made a valid point
when he said "This is the only thing that even God cannot do: undo what has already been done."

Both the rational parts have truth as their object; and
the virtues of both are the dispositions by virtue of which
each part arrives at the truth.

3. Let us start at the beginning and discuss them again.
The means through which the soul comes to the truth,
whether in affirmations or in denials, are five in number.
They are the following: technique, science, practical
sense, wisdom, and intelligence. (In the case of supposition and opinion, it is possible to go wrong.)

The following will make plain what is meant by science, since we must be accurate and not follow analogies. We all suppose, in the case of something we know,
that it cannot be other than it is. But of things that vary,
when they are outside our range it is not clear whether
they exist or not. The object of scientific knowledge ex-

ists necessarily; and it is therefore eternal, since all things that, in the strict sense, exist necessarily are eternal; and eternal things are not subject to creation and destruction.

Also, opinion has it that all science can be taught, and that every object of scientific knowledge can be learned. All instruction starts from things known beforehand, as we said in the *Analytics;* some proceeds by induction and some by syllogistic proof. Induction is a principle, and means induction of the universal; whereas syllogism works *from* universals. There are, therefore, principles from which syllogism works, but which cannot be proved syllogistically. They are known, then, by induction.

Science, then, is a disposition that has to do with demonstrative knowledge (see the fuller account that I have given in the *Analytics*). When a man has a particular sort of conviction, and the principles are known to him, he has knowledge. If he does not have better knowledge of the principles than of the conclusions, he will have knowledge only incidentally. This is sufficient about science.

4. When we come to what can vary, we find that it divides into products and moral actions. Producing and action are not identical (we can accept the popular account of this distinction). It follows that a disposition accompanied by reason and involved in action is different from a disposition that is also accompanied by reason but makes or produces. This is why neither is included in the other, since action is not production and production is not action.

The art of building is a craft, a particular *productive* disposition accompanied by reason. There is no craft that is not a particular productive disposition accompanied by reason, and there is no such disposition that is not a craft; it follows that craft and productive disposition accompanied by true reason are identical.

All craft or skill has to do with bringing something into being: with devising and seeing how something can

be made that can either exist or not exist, and for which
the starting point of production resides in the maker,
not the thing made. Technique does not apply to things
that exist or happen necessarily, or to things that exist
by nature: such things have their starting point in
themselves.

Since producing is different from action, it must be
the case that technique or craft is concerned with producing, not with action. There is a sense in which chance
and skill apply to the same objects, as Agathon says,
viz., "Skill loves chance, and chance loves skill." Skill,
then, as we said, is a disposition that has to do with
producing things, and involves true reason. Lack of skill
is the opposite: it is a disposition that has to do with
producing, but accompanied by false reason. The field of
operation for both is that which can admit of variation.

■   ■   ■

7. In talking about arts and crafts, we apply the term
"wisdom" as meaning "technical mastery" to those who
are most accomplished in their special skill. We say, for
instance, that Phidias is a masterly sculptor in stone, Polyclitus a masterly sculptor in bronze. In these examples,
all we mean by mastery is excellence in the given craft.

But we think that there are some people who are wise
in a general, not a particular sense. They are not masters
of something, in the sense used by Homer in the *Margites*: "The gods did not give him mastery of the spade
or plow; they made him a master of nothing."

Clearly then, wisdom is the most finished of all the
different ways of knowing. The wise man ("master" in
the general sense) must know not only what follows
from first principles but also the truth about the first
principles. Wisdom, then, will be intelligence and science
together; it is knowledge of the highest things, knowledge made complete.

It is absurd to suppose that political science or practical sense is the highest art, since man is not the best thing in the universe. Health and goodness are not the same for men as for fish; but whiteness and straightness are always the same. Everyone would always apply the term "wisdom" to the same thing, but not the term "practical sense." A man uses the term of what serves his own advantage in a particular respect, and he will entrust himself to that. That is why practical sense is attributed to some animals, since they appear to have the ability to take forethought regarding their own lives.

Clearly, then, wisdom and political science are not identical. If one means by wisdom the skill that deals with our own welfare, then there will be a number of "wisdoms." There is no single craft that deals with the good of all animate things; there is a different one for each, unless one says that there is a single art of medicine for all things. It would make no difference if one pleaded that man is better than all other living things. There are other things than man that are more godlike in nature, the most obvious examples being the heavenly bodies.

From what has been said, it is clear that wisdom is science of *and* intelligence about the things that are by nature the highest. For this reason people say that Anaxagoras, Thales, and their like were wise, not that they were men of practical sense. They see that such men do not know what is in their own interest; and they say that their knowledge is clever, marvelous, difficult to obtain, and godlike—but that it is useless, since they do not study the good for man.

Practical sense does deal with human affairs, things about which it is possible to deliberate. Successful deliberation, we say, is the main function of the man with practical sense; no one deliberates about things that cannot be other than they are, or about things that are not subordinate to an end obtainable by action. In an absolute sense, the man who deliberates successfully is able to take a reasoned aim at the greatest good that man can obtain through action. Practical sense is not just concerned with universals; it has to know particulars too. It is concerned with action that, in turn, has to do with particulars. That is why there are cases in which people who do not have knowledge are more successful than others who do; we may cite, among others, those with experience. If a man knows that light meat is easily digested and health-giving, but does not know which meats are light, he will not make you healthy. The man who knows that chicken is health-giving will be more successful. Since practical sense has to do with action, one must have knowledge of both particulars and universals; or, if not of both, then knowledge of particulars rather than of universals. In this case, too, there will be an art that will give directions.

8. Political science and practical sense are the same disposition, although not identical in essence. When practical sense is concerned with the state, it is, in its supreme aspect, the art of legislating; when it has to do with particulars, it takes the common name of political science. This last involves both action and deliberation: a decree, for example, indicates a course of action; it is also the last stage of a deliberation. Such people—those concerned with particulars—are the only ones of whom we say "they are in politics"; they are the only ones who perform actions in the sense in which craftsmen do. Practical sense is also, it is thought, an art concerned with one's own individual affairs; then it is given the name "practical sense," which is common to other things too. Other branches are specified as management, legislation, politics, or statesmanship, the last of which divides into the art of deliberation and legal science.

Knowing what is best for oneself will certainly be one kind of this knowledge, although it is very different from other kinds. There is an opinion that the man who knows his own business and is occupied with that is a man of practical sense, whereas politicians are meddlers.

This is why Euripides said: "Would that be sensible for me? I might have lived without meddling, a mere number like the majority of men, as equal as anyone. As for energetic people, who are busy meddling. . . ."

People of this sort look to their own advantage, and think it right to do so.

This opinion has led to the idea that such people are men with practical sense. But it may be that it is not possible to get one's own advantage or good without bringing in management or even politics. Again, how best to arrange one's own affairs is not clear and should be considered carefully.

This is confirmed by the fact that, although quite young people become good geometricians and mathematicians, and expert in similar subjects, it is not thought that a young person can have practical sense. The reason is that practical sense deals with particulars, with which we become familiar by experience. Youth, however, is inexperienced; since only the passage of time can bring experience.

We might ask how it is that a child can be a good mathematician, but not a philosopher or a scientist. Is it because the former deals with abstractions, whereas the first principles of the latter subjects are given us only by experience? The young cannot have any depth of conviction about such principles; they can only state them, whereas the meaning of terms in mathematics is quite clear. Here is another point. In deliberation, we can make mistakes about the universal or the particular. For example, we may think that all stagnant water is bad, or that this particular sample of water is stagnant.

It is clear that practical sense is not science since, as we said, it is concerned, as action is, with an ultimate, particular thing. It is the opposite of intelligence. The latter has to do with definitions, which cannot themselves be proved; but practical sense has to do with something immediate and particular (in the sense indicated above), which is not known scientifically but is perceived. It is a particular kind of perceiving or seeing; not simple sense perception, but rather like the way in which we "see" that the last particular figure is a triangle, which will bring the analysis to a stop. Seeing applies more to this than to practical sense, in which it is a different kind of seeing.

●　●　●

13. We must look once more at virtue. There is the same analogy in the case of virtue that there is between practical sense and cleverness. (These are similar, but not identical.) The analogy here is between natural virtue and virtue proper. It is commonly thought that all moral characteristics are, in a sense, given us by nature: we are just, temperate, brave, and so on as soon as we are born. But we expect to find that the good, in the absolute sense, is different from this—that the virtues, in the true sense, come about in a different way. Both children and animals have the natural dispositions, but, without reason, these may prove to be harmful.

We can see with our own eyes that a strong man who is blind falls heavily because he has no sight. There is an analogous situation with regard to these dispositions. Yet, if they acquire reason, they are outstanding when it comes to action. The disposition, which is already similar to a virtue, will then be virtue properly speaking. Just as there are two sides to the "calculating" part—cleverness and practical sense—similarly there are two sides to the moral part: one is natural virtue, the other is virtue proper. Virtue proper does not occur apart from practical sense.

That is why some people say, as Socrates did, that all the virtues are forms of practical sense. His view was partly right and partly wrong: he was wrong in supposing that all the virtues are forms of practical sense; but he was right in saying that they cannot occur without practical sense. Here is further proof. Everyone nowadays, when defining virtue, first states the disposition and its scope and then adds that "the disposition must be in conformity with right reason"—"right" here meaning "in conformity with practical sense."

We must change ground a little. Virtue is not only disposition in conformity with right reason; it is disposition *accompanied by* right reason. Right reason, in connection with such matters, is practical sense.

Socrates thought that the virtues were themselves reason: according to him, they are all branches of knowledge. We, however, say that they are accompanied by reason. It is clear, from what has been said, that it is not possible to be good in the strict sense without having practical sense; nor is it possible to have practical sense apart from moral virtue.

That is how we may solve the dialectical argument that the virtues are all separated from one another—a view that is based on the fact that the same person does not have the greatest aptitude for all the virtues. He will have one virtue already, but will not yet have acquired another one. This is possible with regard to natural virtues, but not with regard to those that properly qualify a man as good. Once the single virtue, practical sense, is present, all the virtues will be present.

Clearly, even if practical sense were not concerned with action, it would still be required because it is the virtue of a part of the soul, and because there cannot be right choice apart from practical sense and virtue. Whereas the latter enables us to achieve the end or purpose, the former enables us to take up the means subordinate to that end.

It is not really true that practical sense controls wisdom or the superior part of the mind, any more than medicine controls health. The point is that medicine does not *employ* health, it works out how to *create* it. It gives instructions with a view to making health, but it does not give orders to health. That would be the same as saying that politics rules over the gods merely because politics gives orders about everything that has to do with the state, including religion.

Book VII

* * *

2. The following question may be raised: How can one both behave in an unrestrained way and at the same time believe correctly that such behavior is wrong? Some people deny that it is possible to do this knowingly. As Socrates thought, it is monstrous, at a time when knowledge is actually present, for anything else to be in charge, dragging knowledge around like a slave. Socrates used to argue wholeheartedly against such a view, his idea being that there is no such thing as lack of restraint, since no one would knowingly act contrary to the good. That could happen only through ignorance.

This theory is obviously at variance with plain fact. We must examine the failing more closely, and see—if it happens through ignorance—what sort of ignorance this is. It is clear that the unrestrained man does not think it right to do what he does until he is actually "out of control."

Some thinkers allow part of this, but not all of it. They agree with the view that nothing can be superior to knowledge; but *not* with the view that no one acts contrary to what, in his opinion, is the best. For this reason they say that the unrestrained man, when he comes under the influence of pleasures, does not have knowledge; he has opinions instead. But if it is opinion, and not knowledge, and if the opposing idea is not strong, but weak (as happens with people who are of two minds), it is an understandable fault not to stick to such ideas in the face of powerful desires. Vice, however, is not in this sense "understandable," nor is any blame-worthy act.

What about the case where practical sense is in conflict with desire? Practical sense is a very powerful thing, and it would be very odd that the same person should have practical sense and lack of control at the same time, for no one in the world would say that men of practical sense deliberately do the vilest acts. Besides, we have already shown that the man of practical sense has to do with action (he is a person occupied with immediate, particular things), and has the other virtues.

Consider this point, too. If restraint consists of having violent and bad desires, the result will be that the temperate man will not have restraint; and the man with restraint will not be temperate. The point is that excess or having bad desires must by definition be bad. After all, if the desires are good, the disposition that prevents a man from following them must be bad—in which case not all control will be good. But if these desires are weak, and not bad, there is nothing admirable about the controlled man; and even if they are both bad and weak, there is nothing really great about him.

Furthermore, if control makes people stick to any and every opinion, it is bad; this will happen if it makes people stick to false opinions. And if lack of control makes a person abandon all his opinions, some lack of control will be good. Take the case of Neoptolemus in Sophocles' *Philoctetes*. He is to be praised for not sticking to the course he was persuaded to take by Odysseus—not sticking because of the pain that telling a lie gives him.

Also, there is the problem created by the sophists. Because they want to reach a paradoxical result, so as to show how clever they are when they succeed, the reasoning they offer leads to a dilemma. The mind is imprisoned, since it does not wish to stay put, being dissatisfied with the conclusion, and yet cannot advance because of its inability to refute the argument.

(1) One of the sophists' arguments reaches the conclusion that practical folly, combined with lack of control, is a virtue: a person in that state, because he has no control, does the opposite of what he thinks; since he thinks that good is bad and should not be the object of action, he will as a result in fact do good, not bad.

(2) Whoever pursues pleasure from conviction and choice will appear to be better than anyone who pursues pleasure not from reasoned principle, but from lack of control. The former can be more easily cured, since he can be persuaded to change; but the unrestrained person is open to the old saying: "When water chokes you, what do you take to wash it down?" If he had had rational conviction about the rightness of his acts, he would have stopped acting as he does, upon suffering a change of conviction. But, as things are, even when he is convinced of the rightness of his course, he still goes on acting in the same way.

Lastly, if control and lack of control can be shown in every sphere, what is meant by "uncontrolled" without qualification? No one has all the vices that we call "lack of control"; but we do talk of people being "uncontrolled," without saying in what respect.

3. These are the problems. Some of these views must be cleared away, others left standing. Solving a problem is a sort of discovery.

First of all, one must see whether unrestrained people act knowingly or not. Then we must define the sphere of action of the unrestrained and the self-controlled man; I mean, are they concerned with all pleasures and pain, or certain selected ones? Is control identical with endurance, or different from it? Similarly with regard to other questions that are associated with the subject.

The starting point for our inquiry is this: does the self-controlled man differ from the unrestrained man in respect to the sphere of action or to his manner of approach to the sphere of action? Is a person uncontrolled just because he lacks control about certain things? Or if that is not the case, is it his attitude or his disposition that counts? Or is it a mixture of both? Then, we must settle whether control and lack of control can be exhibited in regard to everything. The uncontrolled man, in the strict sense, does not show his fault in everything; he has the same sphere as the profligate man. But it is not just that he has the same sphere—in that case he would be the same as the profligate man—but that he has a particular attitude toward it. The profligate man is led on from choice: he thinks that one should always follow the pleasure of the moment. But the uncontrolled man who lacks control does not *think* he should, even though he does in fact follow immediate pleasure.

As for the question whether it is "true opinion" or "knowledge" that is transgressed by uncontrolled men, that is not important to this argument. Some of those who merely have opinion are not in any doubt at all; they think they know for certain. If weakness of conviction is the cardinal factor and if, therefore, it is the people with opinion rather than those with knowledge who act contrary to what they think right, knowledge will be no better than opinion. Some people have as strong conviction about their opinions as others have about what they know. Heraclitus serves as an example.

"Knowing" has two meanings. There is the man who has knowledge but does not make use of it, and there is the man who uses his knowledge; both are said to know. There will therefore be a difference, in doing what one should not, between (1) having the knowledge but not exercising it and (2) having it *and* exercising it. The latter is the shocking thing; it is not so bad if the person goes wrong when his knowledge is not active.

Again, the premises used in reasoning about action

are of two kinds. It is quite possible for a man to have both and still act contrary to what he knows; but in that case he will be making use of the universal premise, not the particular. After all, it is particular things that are the concern of action. There is also a distinction about the universal: one aspect of it is predicated of the person himself, another of the thing. Take as an example the proposition that "dry food is good for all men." The two aspects of the universal are: (1) that the person is himself a man and (2) that this kind of food is dry. But in cases of a mistake, he either does not have the knowledge or does not have it *actively* that this food is of that particular kind.

The difference between these two ways of knowing is considerable. There is no absurdity in the unrestrained man's knowing in one sense; but it would be remarkable if he knew in the other.

Men can have knowledge in another way, as well as in those just outlined. We see that there is a variation in the disposition "having knowledge but not using it." One can both have it, in a sense, and not have it. This is exemplified in being asleep, mad, or drunk; and this is also the state of those people who are swept away by the emotions. Fits of temper, desire for sex, and such things quite patently alter the condition of the body; and some people actually go mad because of them. Clearly, we must say that men who lack control resemble such persons. The fact that they make rational and correct statements means nothing. People who are drunk or mad can recite proofs and quote the verses of Empedocles. Even people who are just starting to learn can string propositions together; but they do not know them. The person and the subject have to grow together—a process that needs time. Uncontrolled persons uttering maxims, as they give way, are like actors speaking their parts.

One can also consider the cause in this way, with reference to the nature of control. The universal premise is an opinion, whereas the other premise has to do with particulars, which are subject to perception. When the two premises are joined to make one, action must follow at once, just as, in scientific thought, the mind must at once agree to the conclusion. Here is an example. If all sweet things should be tasted, and this particular thing is sweet, it follows that the person who can, and is not prevented, should taste this thing. Suppose there is present a universal premise that *forbids* tasting, along with another that says, for example, that "all sweet things are pleasant"; and suppose these to be combined with an active minor premise, e.g., "this is sweet." Suppose, too, that desire is present. Now then, the former universal orders one to avoid this thing; but desire leads one on. Desire can move the parts of the body. The result is that there is an instance of getting out of control, which is due in a way to reason and an opinion that is, not of itself but accidentally, contrary to right reason. (The true contrary is desire, not opinion.)

This is why we do not speak of animals as "uncontrolled." They do not have the universal premise; instead, they perceive images and remember particular things.

How does this ignorance (of the uncontrolled man) come to an end? How does he regain his knowledge? The same thing applies here that applies to being drunk and being asleep. The reason is not peculiar to this case alone; we must look for it in physiology.

The last premise (the minor) is an opinion about what can be perceived. It controls whether we act or not. When the uncontrolled person is carried away, either he does not have that opinion or he does have it, although not in the sense of knowing it, but just of reiterating it, as the drunkard goes on quoting Empedocles.

The final term is not a universal, nor is it of the same scientific status as the universal. Because of this, it seems that Socrates' conclusion is actually the result. This failure (being uncontrolled) does not occur when knowledge proper is present; for it is not knowledge proper that is dragged about by emotion; it is a knowledge connected with sense perception.

This is enough about the question of whether people are uncontrolled knowingly or not, and in what sense one can know the right thing to do and yet be uncontrolled.

* * *

Book X

1. Next, perhaps, comes a discussion of pleasure. Pleasure appears to be closely involved with human beings. This is why people educate young children by steering them with the aid of pleasure and pain. Taking pleasure in the right things and hating the wrong are thought to be of the greatest relevance to forming a good character. They extend throughout our whole lifetime and exercise weight and influence on virtue and the happy life, since people choose the pleasant and avoid the painful. There is little excuse for omitting this subject, especially since it is much debated.

Some say that pleasure is the good; others, on the contrary, that it is utterly bad. Some, perhaps, do think that the latter is really the case; but perhaps others think it is better for our way of living to say that pleasure is bad, even if it is not. They argue that most people incline to pleasure and are slaves of their pleasures; and that is why one should lead them to the contrary idea, since in that way they can arrive at the mean.

This is surely wrong. Arguments about things having to do with the emotions and with actions are less trustworthy than the facts themselves. Therefore, when they disagree with the evidence of the senses, they come to be despised and to drag the truth along in their fall. If a man blames pleasure but is once caught aiming at it, his swerving toward it seems to show that all pleasure is to be aimed at, since most people do not draw distinctions. True statements are extremely useful, not only for knowing but also for living. They agree with the facts and, so, are believed; and therefore they encourage those who understand them to live by their light. But this is enough on such matters; let us examine the received views on pleasure.

2. Eudoxus thought that pleasure was the good. He saw that all things aim at pleasure, both rational and irrational creatures alike. Further, the object of choice is the good, that which is really best. Therefore, since everything inclined to the same goal, that was evidence that this was the good for all things. (Each thing discovers its individual good, just as it finds its food.) What is good for all things, the goal of their desires, must be the good par excellence.

His arguments were accepted because of his excellent character rather than for their own validity. Indeed, he seemed a most temperate person. He did not seem to have this view because he was a partisan of pleasure, so people thought that what he said must be really true.

He thought that his position was equally obvious starting from the contrary. Pain, he argued, was intrinsically avoided by all things, and similarly the opposite was to be sought or chosen. The supreme object of choice is that which we choose for its own sake, not with a view to something else. This, by general agreement, must be pleasure, since nobody asks to what *purpose* anyone is pleased, assuming that pleasure is chosen for its own sake. When pleasure is added to any good thing, it adds to its desirability, as when pleasure is added to just action and to temperance; but good can be increased only by good.

This argument appears to show that pleasure is *a* good, but not more so than another. Every good, when associated with another good, is more desirable than taken by itself. Plato, indeed, uses this argument to *refute* the view that pleasure is the good. The pleasant life is even more sought after when it is combined with wisdom than when apart; now, he continued, if the compound is better than the constituents, pleasure cannot be the good. The good is what we choose without anything having to be added to it.

It is clear that nothing can be *the* good that becomes better for us to choose when taken in conjunction with any intrinsic good. What, then, is there of this kind that is available to us? That is what we are looking for.

Those who object that what all things aim at is not the good are wrong. We say that something is the case when it appears so to all. The man who tries to refute our belief here will not be able to say anything more credible. If only unintelligent beings desire pleasure, there would be some point to the objection. But since intelligent beings also desire pleasure, how can there be? Perhaps even in the lower animals there is some natural good, which is better than they are, and which aims at the proper good.

The argument about the contrary of pleasure seems to be wrong. They argue that pleasure is not the good just for the reason that pain is bad; there can also be opposition between bad and bad (as well as between good and bad), and both evils can be opposed to what is neutral, neither good nor bad. They are right about this, of course, but the truth of what they say is irrelevant to the present case. If both pleasure and pain were bad, they would both be things to be avoided; if they were neither good nor bad, neither would be avoided, or both would be equally avoided. As things are, men avoid one as bad and choose the other as good. That is the way in which pleasure and pain are opposites.

3. Even if pleasure is not a quality, that does not mean that it is not good. Neither are the activities of virtue in the category of quality; nor is happiness.

They say that the good is limited but that pleasure is unlimited, since it admits of degree. If they decide this by examining the way in which we feel pleasure, then the same will be true of justice and other virtues; we do say that men have more or less of such and such a virtue, and act according to the virtues more or less. Some people are "more just," "more brave," and the question of degree applies also to doing just acts and doing temperate acts. On the other hand, if the examination of pleasures themselves leads them to this view, they do not give the reason correctly, since some pleasures are pure, whereas others are mixed.

What is there to keep pleasure from being like health? Health itself, although limited and defined, admits of degrees. Health does not consist of the same balance in all people, or even in the same individual. When it is being dissolved, it still remains for a certain time and varies in degree; the same can be true of pleasure.

They say that the good is complete but that motion and process are incomplete. Then they try to show that pleasure is motion and process. But they appear to be wrong, and it appears that pleasure is not motion. All motion is properly characterized by quickness or slowness: if motion is not in itself quick or slow, like the motion of the universe, it is so in relation to something else. But neither applies to pleasure. One can *become* pleased quickly, just as one can get angry quickly; but one cannot *be* pleased quickly, or more quickly than someone else, even though this usage does apply to walking and growing and such things. Quick and slow, then, apply to the *coming* of pleasure, but the *activity* of pleasure is not quick; I mean, one does not take pleasure quickly.

How can pleasure be a process of becoming? A process is not haphazard in the sense that just anything can come into being out of anything else; but that from which process starts is the very same thing that is left after dissolution. Pain must be the destruction of that of which pleasure is the process.

They say, too, that pain is a deficiency of a natural state, whereas pleasure is the corresponding satisfaction. Now, these effects concern the body. If pleasure is the satisfaction of a natural want, the feeling of pleasure will occur where the satisfaction occurs—that is, in the body. But appearances are against this. It is not, then, that pleasure is satisfaction; when satisfaction occurs, one *feels* pleasure, just as one feels pain when an incision is made.

This view appears to be based on pains and pleasures having to do with food. When people have felt the pangs of hunger, they feel pleasure in satisfying the want. But this does not happen with all pleasures. The pleasures of learning are not a sequence to pain; nor (among the pleasures having to do with the senses) are the pleasures of smelling; nor are many sounds and sights, memories and expectations. If these are processes, what are the results of the process? There has been no deficiency to be followed by satisfaction.

Some people introduce the shameful pleasures into the discussion. In reply to them, one may say that these are not pleasant. One should not suppose, just because they are pleasant to bad people, that they really are pleasant, except for these same people. Similarly, when people are ill, what is healthful, sweet, or bitter to them is not really so; and so too with what appears white to people with bad eyes.

Alternatively, one may say that pleasures are to be sought, but not pleasures from this source; just as wealth is to be sought, but not at the price of treason, nor health at the price of eating just anything.

Or, again, there are different classes of pleasure. Pleasures derived from good things are in a different class from pleasures derived from bad things. You cannot feel the pleasure of the just man except by being just; and so with music and other things.

Friendship, since the friend differs from the flatterer, seems to make it plain that pleasure is not the good, or else that there are different classes of pleasure. The friend associates with us with a view to the good, but the flatterer with a view to pleasure. The flatterer is reproved, but people praise the friend because he associates with us for a different purpose.

No one would choose to live with a child's mentality throughout the whole of his life, even though he took the greatest possible pleasure in the things that children are pleased by. Nor would anyone choose pleasure by way of doing something very dishonorable, even if there were no painful consequences. There are many things one would value greatly even if they brought no pleasure, like seeing, remembering, knowing, possessing the virtues. It makes no difference that pleasures do necessarily accompany these things; we would still choose them, even if no pleasure at all came from them.

Pleasure, then, is not the good, nor is all pleasure to be sought. There are certain pleasures that are worth having in themselves; these differ in kind or in respect to origin. This is sufficient as an account of views about pleasure and pain.

4. If we resume from the beginning, it will be clearer what pleasure is, and what kind of thing. Seeing, for whatever length of time, appears to be complete: it does not need anything to come along later and make its specific form complete. Pleasure is like that, since it is something whole: there is no time at which you can indicate a pleasure and say that its specific form will be complete only when it has lasted for a longer time. This is why pleasure is not motion. All motion is in time and has a goal—the art of building is an example—and it is complete when it fulfills its aim. Completeness, here, refers either to the whole period or to the moment of completion. The parts of the whole motion are incomplete both in themselves and in the time they occupy, and they are specifically different from one another and from the whole. Laying the bricks is different from fluting the column, and both these are different from making the tem-

ple. For making the temple is complete, since nothing
further is needed to satisfy the objective; but laying the
foundation and making the triglyph are incomplete, since
each is the making of only a part. Here, the parts of the
motion are specifically different: you cannot indicate a
motion complete in kind by referring to just a part of
the time; if you can do so at all, there must be reference
to the whole time.

The same is true of walking and other things. If locomotion is motion from whence to whither, there are different species of locomotion as well: flying, walking,
jumping, and so on. That is true not only with reference
to the whole but also to the act of walking itself.
"Whence" and "whither" are different points of reference in the stadium (seen as a whole), and in *part* of
the stadium; they differ, too, from one part to another.
Traveling along this line is different from traveling along
that. A man travels not only along a line, but a line
situated in a place; and this line is in a different place
from that.

There is a detailed account of motion elsewhere. However, it does seem that motion is not complete in just
any and every segment of time. The many separate motions are incomplete and differ in kind, "kind" in this
case depending on "whence" and "whither."

But the specific quality of pleasure is complete at any
moment of time. Plainly, then, pleasure and motion are
different; and pleasure is something perfect and
complete.

It is clear from this that people are wrong to say that
pleasure is motion or process. Motion and process are
not terms used of everything, only of things that have
parts but are not perfect wholes. Process does not apply
to seeing, to point, or to unity; none of these things is
motion or process. Nor is pleasure, since it is a perfect
whole.

All the senses exercise their activity on what is sensed.
Perfect activity is that which is exercised by a sense in

good condition on the finest object that falls within its
scope. (This, above all, appears to be perfect activity. It
is immaterial whether we say that the sense is active or
that the organ is active.) Now, for each sense the best
activity is the activity of what is in the best condition,
exercised on the best of the things that come within its
scope. This will be the most perfect and most pleasant
activity. There is a pleasure peculiar to each sense, just
as there is pleasure peculiar to thought and contemplation. The most pleasant, however, is the most complete;
and the most complete is the activity of the best in condition, exercised on the most valuable object within its
ken. Pleasure completes the activity, but not in the way
in which the thing perceived and the sense perceiving
do when they are both good. After all, health and the
doctor are not both causes of good health in the same
way.

It is clear that pleasure accompanies every sense (since
we say that sound and sights, for example, are pleasant).
It is also clear that this is especially true when the sense
in question is at its best and is actively exercised on the
best object. Provided that what is perceived and what
perceives are both at their best, there always will be
pleasure as long as something to cause it and something
to experience it are there.

How does pleasure complete the activity? Not as a
state does, which is inherent in the agent, but as a kind
of supervening completeness, like the healthy look of
young people.

So long as the object thought or perceived is as it
should be, and so, too, is the discerning or the contemplating faculty, there will be pleasure in the activity.
When what experiences and what causes the experience
are alike, and in the same state with regard to each
other, the same result will naturally follow.

How is it that no one feels pleasure continuously? Is
it because of fatigue? It is impossible for anything in
man to be active continuously. Nor, then, can pleasure

be continuous, since it accompanies the activity. Some things give pleasure because they are novel, although later on they do not have the same effect. At first, the intellect is engaged and becomes energetically active on them, like somebody looking hard at something. Later, however, the activity is not the same, but lapses, which is why the pleasure is dimmed.

It might be thought that all people strive after pleasure because all people have an appetite for life. Life is a kind of activity, and each person is active on those objects and with those faculties that he most likes. The musician exercises the sense of hearing on songs; the lover of mathematics is active with his intellect on problems; and so with each of the others. Pleasure completes these activities, and therefore completes life, which is what people strive after. Therefore, people rightly strive after pleasure, too, since for each person pleasure completes life, which is striven after.

Let us leave aside the question whether we choose life for the sake of pleasure or pleasure for the sake of life. These things appear to be coupled and not to admit of separation, since there is no pleasure without activity and every activity is completed by pleasure.

5. For this reason, the pleasures seem to be different in kind. We think that things that are different in kind are completed differently. This seems to apply to natural things and to the products of art: animals and trees, paintings, statues, houses, and manufactured articles. Similarly, specifically different activities are completed by specifically different things. The activities of the intellect are different from those of the senses, and both are specifically different among themselves; so too, therefore, are the pleasures that complete the activities.

This will be apparent, too, from the fact that each pleasure is closely coupled with the activity it completes, and increases that activity. People who engage in an activity with pleasure are better judges of each question in that kind of activity, and more accurate too: those who like doing geometry become students of geometry, and are better at understanding it. Similarly, lovers of music and lovers of building and the rest improve in relation to their particular field by virtue of enjoying it: the pleasures increase the activities, and what increases something is coupled with it; but things that are coupled to things specifically different are themselves specifically different.

This will be still more apparent from the fact that a pleasure from another source is an obstacle to an activity. Flute lovers cannot attend to an argument if they suddenly hear a flute playing, since they take more pleasure in flute playing than in their present activity. The pleasure that they derive from flute playing ruins the activity of arguing. This happens similarly in other cases, when a man is doing two things at once. The more pleasant of the two drives out the other, and the greater the discrepancy between the two pleasures, the more it does so, so that it is not possible even to exercise the other activity. That is why people who gain intense pleasure from something cannot really do anything else. We do other things as well only when we obtain moderate pleasure from an activity. People who eat sweets in the theater do so above all when the actors are bad.

Now, the related pleasures refine activities, and make them better and more lasting; but alien pleasures impair an activity; it is plain, then, that there is a vast difference. Alien pleasures have roughly the same effect as related pains, which ruin activities. As, for example, when someone finds writing or calculating unpleasant or painful. The one does not write, the other does not calculate, because the activity is painful.

Related pleasures and related pains produce the opposite effect on activities. (By "related" we mean things that occur essentially because of the activity.) But alien pleasures, as we said, have much the same effect as pain, since they bring ruin, although not in the same way.

Activities differ with regard to goodness and badness: some are to be sought, others avoided, and some neither. The same is true of pleasures, since there is pleasure related to each activity. Pleasure related to a good activity is itself good, but the pleasure related to a bad activity is bad. Desire for the good is praiseworthy, for the bad blameworthy. But the pleasures we take in activities are more closely related to them than are our appetites or strivings. The latter are marked off from them in time and in nature, whereas the pleasures are very close to them, and are not marked off, so that it is actually arguable that activity and pleasure are the same. (However, pleasure does not seem to be intellect or perception—that would be absurd; but because they are inseparable, some people think that they are identical.) Therefore, just as activities differ, so too do pleasures. Sight differs from touch in purity; sound and smell differ from taste. Similarly, the pleasures differ too—the pleasures of the intellect from those of the senses, and the pleasures in each class among themselves.

Each animal has a pleasure proper to it, just as it has its own function: it is the pleasure proper to its activity. This becomes evident when we study particular cases. The horse, the dog, and man have different pleasures. Heraclitus says that an ass would prefer sweepings to gold, since asses get more pleasure from food than from gold. Different species, then, have different pleasures, and it is reasonable to expect that the pleasures of the same species will be the same. But there is no little variation in the case of man. The same things please some but pain others; to some they are painful and hateful, to others pleasant and lovely. The same thing happens with sweetness: the man with a fever disagrees with the healthy man about what is sweet, just as the weak man and the man in good condition disagree about what is hot. Similarly with the rest, too.

In all these cases the thing is as it appears to the good man. If this is true, as it seems to be, and excellence and the good man, as good man, are the measure of each thing, then pleasures, too, will be the pleasures of the good man, and pleasant will apply to the things that please him. We should not be surprised to find what is painful to him seeming pleasant to someone else, since there are many forms of perversity and corruption among men; so that they are not pleasant as such, but only to those people, to people in that state.

Clearly, we must not say that those pleasures that are admittedly shameful are pleasures, except for the corrupt. Now, in the case of good pleasures, which one or what kind belongs to man? Is it clear from a consideration of activities, since pleasures follow on them? Whether there is one or more than one activity of the complete, happy man, the pleasures that complete them will rightly be called the pleasures of man. The rest will be secondary or partial, like their activities.

6. Now that we have discussed things having to do with the virtues, with friendship and pleasure, our last task is to give an outline account of happiness, since that is what we make the goal of human activity. If we sum up what we said before, the argument will be shorter.

We said that it was not a disposition: if it were, it could be present in a man who slept out his whole life, living like a vegetable, or who had very great misfortune. If this is unacceptable, we must count it as an activity, as we said before. But some activities are necessary means and to be chosen for the sake of something else; others are chosen for their own sake. Clearly, happiness is one of these activities that are chosen for their own sake, and not for the sake of something else, since happiness is self-sufficient and needs nothing else to complete it. Activities chosen for their own sake are those from which nothing is sought apart from the activity itself. These would appear to be acts in accordance with virtue, since doing fine, good acts is something to be chosen for its own sake. So, too, are those amusements that are pleasant, since people do not choose them for the sake of other things. People are harmed by them rather than helped, since they are led to neglect their persons and their property. Most of those who are called happy take refuge in that way of living, which is why those who are clever at providing entertainment are very well thought of by tyrants. They make themselves pleasant and amusing in deference to their patrons' wishes; and their patrons need such amusements.

These things appear to make for happiness, because those with personal power spend their leisure in such matters. However, these people are not, perhaps, real evidence. Neither virtue nor reason consists in having personal power, and valuable activities come from virtue and reason. Even if such people have not tasted pure and liberal pleasure, and that is why they take refuge in the pleasures of the body, we should not say that the latter are preferable. Children, too, think that what they value is best. It is likely that just as grown men and children differ about value, so too do good and bad men.

As we have often said, valuable and pleasant means what is valuable and pleasant to the good man. The chosen activity for any individual is activity in accordance with his own condition; in the case of the good man, this means activity in accordance with virtue. Happiness therefore does not consist of amusement; it would be absurd if the end were amusement and if trouble and hardship throughout life should be all for the sake of amusing oneself. Except for happiness, which is itself the end, everything we choose is for the sake of something else. It would be stupid and childish to work hard and sweat just for childish amusement. The right thing, as Anacharsis said, is amusing oneself in order to work: amusement is like rest, and men need rest because they are unable to exercise their activities all the time.

But rest is not the end, since it takes place only for the sake of activity. The happy life is thought to be in accordance with virtue, and the virtuous life is accompa-

nied by seriousness, not amusement. We say that serious
things are better than comic, amusing ones; the better
the faculty, or the man, the more serious the activity.
The activity of the better man is already better, more
contributory to happiness. Anyone, a slave no less than
the good, might enjoy the pleasures of the body. But no
one allows a slave a share in happiness, any more than
in political life. Happiness does not consist of such things
but of activities in accordance with virtue, as we said
before.

7. If happiness is activity in accordance with virtue,
then it must be the best activity, i.e., that of the best in
man. Whether it is mind or something else that seems
naturally to rule and to lead, and to take notice of good
and divine things—whether it is itself divine, or the most
divine thing in man—the activity of this in accordance
with its own proper virtue will be complete happiness.
We have said that this is contemplation, which appears
to agree both with our former arguments and with the
truth. This is the best activity (mind is the best in us;
and "intelligible" things, which are apprehended by the
mind, are the best objects in the known world), and also
the most continuous. We are better able to contemplate
continuously than to *do* anything.

We think it essential that pleasure should be mixed in
with happiness, and the most pleasant of activities in
accordance with virtue is admittedly activity in accordance with wisdom. Philosophy has pleasures that are
marvelous for their purity and permanence. Besides, it
is likely that those who have knowledge have a more
pleasant life than those who are seeking it. Sufficiency,
as people call it, will be associated above all with contemplation. The wise man, the just, and all the rest of
them need the necessities of life; further, once there is
an adequate supply of these, the just man needs people
with and towards whom he may perform just acts; and
the same applies to the temperate man, the brave man,

and so on. But the wise man is able to contemplate, even when he is on his own; and the more so, the wiser he is. It is better, perhaps, when he has people working with him; but still he is the most self-sufficient of all.

Contemplation, alone, seems to be admired for its own sake. Nothing comes from it apart from contemplating; whereas, in matters of action, we hope for something more or less apart from the action. Happiness appears to depend on leisure: we work in order to have leisure; and we make war in order to have peace. Now, the activity of the practical virtues is exercised in war and politics; and actions concerned with these are full of work—in the case of war, absolutely so. No one chooses war for the sake of war, or precipitates war with that end in mind; he would seem to be an utter butcher if he turned his friends into enemies just to produce battles and slaughter. However, the politician's life is also full of work. Apart from just carrying on politics, politicians aim at power and honor or even happiness for themselves and for the citizens—a happiness that is different from political activity (and we are investigating it as being plainly different).

Now, political and military activity stand high for nobility and grandeur among the activities carried on in accordance with virtue. However, they are laborious; they aim at an end; and they are not chosen for their own sake. But the activity of the mind—contemplation—seems to be outstanding in its seriousness, and it has no goal apart from itself. It has its own pleasure (which increases the activity), and it also has sufficiency; and it is leisurely and unlaborious (so far as these are possible for man). All the attributes of the blessed man seem to be present in this activity; this will be complete human happiness—if a complete lifetime is involved, for there is nothing incomplete in the case of happiness.

Such a life would be more than human. A man will not live like that by virtue of his humanness, but by virtue of some divine thing within him. His activity is as

superior to the activity of the other virtues as this divine
thing is to his composite character. Now, if mind is divine in comparison with man, the life of the mind is
divine in comparison with mere human life. We should
not follow popular advice and, being human, have only
human ambitions or, being mortal, have only mortal
thoughts. As far as is possible, we should become immortal and do everything toward living by the best that
is in us. Even if it is small in bulk, in power and value
it is far above everything.

It may be thought that each individual is really this,
since this is the master-part, the best thing in man. It is
absurd to choose not one's own life, but the life proper
to something else. What we said before applies now.
What is by nature proper to a thing is best and most
pleasant for that thing. The life of reason will be best
for man, then, if reason is what is truly man. That sort
of man, then, will be the happiest.

8. Next will be the man with the other virtues, for the
activities of these have to do with the human side of
man. We do just and brave acts in relation to one another, observing what is fitting in each case with regard
to associations, services, and all kinds of acts and with
regard to the emotions. All these appear to be purely
human: some virtues seem to occur as a result of the
physical constitution; and moral virtue, in many respects,
is closely related to the emotions. Prudence, too, is coupled with moral virtue, and vice versa; the beginnings of
prudence depend on the moral virtues, and the right
thing in moral conduct is determined by prudence. Since
they are both connected with the emotions, they will be
related to man's composite nature. The virtues of this
composite nature are human; so too, therefore, will be
the life and the happiness that belong to them.

But the happiness of the mind is separate. (Let us be
content with saying that much here, since more detail
lies outside the present occasion.) It seems to require
external advantages to but a slight extent, or less than

moral virtue does. Let us grant that both have equal
need of the essentials of life, even though the politician
is more occupied than the philosopher with man's physical side and such things, for that makes only a slight
difference. The big difference will be in what they need
for their activity. The liberal man will need money for
doing liberal acts, and so will the just man for making
repayments. (Intentions cannot be seen, and even the
unjust make a pretense of wanting to act justly.) The
brave man will need power to do any of the acts proper
to his virtue; and the temperate man will need opportunity. Otherwise, how will he, or any of the others, be
known for what he is? There is an argument as to
whether decision or action is the more valid part of virtue, on the grounds that virtue consists of both. Clearly,
completeness of virtue will consist of both; however, for
actions people need many things, and the greater and
finer the acts, the more they need.

But the man who contemplates needs none of these
for his activity; indeed, there is a sense in which one
may say that they actually impede his contemplation. It
is by virtue of his being human, and associating with
human beings, that he chooses to act in accordance with
moral virtue. He will therefore need external things to
live as a human being. But it is plain from the following,
too, that complete happiness is an activity of contemplation. We assume that the gods are blessed and happy
above all others. What sort of action should we assign
them? Just ones? Will they not look ridiculous, making
contracts, returning deposits, and so forth? Or brave
acts? They will still look strange, facing the fearful and
running risks because of honor. Will it be liberal acts?
To whom will they give? It is absurd for them to have
currency or something like that. What will their temperate acts be? Surely such praise is out of place, since they
do not have wrong desires. A complete examination will
show that all moral acts are petty and unworthy of the
gods.

However, everybody supposes that the gods are alive,

and therefore active, since we cannot suppose them to sleep like Endymion. Now, if practical life and, still more, production are removed from a living being, what else is left but contemplation? Therefore, the activity of a god, which surpasses all others in blessedness, will be an activity of contemplation. Among human activities, that which is closest to it will be most happy. One indication is the fact that other living beings apart from man do not have a share in happiness, for they are completely deprived of such an activity.

The life of the gods is completely happy, the life of men only so far as it has some resemblance to the gods' activity. But no other living thing is happy in this sense at all, since it does not share at all in contemplation. Happiness, then, covers the same scope as contemplation: things that have the activity of contemplation have happiness, not incidentally but by virtue of their contemplation, since this is valuable in itself. Happiness therefore is a kind of contemplation.

But, since the philosopher is human, he will need external goods too. Man's nature is not sufficient for contemplating, but a man's body too must be healthy; food and other necessities must be available. Yet it should not be thought that the man who is to be happy will need many or great possessions, merely because it is not possible to be blessed without external goods. Self-sufficiency or good actions do not involve excess: it is possible to do fine things without being ruler of land and sea. Even with moderate resources, one can act virtuously; and the proof of this is clear to see: private citizens do good acts quite as much as do rulers; indeed more so. It is enough to have a right amount, for in that case the life of a man active in accordance with his virtue will be happy.

Perhaps Solon was quite right about happiness. He said that the happy were moderately supplied with external goods, had done very noble acts, and lived temperately. The point is that one can act rightly if one has only moderate resources. Anaxagoras, too, does not seem to have thought that the rich man or the ruler was the happy man. He said that he would not be surprised if the happy man looked strange to most people, who go by externals alone, since that is all they see. The opinions of the wise, then, agree with our arguments.

Such arguments do have a certain amount of force in them; but in practical matters the truth of a theory is judged by reference to life and to action, since these are what count. We must examine what we have said by applying it to actions and to life. If the theory agrees with the facts, we should accept it; if not, we must suppose that it is just theory and nothing more.

The man whose activity is activity of mind, and who studies that, is thought to be in the best state and to be dearest to the gods. If the gods have any care for human beings—it is thought that they do—it will be reasonable for them to be pleased by the best, by what is most closely related to them. This will be mind. They are likely, therefore, to favor those who esteem and value mind for caring for what is dear to them and for acting rightly and well. It is quite clear that it is the wise man above all who has these characteristics. He is therefore dearest to the gods. It is likely, too, that the man favored by the gods will be the happiest; on this argument, too, the wise man will be the most happy.

9. If we have given an adequate general outline of this topic, of the virtues, and also of friendship and pleasure, should we consider that our proposed investigation is now complete? Or, as is said, since the end in matters of action is not contemplating and knowing each thing, but rather doing it, is it insufficient just to know about virtue? Should we not try to have and use it or, in whatever other way, to become good? If arguments were in themselves sufficient for making people good, they would have earned many high rewards, as Theognis put it, and all that would have been necessary would be merely to supply such arguments. But, as things are, although arguments appear to have the power to encourage and stimulate liberal young people and to render a noble character—one that truly loves good—susceptible to virtue, they are nevertheless unable to turn the mass of the people toward goodness. Their nature is to obey by fear, rather than by right shame; and they do not abstain from the bad because it is wrong, but because of the possible punishment. They live by emotion and pursue those pleasures that are related to emotion, and the means to these pleasures. They avoid the opposite pains, and have no idea of the good or the really pleasant, for they have not tasted them.

What argument would change the character of such people? It is not possible, or at least it is not easy, to change by argument practices long since settled by habit. Perhaps we must be content if we get virtue to some extent even when we have at hand *all* the means whereby we are thought to attain goodness.

Some think that men become good by nature; others, through habit; others, by being taught. As for "nature," it is clearly not within our power, but comes to those who are truly fortunate, as the result of certain divine causes. Argument and teaching, it is to be feared, do not always have the same power. The student's soul must have had good prior training and habituation with a view to taking pleasure rightly and hating rightly, like earth that is to nourish the seed. The man who lives by emotion would not listen to a dissuasive argument, nor would he understand it. How can one change someone like that? In general, emotion does not seem to submit to reason, but to force.

Therefore, there must already be character related in some way to virtue, loving the fine and hating the ugly. It is hard to get the right approach to virtue from youth onwards, unless you are brought up under that kind of law. Living temperately, with restraint, is not pleasant to most people, especially for the young. Therefore, their

training and their pursuits should be matters arranged
by the laws; they will not be painful when they have
become matters of habit. But perhaps it is not enough
to get the right training and care while young. Since we
have to practice these things habitually when grown up,
we shall need laws about adult life, too, and in general
for the whole of human life; for the majority obey necessity rather than reason, and punishment rather than
honor. For this reason, some people think that lawgivers
should urge and exhort to virtue for its own sake, since
those who have had a good moral training will pay attention; but that they should impose penalties and punishments on the disobedient and those with bad disposition,
whereas the incurable should simply be exiled. They
argue that the good man, who lives with a view to what
is noble, will obey reason; but that the wicked man,
whose appetite is for pleasure, is to be punished by pain
like a beast of burden. They say that the pains should
be those most contrary to the pleasures most liked by
such people.

If, as was said, the man who is to be good must first
have had a good upbringing and training and, next, must
live in the same way in good pursuits, acting badly neither willingly nor against his will, this will come about
if people live by a certain rationality and right order—
provided the order is effective. Paternal order has neither the power nor the necessary compulsion, as is true
in general of the orders given by one man, except where
he is king or something of that sort. But the law has
compulsive power, since it is theory derived from a certain wisdom and reason. People hate those human beings who oppose their desires, even if they are right to
do so, but the law does not incur hatred for making right
orders. Only in Sparta (perhaps there are a few other
cases) does the lawgiver seem to have paid attention to
training and pursuits. In most cities, these matters are
quite neglected, and each individual lives as he wishes,
ruling over wife and children like the Cyclops.

Now, the best course is for training to be the subject
of state control of the right kind; but when states neglect
these matters, it seems to be fitting for each individual
himself to contribute toward the virtue of his own children and friends, to have the power to do that or at
least to choose to do so. On the basis of what we have
said, a man would be better able to do that by becoming
a lawgiver. State control, clearly, is produced by means
of laws, and good control by means of worthy laws.
Whether these are written or unwritten makes no difference; nor does it matter whether one or many will be
educated, any more than it matters in music, physical
training, and other pursuits. Just as laws and national
character are powerful influences in states, so customs
and a father's precept and example are powerful in the
home, still more so in fact because of family ties and the
benefits he confers. Those under authority here have a
natural obedience and a natural fondness.

There is another difference between private training
and state training, similar to the situation in medicine.
In general, quiet and fasting are proper treatment for
people with fever; but it may not be so for a particular
individual. The boxer, too, does not impose the same
style of fighting on all his pupils. The particular case
seems to get more precise attention when the treatment
is private, for then the individual is more likely to get
what is suitable. But the best individual treatment can
be given by doctor, trainer, etc., when they know the
general treatment, that is, what is good for all cases or
this sort of case. (The sciences are said to be, and are,
sciences of the general or universal.) However, one may
well be able to give good treatment to an individual
without actually *knowing,* but through having observed
carefully what happens in each case; some people seem
to be their own best doctors, although they would be
unable to cure others. Nevertheless, the man who wants
to be a good craftsman and know the subject must, it
seems, proceed to the universal and know it as far as

possible, since this, as we said, is the object of science. Perhaps, it is also true that the man who wants to make people better by training, whether they be few or many, must try to become a lawgiver—assuming that it is possible for us to be made better by means of laws. It is not just for anyone at all to set a given person right; if anyone can do it, it is the man who knows, just as it is in medicine and in other cases where care and prudence are involved.

Next, then, should we not see whence or by what means one may become a lawgiver? As in other cases, is this not to be learned from the politicians? It has been thought that lawgiving is a part of politics. But can it be that what was true of other sciences and faculties is not true of politics? In the other cases, the same people both teach and practice the activity, as doctors and painters do. Yet, the sophists claim that, although they teach politics, none of them practices it. The politicians do that; and they appear to act by virtue of a certain knack and empirical skill, rather than by reason. They neither write nor speak about the subject (although this might have been a finer task than making speeches in court and in the assembly); nor does it seem that they have made their sons or any other dear ones into politicians. Surely it is reasonable to expect that they would—if they could! They could have left their states no better legacy, nor would they have chosen any other faculty in preference to this one, for themselves or for their dearest ones.

Experience, however, seems to make no little contribution; otherwise, men would not have become politicians simply through acquaintance with politics. Therefore, those who wish to know about politics need experience too. Those sophists who claim to teach the subject seem to be a long way from doing so: they just do not know what politics is or what it is about; otherwise, they would not have identified it with rhetoric or placed it lower, nor would they have thought it easy to make laws, simply by collecting the most famous ones. Their idea was that one

could then choose from among them, as though the choosing itself was not a matter of intelligence, and right judgment the most important thing, as in the case of music. In
each subject, it is those with experience who are the best
judges of composition: they know the means to perfection
and what is in harmony with what. The inexperienced must
be content if they do not fail to judge that the work is
good or bad, as in painting.

In politics, laws resemble such works. How, then, can
someone become a lawgiver through studying laws, or
learn how to pick the best laws? People do not become
doctors through treatises; yet they try to determine not
only what the various treatments are but also how particular people can be cured and how individuals should be
treated, by distinguishing the different states of the body.
To those with experience, this seems useful; but it is
useless to those without. Perhaps, then, collections of
laws and constitutions will be of use to those who can
see the whole subject and judge what is good or bad and
what suits certain people. Those who study such things
without a trained mind will not be able to judge rightly
thereby, except by accident, even though they may become sharper-witted at politics.

Previous writers have neglected the subject of lawgiving. It is better perhaps for us to investigate it, and
the subject of constitutions in general, so that as far as
is possible we may complete our philosophy relating to
man. Let us try first to see if former thinkers have said
anything along the right lines. Then, working from a collection of constitutions, let us see what either preserves
or ruins states, in general, and what sort of thing does
this in relation to each type of constitution; and finally
what are the reasons some states are well managed, and
others badly. When this has been studied, we may be
better able to see what constitution is the best, what the
best arrangement for any given case is, and what laws
and customs each should employ. Let us start, then, and
discuss the matter.

POLITICS

Introduction

The closing sentences of the *Nicomachean Ethics* effect a transition to the *Politics*. Like most Greeks of his own and earlier times, Aristotle could not conceive of a good life for man that did not involve social relations and institutions. "Man is a creature by nature adapted for life in a *polis*, or city-state," he says; so we may paraphrase the famous sentence that is usually quoted as "Man is by nature a political animal." Aristotle is the ultimate authority for the almost proverbial saying, found in the *Essays* of Francis Bacon, that "he that delighteth in solitude is either a wild beast or a god." Aristotle's aspirations after a more-than-human happiness, expressed in Book X of the *Ethics,* do not obscure or contradict his conviction that the specific happiness of man as a *human* being must be aimed at in the life of a community.

Aristotle arrives at this conception by applying his usual philosophical principles. He asks what is the *purpose* of the state and insists, in this as in other fields of investigation, that *nature* is to be understood in terms of purpose. The city is necessary even to the bare survival of mankind because the individual man and the individual family are both too weak and too limited to be self-supporting. But once it has come into being for the sake of *mere* life, the city is preserved for the sake of the *good* life. The city provides an environment in which the individual can achieve the proper *telos* of a man; and this, as we have learned from the *Ethics,* consists in the enjoyment of happiness in the exercise of the intellectual and moral virtues. What is more, the city has its own *telos;* it is complete and finished in itself and does not need to be supplemented by or absorbed in any larger community. There is no further and better term in the series that runs from the individual through the family and the clan to the city-state.

Aristotle followed Plato in thinking that the Greek *polis*, if properly planned and governed, constituted the most natural and therefore the ideal form of human society, perfectly fitted to the nature of the individual man at his best. He neither foresaw nor would have been prepared to tolerate the larger community that was built up by the conquests of his pupil Alexander.

But Aristotle differs from Plato as soon as he comes to consider more specific questions about the nature of the city-state, and much of the interest of this treatise is centered on the reasons that he gives for rejecting some of Plato's main proposals. It is true that he shares Plato's belief in the necessity for specialization and division of function, and he recognizes that the art of government requires native gifts and acquired skills; but he rejects the Platonic conception of moral and political virtue as branches of knowledge, like medicine and navigation.

His most fundamental objection to Plato's ideal republic is based on his conception of happiness as an activity of the *individual* human being. Plato had concentrated on producing a happy *community* and had not given due weight to the overriding claims of individual men. Aristotle thought that the state existed for the sake of the citizen and not the citizen for the sake of the state; accordingly, he rejects the scheme for the communal ownership of wives, children, and property that Plato had prescribed for his guardians. Not only is Aristotle opposed to this proposal for theoretical reasons, he also criticizes it on the very practical grounds that "what is everybody's business is nobody's business" and that men will inevitably show less concern for property, persons, and political and social duties if there are no *personal* ties and *personal* possessions.

This contrast between Plato and Aristotle is seen at its plainest when we consider Plato's revised blueprint for human society in the *Laws,* in which he explicitly maintains that all private concerns must be subordinated to the good of the community as a whole. Aristotle, on the other hand, believed that too much unity was as damaging as too little unity to the well-being of a city, and that *complete* unity would be tantamount to the annihilation of the city. The discussion of happiness in Chapter 5 of Book II is among the best passages of political thought in this or any other work. He is pursuing the same line of thought when he contradicts Plato's view that a community cannot be good unless all its individual members are good.

Like Plato and nearly all other ancient thinkers, Aristotle accepts the institution of slavery almost as a matter of course. His treatment of the topic provides a very good example of the application to politics of his general philosophical doctrine. He maintains that some men are *by nature* fitted only to be slaves, or "living tools," and that they are therefore achieving their own proper *telos* by performing servile duties for other and higher beings. Here he shows the understandable but regrettable prejudice of the Greeks that they were by nature superior to non-Greek, "barbarian" peoples. He is also typically Greek in his reaffirmation, as against Plato, of the superiority of men over women.

On all these points, and on numerous other questions both of principle and of detail, it will be clear that Aristotle is paying very close attention to the institutions of the actual city-states of his own time. Once again we notice the importance to Aristotle of the description of *how things are* as an essential element in any reflection on *how things ought to be*. In the later books, when he makes his own proposals for an ideal community, he is as down-to-earth, as directly concerned with the light that the actual concrete specimens can throw on the abstract consideration of the formal and the ideal, as in his works on biology, ethics, and literature.

Book I

1. We see that every state is a sort of partnership, and that every partnership is formed in order to attain some good. After all, it is universally true that people do act with a view to obtaining what they think good for them. Clearly, then, all partnerships have some good as their objective; and the highest, most authentic good is the objective of the most authentic of all partnerships, the one that includes all others. This is the state: political partnership.

Some thinkers, however, suppose that statesman, king, estate manager, and master of a family have a common character. This is a mistake; they think that the distinction between them is not a difference in kind, but a simple, numerical difference. For example, if a man rules over a few, they call him a master; if more, a manager; and so on with the statesman and king—as though there were no difference between a large estate and a small state. As for the terms statesman and king, they use the latter when a person holds power on his own; and they use statesman when a person follows the principles of the science of statesmanship and takes his turn with others in governing and being governed. However, these views are not true.

Our meaning will become clearer if we follow our usual method. In other cases, too, one must analyze a complex whole into its elements; similarly, if we look at the constituent parts of the state, we shall be clearer about the differences between the different functions mentioned above, and we shall see whether it is possible to arrive at a precise distinction, as in a science.

2. The best way of studying the matter, as in other cases, will be to see how things develop right from the start. First of all, there has to be an association of those persons who cannot exist apart from each other, namely, male and female, in order to reproduce. This is not a matter of choice, but, as with other animals and with plants, it is part of nature to desire to leave something like oneself behind.

There must also be an association between that which naturally rules and that which is ruled, with a view to security. That which is able to plan and to take forethought is by nature ruler and master, whereas that which is able to supply physical labor is by nature ruled, a slave to the above. This is why master and slave have a common interest.

Female and slave are marked off from each other by nature. Nature does not operate like the smiths who made the Delphic knife a multipurpose tool. There is nothing niggardly about her: she assigns a single function to a single thing. An instrument is at the peak of perfection when it serves a single end, not a number of ends. But among barbarians, female and slave occupy the same position. The reason is that a natural ruler is not to be found among barbarians. Association there is a partnership between slaves, female and male. All the more reason, then, for the poet to say: "It is right for Greeks to rule over barbarians," since barbarian and slave are by nature identical.

The first product of these two partnerships is the household. Hesiod was right when he wrote, "First a house and a wife and an ox to plow"; the point being that for poor people an ox is equivalent to a slave. The partnership established by nature for satisfying all daily needs is the household. The members are humorously called "mess-mates" by Charondas, and "trough-fellows" by Epimenides the Cretan.

The first partnership that is (a) the product of several households and (b) not meant just for satisfying daily needs is a village. By nature, the village seems to be par excellence a development of a household: its members are called "fellow-sucklings," "one's children and one's children's children." This is why, to start with, states were run by kings; and it is the reason why "tribes" (as opposed to states) are still ruled by kings. They arose from social forms that were themselves monarchic. Every household has a "king," the eldest member; so too, therefore, does its offshoot or development, because the members are related. This is the point made by Homer about the Cyclopes: "each of them rules over his wives and children." They all live apart from one another; and indeed, in antiquity, this scattered living was prevalent. Besides, everybody says that the gods too are ruled by a king, because some people are still so ruled and others were once; and human beings imagine the gods to live like human beings, just as they imagine the gods to be like men in appearance.

A partnership of several villages is a state; and with that the process is complete. It is a partnership that has already reached the high point of self-sufficiency; it originated so that people could live, but its raison d'être now is that people can live the good life. All states therefore are natural, since the very first partnerships are natural. The state is their end, or the goal they aim at, and nature means end; we use the expression "the nature of a thing" with regard to what it is like when its development is complete, as with "man," "horse," and "house."

Also, the end of an activity, the reason why it is done, is the highest good; and self-sufficiency is the objective of the state and is the highest good.

Clearly, then, the state is natural, and man is by nature

an animal designed for living in states. The person who by nature, not accident, does not belong to a state is either an inferior creature or better than a mere human being. He is like the man criticized by Homer: "without a clan, without law, and without a home." Such a person has also a passion for war; he is on his own, like an isolated piece in a game.

It is now clear why the term "animal designed for living in states" applies to man more than to bees or to any other animal living in herds. Nature, we are always saying, does nothing without a purpose. Now, man is the only animal with the power of speech. The mere voicing of sounds is an indication of pleasure and pain, which is why it is found among animals other than man; the point being that their nature has reached the point where they perceive what is pleasant or painful and can indicate this to one another. But speech is for pointing out what is useful or hurtful; it points out also what is just or unjust. This is peculiar to man, as compared with the other animals—the fact that he is the only animal to have a sense of good and evil, just and unjust, and so on. It is a common partnership in such ideas that brings about a household, and eventually a state.

The state is, clearly, by nature prior to the household or to the individual human being; for the whole must be prior to the part. If the whole body is destroyed, there will not be, for example, a foot or a hand, except in the ambiguous sense in which one speaks of the hand of a statue as "the stone hand"; if that hand is destroyed, it will still be stone. But things are characterized by their function and capacity: when they no longer have their particular character, they cannot be described unequivocally as the same thing. Clearly, then, the state is a natural thing, prior to the individual: an individual is not self-sufficient when separated; and, therefore, the relation between him and the whole (the state) will be that of part to whole. The man who is unable to join in partnerships or does not need to because he is himself sufficient is not part of a state; he is either a beast or a god.

There is therefore a natural and universal impulse toward such partnerships. The man who first formed one was responsible for great benefactions. Man, when he is at the goal of his development, is the best of all animals; but he is the worst of all when he is detached from customs and justice. Injustice, given weapons, is the most oppressive thing there is; and man is given weapons at birth, which are meant to serve prudence and goodness but can easily be turned to the opposite ends. Man without goodness is the most wicked and savage of animals, the most subject to lust and gluttony. Justice, however, is part of the state, since it settles what is just; and political partnership is regulated by legal justice.

3. Now that we have a clear idea about the parts of the state, we must first discuss management of estates, or households, since every state consists of households. The parts of this subject are the same as the parts of the household: a complete household consists of slaves and free persons.

Now, any subject must be studied by taking first the simplest elements. In the case of the household, the prime elements are the following: master and slave, husband and wife, father and children. Our task is therefore to examine each one of these three groups and to see what they mean and what they ought to be. These subjects are: the art of being a master; the art of marriage (we have to say that, since there is no special term for this aspect of the association of husband and wife); and the art of rearing children (here, too, there is no special term for the relation between parents and children).

There are the above-mentioned three relationships; there is also a part that some people think is identical with household management, whereas others think it to be an important branch of it. We must study the matter and see what the position is. The subject I refer to is what is called the art of acquiring possessions.

Let us first, however, take master and slave, in order to see what is required for the basic needs of life. We want also to see if one can get a better idea about the subject than the opinions now current. Some people think that the art of being master is a sort of science: they think that management, mastership, statesmanship, and kingship are identical, as we said at the start. Others think that it is contrary to nature for there to be masters ruling over slaves; they argue that slave and free are determined purely by convention, whereas by nature there is no difference between the two. This is why the relationship is not just, since it is imposed by constraint, or force.

4. Property is part of the household, and the art of acquiring property is part of household management. (After all, without the basic essentials, it is impossible to exist, let alone live the good life.) Now, if we look at the arts, we see that each of them must have its proper tools or instruments in order to complete its function; so too with the manager. Instruments are either inanimate or animate; for the pilot of a ship, the rudder is an inanimate instrument, whereas the lookout man is an animate instrument, the point being that an assistant (such as the lookout man) is to be classed as an instrument in the case of the arts. Similarly, an article of property is an instrument for living; property is a number of such instruments; and the slave is an animate article of property. Every assistant is, as it were, an (animate) instrument prior to (inanimate) instruments. If every instrument could do its job either by anticipating the need or simply on receiving the word "go," if shuttles worked and plectra played the strings on their own—as the statues of Daedalus and the tripods of Hephaestus* are said to have operated—master craftsmen would not need assistants and masters could do without slaves.

An instrument, as the term is usually employed, means something that helps to make or produce something else;

---

*Homer said they came to the meeting of the gods by starting themselves.

an article of property, however, is for action. Take the shuttle. Quite apart from the use of the thing, something else is produced by working it. But in the case of clothes and beds, for example, the use of the thing is the sole result.

Production and action are different in kind; since both require instruments, these too must exhibit the same difference. Life is action, not production; and so the slave is an assistant in matters that have to do with action.

The term "article of property" is used in the same way as "part." Part, for instance, is not only a part of something else; it belongs entirely to that thing. The same applies to "article of property." That is why a master is merely master of the slave, but does not belong to the slave; the slave, however, is not only the master's slave, but belongs entirely to the master.

This shows us clearly what a slave is and what he can do. A human being who by nature belongs to another, not himself, is by nature a slave. One person belongs to another if, though a person, he is an article of property (he is *owned*), for an article of property is an instrument for action that can be separated from the owner.

5. We must now see whether there is such a person as a slave by nature, and whether it is good and just for some people to be slaves or not—whether all slavery is contrary to nature. It is not hard to get the answer either by reasoning philosophically or by working from the facts.

Ruling and being ruled are not only necessary, they are also expedient. From birth onwards, the difference is noticeable; some tend to be ruled, others to rule. There are many kinds of rulers and subjects. (It is always the case that the better the subject, the higher the rule: rule over men is higher than rule over beasts. The function achieved by higher things is itself higher in the scale; and there is such a function when there is a combination of ruler and subject.)

To resume: in cases in which we are dealing with composites, made up of several parts that form a single common whole—whether the parts are continuous or separate—a ruler and a subject can always be found. This is by nature an essential characteristic of animate things; even in things that are inanimate there is a sort of ruling principle, as with harmony in music.

This is, however, more suitable for a less rigorous kind of study. The prime elements of living things are soul and body, of which the former is by nature the ruler, the latter the subject. We should study what is true by nature, taking things that are in a state of nature, and not corrupted; we should examine the person who is in the best state of both soul and body. In him, the truth of our view is made clear. In the case of bad men, or of those who are in a bad state, it will often strike one that the body is ruler over the soul, simply because such people are in a bad state, a state contrary to nature.

At any rate, animate creatures are the first cases where we can see the authority of a master and the rule of a statesman. Soul rules over body like a master; and mind rules over appetite like a statesman or king. This makes it clear that it is natural and expedient for the body to be ruled by the soul, and for the emotional part to be ruled by the mind and by the part that has reason. When both are equal, or the natural relation is reversed, all these functions are impaired.

What is true of man is also true of other living creatures. Domesticated animals are superior in nature to untamed animals; it is better for all the former to be ruled by man, since in this way they obtain security.

Also, as regards male and female, the former is superior, the latter inferior; the male is ruler, the female is subject. It must also be that the same is true for the whole of mankind. Where there is a difference between people, like that between soul and body, or between man and mere animal (this being the condition of people whose function is to use their bodies, manual labor being the best service they can give, for such people are by nature slaves), it is better for the lower ones to be ruled, just as it is for the subjects mentioned above. A man is a slave by nature if he *can* belong to someone else (this is why he does in fact belong to someone else) or if he has reason to the extent of understanding it without actually possessing it. Animals other than man do not obey reason, but follow their instincts. There is only a slight difference between the services rendered by slaves and by animals: both give assistance with their bodies for the attainment of the essentials of living.

Nature tries to make a difference between slave and free, even as to their bodies—making the former strong, with a view to their doing the basic jobs, and making the free people upright, useless for servile jobs but suitable for political life, which is divided into the tasks of war and of peace. The opposite, however, often turns out to be the case: it happens that some have the physique of free men, whereas others have the souls. It is quite obvious that if people showed their differences in their mere physique, as the statues of the gods show the difference between gods and men, everyone would say that the inferior ones ought to be slaves of the others.

If this is true of the body, it is even more just for the distinction to apply to the soul. But it is not so easy to see the beauty of the soul as the beauty of the body. It is clear, then, that people are by nature free men or slaves, and that it is expedient and just for those who are slaves to be ruled.

6. It is not hard to see that people who say the opposite have some right on their side. "Being a slave" and "slave" are both ambiguous. There are also those who are slaves only by convention. Convention here means a kind of agreement by virtue of which what is captured in war is held to belong to the victors. This is said to be a just principle; but many lawyers challenge its legality on the grounds that it is abhorrent for something to be the slave and subject of what can exert superior force

and is merely superior in power. There is disagreement about this, even among experts.

There is a reason for the tangled dispute between the two theories. There is a sense in which virtue, when provided with the external means, is supremely able to use force; and it is always the case that superiority occurs by virtue of having more of some good or other. This leads to the idea that force must somehow be connected with goodness, so that the disagreement on this question is only about the matter of justice. That is why some think that justice is benevolence, whereas others think that the rule of the stronger is itself the principle of justice. But if these views are taken separately from one another, neither has any validity or persuasive force as against the view that it is superiority in virtue that entitles one to rule and mastery.

There are some who hold fast to a kind of justice, as they think—after all, convention or law is a kind of justice—when they count enslavement, as the product of war, as just. At the same time, however, they assert that it may not be just: for it is possible for the start of the war not to be just, and no one would say that the man who did not deserve to be a slave is truly a slave. Otherwise, the consequence will be that people whom we think to be really wellborn will turn out to be slaves and the children of slaves if they happen to be captured and sold.

That is why they do not mean to assert that such people are slaves, but that barbarians are. Yet, in saying that, all they are looking for is the "natural slave," as we said at the start. It is undeniable that there are people who are slaves wherever they are, and others who are never and nowhere slaves. The same applies to noble birth: our nobles regard themselves as wellborn, not only in their own country but anywhere in the world; barbarians, however, are wellborn only in their own country. They thus assume that there is a sense in which noble and free are absolute, and another in which they are not. As Helen puts it, in the play by Theodectes: "Who would dare call me a servant, when I have gods on both sides of my family tree?"

When they talk in this way, they are simply using the ideas of virtue and vice to distinguish between slave and free, wellborn and lowborn. Their assumption is that good parents produce good offspring in the same way that human beings produce human beings and animals produce animals; but although nature tries to achieve this, it is frequently unable to succeed.

There is some reason for the dispute. It is not always true that people who are slaves or free are such by nature. In cases where such a distinction does exist, it is expedient and right for one group to be slaves and the other to be masters, for one set to be ruled and the other to exercise the rule proper to it, which means to act as a master. But ruling in the wrong way is bad for both sides: part and whole, just like body and soul, have a common interest; and a slave is part of his master, an animate, even though separate, part of his body. That is why master and slave have a community of interest and friendship—provided they are what they are by nature; if they are not, but are in this position by convention, because of force, the opposite is true.

7. It is clear from this that mastership and statesmanship are not identical; nor are all forms of power the same, as some thinkers suppose. Statesmanship means ruling over people who are by nature free, whereas being a master means ruling over people who are by nature slaves. Management is monarchic, since every household is controlled by one person; whereas statesmanship is ruling over those who are free and equal.

A man is given the title of "master," not because he has a certain branch of knowledge, but simply because he is of a certain disposition. The same is true of the words "slave" and "free." But there could be a science of being a master and a science of being a slave. An example of the latter would be the subject taught by the man at Syracuse, who, for a fee, used to teach slaves their routine jobs. The study of these subjects could be extended to take in cookery and other kinds of service. There are different kinds of jobs, some being more respectable and others more basic; as the saying goes: "slave before slave, and master before master."

All such subjects are "sciences" fit for slaves. The science of being master is concerned with the use of slaves. A man is not master by virtue of acquiring slaves, but by using them. There is nothing great or important about this science. The master must know how to order what the slave has to know how to do. This is why people who can afford it avoid the trouble: they have a sort of steward who takes over this job, and they, the masters, go in for politics or philosophy. The art of acquiring slaves is different from both the science of being a master and the "science" of being a slave. If it is just, it is part of war or hunting. This is enough on the subject of master and slave.

■   ■   ■

Book II

1. Our chosen subject is the study of political partnership, and we want to know the best form of government for people who can actually live as they would wish. But we must also study other kinds of constitutions: (a) those actually enjoyed by states that are said to be well governed, and (b) those *theoretical* constitutions that are thought to be good. Our object is to discover what is correct and useful in them, and to show that our search for a quite different one is not just a desire to be clever; it will become plain that our study is necessary because none of the constitutions available is satisfactory.

We must start with the beginning natural to this subject (i.e., the system of property). There are three possible cases: (1) all citizens share everything in common; (2) they share nothing in common; (3) they share some things in common, but not others.

The second case is clearly impossible. After all, the state is a kind of partnership and, to start with, the citizens must have locality in common. There is a single locality to a single state, and the citizens are all partners in this one state.

In the well-run state, is it better that: (1) everything should be held in common that can possibly be so held? Or is it preferable (3) for some things to be so shared and others not? It is possible for the citizens to have

441

their children, wives, and property in common, as is the case in Plato's *Republic*. In that work Socrates declares that children, wives, and property should all be shared by all. Is it better to follow current usage in these matters, or should we work in accordance with the rule stated in the *Republic?*

2. There are various difficulties in the way of complete community of wives. To begin with, Socrates gives a reason why this practice should be instituted; but this reason does not itself follow from his arguments. Secondly, the scheme as described does not help toward the end that he declares the state must aim at; and, finally, there is no account of how one ought to develop it. By "the end," I mean the idea that the best thing is for the whole state to be as much of a *unit* as possible. This is the principle on which Socrates bases his argument.

However, it is clear that as the state advances and grows in unity, it ceases to be a state at all. The state is naturally plural; if it grows in unity, it becomes a household instead of a state, and then an individual instead of a household. We would say that a household is more of a unit than a state, and similarly an individual more of a unit than a household. Therefore, even if one could achieve this, one ought not to do so, since the state would then be destroyed.

Not only does the state consist of a number of human beings; it also consists of a number of different kinds of individuals. The state is not an association of like people, since there is a difference between the state and an alliance of states. The latter is of value through sheer quantity, even if the member states are identical in kind, since the natural purpose of an alliance is for resisting aggression; and it is as if there were more weight in the scale.

There is the same difference between state and tribe that there is between state and alliance of states. A tribe can have more weight if its members are not isolated in separate villages but organized like the Arcadians. But if there is to be a unity, the elements composing it must be different in kind. This is why the principle of reciprocal equality is the lifeblood of the state. This practice must be in force among those who are free and equal, since it is impossible for all citizens to hold office at the same time: they have to hold it annually or for some other period of time.

The result of this method is that all hold office. It is as though shoemakers and builders exchanged jobs and were not always either shoemakers or builders. The principle of "one man, one job," however, is just as valuable in political partnership, so that clearly, where it is possible, it is better for the same people to hold office all the time; but where this is not possible because all the citizens are equal in nature, it is only right for all to hold office (whether the governing is a good or a bad thing). A society of equals, in which office is held in rotation and all the members are equal outside of their period of office, is an approximation of the idea of all taking part in the government. The point is that some hold office while others take their turn at being ruled, as though they had changed their identity. Similarly, there is a difference of status among the actual holders of office, depending on the kind of office they hold.

This all goes to show that it is not a matter of "nature" for the state to be a unity in the sense maintained by some writers, and that what has been called the greatest good for a state is really its ruin and destruction. Yet the good of a thing is what keeps it in being.

There is another line of thought from which it is evident that it is not good to attempt to make the city too much of a unity. A household is more self-sufficient than an individual, and a state more self-sufficient than a household. Indeed, a state comes into being only when an association of many different kinds of people turns out to be self-sufficient. The greater the self-sufficiency, the more desirable the institution; therefore, a lesser degree of unity is more desirable than a higher.

*   *   *

3. Even if it is best for the partnership to have as much unity as possible, this does not seem to be proved by the slogan "If all men say 'mine' and 'not mine' at the same time," which Socrates takes as indicative that a state is a complete unity. The point is that "all" is ambiguous. If it means "each separately," it may well be that Socrates' scheme will be realized. Each one will speak of the same person as his son and the same woman as his wife, and similarly with property and everything else. But it is not in this sense that people who have wives and children in common will speak. They will all say "mine," but not, as each of them separately. Similarly, in the case of property they will all say "mine," but not as each separately.

It is clear that there is a fallacy in using the term "all"; "all," "both," "odd," and "even" are terms that lead to eristic arguments even in philosophical discussions. Therefore, for "all to say mine" is in one sense splendid but impossible; in another sense it is not even productive of harmony.

Also the idea has another drawback: attention to things is in inverse proportion to the number of people responsible. People take most trouble over their own affairs, less over public matters; or they take trouble, but only insofar as it touches them individually. Apart from other reasons, they pay less attention on the grounds that someone else is doing it; there is an analogy with servants, for a large number often gives worse service than a lesser number. Each citizen has a thousand sons; these are not sons of a citizen as an individual, but any of them is equally the son of any citizen, with the result that the neglect will be equal too.

Again, each of them says "mine" of someone who is succeeding or doing badly, but only in a fractional sense: he says "mine" or "so-and-so's" only in the sense of a thousandth, or whatever number the state consists of; and even here he is doubtful, since it cannot be known who has had a son born, and not only born but reared.

Is it better to use "mine" in that way, with each one of
two or ten thousand calling the same thing mine; or is
the usage now current in states preferable? As things
are now, the same person is called "my son" by one,
"my brother" by another. Another says "nephew" (or
whatever the relationship is, whether by blood or by
marriage); he uses the term because the person is a direct relation or a connection. Also others will say of him
"my clansman" or "my tribesman." It is better for a
person to be someone's real cousin rather than a son in
the sense discussed.

Indeed, it would be impossible to avoid the case of
some people recognizing that certain others are in fact
their brothers, children, fathers, and mothers. People
could not help forming beliefs about one another on the
basis of the likenesses between children and parents.
Some of the writers on world geography say that this
actually happens. It is said that some of the Upper Liby-
ans have their wives in common, but that their children
are shared out by resemblance to parents. There are
some females, both in the human species and in others,
with a strong natural tendency to produce offspring like
the parents. This was the case with the mare at Pharsalus
called Fair Return.

4. It is not easy for people setting up a partnership of
this sort to avoid troubles like assault, unintentional and
intentional homicide, fighting, and insulting language.
These are offenses against piety when committed against
father, mother, and those not far removed from close
blood relationship; they are different when committed
against those who are more remote. When the citizens
do not know their relations, there must be more such
cases than when they do. If they occur, it is possible to
make the usual expiations if people know who is who,
but if not, they do not.

It is absurd to make the sons common to all citizens
and prevent lovers from having intercourse, without pro-

hibiting love as such or other familiarities that are quite shameful, as between father and son or two brothers; since love even without intercourse is shameful in those cases. It is absurd to prevent intercourse for no reason other than that the pleasure is excessive and to think that it makes no difference that here we have a father and son, there two brothers.

It seems that having wives and children in common is more useful for the farmers than for the guardians. If their wives and children are held in common, there will be less friendship among them; and it is good for subjects to be in that condition, with a view to their being obedient and not making revolutions. In general, a law of this kind is certain to create a condition opposite to that which properly made laws should produce and opposite to what Socrates intends when he makes such legislation about children and wives. For we think that friendship is the greatest good in a state; and the unity of a state (which Socrates praises highly) is thought by most people, and is asserted by Socrates, to be the achievement of friendship, just as we know that in Plato's *Symposium*, Aristophanes says that lovers want to unite and to become one instead of two because of their excessive affection. In this case both, or at least one, must be destroyed; and in the state the friendship would necessarily become watery as the result of such a partnership. There would hardly be a case of a son saying "my father" or of a father saying "my son." If a little sugar is mixed into a vast quantity of water, the mixture has no taste of sugar; the same will happen to family feeling based on these names when, in a state like Plato's, there is hardly any need for people to care for each other, as a father for his sons, a son for a father, or a brother for a brother. There are two feelings that make people care for and love one another; these are the feeling of owning something yourself and the feeling of affection for things. Neither of these can exist for people in Plato's *Republic*.

As for transferring children from the class of farmers and craftsmen to the guardians, and vice versa, it is quite confusing to see how that can be arranged. Those who give the children and those who transfer them must know whom they are moving and where they are being placed.

Also, the difficulties mentioned earlier must arise even more often with such people: I mean assault, homosexual love, and homicide. Those who are transferred to other classes will no longer speak of the guardians as brothers, children, fathers, and mothers; and, again, those who are in the guardian class will no longer speak of other citizens in that way, so as to avoid committing such mistakes because of their being related.

These remarks may stand as our conclusion on the question of sharing wives and children.

5. Property is a connected subject. We must consider how property is to be organized by those who are going to live in the best state. Should it be in common or not? This question may be regarded as a separate issue, apart from the legislation having to do with children and wives. The question is: even if there are separate families, as is now universally the case, would it be better for property and the management of property to be common? Or should there be a compromise system? For example, should the farms be owned separately and the produce contributed to a common pool? (This is the practice of some barbarian tribes.) Should the land be owned and farmed in common, but the produce divided for private use? It is said that some barbarians have this kind of partnership. Or should farms and produce both be common?

Now, if the laboring class consists of noncitizens, there may well be another system with fewer difficulties; but when citizens are working their own property, there may be considerable difficulties raised by ownership in common. If there is inequality both in the rewards and in the work done, there are certain to be complaints by those who get less but work more against those who do little but receive a large reward. In general, association and partnership in affairs is one of the most difficult things, especially when these concern property. This is exemplified in the partnership of people traveling together: most of them come into conflict with one another as the result of trivial and ordinary incidents. Secondly, we tend to fall out most readily with those servants that we employ most frequently in everyday service.

These and similar difficulties occur when property is held in common. The present way of holding property, if improved by good customs and a good legal system, would be much better. It will have the advantages of both schemes, namely, the advantage of property being both common and private. Property *should* be common in a sense; but generally it ought to be private. If management is divided among individuals, there will not be mutual complaints; and the properties will be improved because each individual runs his own private section. As regards use and enjoyment, virtue will guarantee the fulfillment of the proverb "friends' goods are common goods." Even now such a scheme exists in outline in some communities, so that it is clearly not impossible. In states that are well run, some parts of the scheme are already working, and other parts could easily be put into operation. An individual owns property privately, but makes his property available to his friends and uses theirs as common property. This happens in Sparta, where people use one another's slaves as though they were their own; and similarly their horses and dogs. They take food, if they need it on a journey, from the farms in the country. Clearly, the best course is for property to be privately owned but open to common use and enjoyment. It is for the legislator to see that people are trained to be capable of this.

Thinking that you own something yourself makes an enormous difference in the pleasure that it provides. The love that each of us feels for himself is not just pointless, but rooted in nature. Self-love is rightly criticized, but that is not the same as love for oneself; it means loving oneself more than one should, in the same sense that we use it disparagingly of the "money lover," for feeling love for such things is found among all men.

It is a very great pleasure to do favors and to help friends, visitors, or associates. This can be done when property is privately owned, but not when people make the state too unified. Besides, that plainly ruins the activities of two virtues: one is self-control in relation to women, for it is morally good to keep away from someone else's wife because one is self-controlled; the other is generosity in matters of property. In these other systems, one will not be able to prove one's generosity or to do any generous action at all: the practice of generosity consists in the use made of money.

Such legislation as Plato's looks attractive and benevolent. He who hears of it welcomes the news with pleasure, thinking that everyone will have a wonderful feeling of universal brotherhood, especially when it is argued that the evils now existing in states are due to the absence of property held in common. (By "evils," I mean lawsuits about contracts, trials for perjury, and the parasitic flattery of the rich.) But in fact these are not caused by the absence of a system of common property but are due to the evil in man; we see many more disagreements among partners and property owners in common than among private owners, although we notice also that the number of those who quarrel because of partnership is relatively small compared with the large number of private owners. Also, it is fair to mention not only the evils of which men would be rid by a common system but also the advantages that they will lose. Life in such conditions seems to be quite impossible.

We should consider that the reason for Socrates' mistake is that his starting point is incorrect. There is a sense in which both the household and the state ought to be a unity; but neither should be an entire unity. In one way, by increasing in unity, the state will cease to be a state; in another way, as it gets near to not being a state, it will be an inferior state, just as if one turned a harmony into unison or a rhythm into a single foot. The right thing is for the state to be a plurality, as we said before, unified and integrated by education. It is absurd for a man who is about to introduce education, and who thinks that the city will thereby be made good, to suppose that he can set things right by such measures as those described, instead of by social customs, culture, and laws; consider Sparta and Crete, where the legislator introduced the idea of common property by means of public messes. We must also bear in mind that we should pay close attention to the question of time, and to the number of years during the course of which it would surely have been noticed if these proposals were sound. Almost everything has already been discovered; but some ideas have not been connected, whereas others, though known, are not used. We would have a really clear picture if we could see Plato's state actually in operation. It would not be possible to found such a state without making divisions and parts—that is, messes, clans, and tribes. The only result of the legislation will be the exemption of the guardians from farm work, which is something that the Spartans are attempting to achieve, even as their regime now stands.

Socrates has not defined—nor is it easy to work out—the manner in which the whole state will work. The fact is that the mass of the other citizens will form the bulk of the state, although their position has not been defined. Will the farmers, too, have property in common, or own it individually? Will they have their own wives and children, or have them in common? If they have everything completely in common in the same way, how will they be different from the guardians? What advantage will there be for them in submitting to the guardians' rule? What is to make them submit, unless the guardians make use of a device like that of the Cretans, who allow their slaves everything, with two exceptions: they forbid them athletic exercises and they forbid them the right to acquire arms.

But if the farmers are to have the same institutions as are found in other states, what kind of partnership will there be between the two groups? There are bound to be two communities in the one state, opposed to each other. For Socrates makes the guardians a sort of police force, whereas the farmers, craftsmen, and the rest are citizens; and these people, like the citizens in other states, will have quarrels, lawsuits, and all the other ills that states are said to be heir to.

Socrates says, however, that with their education they will not need many police and market regulations, etc., although this education is in fact for the guardians exclusively. Also, he makes the farmers masters of the land on condition that they pay rent; and they are likely to be far more recalcitrant and spirited than the classes of helots, serfs, and slaves actually found in some states.

However, there is no clear guidance on whether the farmers are to have the same system or not. Nor is there anything on the related topics, what their political role will be, their education and laws. It is not easy to work out—and it is an important question—what character these must have with a view to preserving the common system of the guardians. If he makes the farmers have their wives in common but their property separately, who will manage the house in the way that the menfolk look after the farms? It is absurd of him to use animals as an analogy to show that women should have the same pursuits as men. Animals have no households to manage.

There is a source of danger in the manner in which Socrates appoints rulers. He makes the same people hold office all the time, and since this is responsible for internal disturbances even among people of no distinction, it will be so far more among men who are spirited and warlike. Yet it is clear that he is forced to make the same people hold office: the divine gold* in the soul does not shift from group to group, but is found permanently in the same people. He says that, at the moment of birth, "some received an admixture of gold, and others of silver, whereas bronze and iron were allotted to those who would become craftsmen and farmers."

Also, he deprives the guardians of happiness, but says that the legislator must make the state happy as a whole. It is impossible for the state to be happy as a whole unless most people or all the constituent parts are happy. "Happiness" is not the same kind of term as "even." "Even" can apply to a whole without its being true of any part; but this is impossible with "happiness." If the guardians are not happy, who is? Surely not the craftsmen and the general mass of ordinary workers.

There are these difficulties, and others as great, in the way of Socrates' *Republic*.

* * *

*Republic, vii, 415.

Book III

1. In a study of constitutions, which deals with such questions as what each constitution is and what kind of constitution it is, the first question to decide is what is meant by "state." At present, this is disputed: some thinkers argue that one should say "the state did the act," whereas others deny that it is the state and say "the oligarchy did it," or "the tyrant did it." Secondly, we can see that the statesman and lawgiver spend all their energy on the state, the constitution being a way of organizing the inhabitants of the state.

The state is a composite thing, like anything else that is a whole but composed of many parts. Clearly, then, there is a prior question, "What do we mean by citizen?" since the state consists of a number of citizens. We should therefore consider what person should rightly be called citizen; what do we mean by the term? This question has to be put, since even "citizen" is a matter of much dispute. Not all thinkers give the same definition: the sort of man who is a citizen in a democracy would often not be a citizen in an oligarchy.

We should leave to one side those who get the name citizen in a sense other than the strict one—e.g., those who are citizens by naturalization. The citizen as such is not a citizen simply by virtue of inhabiting a certain place; in that sense foreigners and slaves share with citizens a common place of residence. Nor should the name be given to those who share in legal rights, having the right to bring cases in the courts and to stand trial, for this right is found among those who share in citizenship by virtue of a commercial treaty. (Indeed, there are many places where resident aliens do not even have these rights completely, but have to have a patron to look after them; they share in the rights only partially.) We have to speak of these as we do of children, who are not yet on the citizen register, or of old men, who are excused the obligations of citizenship. They are citizens in a sense, but not in the strict sense. We say that, in one case that they are minors, in the other that they are "retired" or some such expression; we do not have to be exact, since the meaning is plain.

We want to define citizen in the strict sense of the word, meaning the person who does not suffer any impediment that needs to be corrected before he can receive the name. (Similar problems can be raised and solved with regard to disfranchised citizens or exiles.) Strictly speaking, the defining mark of a citizen is whether a man has a share in the administration of justice and in holding political office. Some offices are limited in time—i.e., some cannot be held more than once by the same man, whereas others can, but not without an interval. However, other offices have no time limit; take, for example, the posts of juror and member of the assembly. It might be argued that such people are not in fact officeholders, that they do not thereby share in the holding of office. But it is ridiculous to deprive those who have ultimate authority of the title of officeholders. It need not make any difference, as the disagreement is about only a name: juror and assembly member do have something in common, but it is not a common name. Just to complete the idea, let us call it "office without time limit." We count as citizens people who share in holding office in this sense.

This is the definition that will best suit all those who are called citizens. We must remember, however, that we are dealing with things (such as types of constitutions) that differ in kind, and about which we can speak of "first," "second," and so on; in such cases there is either nothing common to the things as such or hardly anything common. We see that constitutions actually differ in kind from one another, and that some are "later," some "prior." Constitutions that are wrong, and those that have gone wrong, must be later than those that are not wrong. (What we mean by "gone wrong" will appear later.) Therefore, there must be a different citizen corresponding to each different constitution.

The term "citizen," as we defined it above, applies above all to a democracy. In other forms of state it is possible, although not necessary, for the same kind of person to be a citizen. There are states, for example, in which the people do not meet; they have a senate, not an assembly; and judging law cases is confined to certain sections. In Sparta, the ephors deal with cases relating to commerce; one of them deals with one branch, another with another. The senate of elders decides cases of murder; and no doubt other cases come under other offices. The same kind of thing happens at Carthage, where some officers deal with *all* judicial cases.

However, our definition of a citizen can be corrected to cover these exceptions. In these cases, the functions of legislating and judging are not left to citizens with no definite office; they are exercised by officials appointed for the purpose, to some or all of whom the consideration of some or all questions is reserved.

It is clear from the above what is meant by the term "citizen": he is a person who has the right to participate in deliberative or judicial office. We call such a person a citizen of his state; and by the state we mean, broadly speaking, the number of such citizens that is adequate for a self-sufficient existence.

2. For practical purposes, people define a citizen as "the child of parents both of whom—not just one only—are themselves citizens." Some people extend this requirement beyond the parents to two, three, or more generations back. With this rough, general definition there arises a difficulty; the question is, how did the ancestor three generations back become a citizen? Gorgias of Leontini had a remark about this, which was partly serious and partly a joke. He used to say that there was a similarity between mortars—vessels made by mortar makers—and citizens of Larissa, who were made by the magistrates of that place. The point was that some of the magistrates were "larisopoioi"—mortar makers.

The question is quite simple. If people share in the functions of citizenship in the sense we have indicated, they are citizens. (It is obviously impossible to make sense of the "ancestry requirement" when it is applied to first inhabitants or to founders.)

Perhaps there is a more serious difficulty about people who come to be citizens as the result of a revolution. One example is the enfranchising carried out by Cleisthenes at Athens after the expulsion of the tyrants: he enrolled many foreigners and resident slaves on the tribal lists. But the question in this case is not one of fact—"Is he a citizen?"—but rather, "Is he a citizen *rightly or wrongly?*" However, you can go then on to the difficulty, "Is a man not a citizen at all, if he is not a citizen *rightly?*" on the grounds that "wrongly" is the same as "not really."

We do know of instances in which people hold office unjustly. Of them we shall say that they are officeholders, but that their title is not justly held. Since we defined "citizen" with respect to office (we said that a person having a share in a particular sort of office was a citizen), it is clear that we must count such people as citizens, too.

3. As for the question of whether they are citizens justly or unjustly, this is connected with the problem raised earlier. Some people ask the question "When is an act done by the state, and when is it not?" This situation would occur with a change to a democratic constitution from an oligarchy or a tyranny. In such a case, some people are unwilling to settle trade debts on the grounds that they were incurred not by the state but by, for example, the tyrant. They make similar repudiations throughout, on the grounds that some constitutions are imposed by force and with no reference to the common interest.

Well, if a democratic constitution is imposed by force, we shall have to say that the acts of this regime are no more acts of the whole than were the "acts of the oligarchy" and "the acts of the tyranny" in the examples above. The problem seems to be linked with yet another, namely, the question of when we should speak of a state as retaining its identity and when of its having lost it and changed.

The most obvious way of dealing with this is to refer it to the place inhabited and the inhabitants. It is possible for the place to be divided in two, and hence too the inhabitants, so that some will live in one quarter and some in another. This way of putting the difficulty is easier to treat. If we note that "state" has more than one meaning, it will be quite simple to solve the problem.

Similarly, in a case where all the inhabitants reside in the same place, the question is, "Under what conditions does their state have a single identity?" Identity does not depend on having fortified walls; after all, it would be possible to throw one wall right around the whole Peloponnesus. It may be that Babylon is like that; and so too is any city with outer dimensions more appropriate to a "tribe" than to a state. Indeed, the story is that when Babylon was captured, part of the city still did not know it three days after it had happened.

However, there will be another opportunity to examine this problem. The statesman ought to keep his eyes open to questions of size of state, and whether there should be one or more than one separate people.

Let us take the case where we have a single, identical people continuing to inhabit the same territory. Should we say that the state is identical as long as the race of inhabitants stays the same? Admittedly, it is always the case that some members are dying and others are being born. However, should we speak of states being the same as we speak of rivers and springs being the same, even though water is constantly flowing on as well as being lost? Or should we say that the human beings are the same but that the state is different? The state is a kind of partnership, a partnership of citizens in a form of government. It seems that if the constitution changes in kind and becomes different, the state, necessarily, can no longer be identical. We speak of the chorus being different when it appears first in a comedy and next in a tragedy, even though the members of the chorus may be the same in both cases. The same applies to all other partnerships and compounds. If there is a change in the kind of compound, the compound itself changes identity. Even though the notes are the same we speak of a different harmony, depending whether it is the Dorian or the Phrygian mode.

If that is the case, we can decide the identity of a state only by examining the form of its constitution. As regards the question of race, we can do as we like: we can speak of the state remaining identical or changing, whether the inhabitants remain the same or change entirely. And as for the question whether it is right to settle debts or not after a change of government, that is another matter too.

■   ■   ■

4. Our next question to consider is whether the virtue of "a good man" is the same as that of "a good citizen" or not. If we are to look into this, we must first work out a general idea of what we mean by the virtue or goodness of a good citizen.

There is an analogy between the citizen and the sailor: the latter is one of a number of associates, each of whom has a different function; there are rowers, helmsmen, lookout men, and people with other special names. The most precise definition of each will correspond to his particular ability; but it is still true that there will be a common definition covering them all: the function of all of them is to achieve the safe conduct of the expedition, this being the objective of all the sailors.

The same sort of thing applies to citizens, who also differ in their abilities: their common task is to make their association last, association here meaning their community or states. That is why the goodness of a citizen is relative to the state in which he lives. Since there are several kinds of states, it is clear that there cannot be a single, complete goodness proper to the good citizen; but when we speak of a good man, we mean that he is characterized by a single virtue, which is complete.

Clearly, then, it is possible for someone to be a good citizen without having that virtue that would entitle him to be called a good man. There is another way of covering the same ground—namely, by raising the question of the best form of the state. If it is not possible for a state to be composed of citizens all of whom are good men, it must be true at any rate that each citizen performs his function well; and that can be due only to goodness. Since it is impossible for all the citizens to be absolutely alike, the goodness of the citizen will not be identical with that of the good man. All the citizens must have the goodness proper to the good citizen: only if this is so will it follow that the state is as good as possible; but it is impossible for them all to have the goodness of the good man, unless it is required that all the citizens in a good state should be good men.

Further, the state consists of people who are not alike. Just as an animal (taking this case first) consists of soul and body as elements—and soul consists of reason and appetite, household of husband and wife, property of master and slave—so too a state consists of all these, and of other classes, which are not alike. Necessarily,

therefore, the citizens do not all have a single virtue—
as in a chorus, where the ability of the leader is different
from that of a subordinate.

It is clear from the above that in the strict sense the
two virtues are not generally identical. But will there be
a particular case in which the goodness of a good citizen
will be identical with that of a good man? We say that
a serious ruler is good and wise, and that it is essential
for any who would seek to be a statesman to be wise.
Besides, some people say that a ruler has to have a different education; indeed, we can see for ourselves that
kings' sons are taught riding and studies connected with
the art of war. Euripides says: "Not for me that clever
stuff . . . but what the state needs," meaning that there
is a type of education proper to a ruler.

But even if the goodness of a good ruler is identical
with that of a good man, it must be pointed out that a
subject, too, is a citizen. In the strict sense, there is no
general identity of goodness in the case of the good citizen and the good man; but there is in the case of a
particular citizen. There is a difference between the
goodness of a ruler and that of a mere citizen. Perhaps
that is why Jason said that he was hungry when he was
not a tyrant, meaning that he did not know how to be
a private citizen.

We praise the ability to rule and to be ruled. The
goodness of a reputable citizen is thought to consist of
the right use of ruling and of being ruled. If we maintain
that the goodness of the good man is exhibited in ruling,
and that the goodness of a good citizen is exhibited in
both ruling and being ruled, then they cannot both be
equally praiseworthy. It is sometimes held that: (1) the
ruler should not learn the same things as the subject;
but (2) the citizen should know both and have a share
in both.

We can now see the next stage in the argument. There
is a type of rule exercised by masters: I mean the rule
concerned with essential duties. It is not necessary for

the ruler to know how to carry these out; he must, however, know how to make use of others in carrying them
out. The other thing—knowing how to carry out menial
jobs—is actually servile. There are several kinds of
slaves, corresponding to their several kinds of jobs. One
class consists of manual workers: these are people, as
the name indicates, who live by their hands; and among
their number is the laborer. That is why there have been
states in which the laborers were not allowed to hold
office—not, at least, until the most extreme form of democracy was established. The tasks of those who are
subjects in this sense should not be learned by the good
man or the statesman or the good citizen, except at times
for his own personal need. Otherwise, it is no longer the
case that one is master and the other slave.

But, besides the above, there is another type of rule.
It is that by virtue of which a man rules over people
who are similar by birth and are free men. This is what
we mean by "political" rule: the ruler has to learn it by
being ruled, just as one learns how to lead cavalry by
serving in the cavalry or to become a general by serving
under one; and similarly in the case of a company commander or a platoon commander. That is why there is a
lot in the saying that you cannot learn how to rule properly without having been ruled. There are different virtues in each case, but the good citizen must know how,
and be able, to rule and be ruled. This is the virtue of
a good citizen, knowing about rule over free men from
both sides. The point is that the good man is characterized by both, even though the temperance and justice of
a ruler are different in kind from the temperance and
justice of a subject. Clearly, the virtue of a good man
will not be one and indivisible; the virtue of a subject
differs from that of a ruler. Take justice, for example:
there will be different kinds, the justice appropriate to
a ruler and the justice appropriate to the ruled. Compare
the virtues of temperance and courage as shown by men
and by women. A man would be thought cowardly if he

were courageous in the way appropriate to a woman; and a woman would be considered a chatterbox if she showed restraint in the manner appropriate to the good man. Similarly, the virtue of management is one thing in the case of a husband, another in the case of a wife: it is the husband's duty to acquire goods, the wife's to keep them.

Practical wisdom is the only virtue peculiar to a ruler; it seems that all other virtues must be common to both rulers and ruled. Wisdom, however, is not a subject's virtue, but right opinion is. The person ruled corresponds to the instrument maker, whereas the ruler corresponds to the player making use of the instrument.

It is clear from the above whether the virtue of a good man is identical with or different from that of a good citizen, and in what sense it is identical or different.

∎ ∎ ∎

POETICS

Introduction

Even if Aristotle's little book on poetry were no longer of any intrinsic interest, it would still deserve the prominent place that it holds in literary studies for the immense influence that it has had on the theory and practice of literature in earlier ages. Theorists and practitioners as various as Ben Jonson, Racine, Shelley, Sir Philip Sidney, and Dr. Johnson have been affected by it, or have reacted against it.

But, in fact, the *Poetics* remains an absorbing and illuminating work in its own right, and here as in other fields, Aristotle's true achievement is in danger of being obscured by the adulation that has been given to what he said, or what he was mistakenly thought to have said, in a few particular passages. The barbarous tyranny of the unities of time, place, and action is only one example, but perhaps the worst, of the perils of ossifying into an unalterable law the fresh, agile, and open-minded discussion that is to be found in this little treatise.

The greatest literary works known in Aristotle's time were the Homeric epic and Attic tragedy and comedy, and it is inevitable that his reflections on literature and the arts should center on them. The scope of the surviving portions of the book is even more limited than this would suggest because parts of the work are lost and what remains is almost exclusively devoted to tragedy. But Greek epic, tragedy, and comedy were all of the highest class, as we can see even from the relatively scanty collections that have survived; and there was quite enough stimulus for the mind of Aristotle to enable him to make a permanent contribution to the philosophy of literature.

The *Poetics* has naturally attracted more attention from those whose primary concern is with literature than from students of Aristotle's philosophical thought. A large selection of passages from the book is included here because the work can be fully understood only in the context of his general philosophical system and because that system is itself illuminated by being seen in its application to a special department of philosophical inquiry that does not always receive from philosophers the attention that it deserves.

As we would expect, if we remember the nature of his general philosophy, Aristotle gives a central place in his discussion to the question of the *end,* or *purpose,* of tragedy, which he sees as the purgation or cleansing of the emotions of pity and fear. The word *catharsis,* like its English equivalent, "purgation," is a medical term; according to the most likely interpretation, Aristotle thought of tragedy as a means of removing excess amounts of these emotions rather than of removing them altogether. In fact, this conception can be seen to be related to his account in the *Ethics* of the need for avoiding both excess and defect in the degree of human passions and emotions.

We are also reminded of the *Ethics* by the central place that Aristotle gives to the plot, or *action,* of a tragedy. Character is important for him, but the plot is the very *soul* of a tragedy, since for Aristotle it is in its own proper *activity* that every creature is fulfilled; and the artist can imitate or represent men most effectively and completely only if he portrays them as engaged in characteristically human activities. In the same passage, he extends the parallel between soul and plot by speaking of the plot as the end, or *telos*, of a tragedy, to which character is the *means*.

When Aristotle prescribes that a tragedy must have a beginning, a middle, and an end, he is again being faithful to one of the principles of his general philosophy. A tragedy, like every other product of art or nature, has its own unity as an individual thing, although it does of course also exhibit features that make it characteristic of its kind. The action of a play must be complete (*teleios*), just as the life of the good and happy man in the *Ethics* must be complete.

As in the ethical, political, and biological writings, so also in his discussion of literature Aristotle pays careful attention to actual concrete instances. He constantly bears in mind the actual examples of tragedy that were known to him, and uses them as the basis of his judgment on what tragedy *ought* to be like, on what is most typically and essentially tragic.

The famous remark that poetry is more philosophical than history is to be understood in the same light. The historian or chronicler is compelled by his material and his purpose to set down what actually happened, even if the actual order of events exhibits no unity or pattern. The poet or dramatist can leave out what is marginal or irrelevant and can thus reveal what is central and important; he can compose an artistic unity out of the story he has to tell. The historian deals with particular actual events and characters; the poet fashions his own events and characters, not indeed in such a way as to make them lifeless, stylized *types,* but so that they can throw light on other individuals and hence increase our knowledge and understanding. It is in this sense that literature is concerned with the universal.

Aristotle's theory of knowledge also contributes to his reflections on what kinds of characters and events go to make up an effective tragedy. Knowledge is of "what is always or for the most part so," that is, of what is either necessary or probable. The aim of the dramatist can therefore best be achieved by constructing a plot in which there is an intelligible sequence of events, one in which the spectators can see *why* the later events naturally would or inevitably must follow from the earlier. A mere catalog of disconnected episodes is not a play. Aristotle himself shows the connection between his view of tragedy and his general metaphysical views when he remarks, in Book XIII of the *Metaphysics,* that the world must be understood as a unity, not portrayed as "episodic," as in a bad tragedy.

The remark about poetry and history is itself sufficient to show that Aristotle is not one of those philosophers who demean literature and the imagination in order to glorify the analytical intellect as the only faculty by which knowledge can be pursued. In the same spirit, he remarks that metaphor, the perception and revelation of hidden similarities and differences between things, is an essential task of the poet. The capacity for coining good metaphors cannot be learned or taught; when it is found in a high degree, it amounts to poetic genius.

Here and throughout the *Poetics*, we see Aristotle's own genius for marking similarities without forgetting differences, for making distinctions without obscuring connections. The art of poetry is neither left to one side as something wholly different from other human skills and activities nor browbeaten to conform to standards drawn from other fields. Like everything that Aristotle examines, it is set in such a light that we can see both its connections with other things and its own individual characteristics.

1. Let us discuss the art of poetry and its species. We shall consider the capacity of each species, and the arrangement of plot necessary for the production to be correct. We shall also deal with the number and kind of parts in a poem and other questions connected with the same subject. Let us make the natural beginning and take first things first.

Epic poetry, tragedy, comedy, dithyrambic poetry, and most flute playing and lyre playing are all forms of imitation, generally speaking. They differ from one another in three ways: the media in which they imitate are different in kind; the objects they imitate are different; and they do it in different ways. Here is an analogy: some people imitate many things by making likenesses in colors and shapes (in some cases by deliberate art, in others by mere experience); others do so by means of voice. Similarly, in the case of the arts just mentioned, all of them achieve their imitating by means of rhythm, speech, and melody, either separately or mixed. For example, the arts of flute playing and lyre playing and other such arts (e.g., playing the pipe) make use of melody and rhythm. The arts of dancing imitate by rhythm alone, apart from melody: dancers, by means of rhythm embodied in figures, imitate character, emotion, and action.

467

But the art that uses words only—either in prose or verse, and whether the verse is in one meter or in a mixture of several—has not so far received a name. We cannot give a common name to the mimes of Sophron and Xenarchus and to the Socratic dialogues; nor can we in cases where people do their imitating in iambic trimeters, elegiacs, and so on, except that people add the term "poet" to the meter and speak of "elegiac poets" and "epic poets." They do not call them poets in respect to their imitation, but speak of them in common by virtue of the meter used. This custom holds, even when the writer produces a medical treatise or a book on natural science in verse. But Homer and Empedocles have nothing in common except their meter; that is why it is right to call one a poet and to refer to the latter as a natural scientist rather than as a poet. Similarly, if he imitates by combining all the meters, a writer should be called a poet: that is what Chaeremon did with his *Centaur*, a rhapsody that was a medley of all the meters. These distinctions will serve on this subject.

But there are some arts that use all the means described; these are dithyrambic poetry, the composing of "nomes," tragedy, and comedy. The difference is that some use all at once, whereas others employ them in turn. That is what I mean by the differences between arts, as regards the media of imitation.

.   .   .

4. Generally speaking, it seems that there are two causes that account for the origins of poetry, both of them natural. Imitating is natural to human beings from childhood onwards: man differs from other animals in being extremely imitative; his first steps in learning are made through imitation, and all people get pleasure from imitations. An indication of this is what happens with works of art: there are things that give us great pain when seen in the flesh, yet we enjoy looking at pictures of them that are exact likenesses—things such as the most repellent animals and corpses.

Another reason is that not only do philosophers get great pleasure from learning, but other people do so too, even though they do not have an interest in it to the same extent. This is why people enjoy looking at pictures: one consequence of their looking is that they learn and realize what each thing is, e.g., "this is so-and-so." If a person has not previously seen the original, his pleasure will not be caused by the imitation, but will be because of the execution or the color or some such reason.

Imitating, melody, and rhythm are natural to us (clearly verse meters are part of rhythm). People had a natural bent for them to start with, advanced them by slow degrees, and produced the art of poetry as a result of their improvising. Poetry then became subdivided, according to the character proper to each kind of poet: serious people imitated fine actions and the actions of good men, whereas more ordinary people imitated the actions of inferior men. First, these latter wrote invectives, just as others wrote hymns and songs of praise. Now, we cannot name any such poem (i.e., invective) before Homer, but we meet it starting with Homer. There is, for example, his *Margites,* as well as other such poems. In these works, in accordance with what was appropriate, the iambic meter developed. This is why it is still called "iambic"—because they used the meter to "iambize," or lampoon, one another. Some of the early writers were heroic poets; others were iambic poets.

Homer was the poet par excellence on the serious side, for he was the only one to write well and to make dramatic imitations; so, too, he was the first to outline the forms of comedy, by making a story not out of invective but out of the laughable. The *Margites* stands in the same relation to modern comedies as the *Iliad* and *Odyssey* do to tragedies.

Once tragedy and comedy had appeared, people pur-

sued each according to their own true character: one
group became comic poets instead of iambic poets, and
the other became writers of tragedy instead of epic, the
former kind in each case being more important and
more valuable than the latter. As for deciding whether
even tragedy is adequate in all its forms or not, both in
itself and with regard to the audience, that is another
question.

5. As we said above, comedy is an imitation of inferior
things and people. They are not absolutely bad, however;
the point is that the laughable is part of the ugly. It is
a sort of mistake, an ugliness that does not give pain
or cause destruction. For example, the comic mask is
something ugly and distorted, but causes no pain.

Now, the main stages in the development of tragedy
are known to us, as are the persons responsible for each;
but comedy has gone unnoticed because it was not taken
seriously at first. It was relatively late when the Archon
appointed a state chorus for comic writers; previously
they had supplied it on their own initiative. Comedy had
already acquired its present features by the time of those
writers that we know about. We do not know who decided on masks, prologues, the number of actors, and so
forth. The making of plots came originally from Sicily;
at Athens, Crates was the first to abandon the form of
the personal invective and to make plots and stories with
a general reference.

Epic agrees with tragedy insofar as it is an imitation
of serious events in meter; the difference is that it has
one meter only and uses the narrative form. There is
also a difference in length: tragedy endeavors as far as
possible to fall within one day or not much outside that;
epic, however, has no limit as regards time. Clearly, that
is a difference too, although at first the practice was the
same in tragedy as in epic.

As for their parts, some are the same and others are
peculiar to tragedy. Therefore, the person who knows

what is good or bad tragedy also knows about epic. All the elements of epic occur in tragedy, but not all the elements of tragedy are to be found in epic.

6. We shall discuss later the art of imitation in hexameters and in comedy. Let us now discuss tragedy, taking up the definition of what it is from what we have said. Tragedy is an imitation of a serious and complete action of some magnitude. It uses language adorned with different kinds of ornament, separately in its various parts. It deals with people performing the action, and not with reported action. By means of pity and fear, it contrives to purify the emotions of pity and fear.

By "adorned language" I mean language that has rhythm, melody, and song. By "separately" I mean that some effects are achieved by verse only, others by song.

Since this imitation is achieved by people doing things, it is true that one part of tragedy is necessarily the spectacle; melody and speech are other parts, since these are media of imitation. By "speech" I mean the composition of verses, and "melody" has its full and obvious meaning.

And since it is an imitation of action, and is performed by people doing actions, these people must have a certain quality, in respect to character and mind alike. That is how actions come to have a quality, for there are by nature two sources of action, character and mind; and it is by virtue of these that people succeed or fail.

Plot is the imitation of the action. By "plot" I mean the composition of events; by "character," that by virtue of which we say that people have a certain quality or stamp; by "mind," what is present when people try to prove something or to deliver a judgment.

Every tragedy, then, must have six parts on which its quality depends: plot, character, speech, mind, spectacle, and melody. Two of these are media; one is the manner; and three are the objects imitated—and with that, the list is complete. Quite a few writers employ these elements, since every tragedy has spectacle, character, plot, speech, melody, and mind.

The most important of them all is the combination of events: tragedy is an imitation, not of human beings but of action, life, happiness, and unhappiness. Both the latter are exhibited in action; and the point and purpose of the story is a particular kind of action, not a quality. It is by virtue of character that men have a certain quality; but it is action that gives them the name happy or the opposite. People do not act in order to imitate character, but character is included for the sake of the action. The events and the plot are the end of tragedy, and the end is the most important thing of all.

Also, tragedy would not be possible without action, but it is possible without character. Most tragedies of the modern school do not have "character study"; generally speaking, there are many such writers. Their position is like that of Zeuxis, among painters, as compared with Polygnotus: Polygnotus depicts character well, but Zeuxis' work does not study character in that way.

Again, in the case of juxtaposed speeches exhibiting character, even assuming that they are masterpieces of speech and ideas, the proper function of tragedy will not be achieved. It will be achieved far more by a tragedy that is worse off in these respects but has plot and an arrangement of events.

Also, the principal means whereby tragedy makes its effects are the parts of the plot: reversals of fortune and recognition scenes. Another point in our favor is that aspiring writers of tragedy achieve competence in the spheres of speech and character before they are able to put together events. This was true of almost all the early poets.

Plot, then, is the starting point, the soul as it were, of tragedy; and character comes next. A similar situation exists in painting: a confused mess of the most attractive colors will not give as much pleasure as a likeness in black and white. Tragedy is an imitation of actions and, because of that, an imitation of people performing acts. The third element is mind. This is the ability to say what is contained in the situation and is proper to it; in the case of the speeches of tragedy, this is the function of the arts of politics and rhetoric. Early writers gave us people speaking like true politicians, whereas the moderns give us people speaking like teachers of rhetoric.

Character discloses choice: it shows the kind of choice in cases in which it is not obvious what a man is choosing or avoiding. That is why there is no character in speeches in which the speaker has nothing to choose or to avoid. Mind is exhibited where people argue that something is or is not the case, or make some general affirmation. The fourth of the elements of tragedy is speech: I mean, as I said before, the communication of the story by means of language, which has the same role to play in verse and in prose.

Of the other parts, melody is the greatest attraction. The spectacle may be attractive, but it is remote from the art as such, having least to do with poetry. The power of tragedy is quite independent of performances and actors; what is more, the art of stage design has more to do with the good quality of the spectacle than does the art of poetry.

7. With these distinctions complete, let us next discuss the right kind of arrangement of events, since this is the first and most important part of tragedy. Our position is that tragedy is an imitation of a serious and complete action of some magnitude. (It is possible to have something complete or whole without magnitude.)

Now, a whole is that which has a beginning, a middle, and an end. A beginning is that which does not necessarily follow something else, but after which something else naturally is or follows. An end is the opposite; it naturally follows something else, either necessarily or for the most part, and has nothing after it. A middle both follows something else and has something else follow-

ing it. Well-composed plots, therefore, should not start
or end just anywhere, but should exhibit the features
mentioned.

Also, a fine picture or any fine thing that is composed
of parts should have these parts regulated and should
also have an appropriate magnitude. What is fine appears in magnitude and order—which is why there cannot be a fine picture of infinitesimal size, since the
observation of it approaches the imperceptible and becomes confused. Nor can there be a fine picture of enormous size, since one cannot see it all at once; unity and
wholeness vanish out of sight for the spectator, as might
well happen if there were a picture a thousand miles
high. Composite things and pictures therefore must have
a magnitude such that they can be easily perceived; similarly, plots should have a length such that they can be
easily remembered. The length of plot relative to performances and spectators watching is not properly part of
the art of tragedy. If it were necessary to put on a hundred plays, people would have worked by the clock, as
is once said to have happened. The limit determined by
the nature of the thing is this: the greater it is, compatible with comprehensibility, the more suitable is its size.
To give a rough idea, a sufficient limit of size is that in
which, by a succession of events, there is a probable or
necessary change from bad fortune to good, or vice
versa.

8. A plot is not a unity, as some think, as the result of
being concerned with one man. Many undefined things
happen to an individual, some of which add up to no
unity at all; similarly, one individual can commit many
actions, which do not make a single unified action. This
is why all those poets seem to have gone wrong who
have written a "Heracleid," a "Theseid," or some such
work. They think that simply because Heracles was one
individual, their plot must have unity.

Homer, however, outstanding in other respects, seems

to have realized this clearly as well, either by art or natural talent. When he wrote the *Odyssey,* he did not include everything that happened to Odysseus, such as his being beaten on Parnassus or pretending to be mad when the army was gathering; neither of these was a probable or necessary consequence of the other. He worked his plot around one action, which we call the *Odyssey;* and the same is true of the *Iliad.*

The plot, too, should be one, just as in other arts of imitation there is a unified imitation of one thing. Since it is an imitation of action, it should be about one whole action; the parts should be combined in such a way as to make a difference to and disturb the whole if one part is moved from its position or taken away altogether. Anything the presence or absence of which goes unnoticed is no real part of the whole.

9. It is clear from the above that it is not the poet's function to describe what actually happened. He has to describe what can happen, that is, what is possible because it is either likely or necessary. The historian and the poet do not differ by virtue of one's using prose and the other verse. You could versify Herodotus, but even in verse it would still be a history, just as it is without verse. The difference is that one describes what happened, the other describes what can happen.

That is why poetry is more philosophical and serious than history. Poetry describes the universal, whereas history deals with particulars. There is universality when we have to deal with likely or necessary sayings and deeds of a man of a certain stamp. It is this that the art of poetry aims at, even though it adds proper names. But what Alcibiades did, or had done to him, is particular.

In the case of comedy, this is immediately obvious. Writers make up the plot out of a series of likely events and then apply names at random. They do not write, like the iambic poets, about particular individuals. But in tragedy, writers still adhere to genuine names. The reason is that the possible is credible; and although we do not believe that what has not actually happened is possible yet, quite clearly, that which has happened is possible. It would not have happened had it been impossible.

However, there are some tragedies with one or two established names, while the rest are invented; and in some there are no known names, as in Agathon's *Anthos*. In this work, both the situations and the names alike are invented, but it still gives as much pleasure. The conclusion is that one does not have to adhere at all costs to the traditional plots with which tragedies deal. It is absurd to try for that, since even the well-known themes are known to a few only; but they nevertheless give pleasure to everyone.

It is clear from the above that the poet must be a maker of plots rather than of verses; he is a poet by virtue of imitation, and what he imitates is action. Even if he happens to take actual events as his theme, that does not make him any the less a poet. With some things that actually took place, there is nothing to prevent their having the kind of possibility or probability by virtue of which he is their poet.

Of simple plots and actions, the worst are the episodic ones. By "episodic" I mean a plot in which the succession of incidents is neither likely nor necessary. Such works are composed by bad writers because they cannot help it and by good writers so as to please the actors. Writing for a competition, they extend the plot beyond its capacity and are forced to distort the proper sequence. Tragedy is not only an imitation of a complete action, however; it is an imitation of things that arouse fear and pity, and the maximum effect is obtained when these things happen *contrary to* expectation and yet *because of* one another. In that way, they will contain the element of surprise more than if events happen at random or by chance. Even with chance events, the most remarkable are thought to be those that seem to have happened from a deliberate purpose. An example is the statue of Mitys at Argos, which killed the man responsible for Mitys' death by falling on him at a ceremony. Such things do not look like happenings at random; consequently, plots of this type must be superior.

* * *

13. After what we have just said, the next thing to be discussed is what one ought to aim at and what one ought to avoid in the construction of one's plots, and how the function of tragedy can best be fulfilled. Since the structure of the finest tragedy must be not simple but complex, and since it must imitate things that arouse fear and pity (for that is the special quality of this kind of imitation), it is clear, firstly, that good men should not be shown moving from good to ill fortune, since this does not arouse pity or fear but only appalls us. Nor, secondly, should bad men be shown changing from ill fortune to good fortune; there is nothing more untragic than this—it has none of the necessary characteristics; and it does not make us have any feeling for our fellow men, nor does it arouse any pity or fear in us. Nor, again, should the thoroughly unprincipled man be shown moving from good to ill fortune; a structure of this kind would, indeed, make us feel for our fellow men, but it would not arouse pity or fear. For we feel pity for someone who has ill fortune without deserving it, and fear when the person is like ourselves; and therefore what happens in this case will arouse neither our pity nor our fear.

The only possibility left, then, is for tragedy to be about the man who is in an intermediate position. Such a man is not outstanding for virtue or justice, and he arrives at ill fortune not because of any wickedness or vice, but because of some mistake that he makes. He will also be a man of high reputation who has been enjoying good fortune, like Oedipus or Thyestes or the famous members of some family of this kind.

The well-constructed plot, then, must involve one process rather than the two that some say that it should have; and it should involve a transition not from ill fortune to good fortune, but from good to ill fortune; and this transition should not be due to the man's badness, but to some great mistake, made either by the kind of man that we have specified or by one who is better rather than worse than he is. There is evidence of this in what actually happens. At first, poets used to recount any plot; but at the present time the finest tragedies that are composed concern only a small number of families: they concern such people as Alcmeon, Oedipus, Orestes, Meleager, Thyestes, Telephus, or anyone else who has had terrible things done to him or has done terrible things. The tragedy, then, that is artistically the finest is that which has this kind of structure. Hence, those who reproach Euripides for doing this and for letting many of his tragedies end with the ill fortune of the hero are making a mistake, since, as we have said, this is the right thing to do. There is powerful evidence to support this: on the stage and in competitions, tragedies of this kind appear the most tragic if they are successful; and Euripides, even if he does not manage very well in other respects, is certainly the most tragic of the poets.

The second best kind of composition is the one that some people regard as the best: it is the kind that has a double structure in the way in which the *Odyssey* does, ending up in opposite ways for the good and the bad people portrayed in it. The reason why this kind of structure seems to be best is the inferiority of the audiences; for poets follow their audiences and do what they want them to do. But the pleasure that is gained here is not the pleasure derived from tragedy; it is, rather, the one proper to comedy: the people who are most hostile to each other in the plot, like Orestes and Aegisthus, go off as friends at the end, and nobody is killed by anybody.

14. Fear and pity can be aroused by purely visual effects, or they can be aroused by the actual structure of the plot; the reaction is more fundamental in the second case, and he will be the better poet who brings it about. For quite independently of what one may see, the plot should be so composed that anyone who hears the events related shudders and feels pity at what is happening; this certainly happens to anyone who hears the story of Oedipus. But to bring this effect about visually demands less of art and more of showmanship. And those who produce a visual effect that is not a source of fear, but simply monstrous, are doing something that has no relation to tragedy. One should not seek every kind of pleasure from tragedy, but only the kind that is appropriate; and since the poet must produce, by means of imitation, the pleasure that comes from pity and fear, he must plainly put this quality into his plot.

Now, let us see what kinds of events seem terrible to people, and what kinds seem pitiable. The actions involved must concern either friends or enemies, or those who are neither. If the action is that of an enemy toward an enemy, there is nothing pitiable either in the man doing it or in his intending to do it, except insofar as the thing that happens is itself pitiable; nor is there anything pitiable where the people concerned are neither friends nor enemies. The kind of actions that the poet should seek are those that involve people between whom there are ties of affection, as when a brother kills or means to kill or to do some other such thing to his brother, or a son does this to his father, or a mother to her son, or a son to his mother.

It is not possible for the poet to do away with the traditional stories such as those of Clytemnestra being killed by Orestes, or Eriphyle by Alcmeon: but he should show invention and make good use of the traditional material. We must, however, explain more clearly what we mean by good use. It is possible for the action to come about in the way that the ancients used to make it do so, with the characters conscious and aware of the situation that they are in, as Euripides' Medea was when she killed her children; or it is possible to make the characters act in ignorance of the terrible things that they are doing, and then later to recognize the ties of affection that are involved, as happens with Sophocles' *Oedipus.* Admittedly, in this case the action is outside the play; but it can be in the tragedy itself, as it is with Astydamas' *Alcmeon,* or with Telegonus in the *Wounded Odysseus.* There is also a third possibility: that a character who is intending, through ignorance, to do something fatal recognizes how fatal it is before he does it. There is no possibility apart from these; the characters must either act or not act, and they must do so either wittingly or unwittingly.

Of these, the weakest situation is the one in which a character intends an action in a state of complete awareness, and then does not do it; for the outrageousness is all there, but it is not tragic, since there is nothing done; and so nobody makes his characters act in that way, except rarely, as with Haemon and Creon in the *Antigone.* Second to this in weakness is the situation in which the character does act, and acts wittingly. Better than that is the one in which the character acts in ignorance, and then, when he has acted, recognizes the facts; for there is nothing outrageous involved, and the recognition does have a shattering effect. But the best situation is the last: I mean the one like that in the *Cresphontes,* in which Merope, intending to kill her son, still does not do so, since she recognizes him instead; or like that in the *Iphigenia,* in which the sister does the same with her brother; or like that in the *Helle,* in which the son, intending to give his mother up to her enemy, recognizes her. (This is the reason why, as we said a while back, tragedies are not concerned with a great number of families. In their earlier searches, it was not according to the rules of art, but quite by chance, that poets used to find that they could incorporate such a situation in their plots; hence, they are still compelled to turn to those families that have had such things happening to them.)

So much, then, for the structure of the events and the kind of plots that one ought to have.

15. As far as the characters are concerned, there are four things to aim at. The first and most important is that the characters should be good. A person will have a given kind of character if, as has been said, his words or his actions reveal a given kind of choice; and he will have a good character if they reveal a good choice. But goodness exists in every class of person: a woman can be good, and so can a slave, although the one is inferior and the other altogether worthless. A second thing to aim at is suitability of character; there is such a thing as a brave and manly character, but it is not suitable for a female character to be brave or clever. The third thing is for the character to be plausible. (This is different from its being good or suitable in the way that we have described.) The fourth thing is for it to be consistent; even if the person being imitated is inconsistent and therefore suggests a character of that same kind, there must nonetheless be consistency in his inconsistency. An example of unnecessary badness of character is Menelaus in the *Orestes;* an example of what is unfitting and unsuitable is the lament of Odysseus in the *Scylla* and also the speech of Melanippe; and an example of inconsistency is the *Iphigenia in Aulis,* for Iphigenia is quite different when she is a suppliant from what she is like later on. Further, in the characters as in the structure of the plot, the poet should always look either for what is necessary or for what is likely, so that it is either necessary or likely for a particular kind of person to say or do particular kinds of things and for one thing to happen after another.

Plainly, the unraveling of the plot should spring from the plot itself, and not from the *deus ex machina,* as in the *Medea,* or in the way in which the events concerning the sailing away in the *Iliad* do. The *deus ex machina* should be used to deal with events that lie outside the drama—either things that have happened beforehand, but of which humans cannot know; or things that are to happen and need to be announced; for we do credit the gods with seeing everything.

There should be nothing unreasonable in the events of the play; or, if there is something unreasonable, it should be outside the tragedy itself, as it is in the *Oedipus* of Sophocles.

Since tragedy is an imitation of men who are better than ordinary, we ought to imitate the good portrait painters: although they reproduce the figure of a particular person, they nonetheless make it, as they paint it, more beautiful than it really is. In the same way, when the poet is imitating irascible or lazy people, or people with any traits of that sort in their character, he should make them decent people, as Agathon and Homer have made Achilles.

■   ■   ■

21. Metaphor is transference of an alien term: transference from genus to species, from species to genus, from species to species, or by analogy. I mean by "from genus to species," for example, "This is my ship *standing* here"; lying at anchor is a kind of standing. "From species to genus" is exemplified in "Odysseus did a *thousand* splendid deeds"; for thousand, which is used here instead of many, is a species of many. "From species to species" is exemplified in "*drawing off* his life with the bronze" and "*cutting* with the tireless bronze"; drawing off means cutting, and cutting means drawing off, both being species of "taking away."

Analogy means that the second term stands to the first in the same relation as the fourth to the third. (And sometimes people add that to which the term supplanted is relative.) For example, a cup is to Dionysus what a shield is to Ares; one can speak therefore of the cup as "the shield of Dionysus," and of the shield as "the cup of Ares." Again, old age is to life as evening is to day: one can speak therefore of evening as "the old age of day" or as Empedocles put it; and one can speak of old age as "the evening, or sunset, of life." There are cases where some of the terms have no name, but metaphor by analogy can still be used. For example, to scatter seed is to sow, but there is no name for what the sun does with its fire. However, this action is to the sun what sowing is to seed, and so we have the expression "sowing the god-created flames."

There is also another way of using metaphor. One can call the thing by an alien name and then deny it an attribute peculiar to the name. This would be the case if you spoke of the shield not as "the cup of Ares" but as "the wineless cup."

* * *

23. Let us now turn to the kind of imitative art that is narrative and uses meter. Here, as with tragedies, one should construct plots that are dramatic and that involve a single action with a beginning, a middle, and an end, so that it may produce the appropriate pleasure just as if it were a single and complete picture. It is clear, too, that the composition here should not be like that of histories, in which one has to give a clear account, not of a single action, but of a single period of time and of all the things that happened in it to one or more people—things whose relation to each other may be entirely fortuitous. For just as the sea fight at Salamis and the battle against the Carthaginians in Sicily occurred at the same time without contributing at all to the same result, so too in successive periods one thing sometimes happens after another without any single result emerging from them. And yet, most poets do this. Hence, as we have remarked above, Homer seems in this respect to be a genius as compared with other poets: he did not try to write an account of even the whole of the war, even though it had a beginning and an end, for that would have been too big, and not at all easy to view as a whole; and even if there had been some moderation in its length, it would have been too complex in its variety. In fact, he cut off one part of the war and then used a number of episodes, like the catalogue of the ships, and with that and other episodes divided up the poem. But the others write about a single man or a single period of time or a single action with many parts. . . .

24. Further, epic poetry must have the same varieties as tragedy: it must be either simple or complex, and it must turn either on character or on a calamity; and, apart from the songs and the spectacle, it must have the same parts as tragedy—there must be reversals of fortune, recognitions, and calamities; and then both the thoughts and the diction must be good. Homer was the first to make use of all these qualities, and he did so quite adequately. For, of his poems, the *Iliad* was composed as a simple poem turning on a calamity, while the *Odyssey* was a complex one (for there are recognitions throughout the work) turning on character; furthermore, they have surpassed all poems in diction and thought.

Epic poetry differs from tragedy in the size of its structure and in its meter. What we have said is enough to determine the limits of size: one must be able to gain a single view of the beginning and the end. This would come about if the structures were more modest than the ancient ones were and if they approached the length of tragedies composed for a single hearing. But epic poetry has a special feature that tends toward its being greatly extended in size: in tragedy, it is not possible to portray a number of different parts of the story going on at the same time—one can portray only that part that is being enacted on the stage and that concerns the actors; but in epic poetry, because it is a narrative, it is possible to write about many parts of the story that are going on at the same time—by these parts, which are entirely germane to the whole, the bulk of the poem is increased. Thus epic has this advantage for the attainment of grandeur, that the hearer can switch from one thing to another, and thus the poem can be filled with the most diverse episodes. For what makes tragedies fall out of favor is a general uniformity, which quickly sates one's appetite. . . .

Homer deserves to be commended on many grounds, but mainly because he alone among the poets knew what his own role should be. The poet himself ought to say very little; for it is not by virtue of what he says himself that he is an imitator. The other poets play a part themselves throughout their works and imitate only a little and rarely; but after a short introduction, Homer at once introduces a man or a woman or some character; and these are not characterless either; they all really do have characters.

Amazing events should certainly be put into tragedies; but it is more possible in epic to put in what is highly improbable (which is the chief source of amazement), since one does not see the character in action. The incidents surrounding the pursuit of Hector would be manifestly absurd on the stage: the Achaeans standing still and not joining in the pursuit, and Achilles signaling to them to stay back; but in epic this is not noticed. The amazing gives pleasure, too; there is evidence of this in the way that anyone who is telling a story adds to it, thinking that he is giving pleasure thereby.

Homer, more than anyone else, has taught other poets how to say what is false in the right way. This is by use of false reasoning. People think that if "x" always follows "y;" then "y," will always follow "x." But this is false. Hence, if "x" is false but "y" is true when "x" is true, the poet should add on the statement that "y" is true. Then our minds, knowing that "y" is true, will falsely infer that "x" is true as well. There is an example of this in Homer's "Bath Scene."

The poet ought, too, to choose what is impossible but

plausible in preference to what is possible but implausible. Plots should not be made up of parts that are highly improbable; preferably, they should contain nothing of that kind. But if they must, it should be outside the action of the story. It should, in fact, be like Oedipus' ignorance of how Laius died, which is outside the action of the play; or the report of the Pythian games, in the *Electra;* or the man who came from Tegea to Mysia without uttering a sound, in the *Mysians.* Thus, it is absurd to say that without such parts the plot would have been ruined; the plots should not be constructed in this form in the first place; and it is also absurd for someone to construct a plot in this form when it is evident that it could have been done more plausibly. For the improbabilities in the *Odyssey* about the landing would have been manifestly intolerable if they had been written by an indifferent poet; but in fact the poet with his charm manages to conceal beneath the other merits of his work what is absurd.

One should elaborate one's diction only in the slack parts of the poem, not in those parts that portray character or present thoughts; for characters and thoughts are concealed by a too brilliant style.

25. With regard to criticisms and the answers to them, we shall be clear about how many of them there are and what varieties there are if we look at the matter in this way. Since the poet is an imitator in the same way in which a painter or any other maker of likenesses is, what he is imitating must always be one of three things. It must be things as they actually were or are, things as people say and think that they are, or things as they ought to be. These things are all expressed either by familiar diction or with the addition of rare words and metaphors; there are many modifications of ordinary diction that we allow to the poets.

Furthermore, correctness in the art of poetry is not at all the same as that in the art of politics or, indeed, that in any other art. In the art of poetry itself there are two kinds of error, the one essential to the art, the other accidental to it. If a poet has chosen to imitate something, but has failed through lack of ability, this is an essential failure or error; but if he has failed through an incorrect choice (through deciding, for instance, to portray a horse with both its right legs forward; or through making a mistake relevant to whatever art he was imitating, whether the art of medicine or some other; or through portraying something that was impossible), then his error is not essential to the art. Hence, we must deal with critical objections with all these considerations in mind.

Let us first take the charges brought against the art itself. If what has been written is impossible, then an error has been committed. But it is all right if the art achieves its own end (we have already said what the end is) and if in this way that part itself (or some other part) is made more striking. An example is the pursuit of Hector. Yet, if the same end could have been achieved better, or at least no worse, by following the requirements of the appropriate art, then it is not all right; for if possible no error should be committed at all. To which of the two classes of error, then, does this error belong? To those that are essential to the art, or to those that are accidental to it? It is less of an error not to know that the female deer has no horns than to paint a picture that is a poor representation.

As for the charge that what is said is not true, we can meet that by saying that perhaps it ought to be, just as Sophocles said that he portrayed men as they ought to be, whereas Euripides portrayed them as they actually are. But if anyone objects that what is said is neither what is true nor what ought to be true, we can reply "Well, that is what people say," as with the stories about the gods. Perhaps these stories are neither edifying nor true, as Xenophanes remarked; nonetheless, people tell these stories. Some stories are perhaps no better than the truth, but nonetheless reflect an actual state of affairs, as with the arms, where "the spears stood upright on the butt spikes"; for that was the custom then, as it still is with the Illyrians.

As for the question whether what has been said or done is good or not, we must not only look at what has actually been done or said and see whether it is fine or worthless, but also at the person who said or did it, the person he did it or said it to, and when, how and why he did it—whether, for instance, it was to bring about a greater good or to avoid a greater evil. . . .

26. The question may be raised whether the tragic or the epic form of imitation is the better. If the better form is the one that is the less vulgar, and if the less vulgar is always the one that is addressed to the better audience, it will be only too clear that the one that is addressed to anyone at all is the one that is vulgar. For, on the assumption that the audience will not understand unless the actor adds something, actors engage in a great deal of movement, like indifferent flute players who roll about when they have to imitate a discus or pull the leader of the chorus about if they are playing the *Scylla*. Tragedy, then, is like that; it is like what the older actors used to think of their successors. For Mynniscus used to call Callippides an ape because he overacted, and Pindarus enjoyed a similar reputation. The relation of these later actors to their predecessors is paralleled by that of tragic art to epic. People maintain, therefore, that the latter is addressed to a cultivated audience that has no need of posturings, whereas tragedy is addressed to the less cultivated. If tragedy, then, is vulgar, clearly it is the inferior of the two.

But in reply to all this we can say that it is not a criticism of poetry, but of the art of acting; it is possible to exaggerate one's gestures even if one is a rhapsode, as Sosistratus did, or in a singing competition, as Mnasitheus of Opus used to. Also, we ought not to disapprove of every kind of movement unless we are going to disapprove of dancing; we ought only to disapprove of the movements of inferior people; this was the reproach that was leveled against Callippides and is now leveled against others: that they imitate women who are not freeborn. Further, tragedy can do its job without any movement just as well as epic can; one can see what it is like from reading it. So, if it is superior in other respects, this disadvantage is not inescapable. Further, tragedy contains everything that epic contains (since it can use meter, too), and it also possesses things that make a considerable contribution to it, in the form of music and visual effects, by means of which its pleasures are made even more vivid. Further, it has this vividness both when it is read and when it is on the stage. There is also the advantage that the goal of the imitation is attained in a shorter length of time. For what is more compact is always more pleasing than what takes up a lot of time. I am thinking of what would happen, for instance, if one were to put the *Oedipus* of Sophocles into as many verses as the *Iliad*. Further, the imitative work of an epic poet is less of a unity; there is evidence of this in the fact that several tragedies can be got out of any single piece of epic imitation; the result is that if epic poets take a single plot, either it is expounded briefly and seems too short or it conforms to the length required by the meter and seems watery and thin. When I say that the epic has less unity, I am thinking of cases in which the whole is composed of several actions: the *Iliad*, for instance, has many such parts, and so does the *Odyssey;* and these parts in themselves have considerable magnitude. Yet, these poems have been composed in the best possible way, and are imitations of a single action as far as that is possible.

If, then, tragedy surpasses epic in all these points, and also in the job that it does—since it is not just any chance kind of pleasure that it ought to produce, but rather the kind that we have mentioned—clearly, if it attains its goal, tragedy will be superior to epic.

So much, then, about tragedy and epic—about their

kinds and parts, how many of them there are, how they differ from each other, the causes of their success or lack of it, and the criticisms leveled against them and the answers that can be made to these criticisms.

AFTERWORD

Are you listlessly glancing at this afterword, since you couldn't find a foothold in Aristotle's text? Because he doesn't "speak to you"? Or with desperation or disappointment, as it all seems to make little sense? Are you bored with your reading assignment? Or have you read from cover to cover, and still wonder "so what?", feeling somewhat perplexed or befuddled? Don't give up on Aristotle just yet. There must be *something* that made you pick up the book in the first place. Hold on to whatever that was.

Aristotle is food for thought. If you haven't a hunger for thought, or at least a certain appetite, you will likely not develop a taste for Aristotle's work. But how does one build up such an appetite? First, unlike a French meal, the sequence of courses (works) to read isn't set in stone for Aristotle. If you hunger for answers to the question of what kind of life you should lead, have *Ethics* I, II and VI as an appetizer. Are you fascinated by the problems of what the soul is, or what life is? Read *Psychology* II. Literature or theater is your thing? Delve into the *Poetics*. The science of nature has always interested you? Start with the *Physics*. Logical questions are your pastime? Begin with *On Interpretation* and *Metaphysics* IV.4–6. You get the gist. As an appetizer awakens your hunger for the subsequent courses, so reading one part of Aristotle often makes a reader hungry for another.

Don't eat too fast, though. Take small bites. Chew carefully. Pause between sections, paragraphs or even sentences. Aristotle is a complex, highly nutritious diet. Some of the taste nuances open themselves up only to the more experienced palate. Some flavors will fully reveal themselves only after repeated ingestion.

There are some basic Aristotelian ingredients that help coat the stomach, thus aiding the digestion of more substantial morsels. If you spend some time studying the ten categories (*Cat.*4), the distinctions between primary and secondary substances (*Cat.*5) and between potentiality and actuality (*Met.*IX.6) and the theory of the four causes (*Phys.*III.3), this will pay off manifold when you read other parts of Aristotle's oeuvre. For these form the foundation of much of Aristotle's philosophy.

Still not hungry? How can you stimulate your appetite? Here's one recommendation. When Aristotle says he wants to investigate, say, what courage is or literary art—pause right there. Spend a few minutes thinking about what *you* think courage or literary art is. Only then explore what Aristotle offers. Sometimes the differences may surprise, even shock; sometimes the similarities may amaze. Either way, your interest should be piqued.

Often Aristotle deals explicitly with philosophical problems that contemporary philosophers still discuss and to which no generally accepted solution has been found. But what happens when we want to know Aristotle's view on a philosophical issue where he himself, in his extant works, does not ask the same questions, but merely provides some material relevant to how he may have answered it? Here we enter an area of ancient philosophy where the prejudices, conceptual structures and beliefs of the reader may unduly impact the interpretation of the text—leading to misconceptions, based on the reader's inability to see a philosophical of issue afresh, unadulterated by post-Aristotelian preconceptions and ideas. We may miss what Aristotle says and replace it with what we want him to say or what we cannot imagine him not saying.

The remainder of this afterword provides an illustration of this pervasive phenomenon. One complex of problems still at the forefront of philosophical debate, without a generally accepted solution in sight, is that of freedom and determinism. Aristotle never presents a theory of these problems or even displays clear awareness of their existence. Still, there are plenty of passages in his philosophical writings—in fact, some in every chapter of this book—where Aristotle discusses directly related issues. The following remarks thus also illustrate the many systematic connections among Aristotle's writings. They are structured around a series of common misconceptions regarding Aristotle's position on issues of freedom and determinism.

Misconception 1: Aristotle was a causal indeterminist since he postulated chance events.

A basic distinction in Aristotle's philosophy is between necessary events, like the movement of the stars, and contingent events, which include what happens mostly, what happens as often as not, and what mostly does not happen. Spontaneous and chance events fall in the last category (*Phys*.II.5). They cannot be scientifically explained, like some astronomical and biological facts (*Met*.VI.2, *Phys*. II.5). But they do have efficient causes: efficient causes that are accidental to their effect. If I owe you twenty dollars and you incidentally run into me at the supermarket, then your running into me is the cause of my paying my debt. The payback is a *chance* event, since its cause is accidental, and involves a choice (yours, of going shopping then). If a dagger incidentally falls off your shelf, and injures your friend, then the dagger is the cause of the injury. The injury is a *spontaneous* event, since, although the purpose of the dagger is to injure, it caused *this* injury accidentally. Thus for Aristotle, chance and spontaneous events have accidental efficient causes. From a current scientific viewpoint, too, such events would be considered caused. From either perspective, Aristotle doesn't emerge as a causal indeterminist, i.e., as someone who assumes uncaused events.

Moreover, for Aristotle, necessity and causal determinism (the theory that all events are determined by preceding causes) thus come apart. The fact that an event is causally

determined doesn't make it necessary in Aristotle's understanding of necessity. By contrast, contemporary theories of
determinism usually consider causally determined events
to be necessary. That matters for the next misconception.

Misconception 2: Aristotle is an indeterminist, since he
denies that all events happen by necessity.

This misconception is based on the confusion of necessitarianism (the theory that everything happens by necessity) with causal determinism. Aristotle vehemently rejects
necessitarianism, most famously by refuting logical determinism (the theory that all future events are necessitated
by the fact that statements about them are already true
now) in *Int.*9. He reports this argument for logical determinism: If something is happening now, then it was in the
past always true to say that it would happen. But if it was
always true to say that it would happen, then—whether
or not anybody actually ever said it—it necessarily had to
happen. This holds for all events, past, present or future.
Hence all events, including future ones, are necessary.

Aristotle attempts to show what is wrong with this and
related arguments. He correctly notes that from the fact
that necessarily one of a pair of contradictory statements
is true, it doesn't follow that one of the individual statements is necessarily true. What is quite unclear is how this
provides a refutation of logical determinism, and literally
hundreds of Aristotle scholars have tried to answer this
question. The logical determinist's argument seems to run
from the truth of past statements about future events to
the necessity of the future events. What remains in dispute
even today is whether Aristotle argued (i) that the fact that
a statement "this will happen" has always been true doesn't
entail that it is now already settled that this will happen,
or (ii) that the fact that "this will happen" has always been
true (and it thus will happen, and it is already now settled
that it will happen) does not entail that it happens by necessity. (i) is an argument against the predetermination of
all events; (ii) is an argument against necessitarianism and
compatible with the predetermination of all events. As we

saw in *Misconception 1*, for Aristotle necessity and causal determination come apart. Thus, in Aristotle's own terms, (ii) suffices to refute necessitarianism.

Misconception 3: Aristotle believes that agent causation is necessary for moral responsibility.

For Aristotle, a necessary condition for moral responsibility is that agents are the efficient causes of their action and the action has its beginning in the agent (*Eth*.III.1). *Misconception 3* is the result of misconstruing this condition. Aristotle's statement that the beginning, or principle, of the action is in the agent is wrongly taken to mean not only that the agent is the action's efficient cause, but also that the agent, in turn, is not caused to act by a prior efficient cause. The agent is envisaged as initiating the action, where this initiation itself is causally undetermined. Such causation, where agents are causally undetermined causes of their actions, is called agent causation.

However, for Aristotle, agent causation is not required for moral responsibility. First, when Aristotle elsewhere says that something is the beginning and efficient cause of something else, he doesn't mean that the first thing did not have an efficient cause that caused it to be the way it is. Thus a father is the origin and efficient cause of a child (coming into being), but has himself a father as origin and efficient cause of him (coming into being).

Second, Aristotle himself explicates what he means by the agent being the beginning of action, and this doesn't involve agent causation. Negatively, he explains it as (i) the absence of external force that makes you "do" what you don't intend to do or prevents you from doing what you intend to do plus (ii) the—nonculpable—absence of ignorance of relevant specific circumstances of the actions (*Eth*. III.1, 5). Positively, he explains that the agent deliberates and chooses an action in accordance with the deliberation, where the deliberation and choice are determined by the agent's character (*Eth*.III.2–3, 5). The character is caused by natural dispositions together with upbringing, education, other external circumstances, and the agent's prior actions (*Eth*.II; III.5, X.8). Whether the agent's prior actions are in turn caused by the agent's prior character is a question Aristotle doesn't discuss. But even if they aren't, Aristotle's theory does not require agent causation for moral responsibility.

Misconception 4: Aristotle believes that freedom to do otherwise is a necessary condition for moral responsibility.

This misconception is the result of misunderstanding Aristotle's statement that if acting is in our power (*eph'hemin*), so is not acting, and vice versa (*Eth*.III.5). This is interpreted as meaning that in exactly the same circumstances, and with exactly the same character, the agent could have done otherwise (i.e., has freedom to do otherwise). However, Aristotle's own account of what it means for something to be in our power is quite different. He contrasts the things in our power with things that are impossible or out of our reach (e.g. I cannot square the circle or bicycle on Mars) (*Eth*.III.2, 3); and with things that aren't in our power because we are forcefully prevented from doing them (*Eth*.III.1). Thus with the things in our power Aristotle simply provides the general domain of things on which we focus when deliberating and choosing what to do. Since, in addition, Aristotle never indicates that the same agent, with the same character and in the same circumstances, could do otherwise than he or she actually does, we have no reason to assume that he regarded freedom to do otherwise as necessary for moral responsibility.

Misconception 5: Aristotle claims that humans have freedom of choice.

Freedom of choice is the freedom to choose between alternative options. In Aristotle's terms, this would be to say that it is in our power to choose between performing an action or not performing it; or alternatively to choose between performing one action or another. But Aristotle only ever says that it is in our power to act or not to act, never that it is in our power to choose between doing this or that. His focus is on freedom of action; there is no indication in his *Ethics* that Aristotle is concerned with the question of freedom of choice at all. The way he presents our choices (*prohaireseis*), they follow upon our deliberation, and are in accordance with the result of our deliberation. Our deliberations, in turn are the result of our ends and desires (which are determined by our state of virtue) and our capacity for practical reasoning (which is determined by the condition of the part of our soul responsible for such reasoning), as well as the circumstances that got them started. If someone's—presumed—choices are not in line with the result of his or her deliberation, in Aristotle's view they may not even qualify as choices. Freedom of choice (*prohairesis*) became a philosophical topic only a few hundred years after Aristotle's death.

Misconception 6: Aristotle is a teleological determinist and believes in intelligent design.

Teleological determinism is the theory that all events are *pre*determined by an intelligent being, usually a divinity. This kind of determinism is called teleological, because the intelligent being has a *telos*, an end or plan, as to what should happen, and then—somehow—causes it to happen.

Misconception 6 comes to be as follows: Aristotle distinguishes natural objects (hydrangeas, hamsters, humans) from artifacts or products (houses, hoes, hymns). He says every object, whether natural or artifact, has a final cause or end. For artifacts, the final cause is the "image" of the artifact-to-be in the producer's mind, which, together with the producer's desire to realize the object of imagination, causes the producer to bring about the artifact. Thus an intelligent being's plan, together with its desire to realize it, determine the resulting product.

Now, Aristotle says that if things that happen through art have a purpose, so do things that happen by nature (*Phys.* II.8). The misconceived reasoning expands this analogy, stating that Aristotle thought that the final cause of natural things is the design of an intelligent god. In accordance with this design, acorns become oaks, human embryos fully developed adults, etc. However, this analogy is mistaken. Nowhere in Aristotle's work appears an intelligent god's design that unfolds, and in accordance with which natural beings are fully developed. Aristotle's god does not think about contingent things (*Met.*XII.9). Moreover, Aristotle states that the final cause or purpose of natural objects is *in* those objects and that no deliberation is involved in its actualization by its efficient cause (*Eth.*VI.4; *Phys.*II.8). The plan for the oak is *in* the acorn. And the acorn, with this plan in it, doesn't need to deliberate for an oak to grow from it. Thus comparisons with DNA are more appropriate than with intelligent design.

Aristotle is also aware that nothing guarantees that all acorns become oaks. When the circumstances, e.g., a hungry squirrel, prevent it, no oak comes to be (*Phys.*II.8). If Aristotle was a teleological determinist, he would have to postulate a divine plan for the world as a whole, with acorn-munching squirrels and acorns growing into oaks side by side. The Stoics had such a theory, but not Aristotle. Thus, although for Aristotle all natural objects have an end, these ends are not those of an intelligent being, and Aristotle is not a teleological determinist.

Misconception 7: Aristotle has no room for the freedom of artistic creativity, since art is mere imitation of nature.

Aristotle indeed says that art imitates nature (*Poet.*1, 4–6). But this does not prevent artists from creating something new. Artists are producers, as opposed to mere agents. They have an artistic skill (as poets or sculptors), which they use to produce works of art. The starting point of their production resides in the producer, not in the product (*Eth.* VI.4). The artist's skill is the efficient cause of the artistic product (*Phys.*II.3). In the production process, artists have an image of the product-to-be in their mind, thus employing their faculty of imagination (*Psych.*III.10). This image is the final cause of the artistic product. Hence a work of art is the result of the artists' imagination of the product-to-be, their desire to actualize it and their skill, which makes the actualization possible.

The *Poetics* elucidate how the artistic process is creative rather than merely imitative. There Aristotle states

that poets are the *makers* of plots and *invent* situations
and names. Dramatists are somewhat restricted by what is
stageable. But they can put familiar events together in surprising new ways (*Poet*.9). Novelists can introduce plot elements that are highly improbable, even impossible, as long
as they preserve overall plausibility (*Poet*.24). Moreover, in
Physics, Aristotle acknowledges that artists can be creative
and surpass imitation of nature by perfecting nature (*Phys*.
II.8); and in the *Ethics*, Aristotle may hint that chance
events can cause artists to adjust their original plans (*Eth*.
VI.4), thus leading to unexpected, and pleasing, results.

Hence Aristotle believes that artists can create unique
works of art, within the limits of their imagination, skill,
the specific physical restrictions of their art and possible
chance events. None of these would be without efficient
causes. Does such a theory of art do justice to the aptitude
and creativity involved in artistic production? Or does
true art require uncaused spontaneity, supernatural genius
or divine inspiration? As the presence of none of these is
provable, Aristotle seems on safe ground.

Misconception 8: The freedom of action of the *Ethics* is
the same as the freedom discussed in Aristotle's *Politics*.

Since Aristotle's theory of moral responsibility in *Eth*.
III.1–5 is frequently paraphrased in terms of freedom, and
Aristotle explicitly discusses freedom in the *Politics*, this
mistake is not uncommon. Often it is based on the more
general confusion of the family of notions of freedom related to the determinism debate with those related to discussions of social and political freedom, and of freedom
as autonomy. Some later philosophers (e.g., Kant) tried to
show that a person's potential for freedom *qua* autonomy
is necessary for moral responsibility. But Aristotle never
draws a connection between freedom of action (which is
essential for moral responsibility) and the freedom of the
Politics. If he had, he would have stated that freedom of
action is necessary for the freedom of the *Politics*, but not
vice versa. Aristotle never confuses freedom of action with
social or political freedom. As is standard at his time, he

uses the Greek word for freedom (*eleutheria*) solely for the latter two. Its discussion is restricted to the *Politics*.

Misconception 9: The theory of freedom Aristotle develops in his *Politics* is a theory of political freedom or of civil liberty.

Aristotle briefly discusses contemporary accounts of political freedom that characterize democracies. However, his own notion of freedom is not one of political freedom. Aristotle defines a free (*eleutheros*) person as "one who exists for their own sake and not for anyone else's" (*Met*.I.2). A person's freedom is manifested in the purpose of their existence. *Pol*.I.1–7 provides details about what makes humans free. At the base of Aristotle's theory is the contrast between being free and being enslaved *within a household*. A slave is a person owned by another person. Aristotle defines being free negatively as not being a slave. His positive account of freedom is based on his distinction between being *by nature* free or slave. This distinction doesn't always tally with who is *de facto* slave or free in a given society (*Pol*. I.6). For Aristotle, what makes someone naturally free is having virtuous dispositions that are superior to those of natural slaves (*Pol*.I.6).

Aristotle's natural freedom is related to political theory as follows. A person has to be naturally free to qualify as a citizen (*Pol*.I.7). What makes someone qualify for citizenship is hence superiority in virtue. Aristotelian freedom is then neither political freedom—which may include things like freedom from poverty or oppression—nor civil liberty, which may include things like freedom of religion or speech. For such freedoms are *not defined* by a person not having the natural dispositions of a slave: there could be laws in a slave society that guarantee slaves freedom of religion or freedom from torture. In Aristotle's *Politics*, freedom is, at its core, a social concept, defined relative to households rather than States. It is a virtue-related disposition that justifies *de facto* freedom, as opposed to enslavement, of humans in a household.

In conclusion, a general remark about reading Aristotle. Aristotle never doubts that there are humans who are natural slaves, and for whom it is good and just to be the property of another human being. As justification he invokes the natural inferiority of women to men, which he equally never doubts, thus adding insult to injury. There existed thinkers contemporary with Aristotle who questioned one or both assumptions. Not so with Aristotle. His philosophical imagination has deplorable limits. This fact is a useful reminder. Even the greatest thinkers are prone to fall for the prejudices of their times and err on essential issues. How should we respond? For one thing, it is useful to distinguish between an author and his or her work. What you have in your hands is a copy of a selection of Aristotle's surviving philosophical *works*. And whereas with people, we sometimes have to take them or leave them, with a philosopher's theories, we neither have to adopt nor reject them wholesale. We can pick and choose—just as in the case of an elaborate buffet meal. More than that: The fact that there are some obvious (to us!) errors in a thinker's work should remind us to be on our toes with respect to everything he or she says. Aristotle has been studied for over two thousand years, but slavery and the subordination of women were still justified *with reference to Aristotle's works* less than two hundred years ago. The point of reading philosophical works is never to just memorize and believe the theories expounded in them, nor to put their author on a pedestal. Rather, critical study of Aristotle should lead us to form our own reasoned opinions, with truth trumping Aristotle, where there is a discrepancy between the two. Undoubtedly, Aristotle would agree.

—Susanne Bobzien

BOOKS FOR FURTHER READING

The Loeb Classical Library editions of the works of Aristotle (Greek text and English translation).

Allan, Donald James. *The Philosophy of Aristotle.* New York and London: Oxford University Press, 1985.

Anscombe, G.E.M., and Geach, P. T. *Three Philosophers.* Oxford and Malden, MA: Blackwell Publishing, 2002.

Banes, Jonathan, ed. *The Complete Works of Aristotle: The Revised Oxford Translation.* Princeton, NJ: Princeton University Press, 1995.

Irwin, Terence H. *Classical Thought.* Oxford and New York: Oxford University Press, 1989.

Lear, Jonathan. *Aristotle: The Desire to Understand.* Cambridge and New York: Cambridge University Press, 1988.

Lloyd, G.E.R. *Aristotle: The Growth and Structure of His Thought.* Cambridge and New York: Cambridge University Press, 1968.

Ross, Sir David. *Aristotle*, (sixth ed.) New York: Routledge, 1995.

Taylor, C.C.W., R. M. Hare, and Jonathan Barnes. *Greek Philosophers: Socrates, Plato, Aristotle.* New York and London: Oxford University Press, 2001.

Thomson, Garrett, and Marshall Missner. *On Aristotle.* Belmont, CA: Wadsworth, 2000.